Who's Who in
Late Medieval England

Who's Who in Late Medieval England

(1272-1485)

being the third volume in the
Who's Who in British History series

MICHAEL A. HICKS

Series Editor:
GEOFFREY TREASURE

SHEPHEARD-WALWYN

First published 1991 by
Shepheard-Walwyn (Publishers) Ltd
Suite 34, 26 Charing Cross Road, London WC2H 0DH

British Library Cataloguing in Publication Data

Hicks, Michael A.
  Who's Who in Late Medieval England. — (Who's Who in
  British History Series).
  1. England, History, 1399–1485
  I. Title   II. Series
  942.040922

ISBN 0-85683-092-5 *cased*
ISBN 0-85683-125-5 *limp*

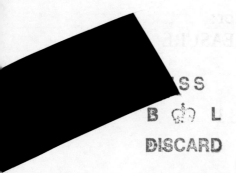

Typesetting by Alacrity Phototypesetters,
Banwell Castle, Weston-super-Mare.
Printed in Great Britain by BPCC Wheatons Ltd., Exeter

CONTENTS

GENERAL INTRODUCTION

The original volumes in the series *Who's Who in History* were well received by readers who responded favourably to the claim of the late C. R. N. Routh, general editor of the series, that there was a need for a work of reference which should present the latest findings of scholarship in the form of short biographical essays. Published by Basil Blackwell in five volumes, the series covered British history from the earliest times to 1837. It was designed to please several kinds of reader: the 'general reader', the browser who might find it hard to resist the temptation to go from one character to another, and, of course, the student of all ages. Each author sought in his own way to convey more than the bare facts of his subject's life, to place him in the context of his age and to evoke what was distinctive in his character and achievement. At the same time, by using a broadly chronological rather than alphabetical sequence, and by grouping together similar classes of people, each volume provided a portrait of the age. Presenting history in biographical form, it complemented the conventional textbook.

Since the publication of the first volumes of the series in the early sixties the continuing work of research has brought new facts to light and has led to some important revaluations. In particular the late mediaeval period, a hitherto somewhat neglected field, has been thoroughly studied. There has also been intense controversy about certain aspects of Tudor and Stuart history. There is plainly a need for fuller treatment of the mediaeval period than was allowed for in the original series, in which the late W. O. Hassall's volume covered the years 55 B.C. to 1485 A.D. The time seems also to be ripe for a reassessment of some Tudor and Stuart figures. Meanwhile the continued requests of teachers and students for the series to be re-printed encourages the authors of the new series to think that there will be a warm response to a fuller and more comprehensive *Who's Who* which will eventually include the nineteenth and early twentieth centuries. They are therefore grateful to Shepheard-Walwyn for the opportunity to present the new, enlarged *Who's Who*.

Following Volume I, devoted to the Roman and Anglo-Saxon period, two further books cover the Middle Ages. The Tudor volume, by the late C. R. Routh, has been extensively revised by Dr. Peter Holmes. Peter Hill and I have revised for re-publication our own volumes on the Stuart and Georgian periods. Between Edward I's conquest of Wales and the Act of Union which joined England and Scotland in 1707, the authors' prime concern has been England, with Scotsmen and Irishmen figuring only if they happened in any way to be prominent in English history. In the eighteenth century Scotsmen come into the picture, in the nineteenth Irishmen, in their own right, as inhabitants of Great Britain. It is hoped that full justice will be done to Scotsmen and Irishmen – and indeed to some early Welshmen – in subsequent volumes devoted to the history of those countries. When the series is complete, we believe that it will provide a comprehensive work of reference which will stand the test of time. At a time when so much historical writing is necessarily becoming more technical, more abstract, or simply more specialised, when textbooks seem so often to have little room to spare for the men and women who are the life and soul of the past, there is a place for a history of our country which is composed of the lives of those who helped make it what it was, and is. In contributing to this history the authors can be said to have taken heed of the stern warning of Trevor Roper's inaugural lecture at Oxford in 1957 against 'the removal of humane studies into a specialisation so remote that they cease to have that lay interest which is their sole ultimate justification'.

The hard pressed examinee often needs an essay which puts an important life into perspective. From necessarily brief accounts he may learn valuable lessons in proportion, concision and relevance. We hope that he will be tempted to find out more and so have added, wherever possible, the titles of books for further reading. Mindful of his needs, we have not however confined our attention to those who have left their mark on church and state. The man who invented the umbrella, the archbishop who shot a gamekeeper, a successful highwayman and an unsuccessful admiral find their place among the great and good. Nor have we eschewed anecdote or turned a blind eye to folly or foible: it is not the authors' view that history which is instructive cannot also be entertaining.

With the development of a secure and civilised society, the range of characters becomes richer, their achievements more diverse. Besides the soldiers, politicians and churchmen who dominate the mediaeval scene there are merchants, inventors, industrialists; more scholars, lawyers, artists; explorers and colonial pioneers. More is known about more people and the task of selection becomes ever harder. Throughout, whether looking at the mediaeval warrior, the Elizabethan seaman, the Stuart radical or the eighteenth century entrepreneur, the authors have been guided by the criterion of excellence. To record the achievements of those few who have had the chance to excel and who have left a name behind them is not to denigrate the unremarkable or unremarked for whom there was no opportunity to shine or chronicler at hand to describe what they made or did. It is not to deny that a Neville or a Pelham might have died obscure if he had not been born to high estate. It is to offer, for the instruction and inspiration of a generation which has been led too often to believe that individuals count for little in the face of the forces which shape economy and society, the conviction that a country is as remarkable as the individuals of which it is composed. In these pages there will be found examples of heroism, genius, and altruism; of self-seeking and squalor. There will be little that is ordinary. It is therefore the hope of the authors that there will be little that is dull.

GEOFFREY TREASURE
Harrow

FOREWORD

The Late Middle Ages comprises two hundred years of our history. It spans the reigns of ten kings. It covers the whole of the Hundred Years War, the Wars of the Roses, the Black Death, and the conquest of Wales. It was an age of faith and crusades, of castle-building and Perpendicular Gothic, of plague and famine, of jousting and of private war. It was crucially important for our political, economic, social, religious, intellectual and architectural development. From our vantage point the whole period is immensely distant, shadowy, and therefore difficult to understand. The assumptions, conventions, and standards that prevailed are quite different from our own. The great changes that occurred inevitably seem much smaller and perhaps also less significant than those that have happened since. Yet the Late Middle Ages is part of our past and makes a vital contribution to our modern world. To study it serves to recall our origins. It reminds us how different attitudes, standards of conduct, and patterns of thought could be from our own and warns us that someday someone will look back on us with as great a disbelief and incomprehension as we now show for the Late Middle Ages. It is this world, so similar in so many ways and so different in others, that this book sets out to evoke, explain, and portray through the lives of people of the time.

This is not an easy task. If source materials are much more copious than for Early Medieval England, the Late Middle Ages nevertheless precedes the invention of diaries, and such revealing sources as biographies, personal letters, and portraits are rare indeed. We seldom know about the birth, childhood, upbringing, or family life of even quite important people, and we rarely know even their appearance. Late medieval Englishmen and Englishwomen have little to offer the psychologist and psychiatrist. But the sources are not meagre. There survives today an enormous quantity of contemporary evidence in the form of histories, manuscript books, and records, which historians have used to study many different people. Frequently there is not too little material but too much. But do these materials allow us to write biography in any meaningful sense? For what we possess is overwhelmingly a record of what people were and what they did, not why they acted or what kinds of people they were. Too many are mere types and we cannot explain the crucial decisions in their lives. In a few particularly well-documented cases, like Margery Kempe and Margaret Hungerford, we know the answers, but more commonly we must deduce motives from actions and make our own interpretations that may not only be wrong, but which may vary with fluctuations in our historical understanding or the fashions of historians. It is the contention of this book that people cannot escape from the preconceptions and conventions of their own age and that few are genuinely single-minded in the sense of having only one interest. These biographies seek not to record merely what is important about their subjects — the greed of Piers Gaveston, for example — but their activities, whether religious, recreational, or dynastic. Perhaps this does not always add up to a personality, for there can be no complete answer to the problems outlined above. It does indicate a spread of interests and activity that is not confined to what we historians in our arbitrary way have found significant about people who lived 500 years ago. All such material will find a place in definitive lives yet to be written.

Of course no collection of biographies can capture everyone of interest and importance in any period and probably every reader will find omissions here. This book presents my selection of lives, not necessarily better than the choice of anyone else, but one that I am happy to justify below.

First of all, the framework is geographically England rather than Britain, with Irishmen and Welshmen figuring only if prominent in English history. The careers of most Celts were confined to Scotland, Ireland, and Wales and to social and political systems scarcely relevant to England. Those included below are either native English people active in England, or Englishmen who distinguished themselves abroad, or foreigners who made their mark in England.

Most of those selected were Englishmen and Englishwomen through and through. Within this principal group, I have confined myself to those for whom sufficient material survives for the biographer, leaving out, for example, the substantial figure of William Langland and almost all peasants. An effort has been made to represent the whole country and to avoid over-representing London and the south-east. Just as historians have increasingly turned from political and religious topics to the study of Urban History, Women's History, and History from Below, so I have depicted a variety of different ranks, styles of life, and occupations. Here, inevitably, my selections are controversial. Not all were distinguished in their own day. Often they are merely representatives of particular types — small landowners, heretics, widows, or gentlemen — and of those that can be studied. Frequently such people have been preferred to those of genuine eminence in their own day. I have tried to treat shadowy earlier periods as fully as the fifteenth century.

Of course, any selection is bound to arouse controversy. Whilst I have been writing, different people have told me to treat all queens, all cardinals, all archbishops, and all royal dukes, whilst only kings have been automatic choices for me. I have been urged to include the mystics Walter Hilton and Juliana Norwich as well as Richard Rolle; to include the singularly obscure if brilliant William Langland; and to find space for more townsmen, more women, and more peasants. There will be those who find my selection too traditional, with too much emphasis on politicians and churchmen, and others who will find my efforts to include women and ordinary people do not go far enough. I have tried to balance these differing requirements and to represent every interest.

This book makes no claim to original research and depends overwhelmingly on the labours of others acknowledged in the sources that I have cited. Had I written twenty years ago, my selection would have been quite different. It would certainly be transformed if repeated twenty years hence. Out would have to go more noblemen and politicians to make room for the women, gentry, and peasants, about whom so much more is being learnt.

If medieval people are too easily regarded as types, this is partly because of the lack of individuality in medieval portraiture. The portrait accurately depicting a distinct individual is the product of the Renaissance and only a handful — mainly of kings — exist for the later middle ages. Such portraits of Richard III, Queen Elizabeth Wydeville, John Howard Duke of Norfolk, and Bishop Waynflete feature here. It is questionable how true even these are to life. In addition there are many pictures of medieval people among the wealth of surviving sculpture, funerary monuments, brasses, stained glass, coins and medals, and (above all) illuminations. Very few are genuinely representational: the illumination of Geoffrey

Chaucer is a good example. Most of these representations are stylised stereotypes, often produced posthumously by artists unacquainted with their subject, and cast little light if any on the appearance of those concerned. It is not their unique facial features that distinguish the Black Prince, Abbot De La Mare, the Earls of Salisbury or Warwick, but their coats of arms, which identified them precisely at the time and which are a foreign language to us. Individuality mattered, but individual appearance did not. In this book I have drawn on the full range of visual media available at the time to depict my chosen characters. Here you will find individuals depicted in illuminations, panel paintings, paintings, stained glass, sculpture, seals and a medallion, and brasses. As befits the period, illuminations and sculpture predominate.

Most surnames in the 13th and 14th centuries were preceded by 'de' and historians have sometimes translated this as 'of'. Thus past histories generally speak of Gilbert *de* Clare and William *of* Ockham. By the fifteenth both 'de' and 'of' have generally been dropped. In the interests of consistency, I have dispensed with both 'de' and 'of' in surnames except in three cases: for surnames like De La Mare and De La Pole; for French-speaking foreigners; and for princes of the English royal house, which lacked a surname and thus called each prince after his place of birth, e.g. Henry of Bolingbroke, Henry of Monmouth, and Henry of Windsor. Quotations in the text are derived from sources listed with each biography; only where this is not the case have they been attributed to a specific author.

It is a pleasure to acknowledge the assistance of those who have made this book possible. High on the list must be Jim Bolton, who put forward my name, Geoffrey Treasure as General Editor, and Anthony Werner my publisher. My colleague Dr Tom James suggested several of the individuals and sources appropriate for their study. Much of the research was undertaken in the libraries of King Alfred's College and Southampton University, whose staff helped me to locate or borrow much indispensable material. Those repositories that supplied the illustrations gave freely of their advice in a field in which I lack expertise. My wife Cynthia read every biography, some several times over. My greatest debt must be to those who suffered most while it was in gestation, my children Ralph, Francis and Isolda, to whom I dedicate it.

MICHAEL HICKS
December 1990

LIST OF ILLUSTRATIONS

The author and publisher wish to thank the following for permission to reproduce materials in their care and possession:

The British Library Board for illustration nos. 1, 6, 12, 15, 16, 17, 19, 20, 21
The National Portrait Gallery, London for illustration nos. 2, 4, 5, 7, 13, 14, 24, 29
The Board of Trustees of the Victoria and Albert Museum for illustration nos. 23, 25
The Royal Commission on the Historical Monuments for England for illustration nos. 8, 9, 10, 11
His Grace the Duke of Norfolk for illustration no. 28
A Private Collection for illustration no. 26
The Provost and Fellows of Eton College for illustration no. 22
Courtauld Institute of Art for photograph nos 22, 26, 28
Geoffrey Wheeler for illustration no 30
Peter Jacobs for illustration nos. 3, 18, 27

LIST OF PRINCIPAL EVENTS

1322   Battle of Boroughbridge. Execution of Thomas of Lancaster and Bartholomew Badlesmere.

1322–
1326   The rule of the Despensers.

1327   Deposition of Edward II. Accession of Edward III.

1327–
1330   Rule of Isabella and Mortimer.

1328   Treaty of Northampton: Recognition of Scottish independence and of Robert Bruce as king.

1337   Outbreak of the Hundred Years War.

1340   Edward III lays claim to the crown of France. Dismissal and trial of Archbishop Stratford.

1346   Battle of Crécy. Edward III defeats the French.

1348–
1349   The Black Death.

1356   Battle of Poitiers. The Black Prince defeats and captures the French King John II.

1359–
1360   The great chevauchée.

1360   Treaty of Brétigny. Peace with France.

1367   Battle of Najera. The Black Prince defeats a pretender to the throne of Castile.

1369   Resumption of the Hundred Years War.

1376   The Good Parliament. The first speaker: Peter De La Mare. Impeachment of Latimer, Lyons and others. Death of the Black Prince.

1377   The Bad Parliament: a reaction is staged by John of Gaunt. The first condemnation of doctrines of John Wyclif. Death of Edward III. Accession of his grandson Richard II.

1378–
1415   The Great Schism. The Church is divided between two or more rival popes.

1381   The Peasants Revolt.

1382   Archbishop Courtenay's Earthquake Council at the London Blackfriars against the Lollards.

1383   Crusade of the Bishop of Norwich to Flanders.

1384   Death of John Wyclif.

1385   Death of Joan of Kent, mother of Richard II.

1386   The Wonderful Parliament. Impeachment of the Lord Chancellor, Michael De La Pole, Earl of Suffolk.

1387   Richard II's questions to the judges. The Lords Appellant defeat Richard II's favourite Robert Vere, Duke of Ireland, at Radcot Bridge.

1388   The Merciless Parliament. The Lords Appellant arrange the trial and execution of Simon Burley and Nicholas Brembre and drive Richard II's other favourites into exile.

1389   Richard II declares himself of age.

1397   Richard II destroys the Lords Appellant in Parliament. Creation of Richard's favourites as duketti [little dukes].

1398   The quarrel of Henry of Bolingbroke and the Duke of Norfolk. Both are exiled.

1399   Death of John of Gaunt, Duke of Lancaster. Deposition of Richard II. Accession of Henry IV, first Lancastrian king.

1400   Rebellion of Richard II's favourites at Cirencester.

1401   The statute *De Heretico Comburendo* allows heretics to be burnt at the stake.

1403   The Percy Rebellion. Defeat of Hotspur at the Battle of Shrewsbury.

1405   Rebellion and execution of Archbishop Scrope.

1408   Rebellion and death of Earl of Northumberland.

1413   Death of Henry IV. Accession of his son as Henry V.

1414   The Lollard rebellion of Sir John Oldcastle.

1414 –   General Council of the Church at Constance ends the
1417   Great Schism and restores unity in the Church.

1415   Henry V's invasion of France. The Battle of Agincourt.

1417 –   Henry V's systematic conquest of Normandy.
1420

1420   The Treaty of Troyes recognizes Henry V as heir to Charles VI, King of France.

1421   Battle of Baugé. Defeat and death of Henry V's brother the Duke of Clarence.

1422   Death of Henry V. Accession of his infant son Henry VI. France ruled by the Duke of Bedford as Regent; England ruled by a council headed by the Duke of Gloucester as Lord Protector.

1429   Siege of Orleans thwarted by Joan of Arc.

1431   Henry VI's coronation at Paris.

1433   Lord Cromwell's statement of account as Lord Treasurer of England.

1435   Congress of Arras. Burgundy abandons alliance with England. Death of the Regent Bedford.

1444   Truce with France. Henry VI marries Margaret of Anjou.

1447   Death of Humphrey Duke of Gloucester and of Cardinal Beaufort.

1450   Loss of Normandy. Jack Cade's Rebellion. Trial and death of the Duke of Suffolk. Richard Duke of York becomes leader of the opposition to the ruling faction.

1453   Defeat and death of the Earl of Shrewsbury at Châtillon. Loss of Gascony and effective end of the Hundred Years War. Birth of Henry VI's son Edward of Lancaster. Henry VI's first bout of madness.

1454   Duke of York's first Protectorate.

1455   Henry VI recovers sanity and ends York's protectorate. 1st Battle of St Albans: the Yorkists kill the Duke of Somerset and other enemies.

1457   Conviction of Bishop Pecock of heresy.

1459   Attainder of the Yorkist lords.

1460   Outbreak of the Wars of the Roses. June: Battle of Northampton. The Yorkists capture Henry VI. September: Parliament recognizes York as heir to Henry V. December: Defeat and death of York at Wakefield.

1461   Battles of 2nd St Albans, Mortimers Cross and Towton. Accession of York's son Edward IV. Decisive defeat of Henry VI and the Lancastrians.

1464   Marriage of Edward IV to Elizabeth Wydeville. Decisive defeat of the northern Lancastrians at Hexham.

1468   Trial of Sir Thomas Cook.

1469   Resumption of Wars of the Roses.

1469–   Rebellions of Warwick the Kingmaker and George Duke of
1470   Clarence.

1470–   Readeption (second reign) of Henry VI.

1471   Yorkist victories at Barnet and Tewkesbury. Restoration of Edward IV for his second reign. Deaths of Henry VI, his son Edward, and Warwick the Kingmaker. Many Lancastrians recognize their cause to be lost and make peace with Edward IV.

1478   Trial and execution of Clarence.
1483   April: Death of Edward IV. Accession of his son as Edward
        V.
        June: Deposition of Edward V. Accession of Richard III.
        Autumn: Buckingham's Rebellion.
1485   Battle of Bosworth. Defeat and death of Richard III.
        Accession of Henry VII as first Tudor king.

GENEALOGICAL TABLES

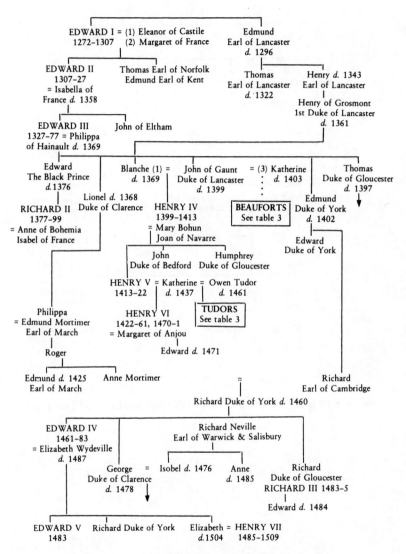

Table 1: The English Royal Family 1272–1485

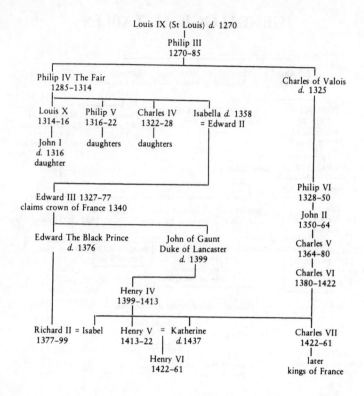

Table 2: Kings of England and France during the Hundred Years War

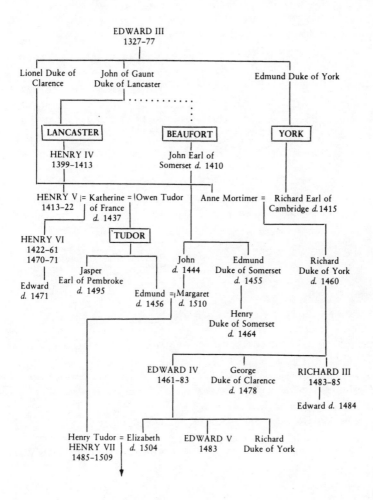

Table 3: Lancaster, York, Beaufort and Tudor in the Wars of the Roses

WHO'S WHO IN LATE MEDIEVAL ENGLAND

EDWARD I (1239–1307) was born at Westminster and ascended the throne in 1272. He was the eldest son of King Henry III and was much better suited than his father for medieval kingship. He was a great soldier, who had all the energy and ruthlessness required of the successful medieval monarch. Proficient in all martial exercises, he had extensive experience of practical warfare in England and on crusade, and could lead his magnates in person on the battlefield or at sieges. Like them he loved jousting, hawking and the chase. His contemporaries supported him loyally in Wales; a younger generation fought for him in Scotland; and a handful — Lincoln, Bek and Grandisson — served him throughout his reign. Edward regularly took counsel from his greater subjects, but he made his own decisions and made them quickly, without procrastination. Tall and imposing, a man to whom one literally looked up, Edward dominated and even terrified the greatest of his magnates. He was quick to take offence and was prone to the shattering rages for which his Angevin forebears were legendary: witness the coronet he cast in the fire and the handfuls of hair that he ripped from his son's head. He could be exceptionally ruthless: his harrying of the clergy in 1297 would stand out in any reign. Offences were not forgotten, but resented: 'He was also a man of strong character, unwilling to submit to injuries, and this made him forget danger when he wanted revenge'. Hence the suspension of Archbishop Winchelsey in 1305 in revenge for actions eight years old. Edward had no fear of personal confrontations. He compelled Archbishop Pecham to retract objectionable canons in parliament in 1279. Another furious altercation occurred in 1297, when the Earl Marshal remarkably — and uniquely? — defied him to his face. Yet Edward could and did accept defeats graciously, particularly over promotions to bishoprics. Disagreements were not always allowed to escalate, for King Edward ordered his priorities and could compromise to achieve his prime objectives. Serious errors were made, inevitable in such an intuitive king, but prudence and foresight also played their part. His ability and energy demanded

1

Edward I
(From his Great Seal)

respect at home and abroad, for he was the greatest monarch of his time.

Edward's career falls into three parts. Before 1272 his political career was distinguished more by his energy than his competence. Untried and inexperienced, he lived extravagantly and ran up debts, failed to control his household and estate officials, and acted perversely and unjustly. During the Barons War he was changeable and inconstant. He was egotistical and self-interested, allowed personal quarrels to clash with issues of principle, and plotted constantly, if ineffectively. Victory at Evesham and the pacification that followed owed much to his efforts, but he did little to reconcile himself to the Disinherited.

In retrospect, the four years he spent abroad, largely on crusade, helped wipe the slate clean. His evil reputation was rapidly erased as king. It was not that his personality had changed, but that his judgement had matured, that he exercised more self-control, and — perhaps above all — that his actions were attended by success. Up to 1290, almost everything went as planned. Wales was conquered, divided into shires and ringed with castles; the Hundred Rolls were compiled; the great inquiry into private franchises called the *Quo Warranto* proceedings was undertaken; a remarkable series of statutes was enacted; Scotland appeared destined to be united to England by marriage; and he acted vigorously to curb corruption in his administration (the trial of the judges, 1289).

In 1290 or soon after, he lost his mother, his queen, his chancellor, and his chief justice and became increasingly embroiled in Scottish affairs. The Scottish wars came to dominate everything, terminating his legislative programme and *Quo Warranto* proceedings and ending any hope of a second crusade. The ruinous expense brought with it heavy taxation, burdensome exactions, chronic indebtedness, administrative decline, and clashes with subjects lay and ecclesiastical, for whom the price to be paid appeared too high. The long term benefits of these years, such as the innovations in taxation and administrative procedure and the development of parliament, were merely incidental consequences of war. Edward died pathetically, still on campaign but unable to ride, leaving virtual bankruptcy and an unwinnable war to his unfortunate heir. It was a disappointing end to a reign that had started so well.

If Edward was indeed a great lawgiver, the man who updated the common law to meet the demands of the later thirteenth century, it was not because he regarded the law as an impersonal standard to which everyone, including himself, was bound. Even before his accession, it was complained that he acted as though above the law and evidence of this attitude throughout his reign is not difficult to find. Six earldoms were diverted by him from their proper course of descent to his own advantage and to the loss of the rightful heirs, who were people of no account. Coercion, fraud, maintenance and perhaps forgery were among the means employed. He used his courts systematically to attack the independent jurisdiction of the church and strove to deny the English clergy the right of dissent to taxation. Never content with routine and the status quo, he was aggressive and constantly strove to extend his powers geographically, at the expense of the Church and private franchises, by stretching traditional rights such as military service, and through erosion of traditional privileges, such as those of the Constable and Earl Marshal. When Archbishop Pecham moved against royal clerks who held several livings, were non-resident and were not properly ordained, Edward treated his action as an infringement of his prerogative. Always impatient of opposition, he objected to Pecham's re-publication of Magna Carta and fought hard to avoid the Confirmation of the Charters. Forced ultimately to give way, he tried unavailingly to escape his obligations and had to concede the *Articuli super Cartas* and give up certain forests, yet in 1305 he recovered by securing annulment of his promise from a complaisant pope on the grounds of duress. He remained to the end 'treacherous as a leopard', as the *Song of Lewes* described him.

Edward dealt in ends, not means. He decided policy and object-ives, but left the details to his officers. This was true of his legislation, which was devised for him by Hengham and his other judges; true of the financing and supply of his forces, which was managed by his department of the wardrobe; and it also applied to the crisis of 1297, which was defused for him by the administrators he left behind. Edward was a good delegator, but he expected results from his servants and made them account for their actions to him. He was fortunate that he was well-served and that solutions were found to most of the problems he posed. He was lucky, for example, that funds were available for his lavish programme of castle-building in Wales and for the escalating cost of his wars, which cost altogether £1.6 millions. Military expenditure cost £100,000 a year from 1294, four times his former annual income. Finally, of course, his problems became insoluble. It was impossible to finance his wars *and* remain solvent, to prosecute the war *and* respect the property of his subjects. As his resources were insufficient, Edward needed to curtail his operations and cut his coat accordingly to his cloth.

Ultimately the war became an obsession to the old tired king, who strove to overcome his difficulties by force rather than to reassess his priorities.

Edward regarded his ministers, judges, and clerks as his servants and expected their devoted commitment to his interests, if necessary in preference to those of his subjects. If they did, he rewarded them generously and condoned their peccadiloes in office and in their private lives. His failure to curb the misdeeds of his household and estate officials had been a charge made against him before his accession. Chancellor Burnell's blatant immorality did not deter Edward from seeking his appointment as archbishop of Canterbury and he defended his Treasurer Langton against enemies at the Curia and at home, granting him a pardon that even covered champerty (abuse of justice). Edward's personal standards, as we have seen, were not above reproach and some of Langton's most reprehensible actions were committed on the king's behalf. The mutual trust established from personal association with the king when wardrobe clerks was the basis of the career of many of his ministers, who went to almost any extreme — including crime — on Edward's behalf, certain of his support and protection. Edward continued to employ Hengham, Stratton, and Langton in spite of their misconduct and conviction of offences and preferred to take fines rather than pursue the trial of the judges to the legal limits. Charges against his servants, such as Langton, were increasingly treated as tiresome distractions from more important business.

Yet Edward was not a lonely and tyrannical egotist, but a man who inspired respect, loyalty and devotion, and even friendship. His confidence, when he gave it, was complete and he was generous to those who offered him good service. His affection for his father, his brother and his queen, and his sorrow at their deaths is well-attested, and he took a close interest in the young children born to him in his sixties. His enthusiasm for the crusade, his splendid new abbey of Vale Royal, his pilgrimages and small expressions of piety, ranked him as a religious man and ensured that the papacy never went to extremes in supporting his archbishops against him. He was literate and well-informed on many different topics. Yet if he had his gentler side, he was primarily a military figure, who eschewed luxurious ease for a bed with canvas hangings secured by nails.

F. M. Powicke, *The Thirteenth Century*, 1962.
M. Prestwich, *Edward I*, 1988.
M. Prestwich, *War, Politics and Finance under Edward I*, 1972.
E. L. G. Stones, *Edward I*, 1962.

WALTER MERTON (*c*.1205–77), Bishop of Rochester (1274–7), was the founder of Merton College, Oxford. His career illustrates how men frequently gravitated from private to royal service, how administrative service to the crown normally led to promotion in the Church, and how churchmen habitually invested their income and employed their patronage to the advantage of their relatives. Born at Basingstoke to prosperous freeholding parents, the only son among seven sisters, Walter was probably not a scholar himself, but was the friend of scholars. Initially known as Walter of Basingstoke, he changed his name about 1236, when in the service of Merton Priory, Surrey, transferring thence to the chancery of the priory's patron King Henry III, perhaps through the patronage of Ralph Neville, Bishop of Chichester. From 1242 he was chancellor of Nicholas Farnham, Bishop of Durham (1241–9). He reappeared in the royal chancery in 1255 and in 1258–9 was the normal deputy of the chancellor. Thwarted of the chancellorship of England by a baronial candidate in 1260, he was chancellor as the king's nominee in 1261–3, but thereafter he gave way to Thomas Cantilupe. Continued employment in the public service led to an unexpected second term as chancellor in 1272–4 during the absence of Edward I, when he was virtually regent of England.

From 1233 Walter was rector of the church of Cuddington (Surrey), where he endowed a light before the high altar in 1274 and whose church he probably rebuilt. Successive patrons rewarded him for his administrative services with further livings, which he held in plurality. Thus in 1246 the pope dispensed him to hold three rectories and in 1268 he held four, certainly without papal approval. From 1259 he was also a canon of St. Paul's, opting to live in a prebendal house nearby, convenient for his work in chancery. In 1274, like most chancellors, he was given a bishopric and was appointed Bishop of Rochester. A superb conveyancer, he was dealing in land in Basingstoke before inheriting his parents' estates and ultimately purchased a large estate for his foundations, besides leaving the large sum of £5,000 in his will.

In accordance with his parents' wishes, Walter established his hospital of St. Mary and St. John, Basingstoke in 1240-5 for the poor and clergy 'whose strength is failing'. When it ran into difficulties in 1262, he transferred the patronage to the king. Merton College originated in 1262-3 as the 'House of the Scholars of Merton' at Malden in Surrey. Consisting of a warden and priests, its role was to support twenty scholars at Oxford. Walter drew up statutes to this effect in 1264, but subsequently changed his mind, transferring the college to its present site in Merton Street, Oxford, and compiling new statutes in 1274. Most students at medieval universities lived in rented lodgings or hall and had to support themselves through their studies, often through non-residence in their benefices. Colleges were endowed halls. Founders established colleges like Merton with sufficient endowments to provide free food and accommodation for their scholars, who were normally graduates with arts degrees reading for higher degrees in theology, law, medicine or music. Walter's scholars, his statutes clearly reveal, were to be drawn mainly from his kin, the numerous offspring of his aunt and seven sisters, whose marriages and dowries he had earlier arranged. Founders kin came first, other scholars from the diocese of Winchester afterwards, a pattern also found in most other early colleges. Walter did not anticipate that Merton College would become an educational institution open to all.

J. R. L. Highfield, ed., *The Early Rolls of Merton College, Oxford*, Oxford Historical Society, new series, xviii, 1964.
C. A. F. Meekings, *Studies in Thirteenth Century Justice and Administration*, 1981.

EDMUND CROUCHBACK, EARL OF LANCASTER AND LEICESTER (1245-96), younger son of Henry III and Eleanor of Provence, was destined for a crown, but became instead the greatest of subjects. Like his uncle Richard, Earl of Cornwall and King of the Romans, Edmund became a pawn in the popes' struggle against the house of Hohenstaufen. Innocent IV gave him Manfred's kingdom of Sicily in 1255, when only nine. With the crown, his father accepted financial commitments for the conquest that he could not deliver and which helped provoke the Barons War. The young Edmund was solemnly invested with the kingdom in 1255, made formal grants and wore Apulian dress, but the grant was cancelled in 1262 and the kingdom was transferred to the French prince Charles of Anjou, who made his crown a reality. Edmund's continental ambitions were at least partly satisfied by his second marriage in 1275-6 to the widowed Queen Blanche of Navarre, granddaughter of Louis VIII of France. This made him ruler of Champagne, a county of cities and great fairs, 64 castles, 2,000 knights, two bishoprics, 21 abbeys, and 200 prebends. Residing principally at Provins, he had an income one-fifth of the crown of France. Even after selling out to Philip III in 1284, he retained land in France, was stepfather to Queen Jeanne, consort of Philip IV (1285-1314), and from 1291 governed Ponthieu on behalf of the future Edward II. No wonder he often acted as his brother's ambassador.

Edmund's disappointed ambitions in Sicily amply explain his return to England in 1265 'burning for plunder and revenge', sentiments that were duly satisfied. Unfaltering loyalty and unstinting service characterised his subsequent career. Military service, often in command, against the Welsh in three wars and in Gascony in 1296, was accompanied by diplomacy and support for his brother in domestic politics. He was Edward I's right-hand man and his death was a grievous blow. In reward his father and brother made him the greatest of English noblemen. Simon Montfort's earldom of Leicester, the honour of Lancaster, the lands of the Ferrers earls of Derby, Kidwelly, Monmouth, the three castles in Wales, and the Savoy in London were principal components in an endowment comprising 632 estates in 25 English counties. He coveted the earldoms of Devon and Aumale, but his marriage to the young heiress Avelina Forz ended with her premature death in 1274. No such mistake was made with the wedding of his eldest son Thomas to the Lacy heiress, as her estates were resettled to ensure Edmund's family benefited even should the union be without issue. Not only did royal favour bring profitable grants and marriages, but it could be counted on to defeat rival contenders, notably the unfortunate Ferrers family, who were repeatedly denied justice over their inheritance.

Not only was Edmund a prince of European stature, but he lived like one. 'A princely giver and spender of money, *flos largitatis*', he was often in debt in spite of his vast income, yet he was also pious in a conventional and princely way. He went on crusade in 1271-2 and seriously contemplated another one later. He was a benefactor of the

Cistercian nuns of Tarrant Crawford and the monks of Grace Dieu and founded a Franciscan friary at Preston and, at Aldgate in 1293, a house of Minoresses. Particularly associated with the French royal family, the latter foundation brought together the international, royal and munificent facets of his character.

W.E. Rhodes, 'Edmund, Earl of Lancaster', *English Historical Review* x, 1895.
R. Somerville, *History of the Duchy of Lancaster*, i, 1953.

ROBERT BURNELL (*d.* 1292), Bishop of Bath (1275–92), was Edward I's chief minister from 1274 until his death in 1292. Typical of ministers of his time, he entered royal service as a household clerk, demonstrating his ability under the eye of his master and earning confidence that never flagged. He was 'above all things the resourceful and faithful household clerk, elevated by his master's goodwill to the highest positions of church and state' (Tout). In Edward's service 'from his earliest years', from 1257 at least, he was left as one of his attorneys during his crusade (1270–2), sealing Edward's English acts with a special seal and witnessing them himself. Edward named him as his executor in 1271, appointed him chancellor of England in 1274, and secured him the bishopric of Bath in 1275. He was seldom apart from Edward and their acts are inseparable: no doubt the minister deserves the credit for many of the king's early achievements. Certainly he promoted his 'master's interests with a zeal and prudence equal to that with which they sought advancement for themselves and their families' (Tout).

Robert Burnell was a younger son of the Burnells of Acton Burnell in Shropshire, inherited a manor there, tried to develop the town, and built a house large enough to accommodate the king for five weeks in 1283, of which the magnificent hall remains. His sense of roots went with a sense of dynasty, as he sought to advance his brothers and nephews as landowners and clerics. He died holding lands in sixteen counties, the endowment of the later barony of Burnell, but much more had been given away already. One nephew became dean of Wells, another was married advantageously. A chronicler claimed that these so-called nephews and nieces were Burnell's illegitimate children and historians have generally assumed that Burnell was the unnamed bishop whom Archbishop Pecham claimed had fathered five children by one concubine, but these charges cannot be substantiated. One 'nephew' *could* have been a son, but he died by 1279. That Burnell's ultimate heir was a genuine nephew shows he had no issue living at his death. We cannot tell whether corruption or extortion helped build up his wealth, but his acquisitiveness and advancement of his family was typical of many contemporary administrators and bishops.

Such conduct did not fit Burnell for a career in the church or for the bishopric that was a common reward for royal ministers. Edward I, indeed, tried to secure his promotion to the archbishopric of Canterbury in 1270 and 1278, but without success. Popes wanted a reformer, which Burnell was not, but he was probably not guilty of the immorality, homicide, usury, or simony with which he was charged. Perhaps he should not be listed with 'negligent prelates . . . sublimely careless of the decencies of their position' (Tout). Probably Burnell visited his diocese each year and may have administered it efficiently through deputies. Certainly he visited monasteries, approved appropriations, settled the longstanding dispute with Glastonbury Abbey, and exerted his political influence on behalf of his cathedral chapter, Archbishop Pecham, and his fellow bishops. He built the splendid hall and chapel at his palace at Wells, organised contributions to the new chapter house, and gave four churches to the chapter. At Bath he took a church for his chapel, giving an alternative site, enlarged the priory's close and improved its access to its fields. That he built two chapels in his palaces, owned magnificent vestments, and founded chantries in his cathedrals indicates that his vocation was more than merely a channel of self-advancement. He even had a conscience, paying £400 to the crusade in 1289 for absolution for pluralism before 1275. Saintly austerity was not common: many bishops lived nobly like Burnell, but few were as kindly, affable, and liberal.

U. Hughes, 'A Biographical Sketch of Robert Burnell with materials for his life', Oxford B. Litt. thesis, 1936.

SIR OTTO GRANDISSON (c. 1238–1328) was one of the most remarkable servants of Edward I. He was the king's closest friend and shared all his interests. The son of Peter Grandisson (d. 1258), lord of Grandson near Lausanne in Savoy, he entered Henry III's service at an early age, probably in the entourage of the king's kinsman Count Peter of Savoy, perhaps in 1252, certainly by 1265. In 1267 he was in the household of the future Edward I, his exact contemporary in age, and in 1268 he was knighted with him. Otto accompanied the Lord Edward on his crusade, serving at the siege of Acre in 1271, and was nominated an executor in 1272. This was immediately after Edward's attempted assassination: one source says that it was Otto, not Edward's consort, who sucked the poison from the wound. Returning to England, he was employed throughout the reign as a soldier in Wales and Scotland — he was Chief Justice of North Wales for a decade from 1284 — and in negotiations with almost all the rulers of Western Europe. When Edward despatched him and Chancellor Burnell to reform the government of Gascony in 1278, he wrote that 'there was no-one about him who could do his will better; nay, it could not be better done if he were to attend to it himself'. So expert was he that in 1283 Edward's brother Edmund borrowed him for his own diplomacy. Otto's loyalty was to Edward I in person and on Edward's death he left England forever. His service lasted somewhat longer, for he represented England at the papal Curia until 1317, when he was still a royal servant. This does not mean that he lost interest in England, for he corresponded with Archbishop Reynolds and Bishop John Langton and in 1323, when well over eighty, he visited the Channel Isles, which he ruled inefficiently as an absentee. Granted for life in 1277 for 'his long and faithful service from an early age and in acquittance of debts owed in the king's service', the islands were his principal reward, but he also received lands in England and Ireland. His religious foundations suggest that he accumulated considerable wealth from his service.

Otto succeeded his father as lord of Grandson, frequently returned there between embassies, and retired there at the end of his life. Surprisingly, in an age when almost everyone married, Otto did not, and was succeeded by a nephew. He employed his embassies, especially those to the pope, to enhance his inheritance. He sought to advance his relatives, some in the church — three in succession were Bishops of Lausanne — and in England, where a nephew succeeded Walter Stapledon as Bishop of Exeter.

Otto was literate, unusual for a knight, and pious. He went on another crusade in 1290 and was thus at the fall of Acre, the final western bastion in the Holy Land, escaping to Cyprus completely destitute. Undeterred, he then went on pilgrimage to Jerusalem. He rated as a benefactor to Edward I's new abbey of Vale Royal and obtained many other favours from successive popes, particularly the grant of priories to endow his own foundations. From 1288 he was increasing the endowment and hence the number of monks at the priory of St. Jean de Grandson. He founded a Franciscan friary in 1289 and a Carthusian abbey at La Lance nearby in 1317. He died at the remarkable age of ninety.

E. R. Clifford, *A Knight of Great Renown: The Life and Times of Otto de Grandson*, 1961.

C. L. Kingsford, 'Sir Otho de Grandison (1238?–1328)', *Transactions of the Royal Historical Society*, 3rd series iii, 1909.

ISABELLA FORZ, COUNTESS OF DEVON AND AUMALE (c. 1236–93), and Lady of the Isle (of Wight), was one of the 'potent dowagers' so prominent in late medieval England. Women were subject to fathers until marriage and subject to husbands thereafter. However effectively they asserted themselves within marriage, it was only with widowhood that they achieved control of their affairs and could thus contribute independently to the historical record. Normally the only ladies who can be studied are widows. Most, of course, chose to marry again and many such took the opportunity to marry beneath themselves, presumably for love, for example Edward I's daughter Joan of Acre, Henry V's queen Katherine of France, and Jacquetta Duchess of Bedford. Others remained single, often — like Cecily Duchess of York and Margaret Lady Hungerford — being distinguished by the piety of their old age. Not all dowagers who remained single were old, however: Isabella Forz, Mary of St. Pol, and Elizabeth Burgh, each last widowed in their twenties, can be studied almost throughout their adult lives.

Isabella Redvers was thirteen when she married William Forz, Earl of Aumale (d. 1260), to whom she bore five children. In 1262 she succeeded as Countess of Devon on the murder of her brother Earl Baldwin. Although a great matrimonial prize, she never remarried, even in 1274 when her last child died. This was a source of great grief for her. Although anxious to promote her offspring, securing a prince for her daughter Avelina, she lost interest in the continuance of her line. This is surprising, for she identified herself clearly with the Redvers family traditions. On her husband's death she settled at the Redvers castle of Carisbrooke on the Isle of Wight, patronised the monasteries of Quarr, Christchurch, Breamore, and Carisbrooke, all of Redvers patronage, and chose to be buried in the Redvers mausoleum at Breamore. Sense of dynasty normally accompanied concern about the succession. Isabella certainly made a distinction between her lands by inheritance and marriage, illegally alienating dowerlands, and allowing Edward I's fraudulent acquisition of the rest of the Forz estates. Her own heritage was different, but without heirs to consider she was tempted to make over-generous grants. Her deathbed sale of the Isle to the king to the disinheritance of her heir had been seriously considered since at least 1276. This highly suspect transaction did benefit her personally, since it gave her executors £4,000 to spend on the good of her soul. Her personal advancement, material and spiritual, her children, and only then more distant kinsmen were her order of priorities. Similar sales were made by other childless dowagers like Lady Mohun (Dunster) and Anne Beauchamp, Countess of Warwick.

Isabella was well able to manage her affairs. Her estates were run efficiently under her close scrutiny. She attended her annual audits and extracted good service from the able but dishonest Adam Stratton. She was not at all fussy about the means pursued to her advantage: violence, coercion and fraud all had a part to play. She doughtily defended all her rights, justified or not, and embarked in frequent litigation, even against her mother. The Barons Wars and Welsh Wars were plausible but untrue excuses occasionally employed. Yet she was remarkably generous to her leading handmaiden and to her knights, some of whom served her loyally for thirty years and beyond the grave: evidence surely that her tough efficiency and hard-headed piety went with more endearing qualities.

K. B. McFarlane, *The Nobility of Later Medieval England*, 1973.
D. E. Pittman, 'A dowager and her lands in the 13th century: The case of Isabel de Forz', M. Litt. thesis, Edinburgh 1974.

JOHN PECHAM (c. 1230–92) is the only Franciscan friar to become archbishop of Canterbury. The case for the thirteenth century as 'golden age of the medieval church' owes much to the triumphal progress of the friars, which was sealed in England by the succession as primates of the Dominican Kilwardby and the Franciscan Pecham in turn. Born at Patcham in Sussex about 1230, Pecham was already an Oxford graduate, when he joined the Franciscans in the 1250s. The preaching of the friars relied on academic training in theology and so Pecham was sent to study and teach first at Paris (c. 1259–72), then at Oxford (c. 1272–5), and finally at the papal Curia (1277–9). Later entitled the 'ingenious doctor', he wrote extensively on theology, criticising the theories of both the Latin Averroists and St. Thomas Aquinas, and contributing to the controversy between the mendicants (friars) and the secular clergy. His sermons are simple and powerful, his poems and hymns deeply religious and technically perfect. He knew the Bible intimately and meditated on the crucifixion, redemption, and on the power and mercy of God. Contemporaries admired as saintly his rigorous fasting and chastity, which caused him to eschew the company of women. To his intellectual and imaginative gifts, he added administrative experience as provincial of the English Franciscans and a range of contacts in academic and papal circles. To the English church establishment he was an outsider and an unlikely papal choice as archbishop in 1279. His role was to initiate reform and to restore ecclesiastical liberties.

As archbishop, his concern for souls extended even to pluralists, he strove to secure the poor their due, and his charity was exceptional in spite of constant financial difficulties. Vigorous, meticulous and efficient, he visited every diocese in his province, a unique achievement, established new training for the parish clergy, sought to exclude the unworthy from bishoprics, and strove to stamp out pluralism and non-residence. His antecedents explain his defence of friars against seculars, his refusal to shorten monastic church services, his correction of theological errors at university, and his anxiety to prevent monks going there from acquiring dangerous learning they did not require. His defence of the Church of Canterbury brought conflict with his subordinate bishops and the archbishop of York. Almost all such actions brought controversy, litigation, and unwanted expense. Often overbearing and caustic, he did not foresee the offence he caused. Naturally irritable, sensitive and impatient of criticism, he responded to challenges with invective, often spoiling a good case through intemperance, and sought to crush his opponents. He lacked tact, forbearance and the spirit of compromise. His concessions were spoiled by the bitterness with which they were made.

Pecham's defence of ecclesiastical liberties began at the Council of Reading (1279), but Edward I compelled Pecham to retract some canons as infringements of his prerogative, ignored Pecham's subsequent assertion of his prime duty to God, and stepped up royal encroachments on the church courts into outright attack. But Pecham's patient negotiation produced a satisfactory settlement in the writ *Circumspecte Agatis* (1285), which defined spiritual jurisdiction generously and precisely. This was perhaps the high point of Pecham's archiepiscopate, as thereafter his physical strength and mental equilibrium declined, leaving him lonely, embittered, and wrongly feeling a failure and betrayed.

D. L. Douie, *Archbishop Pecham*, 1952.
P. Heath, *Church and Realm 1272–1461*, 1988.

ST. THOMAS CANTILUPE (c. 1218–1282), Bishop of Hereford from 1275 until his death, was the last Englishman to be canonised before the Reformation. Born about 1218 at Hambleden in Buckinghamshire, he became a strikingly handsome man, with a big nose and a good beard, both beard and hair being of reddish colour, later streaked with grey. His father had been steward of the royal household and an uncle became Bishop of Worcester. Such a background accounts for his pride in his lineage, his 'aristocratic good manners and unflappability' (Catto), his munificence, and his taste for the chase. Hence too Norman-French, rather than English, was his first language. As a younger son, he was destined for the Church, and about 1237 was sent to the university of Paris, where he lived with his own chaplain, tutor, and two poor scholars. Paupers lived off the leavings from their table and King Louis IX was a visitor. Thomas could afford protracted study. After his M.A. at Paris, he became doctor of civil law at Orleans and studied canon law at Paris and Oxford, where he took his doctorate in 1255 and was chancellor in 1261–3. From 1245 he was appointed to a succession of livings culminating in 1265 in the archdeaconry of Stafford. His brief appointment as chancellor of England by Simon Montfort in 1265 set back his otherwise inexorable progress towards a bishopric, prompting him to study theology in Paris and then at Oxford, where he took his doctorate in 1273 and was again chancellor in 1273–4, finally progressing in his mid-fifties to the see of Hereford in 1275. Nomination to Edward I's council followed.

Thomas was a non-resident pluralist before he became bishop, but was apparently an exemplary one, holding few livings at a time and none without a dispensation, appointing good curates, visiting his livings regularly and conducting services and preaching there, keeping buildings in repair and maintaining hospitality. Similarly as bishop he tried to ensure that all parsons were ordained and adequately educated, attacked unlicensed absentees and pluralists, and visited parishes and monasteries, correcting errors with sympathetic moderation. He himself lived frugally and chastely, giving generously to the poor, preaching and celebrating mass. He was especially devoted to the Blessed Virgin Mary. Thus far he conforms to 20th-century ideas of sanctity, but unlike us his contemporaries particularly admired the self-conscious austerity of his hairshirt and his exclusion of all women from his household including his sister, his intolerance of Jews, his efficient administration, and his defence 'as temporary custodian of the rights . . . of his spiritual spouse, the Church of Hereford' (D. M. Smith). This characteristic, which to us appears mere litigiousness, embroiled him in litigation on which he spared no money nor effort and led to his death far from home in Italy in circumstances akin to martyrdom. The manner of his death, his blameless life, and the miracles at his tomb explain his canonisation in 1320.

His litigation involved successful suits against laymen over hunting rights and for particular estates and against the bishops of St. Asaph and St. Davids over their respective jurisdictions, which were only won by his successor. These pale beside his titanic struggle with Archbishop Pecham, who asserted ecclesiastical jurisdiction against the king in 1279 and his claim as archbishop to hear appeals and settle wills against his subordinate bishops. In both cases Cantilupe opposed Pecham and Pecham excommunicated him in 1282, but only after Thomas had already appealed to the pope. Hence Thomas' journey to the Curia and his premature death. Before he died he was absolved of excommunication, his absolution alone permitting him Christian burial, which Pecham sought to deny him, and subsequent canonisation.

D. E. E. Usher, *Two Studies of Medieval Life*, 1953.
M. Jancey, ed., *St. Thomas Cantilupe, Bishop of Hereford. Essays in his Honour*, 1982.

MASTER JAMES ST. GEORGE, the master mason responsible for Edward I's Welsh castles, 'stands without a rival ... as a military designer of the late thirteenth century' (Harvey) and was 'amongst the greatest architects in English history'.

Edward I's conquest of Wales was consolidated by the construction of fourteen castles, eleven of them royal, that ringed Gwynedd in north Wales with impregnable fortresses that were easily supplied and reinforced from the sea. Built regardless of expense in labour and money, these castles were of the largest size and most advanced design. They brought together three innovations hitherto found singly in Palestine and elsewhere: instead of keeps, they possessed curtain walls with massive towers of bold projection designed to enfillade attackers; their concentric rings of fortification enabled defenders on both walls to fire on the enemy, whilst the inner ward remained a defence of last resort; and their massive gatehouses were points of strength rather than weakness. In four cases they were associated with new walled towns like the *bastides* of southern France. These innovations first appear at the Tower of London in 1274 and at Caerphilly, under construction for many years from 1271, both of which may also be the work of James St. George.

Master James St. George originated at St-Georges d'Esperanche, a favourite residence of the counts of Savoy, and was employed from about 1261 by Count Peter on his castle of Yverdon, which resembles the Edwardian castles in Wales. In 1273, following his crusade in the Holy Land, where the finest existing castles were to be found, Edward I visited the count at St-Georges, where he presumably met James St. George. However that may be, James is generally credited with the overall design of all the Edwardian castles in Wales, although other masons on site implemented the plans and devised the details. From the end of the first Welsh war in 1277, James was employed with Master Richard Lenginour on constructing new castles at Flint and Rhuddlan, where he made his headquarters, and may also have been involved in work at Builth and Aberystwyth. After the second Welsh war of 1282–3, he was responsible for building castles at Conway and Harlech and for the design for Caernarvon that was actually executed by Master Walter Hereford. The rebellion of 1294 resulted in the construction of his masterpiece, Beaumaris in Anglesey, which was completed only after 1316 to his original plans. From 1302 he was responsible for work on Linlithgow Peel in Scotland, perhaps also working at Kildmay Castle, in 1304 he was present at the siege of Stirling, and by 1309 he was dead.

As an indispensable expert, James was well-rewarded for his services. From 1284 he was paid at the high rate of 3s. a day, a pension of 1s.6d. being promised to Ambrosia his wife should she survive him, in 1290–3 he was constable of Harlech with total emoluments of 100 marks (£66.66), and in 1295 he was granted a manor worth £25 a year. Such rewards far exceeded the normal expectations of master masons.

R. A. Brown, H. M. Colvin, and A. J. Taylor, eds., *History of the King's Works* i, 1963.
M. Prestwich, *Edward I*, 1988.

ADAM HORDER is a representative example of the leading citizens of Southampton and indeed many other English towns about 1300. Nothing is known about the origins of Adam or the other Horders who appear in Southampton in the 1270s. They may have been recent immigrants, for Adam at least was an adult of substance in 1277. English trade was then dominated by wool, almost the only export, Southampton was a major outlet for wool exports, and nobody, native or alien, shipped more in 1277 than Adam Horder's 50 sacks, representing the wool of 12,500 sheep: 'It was a commodity such as only the very rich might handle'. Adam was thus a merchant, a trade that implies extensive contacts both in wool-producing areas and in foreign markets about which we know nothing. Typically, little is known of his trading activities, more of his ownership of property, particularly that which later passed to religious houses or abutted on their land. Thus by 1291 he had a shop to the east of Holy Rood church, English Street, which he may have occupied himself for an unknown trade. Two other shops in English Street, rented houses by the fish market, and an important tenement by the south shore brought in income from rents and may themselves represent the investment of profits. To foreign trade, rented property, and perhaps shopkeeping Adam added the new windmill he erected at Full Flood about 1305. His experience in foreign trade equipped him to become a royal customs officer in 1303–5. His son Robert was also a customer in 1303–4 and William Horder, perhaps another son, had the Full Flood mill in 1342.

Many, perhaps most, medieval towns were subject to manors, but many were municipal boroughs independent in law and entitled to run their own affairs. Southampton was such a borough. It had its own corporation and was exempt from interference by the royal sheriff and coroner of Hampshire. The burgesses elected a council of twelve *prudhommes* each year, who selected two of their number to be bailiffs each year. These bailiffs were the main executive officers of the borough and were responsible for keeping the peace, regulating the markets, trading standards, and debts, and observing local customs. There was also an alderman, who took priority in all matters, presided over the town courts, and supervised the other officers. In Southampton, as elsewhere, these offices were passed around a small group of wealthier citizens, an oligarchy, who ran the town in their own interests. Adam Horder was one of the wealthier citizens and became one of the oligarchy. No doubt after serving on the council and holding unrecorded inferior offices, he was bailiff in 1288–9 and 1291–2. In 1303–4, the summit of his career, he was alderman. Clearly, however, he was a relatively minor member of the oligarchy compared with his fellow customer, Robert Mercer, six times alderman, and others aldermen more than once. The oligarchy was closely knit and interrelated, but too little is known of Adam Horder's background to fit him into this family network.

Most leading families lasted only a few generations, going bankrupt, becoming landed proprietors, or failing to produce issue. Adam did none of these, being succeeded by sons and grandsons, but his family did not survive very long. No other Horders were as prominent, the last was recorded in 1351, and at least some of their property was sold before they fade from the record.

C. Platt, *Medieval Southampton: The Port and the Trading Community AD 1000–1600*, 1973.

BOGO CLARE (1248–94) was the most notorious pluralist in medieval England. As the youngest son of Richard Clare, Earl of Gloucester and Hertford (d. 1262), he was destined for the church from an early age and was assured of a particularly successful career within it. His high rank and noble connections assured him of the favour of king and pope, reflected in his appointments as royal clerk and papal chaplain. They enabled him to accumulate a remarkable number of church livings and assured him of dispensations from the pope exempting him from the normal limits on the number of benefices a clergyman was allowed to hold. Many other aristocrats enjoyed flourishing ecclesiastical careers, some becoming bishops, archbishops or even cardinals, yet few if any showed so little sign of a spiritual vocation as Bogo.

Appointed to his first rectory by the age of seven, by 1280 Bogo had accumulated 20 benefices, a total rivalled only by both Ralph Hengham and Adam Stratton. Subsequently he acquired others that placed him in a class on his own. He was presented to at least 34 livings including the dignities of treasurer of York Minster, precentor of Chichester, and chancellor of Llandaff, to all of which he was a non-resident. Bogo's livings, notably his 27 rectories, carried with them the cure of souls or responsibility for the spiritual health of his parishioners or others, which he consistently neglected. Such conduct helps explain why later pluralists such as William Wykeham were restricted to one cure of souls and instead amassed cathedral canonries that carried no such responsibilities and where absenteeism was much less harmful. The harm in Bogo's case did not just result from neglect, like that reported of his deputies in the treasurership of York, who left the cathedral treasures unprotected, failed to supply candles for services, allowed vestments to fall into ruin, and misappropriated them for weddings and other inappropriate purposes. For Bogo maintained a lively interest in the perquisites of his benefices, farming them out at high rent, exploiting his tenants, encroaching on the rights of neighbouring rectors, and rejecting his fair share of running expenses. No wonder contemporaries saw him not as rector but as a ravisher of his livings and described him as 'rich in benefices but poor in morals'. Neglect was to be preferred to exploitation.

Bogo was not even a priest. He consistently refused to be ordained and lived a thoroughly secular life of luxury and pleasure, mainly in

London. He could well afford his lifestyle, as his income rose steadily to about £1,500 at his death and he paid fines of £2,000 in 1290 without apparent embarrassment. His accounts reveal him hawking and hunting, dicing and playing chess, mixing with the nobility and visiting his brother Earl Gilbert at Usk, but not as practising as a clergyman. Bogo applied his considerable energies to acquiring benefices and litigating about them, employing endless money and effort in lawsuits that lasted for years. He was devoted to his family, assisting his mother, Earl Gilbert and other siblings wherever he could, most notably in frustrating the election of Edward I's candidate to the bishopric of Llandaff. His extensive household, which included two knights, appeared committed to his interests and to share his attitude to his responsibilities. On one occasion, apparently unprompted, they compelled Archbishop Pecham's messenger to eat a summons, seal and all. Pecham and two successive archbishops of York strove to bring Bogo to heel, but he easily defied them, secure in his wealth and great connections, uniquely irresponsible and unrepentant.

M. Altschul, *A Baronial Family in Medieval England: The Clares 1217-1314*, 1965.

ADAM STRATTON (*d.*1294), alias Adam Argoyles, the notorious moneylender and forger, was one of several brothers from Stretton St. Margaret in Wiltshire. A clerk, perhaps even a Master of Arts, he became a pluralist to rival Bogo Clare, ultimately holding 23 rectories in the province of Canterbury. An executor and therefore presumably a trusted servant of Baldwin Earl of Devon (*d.* 1262), he entered the service of the earl's sister Isabella Forz, Countess of Aumale by 1263 and controlled all her financial affairs from 1278-88. She gave him annuities and livings, the deputy-chamberlainship of the royal exchequer, in 1276 the chamberlainship itself and its valuable appurtenant lands, and, not least, access to her funds. Henry III and Edward I were satisfied with his service. The chamberlainship involved custody of the royal treasury and of exchequer records and thus offered means to misappropriate royal funds, use royal justice to pursue private debtors, register forged deeds, and generally to coerce and intimidate. From 1260 Adam was buying up the debts of Jews. Henceforth his moneylending and extortion betray not just blatant dishonesty, but also a mastery of financial and legal technicalities that made him very difficult to bring to book. From his headquarters in London's Smale Lane he used the countess' and king's officials and Italian bankers to handle his affairs elsewhere. His success emerges in £12,666 *in coin* alone seized in his possession in 1289, equivalent to half the annual income of the crown, and his payment of a further 500 mark (£333) fine by 1292.

Adam's fall came in three stages. On behalf of the Countess Isabella, he had cut the seal off a charter to Quarr Abbey, but even his conviction in 1278 and other complaints in 1279 did not interrupt his service to her or the crown. Complaints of misgovernment in 1289 brought Stratton as well as the judges to trial. Charged with offences reputedly ranging from homicide to sorcery, Stratton abandoned what the king had seized and paid a fine from what remained. Only his conviction for forgery in 1292 ended his service to the crown, yet although disgraced he retained his livings until his death two years later.

Stratton's career blurs the lines between private and public service and indicates the immense scope for corruption and self-enrichment in the royal administration. Behind the orderly processes and records of government, apparently diligent and devoted officers could oppress and cheat the king's subjects. Contemporaries could not determine whether Adam also defrauded the crown and found it almost impossible to prove even the most blatant crimes.

N. Denholm-Young, *Seignorial Administration in England*, 1937.
M. W. Farr, ed., *Accounts and Surveys of the Wiltshire Estates of Adam de Stratton*, Wiltshire Archaeological Society Record Branch xii, 1958.
State Trials of the Reign of Edward the First 1289–93, ed. T. F. Tout and H. Johnstone, Camden Society, 3rd series ix, 1906.

RALPH HENGHAM (*d.*1311) was 'the greatest and most forthright of Edward's judges'. Apparently from Norfolk, Hengham occurs first as a local justice about 1270, moved to the central courts in 1273, and was appointed Chief Justice of King's Bench the following year. He served continuously until his dismissal in 1290.

Hengham is probably the mind behind Edward I's legislative programme and most likely he devised the great Edwardian statutes. King Edward was not concerned with detailed implementation of his policies, delegating that to others, but he expected good results. 'I have nothing to do with your disputations', he once exclaimed, 'but, God's blood! You shall give me a good writ before you arise hence'. Ralph Hengham, apparently, could give him both a good writ and good statutes. He can be firmly credited with the Second Statute of Westminster (1285), once remarking from the bench, 'Do not gloss the statute; we know it better than you, for we made it, and one often sees one statute undo another'. Hengham's *Summa Parva* showed how Edward I's legislation and particularly this statute had altered the practice of the common law. He was not the author of a second, longer, treatise often attributed to him. In short, Hengham was the sort of expert who could not easily be spared and it is therefore no wonder that he reappeared in royal service in 1300, serving as Chief Justice of Common Pleas in 1301–9.

How then could Edward afford to dismiss him in 1290? The traditional story was that the king was shocked by the revelations of Hengham's corruption. When Edward returned from three years in Gascony in 1289, he was greeted with a popular outcry against misgovernment and abuse of justice. He put the judges on trial. Hengham faced eight charges, was acquitted on five, and was certainly convicted of only one, apparently on a technicality. Such a result hardly justifies the king's anger and can surely have been only a pretext for Hengham's dismissal. The real reason, it has recently been suggested, was that Hengham was too independent, too little the docile executant of royal commands, and therefore his service was terminated in favour of others who would put the king's will ahead of the sanctity of the law. Even if acquitted on the main charges, Hengham can hardly have been innocent of partiality. The king was far from his only master. Others were the archbishop of York, the bishop of Durham, Ramsay and Bury abbeys, and Canterbury cathedral priory, who paid him with annuities, benefices, and gifts, such as the silver cup worth £7 from Bogo Clare. His livings, which included the deanery of Warwick College in 1287–1302 and the chancellorship of Exeter cathedral, numbered fourteen in 1294. In 1303 he was pardoned unlicensed pluralism because he was a royal councillor. The terms of his retainder, explicitly set out by Canterbury cathedral priory in 1284, involved not just advice, but his support in any of the priory's cases before him as judge. Once he stopped a case between the tenants and abbot of Ramsay, denying the former their right 'by cause of a church which the abbot has given to Sir Ralph'. That was about 1270, long before his trial. It is evidence of his guilt that he preferred a massive fine of 8,000 marks (£5,333) to facing further charges. His colleague, the more notorious Thomas Weyland, Chief Justice of Common Pleas, preferred to abjure the realm. The £4,000 that Hengham had paid by 1293 indicates clearly the wealth he had accumulated, obviously not wholly from his paltry official salary.

W.H. Dunham, ed., *Radulfi de Hengham Summae*, 1932.
J.R. Maddicott, *Law and Lordship: Royal Justices as Retainers in Thirteenth- and Fourteenth-Century England*, Past and Present Supplement 4, 1978.
M. Prestwich, *Edward I*, 1988.

ANTHONY BEK (c. 1240–1311), Bishop of Durham from 1283, 'the most valiant clerk in Christendom', was born into a baronial family from Lincolnshire and County Durham. Hence his knowledge of warfare, his love of display, his munificence and magnanimity, and his fondness for falconry and the chase. His self-importance and self-confidence went with a capacity for conciliation and persuasion. He was a king's clerk by 1266. Almost the same age as the Lord Edward, he accompanied him on crusade in 1270, establishing a personal relationship with the future king that lasted all their lives. He was keeper of his wardrobe (in charge of his expenditure) and his executor in 1272 and briefly keeper of his wardrobe as king in 1274. Thereafter, though only constable of the Tower and a royal councillor, Bek was constantly employed on miscellaneous tasks, the arrangement of loans and embassies abroad perhaps predominating. As both a nobleman and a royal clerk, Anthony inevitably attracted benefices, holding at least seventeen at different times and incurring the criticism of Archbishop Pecham for unlicensed pluralism. Aspiring for a bishopric, he submitted to Pecham, who therefore allowed him to become Bishop of Durham in 1283. His elder brother Thomas became Bishop of St. Davids in 1280.

Bek, like Cantilupe, was a man of personal frugality and chastity, who earned a reputation for sanctity by personally handling the bones of St. William of York, which he moved to a more appropriate position in York Minster in 1284, and by defending the rights of his see. He settled disputes between future bishops and Durham cathedral priory, between the bishop and the archbishop of York, and between the priory and archbishop during vacancies of the see. He founded the colleges of Lanchester and Chester-le-Street, thus creating more patronage for his successors, and he founded chantries in honour of the Blessed Virgin Mary at both Norham and Auckland. Particularly appreciated locally was his exaltation of the Church of Durham and his ultimately unsuccessful effort to extend its liberty into Northumberland with lands he had personally acquired. This was recognized by his burial in the cathedral, the first bishop so honoured, and later references to 'St. Anthony'.

It was the king's attorney who asserted in 1292 that 'the bishop of Durham has a double status, namely, the status of a bishop in his spiritualities and the status of an earl palatine in his temporal holding'. This special position was endangered by the vicissitudes of Bek's last years. From 1300 he was at odds with his cathedral priory, whose Prior Richard Hutton sought almost total independence. In a series of unedifying scenes Bek blockaded his own cathedral, deprived Prior Hutton, and was himself suspended. Hutton exploited subordinate issues and Bek's other difficulties and appealed with some success to both king and pope. Bek's officials overzealously disregarded royal protections and messengers and his tenants complained of misgovernment and refused military service to the king in Scotland. At the Curia Bek won over Popes Boniface VIII and Clement V, who made him titular Patriarch of Jerusalem, and was victorious on Hutton's death in 1308, but his absences twice enabled his enemies to secure the confiscation of his liberty. Edward I was not unsympathetic, returning the temporalities in exchange for a charter of liberty to the tenants, and Bek restored the palatinate's autonomy before his death. The monks of Durham remembered him as 'one of the greatest of the prince bishops'.

C. M. Fraser, *A History of Anthony Bek*, 1957.

ROGER BIGOD, EARL OF NORFOLK AND EARL MARSHAL OF ENGLAND (d.1306), led the opposition to Edward I in and after 1297. The son of Hugh Bigod (d. 1266), a former justiciar, Roger succeeded an uncle as fifth earl in 1270. With extensive estates in East Anglia, Wales and Ireland, Bigod was one of the richest of the earls, yet nevertheless ran heavily into debt to the crown, to Italian bankers, and to his brother. He was obliged to relinquish odd manors to the crown in 1291 and to the Italians, in 1293 he publicly protested in parliament against the terms for repayment imposed by the exchequer, and it may have been his brother's demands for repayment in 1302 that prompted him to make the king his heir.

His debts to the crown and the erosion of his rights as Earl Marshal constituted grudges against Edward I. He had participated in all Edward's campaigns in Wales, but in February 1297 at the Salisbury parliament he refused to serve in Gascony in Edward's absence:

Bigod: With you, O king, I will gladly go; as belongs to me by hereditary right, I will go in the front of the host before your face.
Edward I: But without me you will go with the rest.
Bigod: Without you, O king, I am not bound to go.
Edward I: By God, earl, you shall either go or hang.
Bigod: By God, O king, I shall neither go nor hang.

Others joined Norfolk in his stance, notably the Constable of England, Humphrey Bohun, Earl of Hereford (d. 1298). The two earls declined to muster Edward's forces, so Edward replaced them as constable and marshal. After the king's departure for Flanders, both entered the exchequer, where they forbade collection of a tax improperly granted, which they compared to servitude. They pressed for Confirmation of the Charters — Magna Carta and the Charter of the Forest — and demanded that other arbitrary aspects of Edward's government be banned. These points were conceded by the government at home and confirmed by Edward abroad, thus securing the earls' support on the Falkirk campaign of 1298, but Bigod rightly suspected Edward's good faith and continued to press the fight in parliament for implementation of these concessions. His persistent constitutional stand wrung from Edward Confirmation of the Charters, further concessions in the *Articuli super Cartas* of 1300 and partial disafforestation in 1301.

In 1302 Bigod made Edward his heir, disinheriting not just his celibate clerical brother but his cousins the Bigods of Settrington as well. He thus ensured that he was the last Bigod Earl of Norfolk. His reasons are unclear: spite towards his brother, his immediate heir, and the lure of extra lands granted to him for life, may both have been factors. Edward's motives are clearer, for this was not the only case in which inheritances were diverted to the benefit of himself and his family. The ultimate beneficiary in this instance, as Edward may have intended, was his younger son Thomas of Brotherton (d. 1338), later Earl of Norfolk and ancestor of the Mowbray and Howard Dukes of Norfolk.

N. Denholm-Young, *Seignorial Administration in England*, 1937.
K. B. McFarlane, *The Nobility of Later Medieval England*, 1973.
M. Prestwich, *Edward I*, 1988.

ROBERT WINCHELSEY (c. 1240–1313), Archbishop of Canterbury from 1294, was the greatest of the theologically-trained pastor-bishops in England at the turn of the thirteenth century. Born apparently at Old Winchelsea in Sussex, he was educated at the universities of Paris, where he headed the faculty of arts in 1267, and at Oxford, where he was a doctor of theology and chancellor of the university in 1288. He was a famous teacher, a supporter of student rights, and as a writer 'a model example of scholastic thought at its best'. A man of blameless personal life and utter integrity, the generous patron of learning and the poor, affable and good humoured at table, he was above all a man of principle, who resolved what was right and adhered to it regardless of consequences. He was, we are told, 'equitable in all things, severe in his censures and no respecter of persons, nor could many gifts turn him from justice'. 'Stern and determined', inflexible and uncompromising, he is recorded as acting in 'his rough way', with 'his accustomed ferocity', and with 'fury and obstinacy'.

Such a man was a worthy opponent for the equally self-righteous and unyielding Edward I. But Winchelsey was not an impractical idealist. He strove to take an independent line that gave the king and pope their dues and was yet in the best interests of the English church. He led from the front, fully accepting the consequences of his acts, but did not oblige others to proceed so far. In the early years of his archiepiscopate, from 1294–1303, assertion of ecclesiastical privilege brought Pope Boniface VIII into conflict with the kings of France and England, both of whom wished to tax their clergy to finance their war over Gascony. Winchelsey recognized the justice of King Edward's appeal for financial support for defence of the realm and wanted to support him within reason, but Edward's demands were unreasonable and Winchelsey was forbidden to grant anything by Boniface VIII's bull *Clericis Laicos* (1296). Refusal of supply led to the outlawing of the clergy and their harrying, which included the seizure of Winchelsey's own horses. Although most clergy gave way, Winchelsey did not, and Edward was forced to recognize he had gone too far. Subsequently Winchelsey kept taxation to tenths levied only on clerical temporalities, not their spiritual income which he saw as sacred, granted freely by ecclesiastical assemblies, and administered by the clergy themselves.

The archbishop also sought to force royal clerks to reside and be ordained and he resisted deliberate attempts to extend royal patronage, for example in royal free chapels. Winchelsey was committed to the independence of Church and clergy. His 'fight was against *all* lay encroachments upon ecclesiastical rights'. Hence his failure to make common cause with aristocratic opposition in and after 1297, which partly explains why clerical grievances were not satisfactorily resolved. In any case his battles with the crown were not fought on equal terms: firstly, because such issues were settled in royal not church courts; secondly, because Boniface VIII progressively backed down on taxation, making it difficult for Winchelsey to maintain his independent stance; and thirdly and conclusively because Clement V, pope from 1305, placed good relations with his former master Edward I ahead of ecclesiastical principles, conceding most of what the king wanted over Winchelsey's head and suspending the archbishop from office. Although Winchelsey was restored in 1307, the world had changed. Clement V deferred to Edward II's wishes and Winchelsey could not have continued his struggle even had he been physically fit enough to do so. The next archbishop, the non-graduate Walter Reynolds, was a devoted royal official like the unsuccessful Robert Burnell forty years earlier. What had disqualified Burnell was now what was required of an archbishop.

J.H. Denton, *Robert Winchelsey and the Crown 1294–1313: A study in the defence of ecclesiastical liberty*, 1980.
P. Heath, *Church and Realm 1272–1461*, 1988.

HUMPHREY BOHUN, EARL OF HEREFORD AND ESSEX

(*d.* 1298), and constable of England, was intimately involved in Edward I's conquest of Wales and reorganisation of Welsh government. His two earldoms made him a major English magnate and despite his father's death on the baronial side at Evesham he was consistently loyal (if not uncritical) of Edward I. Wider horizons emerge from his French marriage, his pilgrimage to Santiago de Compostella in 1278, and his mission abroad in the 1290s, but it was Wales that demanded most of his attention.

Lands in eastern Wales conquered in the 12th century by Anglo-Norman barons had become marcher lordships within which the king's writ 'did not run' (had no authority). As lord of Brecon Humphrey Bohun was one of the greatest marcher lords. His lordship of Brecon, however, was one of those largely conquered by the Welsh prince Llywellyn by 1267, when his tenure was confirmed by Henry III in the treaty of Montgomery. On his majority in 1270 Bohun started reconquering Brecon and recovered the castles by 1273 in spite of official backing for Llywellyn. The breach between Edward I and Llywellyn enabled Bohun to complete the reconquest and he contributed substantially to each Welsh war.

Each marcher lordship was subject to its own laws, customs, and courts, and disputes between marcher lords were settled by the law of the march, which allowed for private war. Such privileges were acceptable for a frontier zone subject to endemic warfare, but their justification disappeared with the English conquest of Wales. Edward regarded marcher lordships as the greatest franchises to be curbed and treated a dispute between Bohun and the Earl of Gloucester as a chance to impose his authority. While longstanding differences divided the earls, respectively lords of Glamorgan and Brecon, their quarrel focused on a new castle erected by Gloucester in disputed borderlands. Following sporadic conflict, a royal proclamation of 1290 forbade private warfare, but was ignored by Gloucester, who probably rejected royal jurisdiction in the marches. His men seized 1,070 cattle and other beasts and did much other damage on raids into Brecon. Edward's concentration on disrespect to himself rather than settlement of the original dispute caused Bohun to resort to force to assert his marcher privileges and to raid Gloucester's lands. Edward denounced both earls' belief 'that they could escape by their liberty of the march from the penalty they would deservedly have incurred if they had committed such excesses elsewhere in the realm outside the marches'. They were imprisoned and their lordships confiscated, only to be redeemed in 1292 for 10,000 marks (£6,666) from Gloucester and 1,000 marks (£666) from Hereford. They were thus unfortunate victims of Edward's determination to assert novel authority over the Welsh marches.

Even before this humiliation Bohun never enjoyed much favour, but his reasons for becoming an opposition leader in 1297 are unclear. He may well have broadened the opposition's grievances from military service to taxation and other exactions and it was certainly he who was spokesman against those in the exchequer. He foresaw civil war, munitioning Brecon Castle against possible royal revenge. Civil war was averted and both earls served in the Falkirk campaign, withdrawing when Edward failed to fulfil the charters and thus forcing the abandonment of the campaign. Norfolk continued the struggle, ultimately successfully, but Bohun died at Saffron Walden the same year.

G. Jones, 'The Bohun Earls of Hereford and Essex 1270–1322', Oxford M. Litt. thesis, 1984.
M. Prestwich, *Edward I*, 1988.

SIR JOHN SEGRAVE (c. 1256–1325) of Segrave (Leics.) was retained in 1297 by the Earl Marshal, Roger Bigod, Earl of Norfolk. Although it is the first indenture of retainer for life to survive, it was not the first one to be made. It is so like other early indentures that it can be taken as typical of the contracts made between lords and their retainers under Edward I and indeed for the rest of the middle ages. Whereas feudalism, by now obsolete, involved permanent contracts sealed by permanent grants of land, the indenture system involved temporary payment in land or money and has been named bastard feudalism. Segrave promised to serve the earl in person with five knights and ten men-at-arms in peace and in war against all-comers except the king for the earl's lifetime. In peacetime he would bring 16 lances whenever summoned and would receive keep for his men (bouche of court) and his horses and wages for his grooms. If the king fought in Gascony, France or Flanders, then Segrave would bring 20 horsemen, receiving a fodder allowance, but nothing for the men except a lump sum of £80. If the earl did not go, Segrave would serve on the same terms. In return, Segrave received the manor of Lodden in Norfolk for life, two robes annually as the earl's senior banneret and robes for his five knights like those of the earl's own knights. Also implied was support from the earl in his own lawful business. In addition to his own men, the earl recruited unattached bannerets, knights and their retinues, often, like Segrave, from other parts of England. Almost at once Segrave accompanied his lord to the exchequer to stop collection of a tax and soon after he excused the earl's absence from campaign to the king. He was one of the earl's household and he deputised as marshal in the campaign of 1301. Such contracts were normally for the life of the retainer, but as Bigod had no heirs Segrave was retained only for the life of the earl, who died in 1306. Segrave's son Stephen was retained by the Earl of Lancaster by 1308 and Segrave's own contract with that earl may date from then too. He was to serve with 30 men-at-arms for 50 marks (£33.66) and in 1322 was third in Lancaster's list of bannerets, after the Earl of Surrey and another banneret. His brother Nicholas, however, was much more prominent in the earl's service.

Bastard feudal contracts almost invariably reserved the retainer's allegiance to the king. Thus Segrave was entitled to withdraw his service during Lancaster's rebellion in 1321-2. Moreover such contracts were compatible with continued service to the crown. Segrave had served in Wales (1277, 1282, 1285), Ireland (1287) and Scotland (1291), was again in Scotland each year from 1297-1307, and was keeper of Scotland in 1302-5, when he captured Wallace and did much to restore orderly English government. Again keeper of Scotland from 1309 and keeper of the Cumberland marches in 1313, he was captured at Bothwell after Bannockburn in 1314 and was ransomed with royal help. Back in the north in 1318-19, he was in Gascony at his death in 1325.

Segrave attended parliament as a baron from 1296 and was on the continual council set up in 1318. His principal reward from the crown was a grant of lands worth £100 a year or £1,000 to buy lands in 1312. In 1308 he had been appointed justice of the forests beyond the Trent and custodian of Nottingham castle, offices he briefly lost in 1310–12 due to opposition to Gaveston, and in 1314 the custody of Derby was added. Complaints of extortion provoked a commission of inquiry in 1314–15 and presumably also explain why the townsmen of Nottingham besieged him in the castle in 1315. By his death he had extended his estates into Norfolk, Oxfordshire, and other counties, and had improved them by crenellating his houses, creating parks, founding markets, and securing grants of hunting rights.

M. Prestwich, *War, Politics and Finance under Edward I*, 1972.
N. Denholm-Young, *Seignorial Administration in England*, 1937.

HENRY EASTRY (*d.* 1331), Prior of Canterbury Cathedral from 1285 until 1331, is renowned as one of the most successful monastic heads of his day. Monasteries had become great propertied corporations with many economic interests to manage and their heads needed expertise in finance, estate management and handling people more than scholarship or sanctity. Canterbury cathedral priory was one of the greatest of such houses and its prior was a national figure. The years around 1300 were marked by overpopulation and hence high demand for land and food, an exceptional opportunity for those landowners able to exploit their demesne lands fully and ready to invest their profits in improvements to increase production. This was called high farming and Prior Henry as high farmer transformed the fortunes of the priory.

A local man, Henry was elected prior while still young and stayed on 46 years into irascible old age. From the first he proved himself 'an economist of the first order' (Knowles). Debts of £5,000, twice the annual income, were paid off in fifteen years and annual revenues were raised by a quarter. The possibilities of each property were realised, often involving investment on livestock, drainage or marling on a scale more impressive to contemporaries than to ourselves, and the estate was run as a unit, flocks of sheep, for example, being moved around according to season. The monks were more fully involved in running their affairs, whether as monk wardens of groups of manors or in central supervision and audit, and they were encouraged to share in decisions as the prior's colleagues. Prior Henry provided the direction that enabled the priory to take advantages of opportunities, minimise disaster, and transform its finances ready for the harder days that lay ahead.

Henry Eastry identified himself wholly with the Church of Canterbury, whose cathedral he adorned and whose estates he developed. The Church of Canterbury included the archbishopric — he gave good advice to four successive archbishops — but his priory came first. In 1297, when Archbishop Winchelsey defied King Edward I, Henry obediently followed his lead until the priory itself was threatened, but although then submitting he later acted as vicar-general for the exiled archbishop and later campaigned for Winchelsey's canonisation. Prior Henry was too important to keep out of politics, but he disliked it, performing his parliamentary duties perfunctorily. The decline of the political importance of the cathedral priory has been dated from his time. Similarly he was not interested in the affairs of the Benedictine Order as a whole or in uniformity of observance and discipline, but devoted himself to the narrower interests of Canterbury cathedral priory. His youthful interest in scripture has left no mark in his letters, which show no interest either in theology or learning. His priorate was commemorated not by great intellectual or literary achievements, but in the compilation of the splendid administrative registers that remain with us today. Prior Henry's incisive intelligence, his organisational abilities and his cautious pragmatism were fully absorbed by the management and development of the priory estate. He illustrates the way in which monasteries and what was expected of them had changed by the later middle ages.

M. D. Knowles, *The Religious Orders in England,* ii, *The End of the Middle Ages,* 1955.

R. A. L. Smith, *Canterbury Cathedral Priory: A Study in Monastic Administration,* 1943.

WALTER LANGTON (*d.* 1321), Bishop of Lichfield from 1296 until his death, was 'the first treasurer of the Exchequer who was in fact, if not in name, the king's chief minister' (Tout). Probably from Leicestershire, he entered Edward I's service as a youth, establishing mutual trust that lasted all the king's life, and worked his way up the wardrobe from clerk (1281) to keeper (1290-5), serving as treasurer of the exchequer in 1295-1307, ironically as the Scottish war enhanced the financial importance of the wardrobe. Minor reforms at the wardrobe and minor economies in the royal households are attributable to Langton, but his main achievement was the highly efficient management of the Scottish war in spite of escalating royal debts. He was also a frequent ambassador and government spokesman. His devotion to Edward I's interests meant he would go to any lengths, even crime, to achieve his wishes. In return, he enjoyed the complete confidence of the king, who found him 'conspicuous in the maturity of his counsel and full of discretion, useful, nay necessary, to us and our realm', and backed him against all comers.

What this meant in practice emerged at Langton's trial under Edward II. 48 charges alleged all kinds of abuse of power: manipulation of justice, maintenance, extortion, arbitrary seizures and imprisonment. Langton admitted six charges of champerty, the most serious perversion of justice, and was convicted in at least 24 other cases, damages being awarded against him. His mastery of financial and legal technicalities recalls Adam Stratton a generation earlier, but Langton's repertoire was wider. Moreover as treasurer he had more scope: he could exploit royal debts, pressurise sheriffs accountable to him for arrears, and even join the bench to judge his own case. His absolute assurance of royal support and of retrospective pardons when he went too far gave him self-confidence in his immunity and added insolence to his power. Not surprisingly, Langton became very rich, spent lavishly on building (including two churches at his reputed birthplace), acquired extensive estates worth £1,300 a year to pass on to his brother Robert Peverell and nephew Edmund, and later claimed to have lost £20,000 by his trial. Langton's corruption was perhaps not unique, but its scope must have been: surely Langton himself could not have brought all his affairs to a conclusion. The charges of simony, homicide, and devil worship of which he was acquitted at his trial pale beside his documented career as 'the most successful profiteer in the royal administration'. Imprisoned in 1307–8 and in 1311, he was briefly treasurer again in 1312, but thereafter lapsed into political obscurity.

Langton's dishonesty and greed hardly fitted him for an ecclesiastical career. Certainly he was a pluralist and nepotist, perhaps kept a mistress, and must have been normally non-resident as bishop. Yet his cathedral chapter described him as 'a God-fearing man of pure life and devoted to his ministry' and he was remembered, with some justice, as a benefactor to the Church of Lichfield. Not only did he defend the rights of his see, but he built a new palace at Lichfield, reconstructed Eccleshall Castle, and built extensively at his house in the Strand and his manor houses. At the cathedral he founded a chantry, erected the Lady Chapel, walled the cloister, enhanced the common fund, and left plate, jewels etc in his will. He erected a bridge in the town. Tout's comment that he saw 'his bishopric rather as a reward for his administrative skill than as an ecclesiastical obligation' was less than just.

A. Beardwood, 'Trial of Walter de Langton, Bishop of Lichfield 1307–12', *Transactions of the American Philosophical Society*, new series 54(3), 1964.

M. Prestwich, *War, Politics and Finance under Edward I*, 1972.

HENRY LACY, EARL OF LINCOLN AND SALISBURY (*c.* 1249–1311) is a prime example of the nobility of service. The eldest son of Edmund, Earl of Lincoln (*d.* 1257), he acquired the earldom of Salisbury by marriage to Margaret Longsword. He further enhanced his fortune through royal grants, notably the marcher lordship of Denbigh. He was the founder of Whalley Abbey and contemplated establishing an Oxford college in 1307. Unfortunately both his sons died prematurely, one falling in a well at Denbigh and another tumbling from the battlements at Pontefract, leaving his daughter Alice as his sole heiress. On her marriage to Thomas of Lancaster, nephew of Edward I and the greatest nobleman of his generation, Henry resettled his lands, granting the reversion in default of children to the house of Lancaster and thus risked disinheriting collateral relatives should Alice die childless, as indeed she did. This risk, Henry evidently considered, was a price worth paying for such a prestigious match.

While Henry's estates, although extensive, did not place him among the greatest of the earls, his continuous record of royal service over many years was quite exceptional. As a soldier he served in Wales in 1276–7, 1282, and 1293–4; in Gascony in 1294–7, latterly as commander-in-chief, where he was defeated at Bellegarde; and in Scotland in the campaigns of Falkirk (1298), Caerlaverock (1300), 1301, 1305 and 1307. He accompanied Edward I to Gascony in

1286–9 and was one of those commissioned to try the judges on their return. Negotiations with Scotland, France and the Papacy occupied him repeatedly from 1290. In 1279 he acted jointly as regent in the king's absence. Perhaps the closest councillor of Edward I in his last years, he was with him on his deathbed, and was among those the dying king charged with the welfare of his son Edward II.

While Henry honoured his promise to Edward I, he was not uncritical of Edward II's government and particularly of his infatuation with Piers Gaveston. It was Lincoln who assured Edward II of his power to create Gaveston an earl and befriended the young Gascon, but this did not last long as he became 'of all the earls, his greatest enemy and persecutor'. Lincoln recognized the need for administrative reforms, notably of purveyance. He seems to have pressed first for reform by the king and only later, when disappointed, did he become one of the Ordainers imposing Ordinances on the king. Gaveston represented an obstacle to good government and did not endear himself by nicknaming Lincoln 'burst-belly'. Lincoln's opposition was not disloyal. The Ordainers made a distinction between their duties to the crown and king, which it has been persuasively argued represented Lincoln's position. He campaigned for reform whilst remaining loyal to Edward II, may have restrained hotter heads among his younger fellow earls, and even seems to have been ready to tolerate Gaveston, if his influence could be curbed. Remarkably he enjoyed the confidence of both parties, acting both as an Ordainer and as keeper of the realm for the king in 1310–11. His death thus removed a moderating influence that was to be sorely missed.

J. F. Baldwin, 'The Household Administration of Henry Lacy and Thomas of Lancaster', *English Historical Review* xlii, 1927.
J. R. Maddicott, *Thomas of Lancaster 1307–1322: A Study in the Reign of Edward II*, 1970.

CARDINAL THOMAS JORZ (*d.* 1310) was one of three English Dominican friars who were created cardinals of Santa Sabina in 1303–10. All three studied at Paris and Oxford, all probably becoming doctors of theology, all three served in the Oxford convent, and all attended councils abroad. Walter Winterbourne (*d.*

1305), probably the eldest, and Thomas Jorz were successively priors of the Oxford convent, priors provincial (heads) of the Dominicans in England, and confessors to Edward I (1289–1305), to whom Winterbourne was a most trusted servant. Winterbourne probably originated from Wiltshire, William Macclesfield (d. 1303), probably the youngest, from Cheshire, and Jorz from Wales, but all were obscure in origin. Their careers demonstrate not just that high office in the mendicant orders was exceptionally open to the talents, not just the international rather than insular horizons of such men, but also the higher valuation placed by the papacy in comparison to the English crown on those from the religious orders. Several popes and many cardinals were monks or friars and the other two English cardinals of the 14th century, Simon Langham and Adam Easton, were Benedictine monks, yet monks and friars were rarely appointed bishops by late medieval English monarchs.

Thomas Jorz was probably known as Thomas the Englishman at Paris, where he is alleged to have studied under Albertus Magnus and to have known St Thomas Aquinas. He was in the Oxford convent in 1292, when he secured his doctorate of theology and became prior, and in 1297 he became prior provincial of the Dominican order in England. In this capacity he attended Dominican synods at Cologne in 1295, Marseilles in 1300, and Toulouse in 1304. In 1305 Edward I sent him to the General Council of the Church at Lyons, where he was created cardinal by Pope Clement V, thereafter making his home at the papal Curia.

In the fourteenth century cardinals resigned their existing offices on appointment and took up residence at the Roman court. Only in the fifteenth century were they allowed to retain their preferments and remain in their country of origin. Jorz thus became a papal official, serving on papal commissions and embassies; he was on embassy at his death at Grenoble in 1310. Jorz's influence emerges in his dealings with Walter Stapledon, Bishop of Exeter, to whom he was my 'principal lord and promoter', for whom he intervened to assist with his consecration and to avert a challenge to his election, and from whom in return he exacted a pension for a protegé. Similarly Edward II asked him to press for the canonisations of Robert Grosseteste (1307) and Thomas Cantilupe (1308). If appropriate records survived, Jorz would probably be seen intervening frequently in English affairs. He certainly exercised his influence to advance his friends and relatives, no doubt assisting the advancement of his brothers Walter in 1306–7 and Robert in 1311–21 to the archbishopric of Armagh.

EDWARD II (1284–1327) was born at Caernarvon in 1284 and ascended the throne in 1307. He was the eldest surviving son of Edward I and Eleanor of Castile. His reign was a complete failure. The difficulties Edward faced would have taxed any monarch: an unwinnable war in Scotland, an empty exchequer and heavy debts, and the Great European Famine of 1315–17. Edward did little to solve them and much to exacerbate them, clashing repeatedly with his magnates and allowing law and order to collapse. He became a tyrant, was deserted by his queen and heir, and his deposition proved the only practicable solution to his arbitary ineptitude as king. Medieval monarchs had to take a lead in war, govern, and co-operate with their magnates, but Edward would not, from preference not incapacity. It was his personal frailties that made his reign such an unmitigated disaster.

Edward received the military education usual for aristocrats and first impressions were favourable. The *Caerlaverock Roll* records that:

> The fourth squadron, with its train,
> Edward the king's son led,
> A youth of seventeen years of age
> And newly bearing arms.
> He was of well-proportioned and handsome person
> Of a courteous disposition and well-bred,
> And desirous of finding an occasion,
> To make proof of his strength.
> He managed his steed wonderfully well.

'Had he practised himself in the use of arms', we are told, 'he would have excelled King Richard (the Lionheart) in worth'. But his potential was stillborn. Edward cared bitterly about his military defeats, engaging in major campaigns in 1314, 1319 and 1322, but he was a poor general, fostered divisions among the English, and blamed others for his own failures. More important, his interest was sporadic and he regularly subordinated the Scottish war to domestic politics.

Edward II
(From his effigy in Gloucester Cathedral)

Medieval kings had to rule as well as reign. Edward did not lack intelligence or ability, but so rarely did he act effectively that when he did so it excited remark, as when, 'contrary to his usual wont', he rose early in the morning, treated his advisers pleasantly, and contributed constructively in council! He acted energetically on occasion, as in 1321–2, but only briefly. More often he had 'no idea what to do or where to turn next'. He preferred to let things drift or alternatively to allow others to take his burden. What he wanted to make of his reign is suggested by his last years, when he had no rivals. Parliament was not allowed to criticise, only to rubber-stamp, and he accumulated treasure, ultimately £61,981 or a year's revenue: 'The king had plenty of treasure. Many of his fathers amassed money; he alone exceeded them all'. And what did he do with it? In the words of Sir Thomas Gray, he

> kept himself quiet, undertaking nothing in honour and prowess, but only on the advice of Hugh Despenser so as to become rich, keeping for himself as much as he could seize.

No constructive use was made of it against the Scots, the French, or even his domestic enemies.

Unable to rule or fight, Edward enjoyed little respect from his magnates and did not seek their goodwill, rejecting chivalric pursuits for demeaning activities like hedging and ditching and fraternising with low-born artisans. He could not meet his magnates face to face, impose his will on them, curb their private wars, or terrify them into obedience. Nor did he wish to, frequently missing parliaments with feigned illnesses or other excuses. He preferred the company of his favourites.

Edward's personal inadequacies were exaggerated by his reliance on favourites. All kings had them, usually friends or able servants, and they were perfectly respectable providing they conformed to accepted political conventions. Edward II's favourites did not. Their eminence stemmed not from rank, ability or service, but from royal partiality, almost certainly homosexual in origin. Even this could have been acceptable if kept within bounds, but Edward was 'incapable of moderate favour' and his love for them excluded all others. They were promoted, Gaveston acquiring an earldom and marrying a princess, and they monopolised the king's attention, becoming like second kings. Both Gaveston and the Younger Despenser took precedence over Queen Isabella. As their ascendancy was based on royal favour, they were careful to meet Edward's wishes.

> The king preferred his former counsel, because it was more in accord with his desires; indeed it is frequently more acceptable to advise a man to follow his own bent.

Thus too in 1318 it was observed:

> The king is reconciled with his barons. For putting aside trifles, he listens to their advice, and now there is none to incite the king to do evil, because his private following which was hostile to the barons has left court.

Only at such moments could responsible politicians bring Edward back to the serious business of government. Such phases did not last, for Edward was wayward and flighty. Once his affections were engaged, they could not be broken even by death. Only too aware of hostility to his favourites, Edward gave their protection priority over policy at home and abroad. The ultimate absurdity was his proposal that Gaveston should be protected by Robert Bruce against Edward's domestic enemies!

Yet Edward's favourites merely took advantage of their master's weakness and pandered to his wishes. Edward had pronounced opinions and liked having his own way. He did not like being crossed or criticised. Baronial demands, big or small, were resisted or delayed, for Edward was extremely obstinate and incapable of giving way gracefully. He gave way only when the pressure became intense, when magnates came armed to parliament or threatened to withdraw their fealty. He invariably broke his word when the crisis had passed. On one such occasion,

> the king's anger knew no bounds, for he was not allowed to keep even one member of his household at his own wish, but, as is provided for an idiot, the ordering of his whole house should depend upon the will of another.

Such outbursts illustrate his lack of proportion, tendency to overreact, and the violent temper he frequently vented in politically inconvenient directions. His rages usually burnt themselves out ineffectively, but some gave rise to resentments that lasted for years.

Vengeance was important to Edward, who could not let bygones be bygones and constantly allowed personal and public motives to become entangled. To try Walter Langton, his father's corrupt minister, was commendable, to try him in revenge for past slights less so, and to arrest him while escorting the dead king's body was grossly improper. A lack of self-restraint, decorum and timing was a constant weakness. The king's resentments and untrustworthiness coloured relations with his magnates and made genuine reconciliation impossible. Edward's wilful perversity was fertile ground for evil counsellors and brought them all to ruin.

N. Denholm-Young, ed., *Vita Edwardi Secundi: The Life of Edward II*, 1957.

N. M. Fryde, *Tyranny and Fall of Edward II*, 1979.

H. Johnstone, *Edward of Caernarvon 1284–1307*, 1946.

J. R. Maddicott, *Thomas of Lancaster 1307-1322: A Study in the Reign of Edward II*, 1970.

J. R. S. Phillips, *Aymer de Valence, Earl of Pembroke 1307–24: Personal Politics in the Reign of Edward II*, 1972.

PIERS GAVESTON, EARL OF CORNWALL (*d.* 1312), Edward II's notorious favourite, was the younger son of a French knight Sir Arnold Gaveston, head of an ancient family of minor nobility with lands in Béarn on the Spanish border and Gascony. Sir Arnold's faithful and unrewarding service caused Edward I to employ Piers in Flanders in 1297 and Scotland in 1298. A servant of Prince Edward in 1300, he fought with him in Scotland in 1303 and 1305, when he deserted to joust in France. Back in England in 1307, he was exiled because of his excessive intimacy with the prince, presumably homosexual and already of some years duration. Recalled on the prince's accession, Piers was created Earl of Cornwall and granted lands worth about £4,000 a year, married the king's niece Margaret Clare, and was appointed keeper of the realm (regent), all in 1307. He took pride of place at the coronation in 1308. Exiled later in 1308, Gaveston was recalled next year, but he was again exiled in 1311, returning by Christmas. Besieged at Scarborough Castle, he capitulated and was being escorted to Wallingford by the Earl of Pembroke, when he was seized by the Earl of Warwick, condemned by a kangaroo court, and executed (18 June 1312).

Gaveston had much to commend him. He was physically active, brave and skilful in arms, all essential qualities for a good knight, and had the excellent manners of a good courtier. His alien origins and rapid promotion were not disadvantages. The king and most earls had foreign parents and outsiders like Sir Otto Grandisson had pursued successful careers in England. Admittedly Grandisson was never an earl, creation as such having become a rare distinction almost confined to the royal family and the earldom of Cornwall in particular being earmarked by Edward I for a younger son. Hence the significance of Gaveston's marriage, which related him to the king and many noblemen. 'This marriage tie did indeed strengthen his position not a little; for it much increased the goodwill of his friends and restrained the hatred of the baronage'. The Earl of Lincoln, for example, was initially friendly to Gaveston.

Thus Gaveston's downfall was not inevitable. What went wrong? First of all, the favour showed him was excessive. He monopolised Edward's attention to the exclusion of others and cornered royal patronage. 'Nor could the king's affection be alienated from Piers, for the more he was told, in attempts to damp his ardour, the greater grew his love and tenderness towards Piers'. So great were his actual gains that chroniclers — and others too — believed worse of him, that he exported royal treasure and drafted blank charters. Edward's poverty and need for taxes were blamed on him, for 'he almost outdid the king in his extravagance'. Perhaps he did not influence policy, but he impeded both reform and the Scottish war. Unpardonably arrogant, he wore imperial purple at the coronation, whereas other earls wore *only* cloth of gold, and

> lorded it over them like a second king, to whom all were subject and none equal. But Piers did not wish to remember that he had once been Piers the humble esquire. For Piers accounted no one his fellow, save the king alone. Indeed his countenance exacted greater deference than that of the king. His arrogance was intolerable to the barons and a prime cause of hatred and rancour. And indeed the superciliousness which he affected would have been intolerable enough in a king's son.

Hence his scorn for the earls, the rude nicknames he called them, and their determination to destroy him. It was his own fault that 'the country rejoiced and all its inhabitants were glad' at his death.

N. Denholm-Young, ed., *Vita Edwardi Secundi: The Life of Edward II*, 1957.

J. R. Maddicott, *Thomas of Lancaster 1307–1322: A Study in the Reign of Edward II*, 1970.

A. A. Taylor, 'The Career of Peter of Gaveston', London M.A. thesis, 1938.

GUY BEAUCHAMP, EARL OF WARWICK (d. 1315) was both a highly cultivated nobleman and 'one of the most bitter of Edward II's opponents'. His extensive estates in the West Midlands made him a magnate of the front rank. Only the second Beauchamp to succeed to the earldom founded in 1088, Guy took his name from the legendary Guy of Warwick and remembered his roots as a Beauchamp of Elmley Castle (Worcs.), where he founded a college of eight priests, regrettably under-endowed, in the castle chapel. The *Beauchamp Cartulary* reveals many minor purchases of land in Warwick, Berkswell, and elsewhere rounding off existing holdings. He also added to his inheritance through his second marriage to the Tony heiress. He was exceptionally well-educated for his time and class, possessing a particularly good knowledge of Latin. He had a large collection of books and gave 42 of them, including several French romances about Alexander and King Arthur, to Bordesley Abbey, where he founded a chantry of two monks and chose to be buried, deliberately without any pomp.

With his learning went common sense and wisdom that spilled over into his political career. He was variously described 'as a discreet and well-informed man', 'a man discreet and well-lettered, through which the whole kingdom of England shone with wisdom', and 'in prudence and counsel one who has not a parallel'. On their respective deathbeds Edward I confided the future Edward II to him and Lincoln advised Lancaster to be guided by his advice. 'Other earls did many things only after taking his opinion: in wisdom and council he had no peer'. Warwick's public career commenced with the Falkirk campaign of 1298, where he distinguished himself by his bravery, and he served repeatedly in Scotland, earning the high favour of Edward I reflected in his extensive grants of lands in Scotland and, more permanent, the forfeited Balliol lordship of Barnard Castle in County Durham.

Like Lincoln and Lancaster, Warwick's career of committed royal

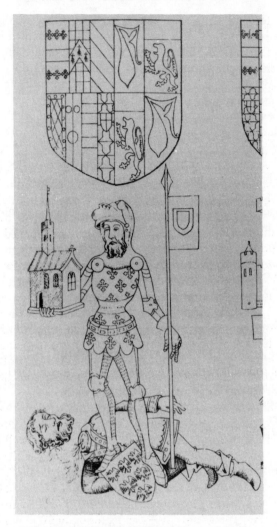

Guy Beauchamp, Earl of Warwick (left)
(Artist: John Rous)

service ended on Edward II's accession. Immediately alienated by Piers Gaveston, who nicknamed him the 'Black Dog of Arden' in allusion to his dark and swarthy complexion, he was the favourite's most bitter and dangerous opponent. Like other noblemen, he supported Gaveston's exile in 1308, but alone opposed his recall from his first exile in 1309. Warwick was an Ordainer and active in compilation of the Ordinances: 'By his advice the Ordinances were framed'. It was Warwick who seized Gaveston from Pembroke's custody at Deddington in Oxfordshire in 1312, bearing him off to Warwick and humiliating him. He shared in the favourite's trial and condemnation but did not attend his execution, which took place on Lancaster's land. He and Lancaster stood firmly together in negotiations for a pardon from the king, absented themselves from the Bannockburn campaign, and then dominated the government, one chronicler describing Warwick as the king's chief councillor. His premature death was widely lamented, although one must doubt whether even Warwick could have brought unity as one chronicler supposed.

J. R. Maddicott, *Thomas of Lancaster 1307–1322: A Study in the Reign of Edward II,* 1970.
N. Denholm-Young, ed., *Vita Edwardi Secundi: The Life of Edward II,* 1957.

AYMER VALENCE, EARL OF PEMBROKE (*d.* 1324) belonged to the international nobility. His maternal heritage comprised lands in England, Ireland, and Wales, which provided an income of £3,000, second only to the Earls of Gloucester and Lancaster. He was briefly lord of Bothwell in Scotland. From his father William, half-brother of Henry III, he inherited four French lordships, and other French property came with his second marriage. Both his wives were French noblewomen, daughters of the constable and butler of France respectively. He visited France almost every year, often on embassies in which his French connections were invaluable. Other missions took him to Scotland and the papal Curia. His military career commenced with Edward I's Flemish expedition of 1297. He served in Scotland each year from the Falkirk campaign of 1298 to 1303, latterly as lieutenant south of the Forth; in 1306–7, when he beat Bruce at Methven, but lost to him at Loudoun Hill; in the Bannockburn campaign of 1314; in 1315, 1319, and in 1323, when he was routed at Byland. In 1320 he was keeper of the realm. Like his older contemporary the Earl of Lincoln,

Pembroke's career was spent in constant service to the crown. Also like Lincoln, he died in harness, on embassy to France.

Historians have identified Pembroke as founder of a 'Middle Party', hostile both to the king's favourites and his enemies, which provided stable government in the years 1317–21. The 'Middle Party', however, is a myth and Pembroke was merely the most prominent of those of Edward II's advisers, who owed nothing to their physical attractions. From Gaveston's death in 1312, Pembroke as royal councillor exercised his influence for moderation. That negotiations with opposing magnates in 1312–13 and 1317–18 ended in agreements rather than civil war is largely to his credit. Edward II valued his advice and often acted on it, but Pembroke's influence varied with that of others. In 1312–14, when he had no rivals, he was the king's chief councillor, but in 1314–16 he was supplanted by Warwick and Lancaster and in 1316–17 by a new court party. The famous indenture of 24 November 1317, traditionally the origin of the 'Middle Party', actually witnessed Pembroke and Badlesmere as royal councillors restraining Damory (the current favourite) from exploiting the king's infatuation and securing Damory's support for their more sensible counsel. From 1318 on the rise of the Despensers progressively relegated Pembroke to secondary importance. Unlike the favourites, Pembroke never established a personal dominance over the king. Lack of authority, rather than moderation, explain why his rewards of office were so meagre and why Edward helped him so little with the ransom Pembroke incurred on royal embassy in 1317.

Like all noblemen, Pembroke preferred co-operation with the crown to opposition. He may have considered Edward's weakness further cause for offering sound counsel. He certainly opposed the malign influence of successive favourites. Twice their dominance strained his allegiance. One such was Gaveston. Pembroke favoured his exile in 1308, was an Ordainer in 1310, and in 1312 fought against him. It was to Pembroke that Gaveston surrendered conditionally and Pembroke therefore who was dishonoured by his execution. Hence his reconciliation with the king, now without Gaveston, the cause of his original defection. Similarly in 1321 he sympathised with the marchers and persuaded Edward to exile the Despensers. By supporting Edward against Badlesmere, he was committed against the marchers and Lancaster, thus inadvertently assuring the Despensers of dominance. If indeed 'he was a man of moderate talents, whose ability was not up to the demands placed upon it in the crises of Edward II's reign', this was because the crises were insoluble without deposition of the king.

J. R. S. Phillips, *Aymer de Valence, Earl of Pembroke 1307-24: Baronial Politics in the Reign of Edward II*, 1972.

THOMAS OF LANCASTER (c. 1278-1322), son of Edward I's brother Edmund and Queen Blanche, was a natural bulwark of the crown. 'As each parent was of royal birth, he was clearly of nobler descent than the other earls'. Greatly favoured by Edward I, he had five earldoms: Lancaster, Leicester and Derby by inheritance; Lincoln and Salisbury by marriage to Alice Lacy. At £11,000 his income was twice that of the next greatest earl, his household cost half that of the king, and his lavishly feed retainers included two earls, nine bannerets, and fifty knights. His lands clustered thickly in Yorkshire, Lancashire and the North Midlands, a 'concentration over a wide area in contrast to those of other magnates which helped to make him the most powerful of the earls'. In 1308 he broke with the king and moved to permanent opposition and henceforth employed his power to frustrate effective government and the war against Scotland. Too strong to repress or coerce, he had to be conciliated: in 1317-18 the government negotiated with him like an independent state and contracted a formal treaty with him at Leake. He was indeed 'the supreme example of the overmighty subject' (McKisack).

Lancaster's misuse of his power reflects 'the repulsive nature of the man'. A generous almsgiver and pious benefactor, perhaps 'more than conventionally devout', he was also sexually immoral, quarrelsome, selfish and vindictive. He was rapacious to his tenants, maintained his retainers beyond the legitimate bounds of good lordship, and seized what he wanted in defiance of right and the law. He readily resorted to brutality, violence and private war in his Thorpe Waterville dispute with Pembroke, his suppression of Adam Banaster's rebellion, his feud with Warenne, Sir Gilbert Middleton's kidnapping of two cardinals, and when wasting Damory's lands. However justifiable, his hatred and distrust of the king soured national politics for years. Incompetent in office, petulantly critical when out, his support declined among the nobility, other north-erners, and ultimately his own retainers. His wife left him in 1316. Having masterminded the Despenser War in 1321, it was his hatred for Badlesmere that enabled Edward to destroy him and his allies in 1322, when he was defeated at Boroughbridge and executed.

To Dr Phillips, Lancaster was a 'muddler and a messer, who nursed his hatred of the King and concealed his own ambitions and lack of constructive ideas behind the facade of the Ordinances and his claim to exercise authority as steward of England'. His claims were thus mere lip-service. Yet miracles were worked at his tomb and some saw him as a martyr, who died fighting a tyrannical government in the cause of reform. This was how Lancaster saw himself, modelling himself consciously on Simon Montfort, promoting the canonis-ation of Cantilupe and Winchelsey. He repeatedly demanded imple-mentation of the Ordinances, the resumption of grants, and the removal of evil councillors: in 1312-14; in power in 1314-16, when they were enforced; and as articles in the 1318 settlement. In 1312 'being of higher birth and more powerful than the rest, (he) took upon himself the peril of the business, and ordered Piers, after three terms of exile, as one disobedient to three lawful warnings, to be put to death'. At least some of his violence had behind it praiseworthy political aims. Lancaster was certainly consistent in his promotion of the Ordinances. If indeed 'his conduct in practice was inconsistent with his lofty claims', this reflects on his ability and character, not his intentions that are, perhaps, his only redeeming feature.

J.R. Maddicott, *Thomas of Lancaster 1307-1322: A Study in the Reign of Edward II*, 1970.
J.R.S. Phillips, *Aymer de Valence, Earl of Pembroke 1307-24: Baronial Politics in the Reign of Edward II*, 1972.

HUMPHREY BOHUN, EARL OF HEREFORD AND ESSEX (c. 1276-1322), exhibits the tensions to which even the most loyal of noblemen could be subjected. Unlike his father, essentially a marcher backwoodsman, Humphrey enjoyed close relations with the court and successive kings. At court in 1285-6 and perhaps even brought up there, the earl married the king's widowed daughter Elizabeth Countess of Holland in 1301 and was appointed to the council and household of his brother-in-law Prince Edward. Hereford was expected to exercise a good influence on the prince and he certainly enjoyed good relations with him before his accession. Although Edward I made Humphrey resettle his estates at his marriage, which could have disinherited the Bohun family, the king also treated the earl generously. His father's substantial £4,000 debt was cancelled and in 1306 Hereford was granted lands forfeited by Robert Bruce, later king of Scotland. These comprised not just Annadale, Lochmaben Castle, and other lands in Scotland, but also Writtle and other valuable properties in Essex. Such grants were not made to him merely as a royal kinsman, but in recognition of his repeated service in Scotland from 1296 onwards.

Hereford thus had every reason to look forward to Edward II's reign. He served against the Scots at Bannockburn in 1314, where he was captured, and again at Berwick in 1319 and helped suppress a Welsh rising in 1316. He was frequently at court witnessing charters, attending council, and dining with the king. He received a constant flow of favours, mainly of limited value, but including diplomatic pressure for payment of his wife's dower from Holland and exceptional assistance with his release in 1314. The influence he exercised, however, was never remarkable — he was never a royal favourite — and it was broken up by two periods of opposition.

Hereford continued his father's campaign for Confirmation of the Charters in 1299 and was both an Ordainer and a serious supporter of the Ordinances. Like most other earls, he was driven into reluctant opposition by the king's excessive favour to Gaveston. Hence, in punishment, his deprivation of his office of Constable of England. Hereford did not share in Gaveston's capture, but he was among the earls who organised his execution. Then, as the most moderate of the earls, he negotiated with the king for a settlement favourable to those responsible. His readiness to compromise shows that his natural place was with the king and that Gaveston's death had removed the cause for his estrangement. He even attended Gaveston's ceremonial reinterment at King's Langley and did not allow the loss of his own Scottish possessions to sour his relations with the king. Again in 1321–2 he took up arms against the Despensers, whose seizure of Gower struck directly at his interests and whose influence doubtless explains why Edward deprived him of his lordship of Builth. Even so, it was with great reluctance that he resorted to force, driven against his will to break with a king, who would not restrain his favourite. This time there was to be no reconciliation, for Hereford was among those killed in 1322 at the battle of Boroughbridge.

Whereas his father was primarily lord of Brecon, Hereford spent much more time in Essex, particularly at Pleshey Castle, and at court. He was an intelligent and competent soldier, councillor and diplomat. He enlarged his estates and provided for his dependant siblings and children. A strong sense of honour and dynasty, conventional piety and generosity round off his character. Genuine conflicts of loyalty, not bad faith, explain his political inconsistencies.

G. Jones, 'The Bohun Earls of Hereford and Essex 1270–1322', Oxford M.Litt. thesis, 1984.

SIR ROBERT HOLLAND (c. 1270–1329) 'reminds us that in the later Middle Ages barons as well as kings had their favourites'. Originating from Upholland near Wigan, which he crenellated and where he established a Benedictine priory, Holland was the eldest son of a county family of purely Lancastrian importance, but his relationship with Thomas of Lancaster transformed the fortunes of himself and his family. He entered Lancaster's retinue for the Falkirk campaign in 1298, thereafter serving him continually in Scotland and in domestic politics, and rose like Sir John Segrave to be one of his nine bannerets. Unlike Segrave, however, his service to Lancaster shaped his whole career. The omnicompetent supervisor of Lancaster's affairs, whose mandates were ranked by estate officials equally with those of the earl himself and who controlled the earl's treasure, Holland was Lancaster's chief confidant and friend. 'He trusts more upon him than upon any man alive. And so much the earl loved him that he might do in the estates whatever he liked.' Hence requests from king and pope for his intercession with Lancaster and hence too his retainder by Audley, Badlesmere and no doubt other magnates, all of whom sought his intercession with his lord. As the closest confidant of the greatest nobleman of his time, 'Holland's relationship with Lancaster cannot be taken as a model of the relationship between a lord and his retainer', but it illuminates in extreme form the character of bastard feudalism.

'Few retainers expected more from their lords than an annual fee together with the use of lordly patronage and influence on their behalf'. Holland, however, received much more than this. From 1300 on he received a stream of grants from the earl of land totalling 25 manors worth perhaps £550 a year, some of which may have been temporary or for ulterior motives. Lancaster's favour explains both his marriage to a baronial coheiress and the highly favourable partition of her estates in 1314. With his grants and wife's inheritance, he had lands in sixteen counties worth about £1,270, which made him one of the richest barons. It was to Lancaster also that Holland owed his summonses to parliament as a baron from 1314, a stream of minor royal favours, and his intermittent appointment as Justice of Chester, his tenure being renewed when Lancaster was in favour and terminated when he was not. Clearly King Edward considered that Holland's ties with Lancaster took precedence over those with himself.

With such a background, Holland's future was closely tied to Lancaster's and the earl's fall was bound to involve Holland as well. So Holland evidently thought, deserting to the crown during the Boroughbridge campaign in 1322, denying him the support of his Midland retainers and thus contributing materially to his destruction. Far from applauding him for giving priority to his allegiance to the crown, contemporaries were shocked by his treachery and Edward II kept him in prison. He had, however, saved his skin and his inheritance, which provided the benefit for further advancement in the next generation, when his son Thomas married into the royal family and became an earl. His own escape was only temporary, however, for it was as a 'false traitor' to Lancaster that he was murdered by the earl's erstwhile retainers in 1329, almost certainly with the backing of Lancaster's brother. The jurors, understandably, would not convict.

J. R. Maddicott, 'Thomas of Lancaster and Sir Robert Holland: A Study in Noble Patronage', *English Historical Review*, lxxxvi, 1971.

SIR BARTHOLOMEW BADLESMERE (d. 1322) rose from provincial obscurity to national prominence and then abruptly fell: a graphic illustration of the uncertainty of Edward II's England. He was born about 1275 into a gentry family from Badlesmere in Kent. His father rose to be Justice of Chester in the service of Prince Edward and died in 1301, by when Bartholomew had also made his mark. He served in Gascony in 1294, in Flanders in 1297, when he became one of Edward I's household knights, and in Scotland in 1303–4. Almost alone among Edward's household knights, he was elected to Parliament, sitting at the Carlisle Parliament in 1307: perhaps evidence of unusual political ambitions. Badlesmere was appointed constable of Bristol in 1307, was granted Chilham castle — henceforth his principal seat — in 1309, and from then on he attended parliament as a baron. One factor here may be his wife's lands as widowed Countess of Angus and heiress in her own right; another may be the patronage of the Earl of Gloucester, whose principal retainer he was, and whom he assisted as keeper of the realm in 1311.

Certainly on Gloucester's death at Bannockburn in 1314 Badlesmere became more prominent in royal service. He was closely associated with the Earl of Pembroke. Thus in 1315 he accompanied Pembroke on his defence of the north; in 1316 Pembroke helped him bring the recalcitrant citizens of Bristol to heel; and in 1317 both went on embassy to Avignon. Late in 1317 it was with Badlesmere that Pembroke strove to restrain the irresponsibility of Roger Damory and with whose assistance in council Pembroke hoped to guide the king more sensibly. The royal grants accompanying Badlesmere's rise culminated in his appointment in 1318 as steward of the royal household, an office of first-rate political importance offering intimate contact with the king. In 1316 the king retained him for life for £400 in peace and 5,000 marks (£3,333) in war, when he was to serve with 100 men-at-arms, and in 1317 added 1,000 marks for his counsel: high valuations indeed for his service. Another sign of his rise are the marriage of his daughter to the heir of the marcher lord Roger Mortimer of Wigmore, for which he paid £2,000.

It was therefore entirely logical that in 1321 Edward II should send Badlesmere to persuade the northerners not to join the marcher lords against the Despensers, but Badlesmere deserted and demonstrated his hatred of the Despensers by concocting the false charge of treason against them. His reasons for rebelling are not clear. Certainly the rise of Despensers to favour with the king deprived

Badlesmere of much of his influence and his marriage ties with the Mortimers may have made him sympathetic towards the marchers. However that may be, the desertion of the steward of his household, bound to him by intimate personal ties, made Edward II into his most vengeful enemy. That Badlesmere's Kentish lands were isolated from those of the other rebels offered Edward the means for revenge. It was probably a deliberate ploy to provoke a crisis that provoked him to send Queen Isabella to Badlesmere's Leeds castle and, when Lady Badlesmere predictably refused admission, Edward reacted to the affront by besieging the castle. Badlesmere's only hope was support from the marchers and northerners, but this Lancaster denied him. The reasons for Lancaster's hostility are not known. Opposed by king and earl, Badlesmere was doomed and was duly executed on 14 April 1322.

J. R. Maddicott, *Thomas of Lancaster 1307–22: A Study in the Reign of Edward II*, 1970.

J. R. S. Phillips, *Aymer de Valence, Earl of Pembroke 1307–24: Baronial Politics in the Reign of Edward II*, 1972.

SIR ANDREW HARCLAY (*d.* 1323) was created Earl of Carlisle for his victory over Thomas of Lancaster at Boroughbridge in 1322. The son of a sheriff of Cumberland, who was not even a tenant-in-chief, he was only a knight until summoned to parliament as a baron in 1321 and, remarkably, as an earl in 1322. 'The direct elevation of a mere knight to an earldom, with no claim to be one either by marriage or well-established status as a major magnate, was quite unprecedented.' Almost his whole career was spent ceaselessly struggling to defend Cumbria against the Scots.

Edward I's death and Edward II's domestic problems handed the initiative to Robert Bruce, who rapidly reconquered Scotland and raided deep into England. Bannockburn in 1314 was merely the worst in a chain of disasters culminating in the fall of Berwick in 1318 and Scottish victories as far south as Yorkshire at Myton-in-Swaledale in 1319 and Byland in 1322. The border counties became a war zone, some protection being offered by pele towers and by buying off the Scots. Cumberland's ransom in 1315 was assessed as for a normal tax and Ripon's ransom was approved by the crown, which stopped levying its own taxes in the north and occasionally sent armies north that were quite unsuited to combat the lightning raids of the Scots. In 1322 Harclay reported new Scottish raids: 'There is none to defend the people, none to stand as a wall in front of the people. Therefore, my lord king, it would be good if, putting aside other business, you came at once to the aid of your hard-pressed people, who without their king's aid cannot resist the savagery of the Scots'. Edward, however, chose first to strike at Lancaster and only then, disastrously, against the Scots. Harclay had no illusions about Edward's capacity as king. It was apparently to bring peace to the borders that Harclay recognized Bruce as King of Scotland, an agreement not dissimilar from the ransoms outlined above, but his action was construed as treason, for which he was executed.

Partition of the Vipont lordships in Cumbria had left a power vacuum for Harclay to exploit. It was as a Vipont client that he had campaigned first in 1303. In 1312 he became keeper of the city of Carlisle, in 1313 keeper of its castle, in 1318 of Cockermouth castle, and at other times keeper of Papcastle, Pendragon, Appleby and Brougham. From 1312 he was repeatedly sheriff of Cumberland. After Bannockburn he saved Carlisle in 1314, when he 'dared not leave his post for fear of Scottish attacks by day or night', and in 1315 he held Carlisle castle though temporarily losing the town. Although quite inadequately resourced, he counter-attacked into Scotland and is credited with organising a force of hobelars (light horse) to combat the Scots on their own terms. Once he was captured and ransomed. Harclay had become indispensable, contributing the principal contingent to the king's army in 1319 and becoming warden of Northumberland and commander of the levies of Cumbria, Lancashire and parts of Yorkshire in 1322. His death left an unbridgeable gap, forcing Edward to conclude a truce. Five years later Edward III recognized Bruce as King of Scotland. Was Harclay's execution necessary?

N. M. Fryde, *The Tyranny and Fall of Edward II 1321–6*, 1979.

J. Mason, 'Sir Andrew de Harcla, Earl of Carlisle', *Transactions of the Cumberland and Westmorland Archaeological Society*, new series xxix, 1929.

J. E. Morris, 'Cumberland and Westmorland military levies in the reigns of Edward I and Edward II', *Transactions of the Cumber-*

land and Westmorland Archaeological Society, new series iii,
1903.

THOMAS RENT (c. 1260–1323) of Ipswich was 'in many ways
typical of the class which directed borough administration in the
early 14th century'. Like Adam Horder in Southampton, John Rent
and his son Thomas apparently moved to Ipswich about 1280 and in
1283 both were taxpayers there, John paying more than average and
Thomas somewhat less. Presumably Thomas succeeded to his
father's fortune, which he then transformed. The list of his
possessions drawn up at his death indicates wide-ranging interests.
He then held six messuages (houses and adjacent land), six shops, a
workshop, quay, garden, and two vacant plots of land in Ipswich
itself; another messuage, some woodland, 120 acres of arable land, 5
acres of meadow, and 17 acres of pasture at neighbouring Stoke.
Together these lands and other rents, mainly acquired in the early
14th century, had a rentable value of £10.7s.4d. a year, a substantial
amount, but not all were rented out. Certainly not his own house in
the town; not the quay where he kept his boat, probably used for
fishing, and stored his timber, perhaps from his own woodlands; not
the 54 acres of land sown with wheat and barley; and not the
meadow and pasture where he kept his 80 sheep. The list reminds us
that even the larger towns of late medieval England like Ipswich
were small in population and physical size by modern standards and
lay among their own fields, enabling townsmen to be part-time
farmers or to keep a few animals on the commons. Thomas Rent was
also a customs collector from 1304–20, a post with a salary and
scope for illicit profit that he apparently exploited. His brewhouse
and bakery probably served more than his family and trading
activities are hinted at by his constant suits for debt. Whatever he
was trading in, he was a slow payer, exploiting free credit for as long
as possible, and building up by his death goods and chattels worth
the large sum of £118, including £4 in cash and £27 in growing
crops. Typically much of his wealth was in moveable goods rather
than tied up in land, typically he bought land as a safer form of
investment than trade, and typically he lived in considerably more
comfort than rural neighbours of similar wealth. His total capital
was less than his half-share of the £666-fine levied by the exchequer
and £200 demanded by the Younger Despenser for his misconduct as

royal customer. His partner was pardoned but Rent was not, dying in 1323. His son John was a prominent citizen, but not in the same class.

As a wealthy citizen, Rent naturally became one of Ipswich's ruling clique. His first known appointment was to a committee to revise the town customs in 1291. He was one of the two bailiffs on twelve occasions in 1297–1321, coroner from 1312, and in 1313 and 1315 represented Ipswich in parliament. His record was exceeded only by Thomas Stace, bailiff eighteen times in 1295–1321, coroner twice, and M.P. ten times. Their monopoly of power, perhaps secured by fixing their annual elections, offered chances for corruption and culminated with reforming ordinances in 1321. They were charged with extorting inordinate fees for use of the common seal of the borough, for using it without common consent, and for levying taxes, some of which they diverted to their own use. Such charges were made in many towns and cannot be proved. The remedies were also commonplace: the appointment of clavigers to keep the keys to the common chest and thus control the use of the common seal and the nomination of chamberlains to control the borough's money. It can be shown however that they admitted new burgesses without common consent and pocketed the entrance fines. Rent, Stace and their clique did not concede victory to the burgesses, but objected vigorously. Rent's house was looted and the crown, accustomed to such urban disturbances, appointed a commission of inquiry. Rent's disaster followed.

S. Alsford, 'Thomas le Rente: A Medieval Town Ruler', *Proceedings of the Suffolk Institute of Archaeology* xxxv.ii, 1982.

WILLIAM MELTON (*d.* 1340), Archbishop of York from 1317 until his death, was both a model civil servant and a model archbishop. Of modest origin, he was one of the many Yorkshiremen recruited into government by Edward I and Edward II. A financial expert, whose first post was usher of the wardrobe to Edward I, he acted as cofferer to Queen Margaret (1298–1300), chamberlain of Chester (1301), controller of the wardrobe to Edward II as prince (1304–7) and king (1307–14), and keeper of the wardrobe (1314–16), which he resigned on his election as archbishop. Subsequently he returned for two spells as treasurer of the exchequer in 1325-6 and 1330-1 and one as chancellor (1333-4), when the royal chancery was at York. His administration was distinguished both by efficiency and honesty, so that he was acceptable both to the king and the Ordainers, and in 1325-6 he was responsible for reforming the exchequer.

A cleric like most civil servants of his time, Melton became a prodigious pluralist, being promoted to a range of ecclesiastical benefices in which he was non-resident, several of which, such as the deanery of St. Martins-le-Grand in London and provostship of Beverley, were normally reserved for royal clerks. Nominated by the king to the archbishopric of York, he immediately resigned his royal offices and departed to his province, where he resided almost continuously till his death. There he proved himself 'one of the best of the medieval archbishops of York' (Grassi), devoting himself to tiresome episcopal duties such as the confirmation of boys and visitation of his parishes, asserting his authority over rival jurisdictions such as the archdeacon of Richmond and York cathedral chapter, and assisting the poor, particularly relieving those poor tenants who could not pay him their debts. He was severe, it was reported, only to the contumacious and to rebels and he tried unsuccessfully to protect the north against the Scots.

Both as minister of the crown and archbishop, Melton patronised his family and fellow Yorkshiremen. In government he was at the 'very centre of the York group', the 'archetype of all the York clerks' (Grassi), and recruited many other Yorkshiremen to royal service, among them a successor as chancellor and archbishop in John Thoresby, who had been receiver of his chamber. Melton was thus largely responsible for the prominence of Yorkshiremen in royal administration for the rest of 14th century. As archbishop, he made at least 388 loans totalling £23,551, some perhaps usurious and others to the crown, but most apparently designed to assist northern monasteries and noblemen through their financial difficulties. He financed the education of his nephews and nieces at Newark, leaving substantial bequests to each of them, and built up a private landed estate for his nephew William, thus raising the Meltons from obscurity into a leading county family. Clerics who were kinsmen or neighbours were promoted to benefices in his gift. As the careers of Anthony Bek and Walter Stapledon show, such nepotism was normal for his time and Melton was even praised for it by the chronicler of the Church of York. By promoting to royal office Yorkshiremen who were both able and thoroughly worthy, Melton was arguably acting in the public interest.

L. H. Butler, 'Archbishop Melton, his neighbours and his kinsmen, 1317–1340', *Journal of Ecclesiastical History* ii, 1951.

J. L. Grassi, 'Royal Clerks from the Archdiocese of York in the 14th Century', *Northern History* iv, 1968.

R. M. T. Hill, *The Labourer in the Vineyard: The Visitations of Archbishop Melton in the Archdeaconry of Richmond*, Borthwick Paper 35, 1968.

MASTER WALTER BURLEY (c. 1275–1345) was a prolific writer, who belonged to two distinguished groups of academics in the early fourteenth century. By this time it was no longer common to study abroad, but he attended the universities of both Oxford and Paris, taught at both and at Toulouse, and engaged in disputations at Bologna. The writer of at least 50 treatises, some very short but altogether of formidable bulk, he was a 'man of impressive energy and versatility, whose literary output was markedly more extensive than that of any other individual of the early-fourteenth century'. Although somewhat overshadowed in retrospect by his younger contemporaries William Ockham and Thomas Bradwardine, he was admired in his own day.

Apparently a Yorkshireman, Burley first attended Oxford in the 1290s. Before moving on to the more advanced subjects of music, medicine, canon or civil law, or, in Burley's case, theology, all students had first to study the seven liberal arts and secure the degrees of Bachelor of Arts (B.A.) and Master of Arts (M.A.). Burley, it appears, was typical, spending four years attending lectures as an undergraduate, three years teaching others under supervision of an M.A., and thereafter teaching as an M.A. from 1301 to about 1307, rather longer than usual. He himself was particularly attracted to logic and philosophy, publishing treatises in 1301 and 1302. He became a fellow of Merton College about 1301, which assured him of resources for further study, and was indeed the first of a highly distinguished group of Mertonians between 1300 and 1360, another being the theologian Bradwardine.

Burley was still only an acolyte in 1309, when his first living enabled him to finance the further seven years study (progressively extended) that he was licensed to undertake, and he was almost fifty when ordained a priest in 1321. He held a succession of livings, probably residing in none of them. Scholarship and diocesan administration were accepted by the Church as so desirable that those engaged in them were permitted to be non-resident, provided that the actual duties were performed for them by curates. Burley's living and licence enabled him to proceed to Paris, perhaps as early as 1308, where he studied theology. It took sixteen years to become a doctor of theology as Burley did in 1324. Initially the student attended lectures on the Bible and the *Sentences* of Peter Lombard, later he lectured on them himself. He also supervised the studies of a nephew of Archbishop Greenfield. After graduating, he spent only a few years lecturing, before returning to England.

About 1327 he became a royal clerk, almoner to Queen Philippa, and the royal emissary sent to the papal Curia unsuccessfully to seek the canonisation of Thomas of Lancaster. He remained primarily an academic, however, joining the distinguished circle of scholars around Richard Bury, Bishop of Durham (1333–45), who included the theologians Bradwardine and FitzRalph and the canonist Acton. Although theology was the 'queen of the sciences' and the arts course merely intended to introduce it, Burley was primarily interested in philosophy and the works of the Greek philosopher Aristotle, writing commentaries on Aristotle's *Ethics, Physics* and *Politics* in these years, dedicating some to Bury and another to his erstwhile contemporary Pope Clement VI. Although ultimately influenced by Ockham, he remained a scholar of marked independence, who was critical of Aquinas and sympathetic on some points to Averroes. He was never an extremist or controversialist.

C. Martin, 'Walter Burley', *Oxford Studies Presented to Daniel Callus*, Oxford Historical Society xvi, 1964.
W. A. Pantin, *The English Church in the Fourteenth Century*, 1955.

ADAM ORLETON (c. 1275–1345), Bishop of Hereford (1317–1327), Worcester (1327–33), and Winchester (1333–45), was one of the first bishops to be translated (moved) from one see (bishopric) to another. Later a commonplace way of promotion to richer sees, at first it led to charges of greedy careerism, particularly as Orleton's appointments were made against royal wishes by Pope John XXII, while he was on missions to the papal Curia. Greed, however, is not the only or perhaps even one explanation. It was papal policy to foster translations and thus strengthen papal control over appointments and increase papal revenue. John XXII was a lawyer who favoured lawyers, particularly Orleton, who had elevated views of the dignity of popes and bishops. A strong pope, he frequently overrode the weak kings with whom he coincided. Later the balance of power shifted decisively, so that popes were reduced to confirming nominees that they did not approve.

Orleton's origins are exceptionally obscure. Born somewhere in Herefordshire and educated at an unknown university, he was an M.A. by 1301 and a doctor of canon law by 1307. Law, so useful for the government of Church and State, became increasingly the route to advancement in the Church and theologians were restricted at best to peripheral and poorer sees. Orleton's legal expertise was appreciated simultaneously by the Bishop of Hereford (1311–13), the future Archbishop Reynolds as bishop of Worcester (1311), as official to the Bishop of Winchester (1312–15), and as a royal diplomat from 1307. Such service took him to the papal Curia and General Council of the Church at Vienne, where in 1311 he was made a papal chaplain. Later he became an auditor of the sacred palace, and ultimately a bishop.

Lawyer-bishops are often charged with legalism rather than a genuine concern for souls, but this is not true of Orleton. Inevitably often on diplomatic business before 1336 and increasingly ill thereafter, 'at many points Orleton is to be found engaged in parochial, judicial and administrative activity'. Visitations, monastic reform, the suppression of illicit pluralism, the encouragement of study, defence of episcopal rights, confirmations and preaching are all recorded. The high point of his episcopal career was the canonisation of Thomas Cantilupe in 1320.

Orleton's reputation has suffered from the enmity of one particular chronicler. Most charges against him are demonstrably unfounded and indeed exaggerate his importance. It is clear that he was never a politician of the front rank. If he did meet Mortimer in 1322, it was not necessarily treasonable, and he was only tried on Mortimer's escape. His conviction proves nothing, for he did not plead, claiming immunity as bishop, and the king shamelessly manipulated the process. His lands and chattels were seized. He hoped for reconciliation and did not plot, but he joined Isabella and Mortimer before victory was assured. Briefly their treasurer, he was sent to the Curia, where he was again promoted. Mortimer's anger at this resembled Edward II's in 1317 and 1333, when Archbishop Stratford was also hostile. Hence, perhaps, Orleton's last brief public appearance to attack Stratford in 1340–1. Blind by then, he resided continually at Farnham Castle and had a coadjutor to assist him with his duties.

R. M. Haines, *Church and Politics in the Fourteenth Century: The Career of Adam Orleton* c. 1275–1345, 1978.

HUGH DESPENSER THE ELDER, EARL OF WINCHESTER (1262–1326) was father of Hugh Despenser the Younger, with whom he established in 1322 a corrupt dictatorship, which collapsed in 1326 to the destruction of themselves and Edward II. Before then, he had a long and distinguished career in public service, in which he established the fortunes of his family as a member of the high nobility. Hugh's father and namesake was royal justiciar at his death at Evesham and his maternal grandfather, Philip Basset, was also justiciar. Endowed with their substantial estates, summoned to parliament as a baron from 1295, married to a daughter of the Earl of Warwick and related to many other noblemen, he was a member of the aristocratic establishment and could not be dismissed as an upstart as Gaveston had been. Moreover he built up his estates throughout his career, both by royal favour and by acquiring lands from others: several times he employed force and maintenance in a manner that foreshadowed his later conduct.

The key to his rise, however, was his consistently good service to the crown. He had obviously acquired some of his justiciar-ancestors' ability and he served not only in war — Gascony 1294, Flanders 1297, and Scotland 1297–8 — but in diplomacy with the Empire, Scotland, France and the Papacy in 1297–1303 and 1305 and at court. He enjoyed the favour both of Edward I and Edward II and never seems to have lost it. Edward I bought the marriage of his son for his eldest granddaughter, which brought the Despensers into the royal family and ultimately gave Hugh the Younger a great inheritance that overshadowed that of his father. Such trust was thoroughly deserved, for Despenser was one of those who served unpaid in Flanders in 1297, in 1305 he sought from Pope Clement V the annulment of the Confirmation of the Charters and the suspension of Winchelsey, and in 1308 he was almost the only reliable baron and several key castles were transformed to his custody. The undue influence he exercised was criticised in 1308 and in 1314 Lancaster excluded him from court.

Back in 1316, he came to dominance from 1318 through his son's ascendancy over the king. 'No baron could approach the king without their consent, and then a bribe was usually necessary; they answered petitions as they wished; they removed household officials without consulting the baronage; and any who displeased them or whose lands they coveted they threw into prison. The King would take advice from none but them' (Maddicott).

It was his son's machinations in Wales that provoked their exile in 1321, but they returned next year on the destruction of their opponents, more powerful and unchallengeable than before. The Elder Despenser was created Earl of Winchester, an appropriate reward for a lifetime of committed service, and was granted forfeited lands worth £1,664 a year, largely those in Surrey and Sussex forfeited by his former enemies. Ultimately his income reached £3,884. Ths was much less than the gains of his son, who was the dominant figure in their partnership, for it was he who controlled the king. Perhaps always unpopular with his fellow peers, the Elder Despenser earned widespread hatred during the years of the Despenser dictatorship, and found in 1326 that his troops would not fight. Humiliation and execution followed.

N. M. Fryde, *The Tyranny and Fall of Edward II 1321–1326*, 1979.

HUGH DESPENSER THE YOUNGER (*d.* 1326) was the evil genius of the Despenser dictatorship of 1322–26. Son of the Elder Despenser and heir to his substantial barony, he was married by Edward I to his granddaughter Eleanor Clare, the eldest sister of Gilbert Clare, Earl of Gloucester. His career was transformed by the childless death of Gloucester at Bannockburn in 1314, which entitled him and his wife to a third of the huge Clare inheritance and made him at a stroke a nobleman of the front rank. The other sisters were married by Edward II to Hugh Audley and Roger Damory, who with the Despensers and William Montagu were the core of a new court party that emerged in 1316. Edward's settlement with Lancaster in 1318 resulted in the exclusion from court of Audley, Damory and Montagu, and enabled the Despensers to take control. The Younger Despenser employed his position as chamberlain of the household to achieve an ascendancy over the king, no doubt homosexual in character, which lasted for the remainder of the reign.

Despenser's share of the Clare inheritance was valued at £1,507 a year, of which £1,276 was in Wales, including the great lordship of Glamorgan, which Hugh saw merely as a basis for future expansion. The king granted him Drysyln and Cantref Mawr for life; Despenser seized Audley's lordship of Newport, forcing him to accept inferior lands elsewhere in exchange; he coveted possessions of Mortimer of Wigmore and Giffard of Brimpsfield; and he secured a grant of the Braose lordship of Gower to which there were better claimants. Such aggression provoked the Despenser War of 1321, in which the marcher lords, backed by Lancaster and Badlesmere, wasted his lands and compelled the king to exile him. Their defeat next year marked Despenser's triumph and ushered in four years of complete political dominance. This ended in 1326, when he was humiliated and horrifyingly executed at Hereford.

Despenser's aim, as he told one correspondent, was to become rich. He aimed at a vast estate to pass on to his three sons. His ruthless methods were foreshadowed by his illegal execution of the rebel Llywellyn Bren in 1316 and his seizure of Tonbridge castle from the Countess of Gloucester in 1315, 'a piece of exceptionally optimistic high-handedness'. He was greedy, arrogant and supremely self-confident. Apart from Glamorgan and Newport, the Clares had held Usk, which was assigned to his sister-in-law Elizabeth Burgh. Despenser compelled her to exchange it for Gower, persuaded Braose as rightful lord to sue her for it and grant it to him, so that he secured both Usk *and* Gower by inheritance not royal grant. Mary of St. Pol, widowed Countess of Pembroke, had to give up £20,000 due to her husband, surrender vast numbers of livestock for a mere £1,000, and lost lands as well. Even the king's brother Thomas, Earl of Norfolk was subjected to an unfavourable exchange of land for Chepstow. Secure in Edward's favour, Despenser imprisoned his opponents with impunity, broke their bones if necessary, and manipulated the legal system with the full co-operation of the royal judiciary. He was blatantly corrupt and untouchable and his regime was a reign of terror.

The surveys compiled on his death are a measure of his success. He died holding lands worth £7,514 a year, more than Gloucester; he and his father had as much as Lancaster with his five earldoms. He had moveables worth £3,136 on his English estates, much more in Wales, and at one time £5,880 was on deposit with Italian bankers. Such wealth brought not support but hatred. His power lacked solid foundations.

N. M. Fryde, *The Tyranny and Fall of Edward II 1321-26*, 1979.

WALTER STAPLEDON (*d.* 1326), Bishop of Exeter 1308-26, was a younger son of a minor Devonshire gentleman. After studying at Oxford, where he became a doctor of both canon and civil law, he returned to his native West Country. Rector of Aveton-Giffard from 1295 and a freeman of the city of Exeter from 1300, he entered the service of Bishop Bytton, becoming his official principal (judge of the consistory court), canon (1301) and precentor (1305) of Exeter Cathedral. On Bytton's death, he was surprisingly elected bishop, perhaps because of his learning and local connections.

Initially ill-prepared for his new office, Walter proved in time an indefatigable diocesan. He spent 40 per cent of his time in the diocese until ministerial office forced him to employ a suffragan bishop. He visited the archdeaconries of Totnes and Cornwall on six occasions and that of Barnstaple four times, defended his rights of patronage against the crown, and gave generously to the rebuilding of the choir of Exeter cathedral. As befitted a university man, he wished to raise the quality of the parish clergy, granting 439 licences for non-residence to potential university students, endowing scholarships for twelve students of grammar in Exeter, and founding Stapledon Hall (later Exeter College) Oxford for thirteen poor scholars from the diocese, twelve in the faculty of arts and another reading for a higher degree. No special rights were reserved for founder's kin, but they played an important role in his foundation, assisted him in his episcopate, and benefited substantially from his elevation. Two clerical brothers and two nephews were advanced in the church, his eldest brother Richard — like Archbishop Melton's nephew — became a substantial landowner, and favourable marriages were arranged for his nieces and other kinsfolk.

As a bishop, Stapledon was inevitably involved in politics. Court connections are suggested by his royal favours and regular diplomatic employment, but he deliberately avoided political commitment until 1320, when he was appointed suddenly — and without appropriate experience — as treasurer of England. Apparently the Despensers' candidate, he resigned on the eve of the Despenser War in 1321, declined to support Edward II's decision to recall them, yet was again treasurer from 1322-5. At the exchequer he calendared and sorted the records, enlarged the staff, and systematically exploited traditional revenues, notably by levying harshly and unreasonably long-forgotten royal debts. Later petitions and his own transactions indicate that he also exploited his office to his personal advantage, admittedly on a much lesser scale than the Despensers themselves. Justly or unjustly, he was blamed for the confiscation of the estates of Queen Isabella, who became his enemy, and for the London eyre of 1321. Although evidently of secondary significance, he thus acquired a reputation for rapacity and covetousness, which explains his murder by the London mob in Cheapside in the revolution of 1326 and his subsequent condemnation in the first parliament of Edward III. Stapledon's fate foreshadows the later murders of Archbishop Sudbury (1381), Bishops Moleyns and Aiscough (1450), who were also too closely associated with unpopular political regimes.

M. Buck, *Politics, Finance and the Church in the Reign of Edward II: Walter Stapledon Treasurer of England*, 1983.

SIR GEOFFREY SCROPE (*c.*1285-1340), Chief Justice of King's Bench, is a 'notable instance of the way in which a medieval common lawyer ... could acquire great wealth and attain an influential position within the most exclusive circles of society'. The younger son of an established North Riding gentry family, Geoffrey married into the same circle and expressed his aristocratic tastes in his coat of arms, his jousting, the crenellation of his principal seat, and above all his acquisition of land. Starting apparently with nothing, Geoffrey built up a substantial estate in thirteen counties, the basis of the barony of Scrope of Masham created for his son, and was a generous benefactor to Coverham and Jervaulx abbeys. Legitimate fees of office and occasional royal bounty alone cannot explain his wealth. He enjoyed retaining fees (latterly perhaps illegally) and payments for legal services from third parties, lent money to embarrassed neighbours, and twice abused his position to seize land and to prevent a legal inquiry into his activities. His behaviour however was never notorious and compared with predecessors like Weyland, Hengham, Stratton and Langton his career suggests that corruption in office and hence the rewards of such office had diminished. Success in the legal profession henceforth raised men only into the ranks of the county gentry and other means were needed to raise even the Scropes of Bolton and Masham into the lowest ranks of the peerage.

It is not clear what was needed to succeed at law. Clerical status was no longer necessary as it had been a generation earlier. An obvious advantage for Geoffrey was that his elder brother Henry (d. 1336), ancestor of the Scropes of Bolton, had already made his mark in legal circles. Henry was a royal justice by 1308 and subsequently became both Chief Justice of King's Bench, the most senior court, and Chief Baron of the Exchequer. Geoffrey was a pleader in 1304, when the lawcourts were at York, a serjeant-at-law in 1316, justice of Common Pleas in 1324, and Chief Justice of King's Bench from 1324. No penalty was exacted for his partisan conduct in the crises of the 1320s. Prominent though he was as a lawyer, overshadowing his brother, Geoffrey was much more than this, with distinguished military, financial, and above all diplomatic service to his credit. From 1319 on he served on twenty missions, securing exemption in 1334 from future embassies except when the king went himself, and was indeed with the king at Ghent at his death. Geoffrey had become one of Edward III's most trusted advisers. His career again shows that ability and royal confidence rather than the particular office held was the key to political importance and hence to the rewards of office and self-advancement.

E. L. G. Stones, 'Sir Geoffrey le Scrope, c.1280–1340, Chief Justice of the King's Bench', *English Historical Review*, lxix, 1954.

B. Vale, 'The Profits of Law: The 'Rise' of the Scrope Family in the Early Fourteenth Century', in *Profit, Piety, and the Professions in Later Medieval England*, ed. M. A. Hicks, 1990.

ISABELLA OF FRANCE (*c.* 1296–1358), consort of Edward II, is normally remembered as the 'She-Wolf of France', who ruled corruptly and tyrannically between 1326 and 1330. This was an uncharacteristic phase in the life of an otherwise conventional queen-consort and queen-dowager. The daughter of Philip IV of France (1285–1314), she was the child-bride of a diplomatic match, which nevertheless seems to have made a successful marriage. Apparently very beautiful, she bore four children, and 'confined herself to being a devoted wife and a loyal queen, a mere spectator of the successive crises her husband had to face both within France and England'. After 1330 she lived in luxurious leisure, principally but not only at Castle Rising, patronised the Franciscans and joined their third order. Only during her son's minority did she defy convention and expose talents and defects otherwise concealed.

Edward II's male favourites twice caused Isabella problems. The king was forced to marry her because of prior diplomatic commitments, not from choice, and spitefully honoured Gaveston rather than her. As Isabella was only twelve, she cannot have been effective politically, but her father was, joining the magnates and compelling Gaveston's exile and respect for the queen. Thereafter Edward was acutely conscious of Isabella's French connections, exploiting them in diplomacy with her father and three brothers, successive kings of France. Such ties enabled the Despensers to disgrace her during the St Sardos war in 1324: her lands and debts were seized, her household purged of Frenchmen, her children were removed, and her household was closely supervised. Again sent to treat with France, she was followed by Prince Edward, and tried to make a bargaining counter of their return:

> I protest that I will not return until this intruder is removed, but, discarding my marriage garment, shall assume the robes of widowhood until I am avenged of this pharisee (Despenser).

When Edward refused, Isabella and Mortimer, from 1325 her lover, used control of the young Edward, whom they betrothed to Philippa of Hainault, to plot an invasion, at which her husband's regime collapsed.

Isabella took over government on her return. She plundered the royal treasury, made massive grants to herself and Mortimer, appointed docile ministers, and then pushed her husband's deposition and Edward III's succession through parliament in as constitutionally regular a manner as possible. Mortimer remained her lover. Parliament also set up a council of regency headed by the Earl of Lancaster, but Isabella circumvented it. 'Edward's youthful loyalty to Isabella was the real mainstay of her rule and no council of magnates could ever equal the influence exerted by the queen on her son'. Parliament was used to rubber-stamp decisions made elsewhere. Naked self-aggrandisement distinguished her regime, like that of the Despensers, whose methods she adopted, and 'subordinated national interests to her own self-seeking'. She lacked policies, concentrating like Edward's favourites on remaining in power, and her treaties with Scotland and France, however desirable, were mere pusillanimous expedients. She relied increasingly on Mortimer to crush opposition. She had not planned what to do on the king's majority, resting content with an ephemeral and adulterous tyranny.

P. Doherty, 'The Date of Birth of Isabella, Queen of England (1308–58)', *Bulletin of the Institute of Historical Research* xlviii, 1975.

P. C. Doherty, 'Isabella, Queen of England, 1296–1330', Oxford D.Phil. thesis, 1977.

H. Johnstone, 'Isabella, "She-Wolf of France"', *History* xxi, 1936.

ROGER MORTIMER, EARL OF MARCH (*c.*1286–1330) moved unexpectedly from the Celtic periphery to the centre of the national stage in 1326, when he became the 'power behind the throne' during Edward III's minority. The Mortimers had been lords of Wigmore since Domesday Book and Roger Mortimer could claim descent from both the Welsh princes and William Marshall, Earl of Pembroke. His wife brought him Ludlow, making him a more potent marcher lord, and he was an obvious candidate to be joint justice of North Wales with his uncle Roger Mortimer of Chirk. Conventionally enough he founded a college of nine priests at Lentwarden and another of two chaplains in Ludlow castle. From his wife he had also inherited extensive lands in Ireland, where he was king's lieutenant in 1315-18, defeating Edward Bruce, and justiciar from 1319. If account is taken also of his service in Scotland (1308-10), Gascony (1313), against Llywellyn Bren (1315) and

Bristol (1316), he emerges as the outstanding soldier of Edward II's reign.

His marcher origins explain his participation in the Despenser War in 1321 and in the defeat next year, when he was spared his life and imprisoned perpetually. Edward's decision to execute him prompted his escape abroad to Hainault, and his alliance with Queen Isabella and Hainault made Edward II's overthrow possible. Thereafter he was an increasingly dominant political figure, initially as Queen Isabella's lover, and latterly as the brute force needed to defeat opponents. Mortimer took his opportunity to enrich himself and revenge himself on his enemies, showing flagrant disregard for the law. He arranged the execution of the Despensers. He is usually held responsible for the very necessary murder of Edward II and the death of his brother the Earl of Kent, but not for the details of policy that remained in Isabella's hands. His abrupt fall in 1330 was followed by his brutal execution as scapegoat of the regime. Edward III ignored Isabella's pleas for clemency.

1326–30 were crucial years in 'the most striking rise in the 14th century of political acquisition of property'. Starting the century merely as marcher lords, the Mortimers ended it with 'an inheritance second only to Lancaster'. Mortimer's rewards from his successful invasion were concentrated in Wales, where he was granted many royal and forfeited lordships, some of which his heirs retained, and the justiciarship of all Wales with power to appoint all officers except the chamberlains. 'They took unto them castles, towns, lands and rents in great harm and loss unto the crown, and of the King's estate also, beyond measure'. In 1328 he was given the new title of Earl of March. So immensely proud was he of his title that, like Gaveston, he insisted on its use rather than his own name. He traced his shadowy connections with the Lusignan Counts of La Marche, claimed descent from the legendary King Arthur and King Brutus, and entertained Edward III and Isabella at Wigmore, where he held a Round Table. A son was married into the blood royal and other children into other great families, alliances that endured and stood his heirs in good stead after his fall. Contemporaries remarked on his pride and arrogance, the splendid and exotic clothes that he wore, and found him as insufferable as the Despensers whom he had destroyed. He shared their fate and thus brought the see-saw of political violence to an end.

P. C. Doherty, 'Isabella, Queen of England 1296–1330', Oxford
   D.Phil. thesis, 1977.
N. M. Fryde, *The Tyranny and Fall of Edward II 1321–26*, 1979.
G. A. Holmes, *Estates of the Higher Nobility in Fourteenth-Century
   England*, 1957.

EDWARD III (1312–77), King of England (1327–77) and
titular King of France from 1340, was the eldest son of Edward II
and Isabella of France. His reign falls into three distinct parts.
First of all, from 1327–30, he was a minor and his government
was dominated by his mother and her lover Mortimer, who used
him as the instrument to destroy his father Edward II in 1326–7 and
then constructed their own reign of terror. Secondly, the years
1330–60 featured his ultimately extremely successful wars with
Scotland and France. Then, thirdly, followed the years of decline,
when the king himself lapsed into senility, becoming again the tool
of others: military defeat abroad was succeeded by financial and
political crises at home. Edward III outlived his triumphs and left
only defeat, debt and division for a grandson too young to rule.
Disaster followed.

King Edward III shared the military tastes and aptitude of his
grandfather Edward I. According to Sir Thomas Gray, the young
king burst into tears at the humiliation of the Stanhope campaign
against Scotland and lamented the treaty of Northampton in 1328,
when Isabella and Mortimer recognized the victorious Robert Bruce
(*d.* 1329) as King of Scotland. Certainly he needed little persuasion
from the disinherited Anglo-Scottish kings to intervene north of the
border and to back Edward Balliol against the young David Bruce,
achieving an important victory at Hallidon Hill in 1333. Conflic-
ting Scottish policies fuelled long-standing disagreements with the
King of France over Aquitaine, and when Philip VI confiscated that
duchy for a third time, outright warfare ensued in 1337, the
traditional starting point of the Hundred Years War. Edward's
French commitments increasingly took precedence over Scottish
affairs, particularly after he laid claim to the French crown in 1340
and the Scottish threat was neutralised by King David's capture at
Neville's Cross in 1346. His dynastic claim raised the stakes, but was
probably originally only as a bargaining counter, to be conceded in

Edward III
(From his effigy in Westminster Abbey)

negotiations for more concrete French concessions. Financial fiascos in the early stages in the Low Countries were followed by more elaborate three-pronged campaigns, as Edward exploited divisions in the other French provinces of Brittany and Normandy. He perfected the strategy of the chevauchée, a high-speed raid deep into French territory designed to cause maximum damage to resources and morale and to force the enemy into battle, in which English tactics proved superior. Also important was the constellation of remarkable commanders, noble and non-noble, to whom he willingly delegated authority and offered scope for self-distinction: the Black Prince, Duke of Lancaster, Earl of Northampton, Chandos, Mauny, Knollys, Dagworth and Calverley. Hence his own great victory at Crécy (1346), his son's stunning triumph at Poitiers (1356), and a host of lesser successes. Not surprisingly, Edward III came to take his claims seriously, declining terms that fell short of the kingdom of France, and in 1359–60 launched a last great chevauchée to make his title a reality. Failing to achieve his purpose, he compromised with a much extended Aquitaine at the Treaty of Brétigny, and ransomed his two captive kings, David Bruce and John II of Valois. 'One of the greatest of English war leaders', Edward's 'fame rests on the achievements of the armies he deployed in his struggle with the Valois kings of France'.

While superior organisation and discipline explain English success as much as good generalship, Edward also earned his reputation as a warrior of great courage and prowess. He loved jousting, taking his lead from his chivalrous friend Salisbury: 'So the King led a gay life in jousts and tournaments and entertaining ladies'. He continued to stage tournaments for the rest of his life, even honouring his mistress Alice Perrers in his last years. He yearned to distinguish himself in war and pledged himself and his knights in the Vow of the Heron to perform great deeds in war. He admired prowess in others, listened enthusiastically to tales of their achievements, and rewarded the best knights among his opponents as well as on his own side. War was an opportunity for personal displays of valour, honour, and knight errantry. His foundation of the Order of the Garter in 1348 created a brotherhood of arms of distinguished knights devoted to such ideals. He thus glamorised the war

as a great adventure pursued by a noble and valiant company of knights against an adversary who was unjustly withholding from their sovereign his rightful inheritance (Keen).

He may have modelled himself on the model of King Arthur and certainly made himself into a chivalric hero of international renown, attracting to his service foreign knights such as Walter Mauny and Enguerrand Coucy, who became his son-in-law and Earl of Bedford.

Edward III thus shared the warlike tastes and aspirations of his nobility. Far from seeing them as rivals, he made them his companions and agents in his wars and rewarded them generously with titles, lands, and other preferment. In 1337, when the Black Prince became England's first duke, Edward created six earls, endowing William Montagu, Earl of Salisbury particularly generously. Later Henry of Grosmont received a dukedom and a palatinate and two of the king's younger sons became Dukes of Lancaster and Clarence. His children were married into the English nobility, precipitating rival dynastic claims in the future, but cementing Edward's alliance with his nobility in his lifetime. King and magnates were as one.

Such collaboration left Edward very much in control. His dignified bearing and military distinction demanded respect and court ceremonial reinforced his sovereignty. On occasion he acted arbitrarily — or even vindictively — in pursuit of his self-interest. He placed service to himself first, forgiving those like Moleyns convicted of crimes. His ascendancy was used principally to marshal support for the French war, not for domestic reforms. He proved a pragmatic politician at home, changing course and compromising when necessary to achieve his ends. Once — and once only — he precipitated a crisis, when in 1340 he returned home thirsting for revenge against those ministers, who had failed to supply his excessive financial demands. 'I believe', he asserted wildly, 'that the archbishop (Stratford) wished me, by lack of money, to be betrayed and killed'. Finding that he had overstretched himself, he was more careful in future and employed ministers — notably Thoresby and Edington — who served him particularly well. What might have been a portent of future conflict became instead an aberration: the king learnt from his mistakes.

His marriage to Philippa of Hainault resulted in twelve children, a secure succession, and ample scope for diplomatic alliances. Before her death, however, Alice Perrers became his mistress and exercised an influence in politics that the queen had never enjoyed. From at least the late 1360s King Edward, now advanced in years, lapsed into mental and physical decline and withdrew into privacy even from his household. He could not provide effective political or military leadership when war resumed in 1369, and yet such direction was increasingly urgent as disasters multiplied. Decisions were taken by those about him — his mistress, son and chamberlain — who acted on informal authority from the king. They lacked, of course, his prestige and inevitably exploited opportunities to their own advantage. Hence the impeachments of Perrers and Latimer in 1376, implicitly critical of the king himself, and hence the impossibility of a regency to see his young successor through the early years of his reign.

C. Given-Wilson, *The Royal Household and the King's Affinity: Service, Politics and Finance in England 1360–1413*, 1986.
G. A. Holmes, *The Good Parliament*, 1975.
M. McKisack, *The Fourteenth Century*, 1959.
M. Prestwich, *The Three Edwards: War and State in England 1272–1377*, 1980.

PHILIPPA OF HAINAULT (*c.* 1314–69), Queen of Edward III, is representative of the majority of late medieval English consorts, who played no significant part in English politics. Typically she was of foreign birth. She was the daughter of William the Good (*d.* 1337) and Jeanne of France (*d.* 1342), Count and Countess of Holland and Hainault. A match between Prince Edward and a daughter of Count William, probably her elder sister Sibylla, had been mooted before the visit of Queen Isabella and Prince Edward in 1326, when Edward and Philippa's betrothal and Hainaulter support for Isabella's invasion of England were agreed. Philippa, it is recorded, wept on Edward's departure, so fond of him had she become in their week's acquaintance, and on his accession their marriage was contracted by proxy at Valenciennes and then concluded in person in 1328 in York Minster. Her coronation and endowment were delayed by Queen Isabella, who understandably did not want to be eclipsed as queen mother, and did not take place until 1330, only shortly before the birth of the Black Prince. Altogether Philippa bore her husband twelve offspring, seven sons and five daughters, thus

Philippa of Hainault
(Sculptor: Jean de Liege)

fulfilling to excess the prime function of any medieval English queen and supplying Edward with endless material for diplomatic marriages.

Philippa was not beautiful, but tall and handsome in her youth, a plump and somewhat heavily-built woman in later life. She was unusually well-educated, writing French and speaking Dutch fluently. Her piety is revealed by her patronage of the hospital of St Katherine by the Tower, St Stephen's College Westminster, and Queen's College Oxford. The latter was founded by the Cumbrian clerk Robert Eglesfield, who persuaded Philippa to give it her name and patronage. She it was who secured Edward's licence for the foundation, the appropriation of various churches, and the diversion to it of other endowments. Such patronage was valuable and perhaps essential, but it involved little loss to the queen except an annuity of £13 from Richmond honour.

Philippa shared in her husband's visit to the Low Countries in 1338–41, supervised the defeat of the Scots in 1346, and witnessed the defeat of the Spanish off Winchelsea in 1350. She apparently shared Edward III's chivalric interests, presiding over many tournaments, and appears to have managed her affairs competently and with due regard for the law. Her best documented quality was compassion, which caused her to intercede for carpenters responsible for staging that collapsed under her at the Cheapside tournament of 1331 and again for the unfortunate burghers of Calais in 1347. Another Hainaulter Jean Froissart, who claimed her patronage but scarcely knew her, praised her as:

> Tall and upright, wise, gay, humble, pious, liberal and courteous, decked and adorned in her time with all noble virtues, beloved of God and of mankind . . . And as long as she lived, the kingdom of England had favour, prosperity, honour and every sort of good fortune; neither did famine or dearth remain in the land during her reign, and so you will find it recorded in history.

Barring the Black Death, this is a description difficult to fault, but so conventional as to add little to our knowledge. Philippa gave Edward little trouble, contributed scarcely at all to national politics, and her kinship network was a diplomatic asset. Their marriage was apparently affectionate. Later when her health gradually faltered, the result of a riding accident and 'dropsy' (1367), she did nothing to impede the transfer of the king's affections to her attendant Alice Perrers, his mistress and dominant influence over him during his last decade.

B. C. Hardy, *Philippa of Hainault and her Times,* 1910.

RICHARD BURY (*c.*1287–1345), Bishop of Durham from 1333, 'was the greatest bibliophile of medieval Europe'. He was born near Bury St Edmunds to Sir Richard Dangerville of Willoughby (Leics.) and was educated by a clerical uncle at Oxford

University, where he did not take a degree. He became a king's clerk in 1312 and was employed in the nominal service of Prince Edward (born in 1312) in a succession of posts at Chester in 1316–24. Gravitating to the prince's household (1325) and accompanying him abroad as constable of Bordeaux in 1326, he established an intimate personal relationship which was the foundation of his subsequent career. Appointed successively cofferer of the wardrobe (1327–8), keeper of the wardrobe (1328–9), and keeper of the privy seal (1329–34), he became the closest confidant of the young Edward III, who in 1332 could not 'be without the presence of his beloved clerk Richard Bury'. He was briefly treasurer and chancellor of England in 1334–5 and was frequently employed on diplomatic missions. Royal favour transformed his fortunes, as the single rectory he held from 1312 was joined from 1327 by a series of canonries, by a papal chaplaincy in 1331 and the deanery of Wells (1333), and in 1333 by the plum bishopric of Durham.

Richard Bury was, we are told, an amiable man, quick of temper but easily appeased. Regarded as an excellent bishop by contemporaries, he adopted a noble lifestyle in preference to austerity and took 20 clerks and 31 esquires in his entourage to the pope at Avignon in 1333. He became renowned for his generous hospitality and almsgiving. His bishopric, one of the richest, also gave him sufficient resources to indulge his literary tastes. As early as 1324 his *Liber Epistolaris* reveals him to be a collector, in this case of letters, and a superb calligrapher. The well-chosen letters and beautiful handwriting, however, cannot conceal that Bury was a careless copyist, who made many minor slips, wrote what he saw regardless of sense, and never checked his work of errors. 'Not in all probability a man of learning as much as a man of literary interests' and 'a promoter in others of knowledge he did not himself possess' (Tout), Bury set out to make himself the greatest book-collector and outstanding patron of learning of his day. He commissioned new books and used all his contacts, official and unofficial, to secure others, caring little about the cost. He kept libraries in each residence, had a book read to him at each meal, and surrounded himself with books even in his bedroom, so that it was impossible to move around without treading on them. His enthusiasm for books is celebrated at length in his book *Philobiblion* or *Love of Books,* which however he is unlikely to have penned himself. It was his love of learning that prompted him to patronise the learned and to surround himself with a circle of outstanding scholars of all kinds including philosophers, theologians and lawyers, with whom he enjoyed holding intellectual conversations. Probably the greatest of them were the two Mertonians Walter Burley and Thomas Bradwardine. Although Bury's project for a college at Oxford University (Durham College) was left to his successor Bishop Hatfield and his books had to be sold to meet his debts, Bury did achieve the lasting fame that he deliberately set out to acquire.

N. Denholm-Young, 'Richard de Bury 1287–1345', *Collected Papers on Medieval Subjects*, 1946.

N. Denholm-Young, ed., *Liber Epistolaris of Richard de Bury*, Roxburghe Club, 1950.

E. C. Thomas, *Philobiblion of Richard de Bury, Bishop of Durham, Treasurer and Chancellor of Edward III*, 1888.

WILLIAM MONTAGU, EARL OF SALISBURY (1301– 44) is 'the most conspicuous example in the fourteenth century of a sudden rise to greatness by royal favour and patronage'. Although established in Somerset by 1086, the Montagus owed their rise to prominence entirely to royal service and patronage. Simon Montagu (d. 1316), the first earl's grandfather, had a long military career in Wales, Ireland, Scotland and Gascony, was custodian of Corfe (1299) and Beaumaris (1309) castles, sheriff of Somerset and Dorset, and an M.P. Apart from military service, his son William (d. 1319) was in Edward II's household by 1306, became captain of his knights in 1315 and steward of the household in 1316. As such, he was one of the new court party, labelled with Audley and Damory as 'worse than Gaveston', and in 1318 was transferred to Gascony as Seneschal. He tripled the family's manors to eighteen and sat in parliament as a baron. The family remained, however, of purely local importance.

Such royal connections explain the future earl's admittance whilst still a minor to the royal household. At first a yeoman, by 1326 he was a knight, and in 1328 a banneret. He established a close personal relationship with the somewhat younger Edward III that lasted all his life. It was Montagu who, on a mission to Avignon in 1329, established a secret mode of communication for Edward with the

William Montagu, 1st Earl of Salisbury
(From the Salisbury Roll)

pope. It was he who devised and led the coup d'état that overthrew Isabella and Mortimer in 1330. Interrogated beforehand by Mortimer, Montagu boldly declared that he had done nothing against his allegiance, then told the king privately 'that it was better that they should eat the dog than the dog eat them', and personally led the dangerous adventure. His reward was an immediate grant of land worth £1,000 a year. He never looked back.

Montagu's career after the coup was marked by continuous service and striking royal favour. He fought in Scotland from 1333–37, sometimes in command and not always successfully, went on diplomatic missions to both Scotland and France, accompanied Edward to the Low Countries in 1338–40, when he was one of his inner council of four and was left as a hostage, and served in Brittany in 1343. He was one of Edward's constant companions, 'always encouraged him to excellence, honour, and love of arms', and escorted him on his secret mission to the French court in 1331. So close was their tie that Montagu was allowed to adopt the king's crest of an eagle, became godfather to his son Lionel of Antwerp, and persuaded Edward to lay the foundation stone of his new priory. Created Earl of Salisbury in 1337 and Earl Marshal in 1338, he was endowed 'with the largesse expected of a chivalrous master' twice as generously as the other five new creations. Besides enhanced West Country holdings, he received the great marcher lordship of Denbigh, the lordship of Wark-on-Tweed, the Isles of Lundy and Man, and (for life) the Channel Isles. For his son he secured the hand of the Monthermer heiress and a daughter married the future Earl of March. As final evidence of his new status, he founded, built and endowed a new priory of Augustinian canons at Bisham as the family mausoleum, where he was buried following a jousting accident when still only 43. Such a flow of favours enabled him to meet without apparent accident the ransom he incurred about 1340. His career demonstrates how one individual 'might make the fortune of his family in one career of brilliance at court and on the battlefield'. His son, less favoured, lost much of his gains.

R. Douch, 'The Career, Lands and Family of William Montagu, Earl of Salisbury, 1301–44', London M.A. thesis, 1950.

G. A. Holmes, *The Estates of the Higher Nobility in Fourteenth Century England,* 1957.

JOHN STRATFORD (*c.*1280–1348), Bishop of Winchester (1323–33) and Archbishop of Canterbury (1333– 48), was 'something of a statesman'. From Stratford-on-Avon and educated at Oxford University, he attended Merton College, and was doctor of canon and civil law by 1311 and assured of rapid employment. The university's proctor at the Curia in 1311, official of the Bishop of Lincoln in 1317, and dean of arches by 1321, he was a royal clerk by 1320 and frequently ambassador thereafter. In 1323 he was promoted Bishop of Winchester while at the Curia rather than Edward II's nominee Robert Baldock. The king furiously accused him of 'acting fraudulently in the affairs committed to him by the king for the profit of himself and his friends and not without the vice of ambition'. Forced to answer for his embassy, Stratford's lands were withheld, he had to buy the stock back, and was bound to pay £12,000. Expertise, not reconciliation, explain further diplomacy and his capacity to advise — fatally — that Queen Isabella should negotiate in France. From 1326 he supported the Earl of Lancaster and thus shared his disgrace in 1329. The fall of Isabella and Mortimer ushered in ten years when Stratford was chief minister and thrice chancellor. His brother Robert, Bishop of Chichester 1337–62, was chancellor twice.

As a minister, Stratford supported the French war, but as a cleric, he was under papal pressure to seek peace and opposed infringements of ecclesiastical and lay liberties. A highly popular stance. King Edward's war effort was crippled by lack of money and so in 1339 he made Stratford head of government with responsibility for providing adequate supply. Stratford satisfied certain popular grievances in return for new taxes, but these proved too little too late and compelled a truce in 1340. Regrettably 'the state lacked the mechanism to control the fiscal arrangements which would ensure the very high receipts from taxation which the king needed', but Edward blamed Stratford, accused him of malice and neglect, and brought him to trial. Edward's attack on the concessions Stratford had made gave the archbishop support in council and parliament, made the clash into a crisis for himself, and turned Stratford into a constitutional hero. The archbishop resisted and escaped unscathed, but his career in government was over.

In 1323 John XXII was impressed by Stratford's 'watchful zeal and careful diligence, his persistent labour and the loyal and skilful way he conducted the royal business'. He was 'sufficiently endowed with the highest gifts, of a conspicuous fairness of manner and refined elegance of life, adorned with honourable behaviour, prudent in spiritual matters and circumspect in temporal business. One who will understand the church, rule it usefully and govern it wisely'. He was a devotee of St Thomas Becket. Yet Stratford's biographer remarks on his worldliness, he was capable of remarkable arrogance and virulence, and he made irreconcilable enemies of two kings and Bishop Orleton.

The archbishop never lost interest in his roots at Stratford, where his parents had founded the chapel of the Guild of Holy Cross and the associated almshouse. John largely rebuilt Holy Trinity Church, established a chantry to Becket there, added a college of priests, and endowed it with the parish church. His brother Robert helped pave the streets and their kinsman Ralph Stratford, Bishop of London 1340–54, built a house for the priests. Locality, family and piety coincided.

N. M. Fryde, 'John Stratford, Bishop of Winchester and the Crown 1323–30', *Bulletin of the Institute of Historical Research* xliv, 1971.

N. M. Fryde, 'Edward III's removal of his ministers and judges 1340–1', *Bull. of the Institute of Historical Research* xlviii 1975.

G. L. Harriss, *King, Parliament and Public Finance in Medieval England to 1369*, 1975.

P. Heath, *Church and Realm 1272–1461*, 1988.

W. M. Ormrod, *The Reign of Edward III*, 1990.

JOHN OXENFORD's 'eccentric and yet typical career' so vividly illustrates the scope for corruption in local government that he has been proposed as the model for the sheriff of Nottingham in the ballads of Robin Hood. Apart from their routine administrative, judicial and financial duties, sheriffs were the obvious people to undertake any exceptional tasks for the crown. All such activities offered opportunities for oppression and profit so tempting that from at least 1170 to 1451 there were constant complaints against sheriffs and repeated attempts to control them through legislation. John Oxenford was repeatedly sheriff of Nottinghamshire and Derbyshire in

1334–9. Commonplace offences that he committed included accepting a bribe to release a thief from prison to the peril of the jurors who indicted him, refusing bail except for payment, charging for the delivery of writs, collecting royal debts more than once, seizure of property, and four times returning himself as MP for the county. Further opportunities were offered by the renewal of war with Scotland and from 1337 with France, which resulted in constant instructions to sheriffs to collect and despatch supplies to the forces, payment to be made later. Oxenford, it appears, took foodstuffs from at least 43 villages without payment in 1338, much of it, it was alleged, for his own rather than the king's use. Wheat, malt and oats levied for the garrison of Perth were instead sold overseas for Oxenford's profit, so that Perth fell. His claim that the supplies were lost in the River Humber was questioned by the exchequer, but fortunately his stepfather John Shoreditch was the exchequer baron assigned to hear the case, not only letting his stepson off, but securing £100 for his losses and trouble. An informer was bribed. Oxenford also seized 200 oxen and 12,000 sheep, afterwards selling them back to their owners, but not before several had been put out of business. 'Even in an age when venality and profiteering were endemic among local officers, Oxenford seems to have been particularly corrupt', yet he was repeatedly reappointed and even escaped unpunished with a pardon from the special inquiry of a fearsome commission of trailbaston in 1341. It may be that Shoreditch secured his appointment, protected him in office, and secured his pardon, or perhaps he had more powerful protectors. Robin Hood, if he existed, lived before 1262, but his ballads were amplified later and may well draw on Oxenford's discreditable and highly unpopular career.

Oxenford was a surprising choice as sheriff. He was the son of Nicholas Aurifaber or Sudbury, who was bailiff and in 1289 mayor of Oxford, and his wife Helen, who remarried to Shoreditch, then an Oxford doctor of civil law, but later a knight, royal councillor, and baron of the exchequer. John Oxenford married a widow by 1327 and thus acquired her dowerlands in Owthorpe (Notts.). Although these qualified him for officeholding in Nottinghamshire, their value — a mere £8 a year — was far below the normal income for a sheriff or knight. Oxenford was besides a townsman and an interloper. No wonder he needed to maximise the illicit profits of office to support himself. Dismissed in 1339, outlawed for non-appearance in court in 1341, and bereft of Owthorpe by 1341, probably by his wife's death, he returned to Oxford to take up his inheritance by 1342, when it was seized as security for his royal debts. He had sold it by 1345, contracted a further debt of £150 in 1348, and thereafter disappears into impoverished obscurity. His origins and fate are thus unusual, but his misconduct in office was exceptional only in scale and fully explains why 'men still had a justifiable distrust' of sheriffs.

J. R. Maddicott, 'The Birth and Setting of the Ballads of Robin Hood', *English Historical Review* xciii, 1978.

WILLIAM OCKHAM (*c.* 1288–1347), the Nominalist, Venerable Inceptor, and Invincible Doctor, was a brilliant thinker, who redefined academic debate for the rest of the middle ages. Apparently of humble origin and from Ockham in Surrey, he became a Franciscan friar about 1308. The Franciscans sent him to Oxford University, where he became a bachelor of theology in 1317 but never actually graduated as a doctor. So novel were his views that he was summoned before the pope at Avignon and in 1326 fifty-one of his propositions were condemned. At Avignon Ockham met the Franciscan Minister-General Michael Cesena, who opposed Pope John XXII's condemnation of the doctrine of absolute poverty of the Spiritual Franciscans. In 1328 both men fled from the Curia to join the pope's enemy Lewis of Bavaria, King of the Romans. For the rest of his life Ockham was an anti-papal propagandist. He died, still defiant, in Germany in 1347.

Ockham's interest in political theory thus dates from his position at the Curia. He was not a political revolutionary and did not seek to sweep away the existing structure of the Church. Instead he sought to define and limit the scope of papal authority within the existing ecclesiastical framework. Obviously of short-term significance, Ockham's political writings were also influential later, but they are not regarded as his principal works, which are theological.

Medieval scholasticism presupposed that human reason could establish more about God than was revealed in the Bible and culminated in the *Summa Theologica* of St Thomas Aquinas, which reconciled theology and philosophy, reason and faith, in an all-embracing synthesis. Not everyone was convinced by Aquinas's conclusions, but his aims were commonly shared. In response, however, Ockham denied that man could know anything except by ascertainable observation — from the evidence of the senses — or by experience. Only the individual thing is real: concepts are mere speculation and cannot be proved to exist. Moreover human reason cannot prove that God exists — only the Bible can do that — and thus in the last analysis our belief in God rests purely on faith. For Ockham God is almighty. That means that he can do whatever he wishes. He cannot be tied down by precedent or even by his promises. He can save the sinful, damn the good, or even make men hate him. He is thus quite incalculable, unpredictable, and beyond human comprehension.

Ockham was a critic of genius and a logician of uncompromising rigour: hence the term 'Ockham's razor'. His new theory of knowledge reduced metaphysics to mere speculation and theology became a matter of faith, not proof. Reason, philosophy, and the intellect had nothing to contribute to knowledge of God. Their union with theology and Aquinas' synthesis were ruined. Ockham did not found a school of thinkers and many disliked his ideas, but he had a profound influence on his critics. Theologians, now uncertain of their powers, restricted themselves to an increasingly narrow range of theological issues capable of conclusion. This scepticism was one of Ockham's principal legacies.

Ockham thus destroyed many of the intellectual achievements of the previous century. Philosophy and theology emerged as different subjects. For Ockham was not purely destructive. Philosophers and scientists were directed to the more fertile areas of psychology, observation and experience. Philosophers were liberated from preoccupation with God and theologians were directed towards the Bible, like FitzRalph, and to God's omnipotence and predestination, like Bradwardine. Wyclif, of course, was directed to both.

G. Leff, *Medieval Thought: St Augustine to Ockham*, 1958.
A. Hudson & M. Wilks, eds, *From Ockham to Wyclif*, Studies in Church History, Subsidia 5, 1987.

ELIZABETH BURGH, LADY OF CLARE, (c.1294–1360), foundress of Clare College, Cambridge, was the youngest daughter of Gilbert Clare, Earl of Gloucester and Hertford (d. 1295) by his second marriage to Edward I's daughter Joan of Acre (1271–1307). She was married first to John Burgh (d. 1313), heir to the earldom of Ulster, to whom she bore her only son William. Following the childless death of her only brother Gilbert at Bannockburn in 1314, she became a great heiress and was abducted in 1316, probably with her consent, by Theobald Verdon, who died later the same year and to whom she bore a posthumous daughter Isabel. A daughter Elizabeth was born by her third marriage to Roger Damory, who died in 1321. Still only in her mid-twenties, with dowers from all three husbands and with an inheritance worth at least £2,000 a year, she was an obvious target both for marriage and for molestation by the Despensers, who defrauded her of her lordship of Usk. This was recovered after their overthrow and she did not marry again, taking a vow of chastity by 1344. At her death her inheritance descended to her granddaughter Elizabeth, wife of Edward III's son Lionel, Duke of Clarence, and thence passed to the Mortimers and house of York.

Elizabeth's widowhood is illuminated by the finest set of household accounts still surviving. These reveal that she lived in stately splendour at Clare in Suffolk, where she received a stream of visitors, including her kinsfolk Edward III and Queen Philippa. 250 people received her livery in 1343, many of them members of her household, and at least £3,000 a year and sometimes more was spent by her wardrobe and household. This was not because Elizabeth was extravagant: she ran her household and estates efficiently, obtained value for her money, and took a strong line with poachers. That 93 esquires took her livery indicates her role as a great local aristocrat, particularly in East Anglia, which also emerges from her religious patronage.

As an heiress, Elizabeth held estates in her own right, not for life, and could thus give generously to the Church without first saving up wealth, as her friend Mary of St Pol had to do. Already before her husbands' deaths she had vowed to go on pilgrimage to Santiago and the Holy Land, a promise she was unable to fulfil, and from the early 1330s was giving property to Ely cathedral priory, Tremenhall and Anglesey priories, and West Dereham Abbey. Her attention was attracted by 1336 to the notoriously under-financed University Hall at Cambridge, which she was persuaded to take over as Clare Hall, to endow (1346), and for which she devised statutes in 1359. All this involved dealing tactfully but firmly with the university and unsatisfactory fellows. Clare College was the first college deliberately planned to include undergraduates. While Elizabeth's example may have prompted Mary of St Pol to found Pembroke College, certainly it was Mary who interested Elizabeth in the Franciscans. In 1343 Elizabeth gave a church to Mary's abbey of Franciscan nuns (Minoresses) at Denney, in 1347 she founded a Franciscan friary at the pilgrimage centre of Walsingham in the teeth of the opposition of the Augustinian canons of Walsingham priory, from 1355 (like Mary) she was authorised to stay overnight in Minoress houses, and in 1360 her will asked for burial at the Aldgate house of Minoresses. Her influence helps explain the foundation of the final English house of Minoresses at Bruisyard by her granddaughter and her husband Clarence with nuns from Denney.

G. A. Holmes, *Estates of the Higher Nobility in Fourteenth-Century England*, 1957.

C. A. Musgrave, 'Medieval Administration in the 14th Century, with special reference to the household of Elizabeth de Burgh, Lady of Clare', London University M.A. thesis, 1923.

MARY OF ST POL, COUNTESS OF PEMBROKE (1304–77), foundress of Pembroke College, Cambridge and Denney Abbey (Cambs.), was fourth daughter of Guy de Châtillon (*d.*1316), Count of St Pol and a granddaughter of Henry III. The Châtillons and Valences, her husband's family, were both of European importance. On the childless death of her husband Aymer Earl of Pembroke in 1324, she received for life lands in England, Wales and Ireland worth £750 and more in France. Young and rich widows normally remarried and indeed her marriage was granted to a son of the Earl of March in 1327, but she remained single throughout her 53-year widowhood. Although defrauded by the Despensers of property later valued at £20,000, this does not adequately explain why Aymer's will remained unsettled in 1377. The estates she bought, her religious foundations, and her evident wealth indicate the low priority given to the husband she scarcely knew.

Mary had four French ladies in her entourage in 1325 and always employed French clerks. She made four lengthy visits to France and bequeathed to the king a sword without a point, a clear indication of her preference for peace rather than war. She provided Pembroke College with external rectors as at the University of Paris and urged it to recruit French scholars. Ultimately forced by the Hundred Years War to choose between England and France, she opted for England, where she had more property, and where her high standing is shown both by the favours received from Edward III and her selection as custodian of the young princess Joan of Woodstock. She pestered successive popes for a stream of privileges for her clerks, her foundations and herself. Her land transactions and her ruthlessness towards the recalcitrant nuns of Waterbeach show her capacity to manage her affairs and have her own way. She remained single because she preferred the independence that her wealthy widowhood gave her.

Mary's foundations comprised a chantry at Westminster Abbey, a house of Franciscan nuns (Minoresses) at Denney, and Pembroke College, Cambridge, besides lesser donations and two abortive Carthusian monasteries. The Minoresses were a highly aristocratic, exclusive and strictly enclosed order originating in a nunnery at Longchamp founded with a special papal rule in 1263 by Louis IX (St Louis)'s sister the Blessed Isabella. Two English houses were founded in 1293 at Aldgate in London (the Minories) and, by Denise Munchensy, at Waterbeach (Cambs.). Initially Mary patronised Waterbeach, then founded Denney (1339) and forcibly transferred the nuns there from Waterbeach. Denney received more land and privileges, becoming a major house with 41 nuns in 1379 and £251 income in 1537–8; Denise received a chantry at Waterbeach. Mary's Hall of Valence Marie of 1347 at Cambridge, later Pembroke College, received generous endowments of £106, a chapel, and other privileges. When aged only 20, Mary took sixteen Franciscans to France and always kept several absentee parsons with her. The pope allowed her first to enter nunneries with female attendants (1333), then with ladies and knights (1334), then with her household, and then to eat and sleep in houses of both men and women (1364). She even built private quarters in Denney Abbey. The final stage in her religious progress was her choice in 1377 to be buried in the habit of a Minoress. Her piety was not the product of old age and proximity of death, but was already present in her twenties.

M. A. Hicks, 'The English Minoresses and their Benefactors 1281–1367, *Monastic Studies — The Continuity of the Tradition*, ed. J. Loades, 1990.

H. Jenkinson, 'Mary de Sancto Paulo, Foundress of Pembroke College, Cambridge', *Archaeologia* lxvi, 1914–15.

J. R. S. Phillips, *Aymer de Valence, Earl of Pembroke 1307–24: Baronial Politics in the Reign of Edward II*, 1972.

SIR JOHN MOLEYNS (*d.* 1361) made his fortune from royal service and crime in the early 14th century. The son of a Hampshire M.P. and thus of gentle birth, Moleyns shared such aristocratic tastes as fighting, jousting, hawking and the chase. He was also literate. As a younger son, Moleyns made his way in life by undertaking difficult and potentially violent tasks, such as arresting people or ships and debt-collection. He entered royal service about 1325 during the Despenser regime and participated in both the revolutions of 1326 and — as Montagu's protegé — of 1330. Just as Montagu rose to be Earl of Salisbury, so Moleyns was in high favour of earl and king in the 1330s, becoming esquire of the household, knight (1334), master of the royal goshawks, and recipient of frequent licences to crenellate, impark and alienate. He went with Salisbury and Edward III to the Low Countries in 1338, travelling frequently to and fro as intermediary with the government in England, but suffered from Edward's wrath against Archbishop Stratford in 1340. His trial, like that of John Oxenford, brought many misdeeds to light. Taking flight, he was pardoned only in 1345 but rapidly recovered his former favour thereafter. He was summoned to a great council as a baron in 1347 and became steward of the queen's household in 1352, but he failed to answer further charges in 1355, pleaded benefit of clergy in 1357, and died in prison in 1361.

John married Gill Mauduit, granddaughter — but not heiress — of Robert Poges of Stoke Poges. During the disturbances of 1326 he murdered Gill's uncle, *induced* her grandfather to surrender Stoke Poges to him, and suborned the judge sent to investigate. This was merely the first of a whole series of crimes including kidnapping, chicanery, seizure of lands, abuse of office and forest offences. Since he was a royal servant, none of his victims dared complain until 1340. He thus resembles the unjust sheriff John Oxenford and the notorious Folville and Coterell gangs of gentlemen-bandits that terrorised the midlands at this time. By 1340 his lands were worth about £800 a year, he had stocks of armour, plate, jewels and wine, and several hundred pounds in coin, which took several days for royal agents to list. In 1357 he was charged both with abuse of office — notably paying himself excessive wages — and straight-forward crime, notably horse-theft. The speed of his second fall suggests improved standards of public order: certainly the criminals gangs declined, partly due to alternative profitable employment as soldiers in France. Moleyns' recall and promotion, like those of Hengham and Stratton somewhat earlier, indicates that Edward III was no more scrupulous about employing discredited servants than his grandfather Edward I. Despite his second fall, Moleyns' heirs succeeded to Stoke Poges and his other estates.

Although ruthless and self-interested, Moleyns performed valued services for others and had genuine religious feeling. He was the benefactor of houses of Augustinian canons at Southwark and Oxford and founded chantries at Burnham Abbey, of which he was patron, Stoke Poges and Ditton. Evidently he was more than merely a man of violence.

J. G. Bellamy, 'The Coterel Gang: An Anatomy of a Band of 14th-Century Criminals', *English Historical Review* lxxix, 1964.

G. R. Elvey, 'The First Fall of Sir John Moleyns', *Records of Buckinghamshire* xx.ii, 1972.

N. M. Fryde, 'A Medieval Robber Baron: Sir John Moleyns of Stoke Poges, Buckinghamshire', *Medieval Legal Records,* ed. R. F. Hunnisett and J. Post, 1975.

E. L. G. Stones, 'The Folvilles of Ashby-Folville, Leicestershire and their associates in crime', *Transactions of the Royal Historical Society* 5th ser. vii, 1957.

WULFSTAN BRANSFORD (*c.* 1280–1349), Bishop of Worces-ter from 1339 until his death, was a Benedictine monk before his election as bishop. Monks still became bishops in the later middle ages, but they seldom secured important sees, being almost invariably confined to those with monastic cathedral chapters. The cathedrals of Canterbury, Durham, Ely, Norwich, Rochester, Winchester and Worcester were managed not by a dean and canons but by Benedictine monks, their bishop being their nominal abbot.

Naturally such monks preferred monks as their bishops and all these 'monastic chapters, great and small, continued to make attempts at electing monk bishops'. Generally they were overruled, by king and/or popes, 'but sometimes they were allowed to have their way, in cases where it could not make much difference and where the sees were not required for "Very Important People"'. Understandably also they tended to elect their priors, the heads of their own monasteries, in preference to heads of other Benedictine houses, and they preferred their own Benedictine order to any other. Thus most monk-bishops had been priors of Benedictine cathedral priories. Monks, who had withdrawn from the world for a life of silent contemplation, were not self-evidently qualified to be bishops. Their horizons tended to be restricted and only gradually did the monastic orders provide university education for a favoured few. All these strictures apply to Wulfstan Bransford. Born just outside Worcester, he was the son of a citizen who named him after a former bishop St Wulfstan, and was clerk of Worcester before entering the priory in 1310. He did not attend university. His election as prior in 1317 brought administrative responsibilities. He undertook extensive building operations, took drastic if dubious action to overcome financial difficulties, and even acted as official and vicar-general of the see, but he did not become less provincial in outlook. Understandably the monks elected their prior as bishop in 1327, but his election was quashed by the pope in favour of Adam Orleton. He was overlooked twice more, and only in 1339, when elected a second time, was he allowed to succeed. He was the only prior of Worcester to succeed as bishop between 1216 and the Reformation. By then he was an elderly man and ill-health dogged his episcopate.

Bransford's monastic background coloured his career as bishop. He supported appropriation of rectories to monasteries, which diverted money from parishes to religious houses, but did not favour licences for rectors to study at university, which diverted the same funds to education, perhaps because sceptical of educational benefits that he had not experienced himself. At his election he obviously possessed an exceptional knowledge of the diocese. He became 'a conscientious diocesan' who 'contented himself with the "minutiae" of administration and the personal care of his parishioners. The most diligent visitor of the bishops of the 14th century', he visited the whole diocese in person once and twice more partly by deputy, and personally conducted 41 ordinations himself. For diligence he compares very well with more scholarly and more politically eminent bishops like Reynolds and Orleton, but his local horizons and avoidance of national commitments justified pope and king, with their wider political preoccupations, in their opposition to the succession of other bishops of his stamp.

R. M. Haines, 'Wolfstan de Bransford, Prior and Bishop of Worcester, c. 1280–1349', *University of Birmingham Historical Journal* viii, 1962.
W. A. Pantin, *The English Church in the Fourteenth Century,* 1955.

SIR WILLIAM DE LA POLE (d. 1366) of Kingston-upon-Hull was the outstanding English merchant of his day and the first to rival the Italians as a royal banker. The identity of William's father is not known, but he may have been a merchant of Ravenser or Hull. It was probably his fortune that launched the successful partnership of his sons Richard (d. 1345) and William as wool and wine merchants. Success led them into royal office at Hull, Richard becoming deputy butler (1317), collector of customs (1321) and then chief butler of England (1327), and into municipal office in Hull, where they were chamberlains from 1321 and where William was mayor in 1332–5 and five times M.P. in 1332–8. Their dominance of Hull made them useful to a government embroiled in Scottish wars and often resident in York. Their services to the crown as munitions suppliers and lenders caused Hull to be incorporated in 1331 and strengthened their hold over it. At that point the partners divided, Richard moving to London, William using Hull to found a new career as royal financier. In 1338–9 he lent Edward III the vast sum of £111,000. Twice, in 1337 and 1344, he organised syndicates to lend unprecedented sums to the crown on the security of the customs. He was rewarded by elevation to the House of Lords, the first merchant to be so promoted, but was also twice imprisoned and prosecuted in 1340 and 1353, scarcely escaping ruin on each occasion. His career nevertheless remains 'one of the most remarkable "success stories" of the fourteenth century'.

William transformed his fortunes by sheer ability. He made money out of the highly competitive wool-trade by close attention to unit costs and economies of scale. His accounts were ideally presented for instant analysis and his mastery of detail enabled him to exploit the opportunities they presented and to rebut the accusations periodically made against him. Such characteristics inspired confidence both among those who put up the money he lent to the crown, trusting in his unrivalled capacity to secure repayment, and among those fellow merchants he lured into his various schemes. These projects were both ingenious and practicable and failed only because of mistrust and misunderstandings, yet each time William emerged unscathed, shrugging off the obligations on his discarded associates. In 1344 they tried to fetter his masterful personality by committing him to support their mutual interests, but he evaded such commitments with relative ease. He manipulated rates of exchange and interest, outwitted friends and rivals alike, and deceived and defrauded the crown. In pursuit of profit he was ruthless and without scruples.

By 1331 William held lands in Hull, elsewhere in Yorkshire and County Durham, and possessed capital worth over five thousand pounds. The great risks of high finance were justified less by the scope for greater profits than for social climbing. Initially William's ambition was focused on Hull, where in 1347 he ranked even above the mayor, but he also wished to establish a landed family. Extensive lands were acquired by purchase and as security for loans and he was even granted the great lordship of Holderness which, however, Edward III took back. Relatively late in life William married a knight's daughter, educated his resultant sons and married his daughters as aristocrats, and thus launched the De La Poles into the hereditary nobility — the only great noble family based on trade in the later middle ages. Hull remained William's home. It was there he founded a hospital and it was in Trinity Church that he was buried in 1366. Twice, decades before, he had ordered his affairs for death.

E. B. Fryde, *William de la Pole: Merchant and King's Banker (+ 1366)*, 1988.
R. E. Horrox, *The De La Poles of Hull*, 1983.

RICHARD ROLLE (*c.* 1290–1349) of Hampole was one of the greatest mystics in medieval England and is certainly the one about whom most is known. Mystics meditated on Christianity and experienced divine revelations that gave them greater understanding of God and Christ. *The* centre of late medieval mysticism lay in the Low Countries, where Ruysbroeck, St Thomas à Kempis and other great mystics lived, but another centre was England. Four important English mystics of the fourteenth century are known by their writings: Walter Hilton (*d.*1396), an Augustinian canon from Nottinghamshire; Juliana Norwich (*d.*1373); Rolle; and the anonymous author of the *Cloud of Unknowing*. Other minor mystics are also known, such as Margery Kempe, and many others read and were influenced by mystical works in the next century, such as Henry VI, Cecily Duchess of York and John Blacman. To judge by surviving manuscripts, mystical writing was widely read both among the clergy and the laity, which is striking evidence for a high standard of religious knowledge among at least some ordinary people.

Richard Rolle has the best documented career of any English mystic. The son of William Rolle of Thornton in Richmondshire (Yorks.), he attended school and was then sent by an archdeacon to Oxford University. He did not take a degree but left prematurely, preferring the spiritual knowledge revealed by his meditations to the abstract learning derived from the speculative theology of the schools. He then became a hermit in a wood, in spite of opposition from his family, who thought him mad and tried to restrain him. He escaped and led a wandering life, until settled at Rotherham by a patron, who met his material needs and enabled him to live a life of contemplation. Subsequently he moved on to Anderby and eventually Hampole by Doncaster near a Cistercian nunnery, where he died, presumably of plague. Although living very simply and ascetically and revered as a saint, at whose grave miracles were supposedly performed, Rolle retained an interest in practical teaching and wrote extensively on a variety of religious subjects.

Rolle is best known from his books, which are numerous and varied in character. He wrote Latin prose and verse *and* English prose and verse. The most popular of his books were apparently the Latin works on immediately useful topics, e.g. commentaries on parts of the Bible, which were presumably read initially only by the ordained clergy. One work indeed was concerned to instruct a parish priest in the basic duties of his post. His English works were apparently less popular and his English lyrics were read least of all. There are almost a hundred surviving manuscripts of his *Amendment of Life* in Latin and 58 surviving commentaries on the Psalms. It was actually in his vernacular works that Rolle developed his more emotional and individualistic interests and in them that he developed his devotion to Christ's Passion and his Holy Name, topics that achieved much greater popularity later in the middle ages. It was even worthwhile for the Lollards to produce pirate editions of Rolle's works to impart heresy unconsciously to the unsuspecting. Rolle's own work was quite orthodox.

A. Bancroft, *The Luminous Vision: Six Medieval Mystics*, 1982.
W. A. Pantin, *The English Church in the Fourteenth Century*, 1955.

SIR JOHN PULTENEY (*c.* 1290–1349) may have been the richest London merchant of the fourteenth century. The son of Adam Neale of Clipston (Sussex) and grandson of Hugh Pulteney of Pulteney (Leicestershire), he was of gentry stock on both sides, yet was nevertheless apprenticed to a London draper. By 1330 he was already a substantial merchant. Characteristically he broadened his activities to include a fulling mill at Stepney, dealt in meat and grain, of which he had £258-worth in store at his death, and high finance. Like William De La Pole, he lent money to the king and several times negotiated with the Flemings on behalf of the king or City. His eminence in London was recognized by the aldermanry he held almost continuously from 1327–38 and his three mairalties in 1331–2, when he was also escheator, 1334, and 1337. Several times he was a commissioner of oyer and terminer in the London area, he was justice of peace for Middlesex, and in 1337 he was knighted with the Black Prince by Edward III — a rare distinction for a townsman — and was granted £66 a year to support his new dignity. No doubt his aristocratic birth, upbringing, and tastes were accompanied by aristocratic manners.

Traditionally trade was considered socially demeaning and those engaged in it were social inferiors of their equals in wealth in the countryside. Investment in trade was speculative and risky and required constant vigilance if losses were to be avoided. Although less profitable, land was a more secure investment and carried with it higher status than trade. Successful tradesmen in medieval England habitually bought land, often becoming substantial landowners, and their sons frequently abandoned trade for the higher social status of rural gentry. As London was the greatest English medieval city and the centre of English overseas trade, it was Londoners who generally made the largest fortunes and therefore Londoners who built up the largest rural estates of all townsmen. Sir John Pulteney was much richer than leading provincial townsmen like Adam Horder and Thomas Rent and was perhaps also the greatest citizen landlord of the fourteenth century. He had a head start on others, for he inherited substantial lands from his mother Maud Napton in Leicestershire and Northamptonshire, but in addition he was buying land as early as 1329. By his death, after he had alienated much in mortmain, he still possessed 23 manors in five countries and had lands in Middlesex, Kent, Cambridgeshire, Leicestershire, Warwick, Suffolk and, of course, London.

Of gentle birth and evidently aspiring to be a gentleman, he also spent his money in an aristocratic way. Much was dispensed in the religious foundations, which he endowed so lavishly: the chantry of Corpus Christi in St Lawrence's church, Candlewick Street, established for a master, thirteen chaplains and four choristers; the smaller — but still substantial — chantry of three priests in St Paul's Cathedral; and the Carmelite friary at Coventry. His plutocratic lifestyle also emerges in his buildings: the church of All Hallows, Lower Thames Street, and his three houses. 'There is no finer or more complete C14 manor house than Penshurst Place' (Pevsner), Pulteney's favourite rural seat built about 1341 and later inhabited by John Duke of Bedford (d. 1435). Coldharbour, near Dowgate, became the city residence of the Earls of Salisbury and George Duke of Clarence, and Pulteney Inn was to be the London house of the Black Prince and his stepson the Duke of Exeter. Pulteney's buildings, estates, and the inventory of his possessions illustrate the remarkable wealth to be accrued by the most successful Londoners, which made them the equals in income and acceptable socially to the greatest noblemen as colleagues and associates, if not yet as marriage partners.

S. Thrupp, *Merchant Class of Medieval London*, 1962.

THOMAS BRADWARDINE (c.1290–1349), briefly Arch-
bishop of Canterbury in 1349, was 'a thinker of a very high order'.
He was a native of Sussex and went to Oxford University. He was
already a bachelor of arts and fellow of Balliol in 1321 and a master
of arts by 1323 and distinguished himself at this stage of his career as
a mathematician. Proceeding to Merton College in 1323 and to the
study of theology, he was proctor of the university in the mid 1320s,
bachelor of theology in the mid 1330s, and doctor of theology in
1348. Long before then, in 1335, he had moved from one centre of
learning — Merton College — to another, the household of Richard
Bury, Bishop of Durham. He became a royal clerk by 1338, when he
accompanied Edward III to Koblenz and persuaded him to contribute to the building of Cologne Cathedral, and served in the royal
household, as confessor, and as diplomat. The usual rewards, ecclesiastical benefices, followed, but not many. Bradwardine apparently
received his first living, a canonry at Lincoln, only in 1333 and his
chancellorship of St Paul's (1337–49) required him to lecture in
theology and was thus no sinecure. Elected as archbishop by the
monks of Canterbury in 1348, Bradwardine did not secure royal
confirmation, but when the king's preferred candidate died next
year, Bradwardine succeeded him. He was consecrated at Avignon
and died of plague next month.

A cool and somewhat inhumane intellectual, Bradwardine
reached his conclusions independently — he had no fear of isolation
— and had supreme confidence in his own ability. His theology
made a great impression on his contemporaries. He was respected by
Wyclif and was mentioned by Chaucer in company with St Augustine and Boethius. His fellow theologians recognized his quality by
dubbing him the profound doctor (doctor profundus), and his
fellow Mertonians urged him to publish his lectures. The result was
his masterpiece De Causa Dei.

Thirteenth-century theologians, culminating in St Thomas
Aquinas, strove to reconcile philosophy and theology in the belief
that human reason could reveal more of God. Ockham and others
rejected this, arguing that speculation could reveal nothing of God,
and were sceptical of anything that could not be proved by experience. Theology had little to offer, being reduced to blind faith, and
could become centred on Man not God, as Man chose whether — or
not — to believe. Such an approach could compel God to accept

what was offered and denied his capacity to refuse. To Bradwardine, this meant that God had ceased to be almighty and he likened the doctrine to the Pelagian heresy of earlier centuries. For Bradwardine, God was almighty, faith was everything, and reason contributed nothing. He believed in predestination, that God had decided everything in advance: God had already determined who was saved and who damned, God had planned every good deed and every act of freewill, and all events were prior programmed. 'God knows everything created externally, no matter how infinitesimal or minute this knowledge may appear. He knows all that is, past, present and future. Nothing can come into being, or change, without His willing.' God can only be known through what he reveals by himself and Man, unable to do anything by himself, is powerless, unable to help himself, and almost irrelevant to God's purpose. Bradwardine's book comprises 900 pages of coherent and systematic argument, none of it unnecessary to his case: 'as a closely reasoned, powerfully argued treatise on a particular topic and with a set purpose, *De Causa Dei* may be claimed as unique during this period'. More than a reply to the Modern Pelagians, it also asserts the supremacy of faith over reason and theology over philosophy, which have nothing to offer. It represents one extreme of the intellectual debate of the fourteenth century.

G. Leff, *Bradwardine and the Pelagians: A Study of his 'De Causa Dei' and its opponents*, 1957.

JOHN CHAUCER (c. 1312–66), vintner of London, was father of the poet Geoffrey Chaucer. The Chaucers were a family who advanced themselves in every generation: their history demonstrates both the importance of migration and of inherited wealth even among townsmen. John himself was one of many tradesmen and craftsmen — another was the master mason Henry Yevele — who never became part of the City oligarchy. The family apparently originated from the Suffolk village of Dennington, whence John's grandfather migrated to Ipswich, became a retailer of drink, and was known as Andrew Dennington or Andrew Taverner. His son Robert was a shoemaker — hence the surname Chaucer — and migrated to the greater city of London, where he became a vintner and died about 1315, when his son John was still in infancy. John's own income was only £1, so it was presumably his prospective inheritance from his mother, the daughter of a London pepperer, that prompted an aunt from Ipswich to abduct him in 1324 with a view to marrying him to her daughter. Although this marriage did not take place, John received £250 in fines for his abduction by 1330 — a very useful accretion of capital. He was wealthier than his father and grand-father largely due to his marriage to Agnes Copton, who unexpect-edly inherited extensive City properties on the death of a cousin in the Black Death. John's son Geoffrey Chaucer, the poet, became an esquire, his grandson Thomas was a knight of the Garter, and his great-granddaughter Alice — after three marriages — ended up as Duchess of Suffolk.

Presumably John Chaucer was apprenticed to a vintner, since he only features as a citizen and vintner himself from 1337, when he was in his mid-twenties. Like most London wine-merchants he lived in the Vintry, a lowlying area near the Thames crossed by lanes leading to the waterfront. From 1345 John Chaucer lived in a house that stretched back from Thames Street to the Walbrook, which served as an open sewer. The house had cellars for storage of wine, which was principally red Gascon wine from Bordeaux (claret). It is likely that John worshipped and was buried at the church of St Martin Vintry. Men like John, who were never rich enough to hold civic office, nevertheless had plenty of scope for public service and responsibility in their livery companies (gilds) and wards. Thus in 1341 John was one of fifteen leading vintners, who consented to an ordinance of the City corporation regulating taverns. At least four times in 1353–64 he was a juryman for the Vintry ward at the Court of Hustings and in 1356 was a collector of a subsidy for war vessels in the ward. He frequently witnessed deeds in the ward and engaged in litigation. His involvement in the wine trade led naturally to his appointment in 1347–9 by the king as deputy-butler, with res-ponsibility for the king's wine, in the port of Southampton. That led to a period as customer for cloth and at least once he dabbled in the grain trade, shipping wheat to Flanders. His career is that of a moderately successful and prosperous City tradesman. There must have been many men in London like John Chaucer for every great merchant and mayor.

His wife's inheritance gave John Chaucer extensive properties in the City. Apart from the house in Thames Street, he held 24 shops in the parish of St Mary Matfelon and fifteen other houses, shops and brewhouses in other parishes in London and Middlesex. Hence perhaps the unusual ambition that caused him to give his only son Geoffrey an education in arms and letters appropriate to an aristocrat and to place him in the household of the Countess of Ulster. It was only this daring ambition that made the poetic career of Geoffrey Chaucer possible.

M.M. Crow and C.G. Olson, eds., *Chaucer Life-Records*, 1946.

JOAN OF KENT (*c.*1328–85), 'Fair Maid of Kent' and Princess of Wales, was renowned for her beauty, love affairs, and as mother of King Richard II. Froissart described her as 'this young lady of Kent [who] was the most beautiful and most amorous lady in the whole kingdom of her time'. The younger daughter of Edmund of Woodstock, Earl of Kent and youngest son of Edward I, Joan was still only an infant at her father's execution in 1330 and was brought up by the Earl and Countess of Salisbury, who doubtless intended her for their own son. Although of the blood royal, she only became an heiress in 1352 on the death of her brothers and sister, at which point her husband Sir Thomas Holland became recognized as Earl of Kent in her right.

A genuine love affair may therefore lie behind the twelve-year-old Joan's exchange of vows before witnesses with Holland and sexual intercourse with him in May 1340. Such a contract, though clandestine and involving no religious ceremony, constituted a valid marriage in the eyes of the Church. Initially it was kept secret and in 1340–1, during Holland's absence in Prussia, Joan — still only thirteen — was married publicly to William Montagu, the future 2nd Earl of Salisbury, who presumably knew nothing of her earlier marriage. They lived together as man and wife until 1347 when Holland commenced a suit of nullity, which Montagu resisted — he appears to have been genuinely fond of Joan — but which Holland successfully concluded with Joan's support in 1349. Following his death in 1360, she remarried to Edward of Woodstock, the Black Prince, eldest son of Edward III. He was the third distinguished soldier and knight of the Garter to become her husband. That he was still unmarried at thirty has been taken as evidence of a prior attachment: was he waiting for Joan? That this union too was clandestine and indeed invalid without a dispensation indicates that it too was a love match and opposed by the king, although Edward III acted vigorously to secure its validity once it had been contracted. That a lady of such high birth could marry irregularly twice suggests that the formality of the arranged marriage may often conceal romantic attachments and shows how ladies could decisively influence their careers in practice, as dowagers indeed customarily did.

Once married, however, Joan almost disappears from the historical record, except for the monotony of childbirth: three sons and three daughters to Holland, two sons to the Black Prince. She accompanied the Black Prince to Aquitaine, her two children being born at Angoulême and Bordeaux. To praise her as 'a devoted wife to the Black Prince and in no sense a political intriguer' (McKisack) is to make a positive statement from the absence of evidence about her activities. With the death of the Black Prince in 1376, Joan again became a dowager, and with the succession of her son Richard next year whilst still under age she became an important independent element on the political scene. Initially, indeed, she continued to care for her young son and was able to contribute to the maintenance of domestic peace: notably in 1377, when she reconciled John of Gaunt and the citizens of London, and in 1378, when she intervened on behalf of John Wyclif. In 1381 she was molested by rebellious peasants in the Tower. Thereafter Richard acted more independently and his declared intention of punishing his brother John Holland, Earl of Huntingdon for murder of another nobleman is said to have contributed to the demise of their mother, still only 57. Presumably she had deliberately decided against any further marriages.

K. P. Wentersdorf, 'The Clandestine Marriages of the Fair Maid of Kent', *Journal of Medieval History*, 5, 1979.

WILLIAM EDINGTON (*c.*1310–66), Bishop of Winchester from 1346, statesman and builder, was born humbly at Edington in Wiltshire, a property of Romsey Abbey. After a brief sojourn at Oxford University, he entered the service of Orleton, Bishop of Worcester, who took him to his new see of Winchester in 1333 and made him master of St Cross Hospital in 1335. By then Edington had entered royal service, rising rapidly to become keeper of the wardrobe, treasurer of the exchequer in 1344, and chancellor of England in 1356–63. He was Edward III's 'most successful and efficient' treasurer and successfully financed the Crécy and Poitiers campaigns. His successes resulted from his personal ingenuity and attention to detail, his willingness to vary his tactics as royal advantage dictated, for example in condoning fraud, and the notable zeal and ruthless lack of scruple with which he prosecuted those who had outlived their usefulness. For such a distinguished public servant a string of benefices, including one at Romsey Abbey, and a bishopric were inevitable rewards. The archbishopric of Canterbury offered shortly before his death was declined on health grounds.

Although he remained a minister after becoming a bishop, it was possible for Edington to reside just within his diocese at his palace of Southwark, then in Surrey. The long periods he spent there testify to the distractions of royal business and certainly explain why he undertook few visitations, but they nevertheless enabled him to keep an eye on his diocese and to avoid excessive delegation. His attention to routine matters such as institutions and ordinations emerges clearly from his register, which was surprisingly well-kept considering the chaotic events of his episcopate: the Black Death killed no less than 48.8% of the beneficed clergy of his diocese in 1348–9. That Edington was more than a mere bureaucrat emerges from his religious foundations, which reveal definite religious preferences, some artistic taste, a willingness to spend his vast income on the good of his soul, and a deep affection for his birthplace and his kinsfolk, some of whom he patronised as bishop.

Edington's elevation gave him the resources to indulge his spiritual preferences. The chantry at his birthplace that he projected in 1348 became in 1351 a foundation of a warden and six chaplains in honour of the Blessed Virgin, St Catherine, and All Saints. His previous contacts with Romsey Abbey doubtless explain why the nuns agreed to amalgamate their prebend of Edington with his chantry, so that the warden became prebendary and Edington's own nominee. Later, apparently to relieve the chaplains of parochial duties, he refounded the chantry as a house of Bonhommes, a variety of Augustinian canons, modelled on Ashridge (Herts.) and probably guided by the Black Prince, whose councillor the bishop was. It was Edington who endowed the priory, secured privileges including exemption from royal taxation, and provided appropriate buildings.

The domestic quarters have gone, but there remains his splendid cruciform church, transitional between Decorated and Gothic. It was not at Edington, however, that the bishop was buried, but in his diminutive chantry chapel — the first of many — in Winchester Cathedral. Its scale shows it was erected between the piers of the Norman nave arcade and thus antedates the great enterprise of his last years, when he demolished the great western towers and initiated the reconstruction of the nave in the Perpendicular style that was completed by his successor Wykeham.

The Edington Cartulary, J. H. Stevenson, ed. Wiltshire Record Society xlii, 1987.

E. B. Fryde, *William de la Pole: Merchant and King's Banker (+1366)*, 1988.

Register of William Edington, Bishop of Winchester, 1346-66, i & ii, ed. S. F. Hockey, Hampshire Record Series vii, viii, 1986-7.

JOHN THORESBY (*c.*1295-1373), Archbishop of York 'is a very interesting example of a great civil servant bishop, who took his episcopal duties seriously' (Pantin). Of gentle birth from Thoresby in Wensleydale and briefly a student at Oxford, he apparently served Thomas of Lancaster (*d.*1322) who presented him to his first living in 1320 and whose canonisation he was seeking at the papal Curia in 1330. He was receiver of the chamber and domestic chaplain to William Melton, the model royal minister and archbishop of York, who collated him to at least three livings. He had become one of the Yorkshire group of royal clerks by 1330. The king's clerk and notary of chancery at £26 a year in 1336, he became master of the rolls in 1341, keeper of the privy seal in 1345, and chancellor of England from 1349-56 — a crucial time to be principal royal minister. Inevitably he was also involved in diplomacy with the Curia, France and Scotland. All his masters had rewarded him with livings, so that he became a notable pluralist: he was master of Gateshead Hospital (1333), archdeacon of London (1339), dean of Lichfield (1346), and held a string of positions in cathedrals and collegiate churches. A bishopric inevitably followed: the remote Welsh see of St Davids in 1347, the bishopric of Worcester in 1349, and then, like his mentor Melton, the archbishopric of York in 1352. Edward III could hardly have placed a higher valuation on his services except Canterbury, which was offered to his successor as chancellor, William Edington.

Probably Thoresby never visited St Davids and he certainly delayed his enthronement at Worcester for two years, but York was different. Yorkshire was his home country, he no longer held ministerial office after 1356, and he appears normally to have resided in his archdiocese. He involved himself in building works at York Minster, particularly the Lady Chapel, to which he contributed generously and where he established a chantry chapel. His reputation for peacemaking is best exemplified in the lasting settlement he reached in the struggle for precedence between York and Canterbury: each archbishop could henceforth carry his cross in the other's province, the Archbishop of York would be entitled Primate of England and the Archbishop of Canterbury Primate of All England. He was also devout and of blameless private life.

Thoresby's main contribution to the spiritual life of the Church was the *Lay Folks' Catechism* of 1357, which was designed to instil basic knowledge of the faith in the laity. Thoresby directed his parish clergy in Latin to teach their parishioners the fourteen articles of faith, ten commandments, the seven sacraments, seven works of mercy, seven cardinal virtues, and seven deadly sins. Based on an earlier model of Archbishop Pecham and imitated later by Archbishop Islip at Canterbury, these instructions were original only in their comprehensiveness. What was novel was that Thoresby then commissioned from the Benedictine John Gaytrigg an English translation in verse, the *Lay Folks' Catechism*, which literate layfolk could read and all could learn, and encouraged them to do so by offering forty days relief from suffering in purgatory to those who could recite it. The success of the English catechism as opposed to the relatively rare Latin instructions is indicated by the later issue of a pirate version by the Lollards containing unacknowledged heretical teachings. Thoresby thus contributed significantly to two important developments of his time: the growth of writings in English and the promotion of Christian knowledge among ordinary people.

T. F. Simmons and H. E. Nolloth, *The Lay Folks' Catechism or the English and Latin versions of Archbishop Thoresby's Instruction for the People,* Early English Text Society 118, 1901.

W. A. Pantin, *The English Church in the Fourteenth Century,* 1955.

EDWARD OF WOODSTOCK (1330–76), the Black Prince, was the eldest son of King Edward III. He was created Earl of Chester in 1333, Duke of Cornwall — the first English duke — in 1337, and Prince of Wales (which he never visited) in 1343, which together gave him an income of £8,600, second only to the Duke of Lancaster. He was the outstanding soldier of the first phase of the Hundred Years War. When only sixteen in 1346 he distinguished himself in battle at Crécy, led daring chevauchées from Bordeaux to Narbonne on the Mediterranean coast and to the Loire in 1355–6, and in 1356 won a crushing victory at Poitiers, where King John II himself was captured. He was appointed in 1362 to be Prince of Aquitaine, maintaining a magnificent court and endeavouring to modernise the archaic government. Intervening in Spanish affairs, he defeated the great Bertrand Du Guesclin at Najera in 1367 and restored Pedro the Cruel to his throne of Castile. An infection contracted there progressively incapacitated him and his last years were spent as an invalid in England.

That the Black Prince became a legend in his own lifetime was not so much for his victories as for his manner of achieving them. A charismatic and inspirational leader, he was a general of skill and discretion and a warrior of personal courage and prowess. His love of jousting, hunting, dicing and fathering bastards were interests that he shared with other noblemen and commanders. He spent lavishly on building, jewellery, and other forms of display. His love of honour made him unstinting in his rewards and in his congratulations, for example to Sir James Audley and King John as the most distinguished warriors on either side at Poitiers. His humble reverence to the captured king was as utterly in character as his remark regarding the bastard King Henry of Trastamare that 'It is not right that a bastard should be king, nor should men agree to the disinheriting of a rightful heir who is of lawful wedlock'. His profound piety emerges in his re-foundation of Ashridge priory and especially in his famous reverence for the Trinity. His belated marriage to the lovely Joan of Kent (fortunately an heiress!) was a love-match. It was his intensely conventional idealism that made him 'one of the best knights of the world and in his time renowned above all' (Froissart) and that later earned him his famous nickname.

Yet such qualities are no longer admired. The Black Prince's

Edward, The Black Prince
(From his effigy in Canterbury Cathedral)

chivalric largesse, self-esteem and courage are transmuted into extravagance, hautiness, cruelty and 'cold indifference to the sufferings of others'. His attempts to make ends meet in England by maximising rents, in Gascony by levying a hearth tax, and in Castile by seeking reparations bring denunciations as a harsh landlord, for precipitating a renewal of war with France, and for undermining his Spanish strategy. All these charges are debatable. His political capacity is doubted — his 'sense of chivalry was not sufficiently tempered by a pragmatic realism' — and even his military record is questioned, greater stress being placed on his technically legal massacre at Limoges (1371) than on all his victories. It has become commonplace to doubt his capacity for kingship and to refuse to lament his premature death. Such charges, however, are coloured by our own standards, which the Black Prince could not share and which are not therefore legitimate touchstones of his conduct. The historic prince was 'the flower of chivalry of all the world' (Froissart): the pattern of the chivalric ideal and practical success.

R. Barber, *Edward, Prince of Wales and Aquitaine: A Biography of the Black Prince*, 1978.
R. Barber, *The Life and Campaigns of the Black Prince*, 1979.
J. H. Harvey, *The Black Prince and His Age*, 1976.
H. J. Hewitt, *The Black Prince's Expedition of 1355–1357*, 1958.
M. Prestwich, *The Three Edwards: War and State in England 1272–1377*, 1980.

HENRY OF GROSMONT, 1st DUKE OF LANCASTER (1310–61) was the greatest nobleman of his day and Edward III's right hand man in the opening phase of the Hundred Years War. He was the only son of Henry Earl of Lancaster (d. 1343), brother and heir of Thomas of Lancaster (d. 1322), whose four earldoms and lands in twenty-six counties yielding £8,380 a year he inherited. The value Edward attached to his services was marked first by his creation as earl of Derby in 1337 and then, far more remarkably, as duke in 1351 — only the second English duke after the Black Prince — and the grant of the county of Lancashire as a palatinate at a time when other franchises were being curbed.

> There could be no greater mark of the king's favour. It was at once the highest recognition of his services and an acknowledgement of his standing in the realm — next to the Black Prince.

So high was his rank and so great his resources that his expenditure on everything — household, buildings, benefactions, retainers, and litigation — were superhuman too. His only — but supreme —

Henry of Grosmont, 1st Duke of Lancaster
(From the choir of York Minster)

failing was in producing a son to continue his line. He died expecting everything to be divided between his daughters, but Maud died and Blanche carried everything to her husband John of Gaunt.

Grosmont was first and foremost a soldier, diplomat and administrator. He served on fifteen expeditions to Scotland,

Flanders, Brittany, and Aquitaine in 1333–60, six times in command, and seven times as king's lieutenant. He missed the great battles only because he was commanding other fronts elsewhere. When war temporarily ceased, he participated in tournaments — he was a founder knight of the Garter — and went on crusades against the Moors at Algeciras and with the Teutonic Knights against the Slavs in Prussia in 1351. He headed six diplomatic missions and participated in twelve truce conferences. Nobody had more influence on the king: the treaty of Brétigny (1360) probably owes much to his persuasions. He was a figure of European stature.

Grosmont records that he was a good-looking youth — tall, fair and slim — who prided himself on his appearance, wearing fine clothes, rings and other adornments. He loved the chase, jousting, dancing, fine food and drink, and the pleasures of the flesh. Properties he coveted he took, employing force and maintenance when ruthlessly removing obstacles in his path. He was a munificent patron to monks, nuns, friars and hospitals and converted his father's hospital in Leicester castle into a great secular college. Chivalry, honour, pride of lineage, and sense of duty shaped his life. Grosmont thus appears almost as an aristocratic caricature, utterly conventional and complacent, except that our principal source is his own writings, his self-critical and highly revealing *Book of the Holy Doctors*. Apparently written as a penance, this allegory

is not remarkable as a work of literature, but it is remarkable in coming from a man in his position and in showing a lively imagination, some traces of originality within a conventional framework, and a gentleness of spirit and humility, which cannot be a literary pose if only because he does not have the literary skill for such an artifice.

By drawing freely on his great experience and acute observation, he emerges as a genial lover of the country and field sports, aware of social divisions and injustice about him, ashamed of his prejudices and frailties, yet understandably content with the privileged station in life that God had given him. The stereotype of the records emerges as a likeable and complex personality.

K. Fowler, *The King's Lieutenant: Henry of Grosmont, First Duke of Lancaster 1310–61*, 1969.

SIR JOHN CHANDOS (d. 1370), 'the bravest of the brave', was 'the most famous of the companions at arms of the Black Prince'. He is representative of those non-noble professional commanders on whom Edward III relied for his successes in the Hundred Years War. Others were Sir Hugh Calverley, Sir Thomas Dagworth, and Sir Robert Knollys; their French counterpart was Bertrand Du Guesclin. Chandos in fact was of gentle birth, the son of the Derbyshire knight Sir Edward Chandos. His prowess explains his appointment both as a founder knight of the Garter and as banneret, yet in 1369 even he was militarily embarrassed by the refusal of the Earl of Pembroke to serve under his command as socially demeaning.

Chandos was not only militarily effective, but also had an international reputation as a model of chivalry:

> for he was a sweet-tempered knight, courteous, amiable, liberal, courageous, prudent, and loyal and valiant in all affairs; there was none more beloved and esteemed than he was among the knights and leaders of his time.

It was the herald of Sir John Chandos, an anonymous Hainaulter, who wrote the metrical French *Life of the Black Prince*. Among many chivalrous incidents in Sir John's career, one may single out his escort of the two Poix ladies during the Crécy campaign from their castle safely away from the combat zone.

'Chandos was the finest English captain of the day'. His military career commenced with the siege of Cambrai in 1337. He distinguished himself in most of the major set-piece engagements that followed: Crécy (1346); Les Espagnols-sur-Mer off Winchelsea (1350); the Black Prince's chevauchée to the Mediterranean (1355); Poitiers (1356), for which he received a substantial annuity and manors from the Black Prince in reward; and east of Rheims on the great chevauchée of 1359–60. He helped negotiate the Treaty of Brétigny and helped implement the transfer of lands conceded by the French in 1362 as constable of Guienne. He was thus the right hand man once more of the Black Prince as Prince of Aquitaine from 1362. Chandos left to take over command of the forces of John Montfort, Duke of Brittany, achieving a decisive victory at Auray in 1364 against the duke's rival Charles of Blois, who was captured together with the great Bertrand Du Guesclin. Returning to Aquitaine and failing to dissuade the Black Prince from intervention in

Spain, he accompanied the expedition, recruiting fourteen squadrons of the Great Company for the purpose. He persuaded the Black Prince to make him a banneret immediately before the battle of Najera in 1367, when he distinguished himself both by his bravery and by again capturing Du Guesclin. Once back in Aquitaine, Chandos opposed the imposition of an unpopular hearth tax on Gascony to pay for the war, but was overruled. He retired to the Norman estate in the Côtentin peninsula that Edward III had given him. But Chandos was genuinely indispensable and was recalled almost at once. He raided beyond Toulouse and helped defend Quercy, before being appointed in 1369 as seneschal of Poitou, a key border area, ready for the French renewal of hostilities. He was mortally wounded next year in a minor skirmish at Lussac-les-Châteaux, typically in a hand-to-hand conflict against larger numbers that could have been avoided. His death marked the beginnings of English defeat just as his rise had paralleled — and facilitated — the earlier English successes.

R. Barber, *Edward, Prince of Wales and Aquitaine: Biography of the Black Prince*, 1978.

J. H. Harvey, *The Black Prince and His Age*, 1976.

WALTER, LORD MAUNY (*d.* 1372), founder of the London Charterhouse, was the most distinguished of the Hainaulters who accompanied Queen Philippa of Hainault to England in 1327 on her marriage to Edward III. Although then only an esquire, he was of noble birth, the son of John le Borgne de Mauny lord of Mauny near Valenciennes and a relative of the counts of Hainault themselves. He inherited lands from both parents in Hainault and continued to visit them even after he became an important landowner in England. His English possessions were the rewards of royal service and of his marriage in 1352 to the great royal heiress Margaret Marshall, Dowager-Lady Segrave and eventually Duchess of Norfolk (1397). This was no *mésalliance*, for Mauny was knighted in 1331, summoned to parliament as a baron in 1347, and became a knight of the Garter in 1359. He was the oldest and perhaps the ablest of Edward III's outstanding military commanders.

Mauny's first campaigns from 1332 were with Edward Balliol in Scotland and from 1337 at sea as admiral. He attacked the Isle of

Cadzand at the mouth of the Scheldt, securing prisoners worth £8,000 and grants of land in reward from Edward III. Henceforth until 1360 he campaigned almost continuously in Brittany (1342), Gascony (1345), Calais (1347), the Low Countries, Scotland, and at sea, always with distinction, but without participating in any of the great battles. He was also frequently engaged in diplomacy with the French. His disgrace in the crisis of 1340 was brief indeed and he held office in Wales and even, in 1368, in Ireland. Resumption of hostilities saw him as second-in-command, in spite of his advanced age, in the expedition of John of Gaunt in 1369, his last campaign.

Mauny was a hardened professional soldier, who made his fortune from war, but he also built up an international reputation for chivalry. He was, we are told, 'one who loved honour more than silver', and his career was punctuated by the quixotic acts of individual courage and prowess that contemporaries so admired. In 1342, for example, when he sallied with a few companions from a Breton castle to destroy a French siege-engine, he was attacked by the French, whom he could easily have evaded. Vowing instead to unhorse one of them, he engaged in unnecessary close combat, and thus had considerable difficulty in returning to the security of the castle. Again in 1346 he released a Norman knight without ransom in return for a safe-conduct from Gascony to Valenciennes. Captured by Philip VI, who wished to execute him, it was only the intervention of the future John II that prevented an abrupt end to his career. In spite of such counter-productive episodes, his career, like those of the Black Prince and Sir John Chandos, shows how the English, unlike the French, somehow reconciled chivalric ideals and individual feats of arms with the organisation and discipline necessary for victory in battle.

Mauny, characteristically, was also a man of deep piety. In 1349 he acquired lands near Smithfield, London for a burial ground, where 50,000 plague victims were reputedly buried. There he built a chapel of the Annunciation of the Blessed Virgin Mary, which Pope Clement VI agreed could become a secular college of thirteen chaplains. Mauny, however, changed his mind by 1361, when he transferred the property to Michael Northburgh, apparently as trustee. Instead in 1371 Mauny secured a licence to found on the site a house of Carthusian monks, the strictest contemporary religious order, still to be dedicated to the Annunciation (La Salutation Mère

Dieu), and left £2,000 in his will for its implementation, which Northburgh duly completed. Mauny was buried in his new monastery.

J.H. Harvey, *The Black Prince and his Age*, 1976.

RICHARD FITZRALPH (*c.*1300–1360), Archbishop of Armagh, was 'one of the most important theological writers of the fourteenth century' and 'the most significant personality linking Ireland with the intellectual world of continental Europe during the millenium between Columbanus and Luke Wadding'. He was a member of an Anglo-Norman family of burgesses called Ralph from Dundalk. Proceeding to Oxford university, he became doctor of theology in 1331 and chancellor of the university in 1332–4 at a time when some scholars seceded and tried unsuccessfully to set up another university at Stamford. Never a royal clerk, FitzRalph owed his advancement to his learning and to another scholar, Bishop Grandisson, becoming dean of Lichfield (1335–46) and Archbishop of Armagh in 1346. If his career thus 'shows how the patronage system could be used by scholars to promote scholars', it also kept FitsRalph away from politically important and wealthy sees. FitzRalph visited the papal Curia four times: in 1334–6 on behalf of the university; in 1337–44 for Lichfield; in 1349–51 for Armagh; and in 1357–60 because of his attack on the friars. He aimed at the 'virtual destruction of the friars', but his cause was doomed by his death, which may indeed have forestalled his formal condemnation.

FitzRalph was a mediocre scholar. He knew little canon law or early theology; he was not an original thinker; and his formal treatises are poorly planned, inconsistent, and often fail to convince. Constant study and debate caused him to develop and continually revise his views. He built up an impressive knowledge and understanding of the Bible, learnt wider perspectives from Greeks, Armenians and Jews, and was influenced by practical pastoral experience. All his works, mediocre though they were, were collected and read, and towards the end of his life he broke new ground with his stress on scripture — but never scripture alone (*scriptura sola*) — and his doctrine of dominion:

So far as I can judge no man in a state of mortal sin has true lordship over other creatures in God's sight until he repents and until the grace of penance has restored him to a state that is acceptable to God.

This doctrine was capable of revolutionary extension, which FitzRalph avoided. Later Wyclif made it and *scriptura sola* prime props of his heresies. For FitzRalph it was a means to attack mendicant privileges, and he moved on in his *Poverty of the Saviour* to deny their claim to emulate Christ's poverty. Originally he had sought to regulate misuse of confessions by friars in his diocese.

FitzRalph's concerns were practical. Profoundly pious and even mystical, he saw himself primarily as a pastor. He was committed to reform and embarked energetically on improving discipline, organisation and observance both at Lichfield and Armagh. Inevitably he was drawn into litigation in defence of his rights as dean and primate. To justify his long absences to the Curia he appealed to his conscience and good motives, but he construed others' motives unfavourably and did not hesitate to denounce them. He was capable of blatant injustice and vituperative scurrility. He was a moralist of uncompromising rigour and a great preacher. Arising from pastoral concerns, his struggle with the friars became an end in itself, distracting attention from his diocese and encouraging his natural obstinacy and intemperance.

W. A. Pantin, *The English Church in the Fourteenth Century*, 1955.
K. Walsh, *A Fourteenth-Century Scholar and Primate: Richard FitzRalph in Oxford, Avignon and Armagh*, 1981.

SIMON PAKEMAN III (*c.* 1306–76) represents the many minor gentry, who ran noble estates and local government in the fourteenth and fifteenth centuries. The Pakemans were a long established family of substantial freeholders from Kirby Muxloe near Leicester. Overshadowed locally by the knightly Herle family, their social contacts comprised families of similar status from their immediate area. Simon Pakeman II held 75 acres in demesne at his death in 1313, when his son Simon Pakeman III was a minor. His wardship was acquired by the Herles, who probably provided him with a legal training. By 1337 he was an attorney in the court of Common

Pleas, where Sir William Herle was Chief Justice. There is no evidence that Simon received any training at arms or that he ever served abroad. Throughout his career he acted for Leicestershire clients in the central courts. Although he was knight of the shire for Leicestershire in 1334, an unusual choice, his career really took off only after 1340.

In 1340 Henry, Earl of Lancaster appointed him steward of the honour of Leicester, which comprised estates in Leicestershire and adjoining shires, and from 1341 he served the Earl of Warwick, becoming steward of his manor of Kibworth Beauchamp and of Merton College's adjoining manor of Kibworth Harcourt. It was presumably such contacts that explain both the widened geographical scope of his activities, as he served on commissions in Warwickshire and Lancashire, and his greater weight in Leicestershire itself, where he became a regular commissioner and served twice more as knight of the shire in 1346 and 1348. Such royal commissions continued in spite of his replacement as steward of Leicester honour in 1346 by Henry of Grosmont, next Earl of Lancaster, who may however have employed him in some other capacity, and the termination of his Warwick stewardship in the late 1350s. He became steward of Leicester honour again in 1362 following the succession of John of Gaunt as Duke of Lancaster and served on his council and in many other capacities up to his retirement in 1375. During these years, Pakeman was continuously employed in local government, sat twice more as knight of the shire, and widened his circle of clients to include Lancaster's retainer Lord Ferrers of Groby, appearing frequently as executor, feoffee and attorney.

Pakeman was thus one of the indispensable experts on whom royal and noble administrations relied. Service to his lords involved him in affairs outside Leicestershire and gave him a prominence in administration of his home county that owed nothing to his personal rank and wealth. Aptitude and expertise were evidently accompanied by a willingness for hard work, which his social superiors eschewed in favour of more aristocratic employment and pursuits. Pakeman's motive was presumably financial. His salaries as estate officer must have brought in much more income over many years than his paltry inheritance. Yet his social position changed little. He extended his lands somewhat, but not substantially. The social status, contacts and outlook of his heir remained those of the minor Leicestershire gentleman. Presumably Pakeman preferred a higher standard of living to investment of his salaries in land. Historians have understandably concentrated on the tiny minority of outstanding successes, who transformed their social position and became national figures like Robert Holland and Thomas Hungerford. Those who did not are less well-documented, more obscure and therefore difficult to study, but there were certainly many more like Pakeman, who enjoyed successful careers without radically altering their social status, landed estates, or provincial horizons. Such people were the mainstay of provincial society and government.

G. G. Astill, 'Social Advancement through Seignorial Service? The Case of Simon Pakeman', *Transactions of the Leicestershire Archaeological and Historical Society*, liv, 1978–9.

THOMAS DE LA MARE (1309–96), Abbot of St Albans, was 'the greatest of the abbots of St Albans and a not unworthy type of the medieval monastic prelate' (Kingsford). He belonged to a leading Hertfordshire family with noble connections and never lost his well-bred ease of manner. His three siblings also entered religion. His education did not include the universities, but he was fluent in Latin, French and English, could preach indeed in Latin and English, and he had learnt the *ars dictaminis*, the skill of composing letters, so that he had mastered even the difficult style required for letters to the papal Curia. His noviciate in a cell, Wymondham Priory, was followed by responsible office at St Albans itself as abbot's chaplain, kitchener and cellarer, and about 1340, still aged only thirty, he became prior of another cell, Tynemouth Priory. The Black Death caused his rapid promotion in 1349 to be first prior and then abbot of the mother house. As abbot of 'the premier religious house in England', Thomas also became President of the English Black Monks, serving with distinction for twenty years and promulgating two sets of statutes for the whole province. His achievements were practical and he avoided involvement in academic controversies. He was also a councillor of Edward III and friend of the Black Prince and King John of France, who dissuaded him from resigning following an attack of plague. His health gradually declined and he was an invalid for the last nine years of his 47 year abbacy.

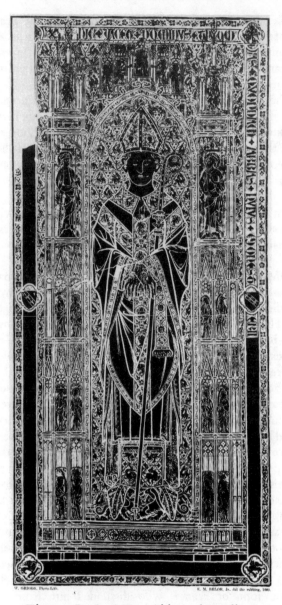

Thomas De La Mare, Abbot of St Albans
(From his brass in St Albans Abbey)

Abbots and priors had separate houses, households, and lifestyles more like gentlemen than monks, but Thomas loved the monastic life and tried to practise it in spite of his eminence. He valued the daily cycle of services, seeking to improve it by slower recitation, more chanting, and less prayers. Business did not prevent attendance at services or observation of the rule of silence and he ate only one meal each day. To such normal austerities he added extra fasts, a rough bed, a hair shirt, regular flogging, early rising, attendance at several extra services a day, and the performance on occasion of the most menial tasks. Unlike other abbots, he eschewed all personal luxury, and unlike many monks did not hunt or hawk, although these had been favourite pastimes as a boy. He was no remote figure, fraternising with his monks, who were devoted to him.

His private piety and humility contrasted with his public face, for he was an 'abbot in the grand style' who enhanced the prestige of his house. He asserted his precedence over other superiors in parliament and vigorously defended his abbey against all encroachments in the courts — temporal, spiritual and at the papal Curia. Particularly noteworthy were his effort to end papal confirmation of abbots, suits with the bishops of Lincoln and Norwich over exemption from their jurisdiction, and his struggle to make Canterbury Cathedral Priory attend provincial Benedictine chapters. He did much to beautify his abbey, constructing the great gateway, a new *lavatorium* (washing-place) in the cloisters, and a new hall and chamber for distinguished visitors. Everywhere he rebuilt, enlarged or repaired, filling the cloister windows with glass, providing studies for university monks, purchasing a great clock, and adding to the stock of vestments and ornaments. Such display, for the glory of God and St Alban, not himself, was facilitated by efficient if oppressive administration, which helps explain why St Albans was a centre of the Peasants Revolt (1381). The rebels destroyed many records and had many grievances annulled, but their defeat resulted in the death of the ringleaders and De La Mare's reassertion of the abbey's authority. Among English Benedictines he was probably more influential than Cardinal Easton or Cardinal Langham.

D. Knowles, *Religious Orders in England*, ii, 1961.

WILLIAM WYKEHAM (*c.*1324–1404), Bishop of Winchester, was the greatest patron of education in late medieval England. Of humble birth, he was born at Wickham in Hampshire and educated at Winchester. He had entered royal service by 1347 and was employed by Edward III to supervise his building projects, especially at Windsor and Queenborough Castles, rising to be clerk of works. His buildings were close to King Edward's heart and brought Wykeham to his attention and favour. From clerk of works he rose in 1363 to be keeper of the privy seal, one of the three great officers of state, and in 1367 he became chancellor of England. It was a 'pre-episcopal career unique among Edward's hierarchy' (Highfield). Inevitably the king rewarded him with ecclesiastical benefices, so he became the greatest pluralist of his day: in 1365 his total income from this source was £873 and in 1367 he became Bishop of Winchester. To secure this last promotion Edward III engaged in a remarkable trial of strength with a hostile pope. Wykeham lacked the university education increasingly expected of bishops, but he was nevertheless literate in English, French and Latin.

Unlike most 'civil-servant bishops', Wykeham did not rise through the great departments of state, but came to ministerial office as an outsider, promoted by the personal favour of an ailing king. In the 1360s, we are told, 'everything was done by him and without him nothing was done'. He was twice chancellor, in 1367–71 and in 1389–91; he sat frequently on commissions of reform in the 1380s; and he was an assiduous member of the royal council, attending on 270 days in the year 1378–79. He had been dismissed as chancellor in 1371 and he joined in the assault on the king's favourites in 1376. This excited the wrath of John of Gaunt and led to accusations against himself for mismanagement of the French war. Fortunately the other bishops united in Wykeham's support. During the political crises of 1386–88 he was a committed supporter of the Lords Appellant and was lucky to escape Richard II's revenge in 1397. It was a political career of exceptional length and importance. 'For long periods Wykeham belonged to a small circle of courtiers whose inside knowledge and influence allowed them to obtain many things by royal grant or licence and to buy cheap what they could get free'. Such opportunities were essential to finance his foundations and to raise his kin into the ranks of the gentry. Even forty years tenure of the richest bishopric in England was scarcely sufficient for such lavish expenditure.

Wykeham's chantry in Winchester cathedral and his two colleges secured prayers for his soul and testify to his piety. His colleges and Winchester cathedral nave, the work of the architects Yevele and Wynford, mark him as a great builder and a great patron of the arts. Only an 'indefatigable man of business' could have financed them and legally secured the necessary endowments. His educational foundations were unique in their conception. Winchester College was the first English collegiate school. It offered free places for the exceptional number of 70 scholars. New College, Oxford was the first college to cater primarily for undergraduates and its 70 students made it the largest college at either university. Together they formed a dual foundation: pupils of Winchester College progressed naturally to New College. These features were imitated before 1500 only by Henry VI's colleges of Eton and King's, Cambridge, which were not on the scale of Wykeham's foundations. Wykeham was thus the outstanding late medieval benefactor of education.

N. Orme, *English Schools in the Middle Ages*, 1978.
P. Partner, 'William of Wykeham and the Historians', *Winchester College: Sixth Century Essays*, ed. R. Custance, 1982.

JEAN FROISSART (*c.*1334–1405), poet and historian, was '*the* historian of the epic struggle between the dynasties of Plantagenet and Valois for hegemony in western Europe'. Born at Valenciennes in Hainault, it was natural that he should seek the patronage first of Philippa of Hainault, queen of Edward III. About 1360 he presented her with a rhyming chronicle, now lost, and remained in her entourage, if not formally in her service, until her death in 1369. Visits to Scotland, Bordeaux and Italy belong to this period. Subsequent patrons included Robert de Namur, who gave him a living; the Duke of Brabant and the Count of Blois. Forced to live by his writings, Froissart's boasts of his achievements and contacts need cautious treatment, not least because of the 'special bond of allegiance between the reader and the chronicler' (Diller) that he forged. He visited England again in 1395 and died sometime between 1404 and 1410.

Froissart was a big producer. His romance *Meliador* has 300,000 lines and he left behind four versions of his vast *Chronicles*. What earned him popularity then and now is his splendid prose style and narrative gift. Froissart was a great raconteur. His *Chronicles* possess dramatic spontaneity, events and characters are sketched vividly and perceptively, and, at his best, he 'integrates vast sequences of far-ranging events into close linked causal patterns. Compared to other contemporary chronicles or annals, the overwhelming superiority of Froissart's prose work becomes immediately manifest' (Diller). Although ruthless in excluding extraneous matter, Froissart took Europe as his canvas, treated peasants and townsmen where appropriate, and was capable of compassion to the victims as well as exalting his aristocratic and chivalrous heroes.

Critical editions and modern historical scholarship have revealed Froissart to be extraordinarily inaccurate. Almost nothing can be taken on trust. All versions of his *Chronicles* date back in their present form from his last years, long after 1356 when he could claim to have become an eyewitness, and much of what he claimed to witness was remembered inaccurately. Froissart claimed to seek sources diligently, to sift what he was told, and to be non-partisan, but gossip and hearsay was acceptable to him and he made little effort to reconcile differences, even preserving contradictory accounts in different versions of his *Chronicles*. Factual information was constantly moulded for dramatic effect, his coverage was not affected by gaps of knowledge, and ignorance was no barrier to his invention. The facts were not sacred to him and he fell far short of modern standards of accuracy. For Froissart history was like romance, a blend of fact and fantasy in a strong story line. Both were literature designed to entertain.

Despite his faults, Froissart remains the best guide to the lost world of chivalric values:

> no single author has more to offer the historian in his efforts to recreate the mental and social dimensions of this world, whether it be contemporary attitudes towards political society, aristocratic mores, social divisions, the social dimensions of warfare, or the nature and techniques of war itself.

His influence on subsequent writers was profound and his *Chronicles* will continue to be read for pleasure.

J. J. N. Palmer, *Froissart, Historian*, 1981.

SIR THOMAS GRAY (*d.c.*1369) was 'the first nobleman since Aethelweard to write a chronicle' (Gransden). He was lord of Heaton near the Bishop of Durham's great castle of Norham-on-Tweed on the Scottish border. In his long and exciting military career Gray's father and namesake fought at Bannockburn, where he was captured, and was constable of Norham castle itself, which he defended successfully during several long sieges. Gray himself probably served in the Low Countries in 1338 with the Earl of Salisbury, lord of Wark-on-Tweed, fought the Scots at Neville's Cross in 1346, and was himself constable of Norham in 1355, when he was ambushed by a much superior force, captured after a desperate struggle, and imprisoned in Edinburgh Castle. Released by 1357, he probably served in France with the Black Prince in 1359–60, and was again responsible for defending the East March from 1367, dying soon after.

It was whilst imprisoned in Edinburgh Castle that Gray read the books in the castle library. There he encountered

> books of chronicles about the deeds of his ancestors, at which he was astonished, and it grieved him sore that, until that time, he had not acquired a better knowledge of the course of the age. So he became curious and thoughtful, how he might deal with and translate into shorter sentences the chronicles of Great Britain and the deeds (gestez) of the English.

That Gray could read all these chronicles and compose such a substantial work indicates an unexpectedly good education and intellectual attainments. Gray was literate in Latin, French and English, but his first language in which he wrote was French: not English, the language into which John Trevisa was translating history for Lord Berkeley only a generation later. Sir Thomas called his history the *Scalacronica*, an allusion to his family crest of a scaling ladder and allegedly suggested by a Sibyl in a dream. It traced English history from the Creation to Gray's own day in four books. Understandably it is of independent value only for the fourteenth century, when it draws on the lives of its author and his father. Gray continued to write on leaving prison and broke off about 1362.

Although Gray drew extensively on chronicles by ecclesiastics, was a religious man capable of ascribing events to miracles, and shared contemporary interest in comets, earthquakes and other marvels, he explained events principally in terms of human actions and focused attention on the warfare that dominated his life and his border homeland. This was described clearly, concisely and extremely vividly. As a warrior and member of the military aristocracy, Gray was embued with chivalric values. He wrote about feats of arms, of glory, of booty, and of courtly love, but he was interested primarily in real war — not the mock conflict of the tournament — and was also aware of both the horrors of war and the sufferings of civilians. His capacity for abstract thought is shown by his discussion of the merits of war v. peace: peace was preferable but just causes must be prosecuted. His independence emerges in his condemnation of the advisers of the young Edward III for not lodging the young king's claim to the French crown in 1328. Gray was a proud man, who admired the exploits of his father and commemorated his deeds in the *Scalacronica*. This may have been why he wrote, but it is the author whom it has made famous.

T. Gray, *Scalacronica: The Reigns of Edward I, Edward II, and Edward III*, ed. H. Maxwell-Lyte, 1907.

SIR JOHN HAWKWOOD (*c.*1320–94) was the outstanding foreign mercenary (*condottiere*) in late-14th-century Italy. His father was Gilbert Hawkwood, a prosperous tanner and farmer from Sible Hedingham in Essex, who left his second son John £20 and quantities of corn. Perhaps through service to the Earl of Oxford, lord of Sible Hedingham, John became a soldier in France by 1343 and was a knight and company commander by 1360. The devastation and dislocation caused by English chevauchées (raids) had permitted the formation of free-lance bands of routiers, who seized what they required or extorted protection money. The treaty of Brétigny of 1360, which brought peace between England and France, left Hawkwood without money or employment and turned him and many others into free-booters too.

Hawkwood accompanied the Free Companies that descended on Avignon in 1361 and were bought off by the pope, who diverted them to Italy, which at this time was riven by constant strife between its many petty states. It was there that Hawkwood made his career as a mercenary soldier. Already commander of the army of Pisa against Florence in 1363, he had spells in the service of Milan,

the Papacy and Florence. Particularly noteworthy among his campaigns were those of the 1360s and his lightning raid deep into
Lombardy in 1392. Although he still fought elsewhere for other
employers, Hawkwood was bound to Florence by a permanent
contract from 1377 and his services in his final campaigns were
recognized by a state funeral and by an enormous mural in Florence
cathedral by Uccello.

Initially Hawkwood employed English veterans from the Hundred Years War. Longbowmen and pikemen gave him an advantage
on the battlefield, although he learnt from experience not to indulge
in sieges, and he equipped them with horses and light armour for
maximum mobility. His renown stemmed not from his personal
prowess, but his generalship: he was primarily a tactician. In 1365
his White Company and in 1367 his Company of St George were
destroyed, but his reputation enabled him to replace them with new
recruits within months. He was careful to keep his troops' pay up to
date. Like most mercenaries Hawkwood changed his loyalties
frequently, serving whoever would pay him, but by contemporary
standards he was reputed to be unusually scrupulous and above
bribery. Naturally his companies lived off the land and caused much
wanton destruction, but his principal atrocity — the massacre of
5,000 inhabitants of Cesena — was undertaken under orders from
the papal legate.

Hawkwood's pay did not always arrive and protection money
was sometimes extorted instead. In 1375 Florence paid him 130,000
florins not to fight them for five years, other towns added 95,000
florins, and he was promised an annuity of 1,200 florins for life.
Originally an alien adventurer, he secured a castle and lands in the
Romagna in lieu of arrears of pay from the pope, which he sold on
taking service with Florence, acquiring instead one estate near the
city and a castle further away. He had no ambition to emulate other
condottiere by establishing a great estate or principality in Italy. In
the 1370s, relatively late in life, he married Donnina Visconti, one of
twenty illegitimate children of Bernabo Visconti, ruler of Milan, by
whom he had a son and three daughters. The two eldest daughters
were married to fellow mercenary commanders. Although he handled vast sums, he was always in debt, particularly in back-taxes to
Florence, and in 1394 he sold his estates and intended returning to
England. At all times he had reserved his allegiance to the English

king, on occasion representing him diplomatically, and he apparently retained contacts with his place of birth. He died before he could come home, but his body may indeed rest at Sible Hedingham.

F. Gaupp, 'The Condottiere John Hawkwood', *History* xxiii, 1939.

N. Ritchie, 'Sir John Hawkwood 1320–94: The First Anglo-Florentine', *History Today* x, 1977.

MARGARET MARSHALL, DUCHESS OF NORFOLK (*c.* 1320–1399) was a dowager 'of remarkable business acumen and spirit' who 'has left distinctive and lasting traces of her colourful career'. Her father was Thomas of Brotherton, Earl of Norfolk and Earl Marshal (*d.*1338), son to Edward I by his second marriage to Margaret of France and half-brother of Edward II, so Margaret was first cousin of Edward III. The successive deaths of her brother Edward by 1337, her sister Alice and her stepmother by 1362, and her niece in 1375 left Margaret ultimately as sole heiress of her father. This was recognized by the crown, which henceforth entitled her Margaret Marshall — holder of the dignity, but not the office, of Earl Marshal — and Countess of Norfolk. Since her father had been amongst the most generously endowed of the earls and since she also enjoyed dowers from her two husbands John Lord Segrave (*d.*1354) and Walter Lord Mauny (*d.*1372), Margaret was the greatest dowager of her time. She outlived all her children and many other descendants, who never realised their hereditary expectations, and thus epitomises 'the problem of late medieval dowagers' to noble families. Her eventual heir at death was a great-grandson. In 1397, when her grandson Thomas Mowbray was created Duke of Norfolk, Margaret was created Duchess of Norfolk in her own right — a remarkable mark of distinction and very welcome to her.

Medieval wives were subject to their husbands and little can be learnt about them. In Margaret's case we know only that she bore each husband a son and a daughter, that she married Lord Mauny from personal choice without royal licence, and that she went overseas in 1350 in defiance of a royal prohibition, perhaps to seek a divorce from Lord Segrave. Edward III's anger was not allayed by her prevarications and she spent several months in detention. Past the age of childbearing by 1372, she deliberately chose to remain single and independent for her last twenty-seven years.

Like other great dowagers, Margaret possessed the resources of great magnates, but not their inclination for high politics. Her acute sense of her exalted ancestry, high rank, and royal connections caused her to seek implementation by the crown of endowments promised to her father and to secure privileges and possessions as Earl Marshal. Both claims apparently failed. To her tenants she probably appeared no different from male lords: like them she was well-served by professional administrators and was concerned to run her property efficiently. One estate exemplifies 'her grasp of administrative affairs; her pursuance of her rights and dues; and a certain harshness stemming from keen self-interest'. She was mean about inessential expenses, such as payment of annuities, and vigorous in enlarging her resources, if necessary by fraud or violence. She could thus afford to live in state at Framlingham Castle very much like the Lady of Clare a generation earlier, entertaining lavishly and pursuing her religious interests. She made no new foundations, but gave generously to several existing ones, including the houses of Minoresses at Bruisyard and Aldgate so fashionable with noble ladies at this time. These gifts were apparently connected to patronage to William Woodford, a Franciscan theologian, and to her provision of stalls for Greyfriars, London, where she chose to be buried. Without obvious functions in their last years, dowagers commonly dwelt on the good of their souls and could afford to satisfy their spiritual as well as their earthly aspirations. If it is therefore strictly true that Margaret 'used her wealth' purely for 'personal advantage', it is also true that some of her activities — such as defence and pursuit of her rights — were of equal or greater value to her successors and their benefit may indeed have been intended.

R. E. Archer, 'Margaret of Brotherton c.1320–1399', *Historical Research* lx, 1987.

HENRY YEVELE (c.1320–1400), master mason of London, has been described as perhaps 'the greatest English architect'. He came from Derbyshire, perhaps from Uttoxeter or nearby Yeaveley, and may have already qualified as a master mason before coming to London, where he became a freeman in 1353 and was an acknowledged leader of his craft in 1355–6. By 1357 he was working for St Albans Abbey and probably also at Kennington for the Black Prince.

By 1360 he was in royal service and directing works both at the palace of Westminster and the Tower of London. Yevele was somewhat older than his great contemporary Wynford and earlier in royal service, which may explain why he was more extensively employed by the crown. However that may be, he worked at several other royal places — Eltham, Sheen, Baynard's Castle in London — and undertook building at half a dozen royal castles. He also tackled tombs with effigies, certainly contracting for those of Richard II, his consort, and Cardinal Langham in Westminster Abbey. He may also have made those of Edward III there and the Black Prince in Canterbury Cathedral. He had an extensive practice with many other clients. Among the more eminent were the city of London, for whom he maintained old London bridge for thirty years from 1365; John of Gaunt, Duke of Lancaster, for whom he worked on the Savoy and the tomb of the Duchess Blanche in 1374–5 and on Hertford Castle somewhat later; William Wykeham, Bishop of Winchester, for whom he worked on New College, Oxford with William Wynford and perhaps on other projects in Winchester itself: Lord Cobham, for whom he designed Cooling Castle in Kent (1380–2) and worked on the parish church of St Dunstans-in-the East in London; Westminster Abbey and the chapter of St Paul's Cathedral. He probably undertook many other private commissions in London's hundred medieval churches, which have now largely disappeared. Yet other projects have been attributed to him on the basis of his distinctive style, which, however, was quickly imitated by others. The most important of these is the nave of Canterbury Cathedral, one of the masterpieces of English Perpendicular, which was built at the same time as Wynford's nave at Winchester Cathedral and yet is stylistically quite different.

Yevele became a Londoner, marrying into a family of London tradesmen and playing a full part in city life. His decision to practise from the capital may explain why he was apparently more extensively employed than Wynford and certainly accounts for his many London commissions. Some at least of his monuments were prepared in London, packed, and despatched for re-assembly locally. He kept a large stock of materials, comprising stone, alabaster, tiles, lead, and latten, some of which were supplied to other London workshops. He has been taken as the model of a skilled London craftsman, albeit an outstandingly able and successful one. He should have made a good living, for he was a royal esquire from 1369, feed by the city from 1365, and doubtless by other clients. Certainly he dealt extensively in city property; on his death he possessed several tenements and quays in the parish of St Magnus. His own house there contained a private chapel, in which he was licensed to hold divine service in 1400, and he could afford to establish a chantry of two priests in St Magnus' church, where he belonged to the fraternity of Salve Regina. He also held lands in Southwark. Like his friend Wynford, he remained in harness until the end.

J. H. Harvey, *Henry Yevele*, 2nd edn. 1946.
E. M. Veale, 'Craftsmen and the Economy of London in the Fourteenth Century', *Studies in London History presented to Philip Edmund Jones*, ed. A. E. J. Hollaender and W. Kellaway, 1969.

ALICE PERRERS (*c.*1345–1400), notorious mistress of Edward III, first appears in history about 1365 as damsel of Queen Philippa. She must have been of gentle birth and may have come from Hertfordshire. Although not beautiful, she was apparently Edward's mistress well before the queen's death in 1369 and enjoyed his unwavering fidelity thereafter. She bore him at least two children: a son John Southerey born about 1364–5 and knighted in 1377, who died obscurely, and a daughter Joan. Another daughter, Joan the younger, was apparently sired by the Westmoreland knight William Windsor (*d.*1384), later a baron, whom she married about 1377, but may have been betrothed to much earlier. Neither daughter was acknowledged by Windsor, who left all his property to three sisters, and both married relatively humbly.

The height of her influence in the 1370s coincided with the king's galloping senility. He treated her with chivalric honour, holding tournaments for her benefit, heaped her with gifts including royal jewels formerly belonging to Queen Philippa, and allowed her to exercise authority within his household like a queen. Her sway over him gave her an influence over his decisions deplored by Bishop Brinton: 'It is not fitting or safe that all the keys should hang from the belt of one woman'. She was apparently uninterested in foreign affairs, but involved herself in court intrigue and distribution of patronage. She was later convicted of preventing investigation of Windsor's misdeeds as ruler of Ireland and of securing a pardon for the merchant Richard Lyons in defiance of parliamentary decree. Descriptions of such events reveal the essentially informal nature of her influence, exercised in Edward's chamber or sitting on his bed, and shows how difficult it was to detect or counter.

Her obscure birth and limited means gave Alice more excuse than most favourites for her rapacity. Certainly she pursued her own advantage singlemindedly and with a shrewd business sense. Edward gave lands and moveables to her, others she borrowed and let him buy, yet others she bought with exchequer loans that he later pardoned. Much else was secured by purchase, in return for influence or by moneylending. She accumulated 22 manors, lands in 17 counties, and a London house. The poet Langland may have made her model for his Lady Meed and the Speaker in the Good Parliament in 1376 declared that 'it would be a great profit to the kingdom to remove that lady from the king's company so that the king's treasure could be applied to the war and wardships in the king's gift be not so lightly granted away'. She also corrupted justice: 'This Alice de Perers had such power and eminence in those days that no one dared prosecute a claim against her'. When not at court, she lived in considerable luxury in her manor of Pallenswick in Hammersmith.

Alice's political influence and greedy self-interest help explain her impeachment in the Good Parliament of 1376 and resultant forfeiture, sentences rapidly revoked by Edward III, but repeated next year after his death. Evidently even her associates disliked her. Although the latter sentence too was set aside, partly because she was tried as single when actually married, Alice did not recover all her wealth despite extensive litigation and died in 1400 a woman of only moderate wealth at her home at Gaynes Park, Essex. She had not forgotten or forgiven her losses, transmitting her by then futile claims to her daughters.

C. Given-Wilson, *The Royal Household and the King's Affinity: Service, Politics, and Finance in England 1360–1413*, 1986.
G. A. Holmes, *The Good Parliament of 1376*, 1975.
G. Kay, *Lady of the Sun: The Life and Times of Alice Perrers*, 1966.

WILLIAM WYNFORD (*c.*1340–1405), master mason, was the great architect who remodelled the Norman nave of Winchester Cathedral into one of the masterpieces of English Perpendicular Gothic. He was apparently a westcountryman, probably from the Somerset village of Winford near Bristol and possibly of gentle birth. He first appears in 1360 as one of the master masons working for the king at Windsor Castle and was promoted next year to joint direction of building there. He was appointed a royal esquire in 1369, feed at £10 a year from 1372, and worked not just at Windsor but also at Orwell and elsewhere. His superior at Windsor was the king's clerk of works William Wykeham, then provost of Wells Cathedral and subsequently Bishop of Winchester. It was probably therefore Wykeham who secured his appointment as master mason at Wells Cathedral in 1365 and he certainly employed Wynford later on his own building operations. Among his other clients were Abingdon Abbey (1375–6), Southampton corporation in 1378–9, and Queen's College at Oxford (1400–2). Work at Wardour Castle, Yeovil church, and Arundel College have also been attributed to him on stylistic grounds, for he is one of the first architects with a personal style quite distinct from those of his fellows. As one of the leaders of his profession, he should have made a good living, certainly married, and fathered a son, probably at Windsor, whom he educated at Wykeham's foundations of Winchester College and New College, Oxford. Perhaps William Wynford's wife was dead by 1399, when he was granted a corrody by Winchester cathedral priory entitling him to free meals for life — not much of a risk for a sexagenarian — but he lived off the premises and possessed a private oratory in 1402.

Wynford's two principal employers were Wells cathedral chapter and William Wykeham. It was also his buildings for them that have survived best. He was architect of Wells Cathedral from 1365 until death, a period which coincided with substantial remodelling of the existing church, for example by inserting tracery in the Early English nave windows, and perhaps also the construction of the Chain Gate and Vicars Close. His most important project there, however, was undoubtedly the great south tower of the west front, which set a model for spireless square-topped towers imitated in the north-west tower of the cathedral and by the many splendid towers of Somerset's parish churches erected during the remainder of the middle ages.

William Wynford (centre), master mason of William of Wykeham,
with the master carpenter (left) and Simon Membury
(From a window in Winchester College)

Some, indeed, may have been his work. For Wykeham he was
probably the designer of New College, begun in 1379, certainly the
architect at Winchester College, commenced in 1387, and worked
also on his castle at Farnham in Surrey. He must have co-operated on
some of these operations with his great contemporary Henry Yevele.
Wynford liaised closely with Wykeham, dining with him thirteen
times in July, August and September 1393, rather more frequently
than Yevele, and was depicted in glass by his grateful employer at
Winchester College. Wykeham had inherited the project of rebuilding Winchester Cathedral nave from his predecessor Edington, who
had completed little more than the west front at his death in 1366.
When Wykeham resumed work on the nave in 1394 it was presumably Wynford, as master mason, who devised the more economical
approach of recasting the original by enclosing the Norman pillars
within Perpendicular mouldings rather than demolishing the existing structure and starting anew. This device was cheaper than total
rebuilding and much quicker. Presumably it explains how operations could be completed within the lifetime of the now aged
Wykeham. Despite cutting corners the result was also one of the
great Perpendicular naves, comparable to, yet quite different from,
Prior Chillenden's splendid nave at Canterbury Cathedral, which is
normally attributed to Henry Yevele. Work on the Winchester nave

was completed only shortly before the deaths of both patron and architect.

JOHN OF GAUNT (GHENT), DUKE OF LANCASTER (1340–99), third son of Edward III, was the greatest noble in late medieval England. Already Earl of Richmond in 1342, he entered his wife Blanche's vast Lancaster inheritance and became Duke of Lancaster in 1362. After her much-lamented death, he remarried in 1371 to Constance of Castile, elder daughter of King Pedro the Cruel (*d.* 1369), and called himself King of Castile and Leon. Invading Spain in 1386, he gave up his realms in 1388 and two daughters became queens of Castile and Portugal. From 1394 he was Duke of Aquitaine. By marrying his mistress Katherine Swynford he legitimised his Beaufort offspring and eased their promotion in the peerage and Church.

Gaunt was a tall, spare, but well-built man, reserved and dignified in manner. 'Conventional in all things', especially in religion, he was typically aristocratic in his love of ceremony and show, his liberality, his love of dicing, falconry, and the chase. Like Edward III and the Black Prince he served in many expeditions from 1355, displayed knightly prowess at Najera (1367), and made his retinue 'a chivalrous company of highly regarded knights conspicuous for their courtly and chivalrous skills' on the model of King Arthur's Round Table. Hence perhaps his sense of honour. Acutely conscious of the dignity of royal and noble birth and rank and the respect due to them, he deeply resented any criticism or hostility from knights, Londoners or other plebeians. Thus he quarrelled with the city in 1377, the Earl of Northumberland in 1381, and King Richard in 1385. Public apologies and ceremonies of reconciliation were required to appease him: from London and parliament in 1377, Northumberland in 1381, the king in 1385 and 1389, and Arundel in 1394. Duties and obligations, like his good lordship to Wyclif, were scrupulously observed. None took priority over allegiance to the crown: 'the King had no more faithful servant than himself and he would follow wherever he would lead'. Gaunt's haughtiness was disliked in England and misinterpreted as ambition for the crown, but abroad his grand manner, exalted birth and rank, international connections and outlook were admired.

After 1370 Gaunt was the senior active royal prince and willingly shouldered military and official burdens that successive kings shirked. Although a poor general, he was a good diplomat and councillor. The ill-health of his father and brother forced him to take the military and political lead, to adopt the French and papal policies condemned by the Good Parliament (1376), and to orchestrate the court's recovery. His unpopularity made a regency impossible, thus permitting Richard II's disastrously premature assertion of power, but his interventions were often decisive. Unable to persuade Richard to campaign in France in person, he walked out of the royal council, thereby giving 'great displeasure both to the king and to the whole council. Yet these temporal lords went in constant fear of the duke of Lancaster because of his great power, admirable judgement, and his brilliant mind'. His seniority, authority, and 200 retainers enabled him to condemn Richard's counsel and government with impunity. No wonder there were plots to kill him. Again in 1394 Gaunt's 'rough and bitter words' in council reportedly prevented others from expressing their views freely. By then, however, Gaunt was recognized as a force for peace and stability and the complaint was quashed. His retainers dominated local commissions because they too contributed to peace and order, for Gaunt, at least, could control his retainers. His absence in 1386 and death in 1399 were followed by political crises.

S. Armitage-Smith, *John of Gaunt,* 1904.
A. Goodman, 'John of Gaunt: Paradigm of the late Fourteenth-Century Crisis', *Transactions of the Royal Historical Society,* 5th series, xxxvii 1987.
G. A. Holmes, *The Good Parliament,* 1975.

RICHARD LORD SCROPE OF BOLTON (1327–1403) raised his family to the peerage by a career of unremitting service on the battlefield and in administration. The eldest surviving son of Chief Justice Henry Scrope (*d.* 1336) and occasionally denigrated for his lowly origins, he inherited his father's military interests and his sense of honour, successfully defending his right to the crest of a crab (1347) and his arms against the Carminowes (1360) and in the celebrated Scrope and Grosvenor controversy (1385). His military career was remarkable for its length, almost forty years, and for its variety, as he fought at sea and on land, in France, Scotland and

Spain, including Crécy and Nevilles Cross in 1346, Espagnols-sur-Mer (1350), and Najera (1367) among his battle honours. He was never in command in France, for he was neither a front rank landowner nor a member of the royal house, but he served repeatedly from 1367 in the retinue of John of Gaunt, Duke of Lancaster, whose retainer he was. As a northerner active in border conflict from his teens, however, he was highly suitable as warden of the West March in 1375 and frequently engaged in negotiations with the Scots. Distinguished military service, local commissions in Yorkshire, and election as knight of the shire for the county led naturally to a series of front-rank ministerial appointments: Treasurer of England in 1371-5, steward of the household in 1377-8, and chancellor of England in 1378-80, and again in 1381-2. Hence his individual summons to parliament from 1371 as a baron and hence perhaps also Henry IV's remission at his request of the forfeiture due on the death of his son William, Earl of Wiltshire. Richard had been loyal to crown and House of Lancaster, both then represented by Henry IV. But such advancement and national exposure left him still a Yorkshireman with predominantly local interests, who sealed his social arrival with a new castle at Bolton in Wensleydale — a status symbol rather than military necessity — and generous patronage of the church, some of which — such as Wensley College — were never fulfilled, but which illustrate his assiduous cultivation of local contacts.

Richard's combination of service to both crown and Duke of Lancaster went with a reputation for complete integrity: a warning to those of us who suppose such ties to be incompatible or to be evidence of self-interest and infirmity of commitment. His appointment as lay treasurer in 1371, itself a remarkable departure from precedent, took place with parliamentary approval on dismissal of his predecessor. The impeachment of his successor in 1376 again left him personally unsullied. Indeed he then agreed to testify — but only if released from his oath of confidentiality as a councillor — and promised not 'to spare any living man but will say the truth entirely to my knowledge'. He presided at the trial of Alice Perrers in 1377. As chancellor in 1381-2 he refused to seal certain extravagant grants made by the young Richard II, resigned his seal only into the hands of the boy king, and declared that he would not take up office under him again. He again spoke up boldly for his brother-in-law

Suffolk at his impeachment in 1386 and supported the Appellants in 1386-9. This is the picture not of a weathercock but of a man of independence and principle, who was not afraid of speaking out in defiance of king, popular or parliamentary opinion. He epitomised the contemporary ideal of the forthright and truthful councillor. Such a model was preferable to kings in theory rather than practice, and several times could have led Scrope to disaster, most notably in 1397, when King Richard chose instead to pardon him for supporting the Appellants. Fortunately he escaped the disgrace experienced by Lord Latimer, whose career otherwise so closely parallels his own.

G. A. Holmes, *The Good Parliament*, 1975.

JOHN UTHRED (*c.*1320-97) of Boldon, 'the most distinguished of all the university monks' and the outstanding northern Benedictine of the 14th century, was never superior of a major monastery. Born at Boldon, a Durham estate, he went to Oxford as a secular clerk and entered Durham Cathedral Priory only in 1341. A brief term at the Durham cell at Stamford was followed by twenty years (1347-67) at another cell, Durham College at Oxford, where he became a doctor of theology in 1357 and was a distinguished teacher. He returned to Oxford only briefly in 1383-6. It was unusual to spend a lifetime in academic study like Walter Burley and still more unusual to remain a lifetime at university. Even when at Oxford in 1350-67 Uthred was prior of Durham College. Subsequently he served three terms as prior of the cell of Finchale (1367-8, 1375-81, 1386-96) and two as subprior of the parent house at Durham (1368-75, 1381-3). Durham priory sent him on visitations, to the convocation of the Church of York, and to General Chapters of the English Black Monks, for whom he also performed commissions. Once, uniquely for a monk who was not head of his house, the king sent him on embassy to Avignon. Such activities reveal Uthred as a busy administrator as well as a scholar and one moreover highly respected and trusted. His career demonstrates the concrete gains in prestige and administrative capacity that monasteries could make from their considerable financial sacrifice in sending inmates to university.

Uthred's reputation originated initially from his academic achievements and he never stopped writing. He was both a daring speculative theologian and a partisan controversialist. At his best he was an independent thinker, who grappled with problems directly and strove to find solutions. He could argue reasonably and persuasively. His best works, on the origins and essence of monasticism, reveal considerable capacity for research, a sense of the past, and 'remarkable serenity and rationality in their treatment'. On the other hand, unlike Adam Easton, he was capable of violent and scurrilous vituperation against his opponents and responded bitterly to criticism. His principal opponents were the friars and his younger Oxford contemporary John Wyclif. Uthred repeatedly defended monasticism against its enemies, attacking the mendicant ideal, defending monasticism and ecclesiastical endowments. Also, like Easton, he asserted the superiority of spiritual over temporal power. In his last years he wrote books of devotion. Before then, perhaps goaded by Wyclif, he defended traditional Catholic doctrines on holy communion and predestination, but his own views were not above criticism. Like many scholars of his time, who lived in an age of uncertainty, his theology was drawn from diverse sources including Ockham. It displayed some of the tendencies condemned by Bradwardine and it included his own doctrine of the clear vision. This asserted deathbed piety over lifetime religion and was condemned by the Benedictine Archbishop Langham in 1368. Uthred was upset, for he felt conventionally enough that academic speculation should be settled in the universities, but his condemnation — to be followed soon after by that of Wyclif — drew attention to the risks of free speculation and may have contributed to the loss of originality among English (and European) theologians. Obviously condemnation damaged Uthred's reputation as a theologian, but it had no apparent effect among Benedictines and he remained in responsible office until death.

D. Knowles, *The Religious Orders in England* ii, 1961.
W. A. Pantin, *The English Church in the Fourteenth Century*, 1955.

THOMAS BRINTON (c.1320–89), Bishop of Rochester was 'the outstanding monk-bishop of the period'. Born humbly at Brinton in Norfolk, he never forgot his origins. He entered Norwich cathedral priory, which was a monastery that placed a particularly high value on learning and which sent him first to Cambridge

University, perhaps in 1352-3, and later to Oxford. He was there with another Norwich monk, the future cardinal Adam Easton, in 1356-7, when both were recalled to preach to the people of Norwich, an unusual task for members of an enclosed order. Back at Gloucester College, Oxford in 1363-4, when Brinton had become a doctor of canon law, he and Easton were the two outstanding monks at the university. Called to be a papal penitentiary by Pope Urban V, a reforming Black Monk and later a saint, Brinton followed him from Avignon to Rome, where he joined Sir John Hawkwood in founding the English College there. He was nominated Bishop of Rochester in 1373 by Urban's successor Gregory XI. He took pride that 'I have this comparatively small and poor church not by money or prayer, not by letters, nor my own importunity, but solely from God and the lord pope'.

Brinton was unusual as a scholar, a monk, and a papal nominee at a time when all these categories among the episcopate were becoming rare. He was well-fitted for office by his learning, his blameless life and religious zeal, and by his utter integrity, a combination which in an earlier age might have made him an archbishop. Like other bishops he acted as a trier of parliamentary petitions and as a royal diplomat and commissioner. He opposed the teachings of John Wyclif and is credited with securing papal condemnation of some of his doctrines, but his career was restricted by ill-health from 1382.

Already a famous preacher in a great age of pulpit criticism, he quickly established himself as the outstanding preacher among the bishops of his day. Two volumes of surviving sermons reveal him denouncing the evils of the contemporary scene without fear or favour. 'Veritas liberabit', the truth will free, became his motto as bishop. He opposed lay interference in ecclesiastical affairs, telling John of Gaunt that he had no right to tax the clergy, opposing the employment of clerics in the royal administration, and lamenting that 'Every day we see Christ being crucified in his members and Barabas set free'. Those bishops and priests who cared for gain rather than the cure of souls were denounced as 'not pastors but mercenaries'. He inveighed against the greed for gold of the papal Curia and of those who sought benefices there. He also condemned the faults of each class of the laity: the rich who oppressed the poor, burdened them with taxes, and manipulated the law; the merchants who practised usury; and the peasantry and poor, for whom he felt most sympathy, were criticised for rebelling in 1381. He did not want fundamental changes in Church or society, but wanted each order to keep its place and perform its proper duties. His moral rigour and passionate eloquence on the most public occasions made him the national conscience of his day and he 'must have exerted a powerful influence upon those who came into contact with him'. Direct evidence is lacking, but it is striking how similar was the message of Langland and how it was developed more radically by Chaucer and Wyclif, to name just three of his contemporaries.

M. A. Devlin, 'Bishop Thomas Brinton and his Sermons', *Speculum* xiv, 1939.

M. A. Devlin ed., *Sermons of Thomas Brinton, Bishop of Rochester 1373–1389*, 2 vols, Camden 3rd Series lxxv–vi, 1954.

W. A. Pantin, *The English Church in the Fourteenth Century*, 1955.

ADAM EASTON (*c.*1325–97), Cardinal of England, was an extreme defender of papal claims to universal power. The formative stages of his career closely parallel those of his older contemporary Thomas Brinton. Both were of humble origin and natives of villages near Norwich, both became Benedictines of Norwich Cathedral Priory, both were sent to study at Gloucester College, Oxford, and both were recalled to undertake preaching duties at Norwich itself in 1356. Easton took his doctorate of theology only in 1365–6, served briefly as head of Gloucester College, and then followed Brinton to the Curia, but in the train of the erstwhile Benedictine archbishop Cardinal Langham. Whereas Brinton became Bishop of Rochester, Easton never returned to England, becoming Cardinal of St Cecilia in 1381. His English origins emerge in his defence of monastic property, his patriotic support of the English in France, and in his alarm about Wyclif.

Unlike Brinton, Easton was a theologian and more of an academic, devoting years to treatises on topics encountered at the Curia. Hence his defence of the mystic St Bridget of Sweden, whose canonisation he expedited, and the service of the Visitation of the Blessed Virgin Mary that he composed. Although exceptionally well-read in modern theology, Easton's preferences were for the more traditional Victorines and for the Bible, especially the Old Testament, which he knew exceptionally well. To assist his biblical studies, he learnt Hebrew with the aid of a Jew and translated the whole Bible from Hebrew into Latin. This contributed to his vast *Defence of Ecclesiastical Power*, completed about 1380, which was intended to introduce five further volumes that were never written. Among other things this book attacks Wyclif, whose works Easton read about 1376 and whose views he may have had condemned in 1377, recognizing their heretical character more quickly than Englishmen in England. Later volumes were to have refuted Marsilius of Padua, Ockham and other heretics. Easton emerges as an extreme papalist, convinced of the superiority of priestly power in spiritual and temporal matters alike, a view still widely held in papal circles but regarded as outdated and impractical elsewhere. He was also a controversialist who was unfailingly courteous and respectful to his opponents, however heretical he considered them to be.

Easton believed Urban VI's election as pope in 1378 to be valid and applauded the end to the succession of French popes. He deplored the subsequent election of another candidate by the French cardinals, which inaugurated the Great Schism of 1378–1415, when there were two or even three rival popes at the same time. Although he found Urban a difficult man to work with, Easton stayed with him and was made a cardinal in 1381, but in 1384 he was imprisoned, tortured, and deprived of all his dignities. Five other cardinals disappeared, presumably killed, but Easton was spared, perhaps because of Richard II's intervention. Easton's integrity was such that nobody except Urban thought him capable of treason and he was speedily restored by Boniface IX on Urban's death in 1389. Easton's sufferings, however, may have broken his health and certainly interrupted his writings. Apart from his provision to ecclesiastical benefices all over Europe, almost nothing is known of his last years.

L. J. MacFarlane, 'The Life and Writings of Adam Easton O.S.B.', London Ph.D. thesis, 1955.

W. A. Pantin, *The English Church in the Fourteenth Century*, 1955.

WILLIAM LORD LATIMER (1330–81) was the villain of the Good Parliament of 1376. Although he succeeded to his father's Yorkshire barony when only five, his mother's longevity — she died only in 1384 — deprived him of most of its income and made him

William Lord Latimer
(From the choir of York Minster)

dependent on the royal favour that he earned by a distinguished career of public service. He was repeatedly in France from Crécy in 1346 until 1381 and was the king's principal representative in Brittany from 1359–67, acting as king's lieutenant from 1361 and sharing in Duke John IV's decisive victory at Auray. He served in Scotland in 1356 and was an active diplomat from 1369. Returning home about 1368, he attended the Lords assiduously, usually as trier of petitions, was a regular royal commissioner, became steward of the household in 1368, chamberlain in 1371-6, executor of Edward III, and councillor both to him and the young Richard II. Always a key officer, the chamberlain controlled 'both written and personal access to the king', which was particularly important in the 1370s as Edward III increasingly lost his grip on affairs. Latimer may therefore have become 'the man most intimately involved in the organisation of the renewed war effort from England'. Certainly he was constantly engaged in mustering and paying troops and administrative tasks of all kinds. Inevitably the government's failures and unpopular policies were also attributed to him and were charged to his account at the Good Parliament of 1376. Latimer pleaded that decisions of policy had been made by the whole council and indeed most charges could not be substantiated.

Latimer undoubtedly profited from his service. He received a £333 annuity during his mother's lifetime in 1354, became a knight of the Garter about 1362, captured the Count of St Pol and others for ransom, acted as captain of St Sauveur-le-Vicomte and lived off the country, was appointed warden of northern forests (1368) and of the Cinque Ports (1372), and purchased several valuable wardships. Hence the wealth that enabled him to lend money to the crown at interest. This loan, supposed to be to the king's loss as another lesser loan without interest was declined, was made a charge against Latimer at his impeachment. So too was his sale of licences to export wool free of custom, which he claimed to have paid into the chamber at a profit, and his purchase of royal debts at a discount, a common enough practice. What was behind these charges was the belief that Latimer exploited his privileged position to profit from the crown at a time of great financial stringency. Such claims could not then be substantiated and cannot now, but they secured Latimer's conviction, fine and loss of office. That was the real intention. The financial and other charges were pretexts to destroy Latimer, Perrers and others who ruled in Edward's last years and whose policies were unpopular. Latimer quickly recovered Edward's favour and resumed his interrupted military and political career, though no longer as chamberlain of the royal household.

Latimer's reputation has been sullied both by his impeachment and by his malicious portrayal by the St Albans chronicler. He may, of course, have been as sexually immoral, avaricious and deceitful as accused, but he was certainly no coward — his military career speaks for itself — and his pious intentions belie the charge of irreligion. On balance it is only the events of 1376 that separate his notoriety from the adulation that befell his colleague at arms and fellow Yorkshireman Richard Lord Scrope of Bolton.

C. Given-Wilson, *The Royal Household and the King's Affinity: Service, Politics and Finance in England 1360–1413,* 1986. G. A. Holmes, *The Good Parliament,* 1975.

SIR PETER DE LA MARE was the first known speaker of the House of Commons in 1376 and was speaker again next year. Apart from these highlights, his career is remarkably obscure. His date of birth is not known, but he was apparently son of Sir Reginald De La Mare and lord of Little Hereford and Yatton in Herefordshire. Any connection with other De La Mares, such as the Abbot of St Albans, must have been distant and his death without issue cannot be dated more closely than 1388/1400. His public career was largely confined to Herefordshire, where he was sheriff in 1372-3, tax commissioner in 1379, J.P. in 1380, and seven times knight of the shire in 1376-83. He visited Ireland once, probably in 1379-80, on behalf of his lord Edmund Mortimer, Earl of March (d. 1381), whose retainer he was by 1373, steward in 1376, feoffee, executor and attorney. As a great nobleman of the blood royal, Mortimer had a crucial political role during Edward III's dotage and Richard II's minority. De La Mare could have been acting on instructions and must have possessed Mortimer's consent or acquiescence.

However that may be, the Commons' victory over the court in the Good Parliament in 1376 owed much to Peter's daring and eloquence. The essential background was military defeat after 1369, which was blamed on English mismanagement rather than the French resurgence, and royal insolvency, which was attributed to speculation and profiteering rather than the ruinous cost of war. Short-term attempts to relieve the pressure, such as a truce with France and an agreement with the Papacy in 1375, were no more popular than defeat and bankruptcy. Understandably the Commons did not want to pay taxes for unsuccessful war and supposed, rather less reasonably, that purging the court would permit victory without any further taxes. The king, De La Mare argued, 'has with him certain councillors and servants who are not loyal or profitable to him or the kingdom and they make gains by subtlety thus deceiving our lord the king'. Corruption was notorious but unremedied because nobody about the king 'wishes to tell him the truth, or to counsel him loyally and profitably, but always they scoff, and mock, and work for their own profit; so we shall say nothing further until all those who are about the king, who are false men and evil counsellors, are removed and ousted from the king's presence; and until our lord appoints as new members of his council men who will not shirk from telling the truth and who will carry out reforms'.

Hence the impeachment of Edward's mistress Alice Perrers, his chamberlain Lord Latimer, the merchant Richard Lyons, and others, the first parliamentary impeachment, and their conviction on the few charges that could be substantiated. They were removed from office, a continual council was appointed, the rapprochements with the Papacy and France were abandoned, and no tax was granted. Popular though such actions were, they contributed neither to military or financial recovery but rather to the further disaster of 1381.

De La Mare's victory was shortlived, for Edward III recalled Perrers and imprisoned De La Mare in Nottingham Castle. Released after 33 weeks on Richard II's accession, for which he was later officially compensated, he was again speaker in 1377, the new king's first parliament, securing restoration of some of the concessions to the Good Parliament and returning thereafter to the provincial obscurity whence he came.

C. Given-Wilson, *The Royal Household and the King's Affinity: Service, Politics and Finance in England 1360–1413*, 1986.
G. A. Holmes, *The Good Parliament*, 1975.
J. S. Roskell, *Parliament and Politics in Later Medieval England*, ii, 1981.

RICHARD LYONS (*d.*1381), vintner and alderman of London, was impeached in the Good Parliament of 1376 and murdered in the Peasants Revolt four years later. Lyons' origins are obscure: perhaps from Winchelsea and certainly illegitimate, he was buying property in London from 1359, when he had presumably completed his apprenticeship and established himself as a vintner. By 1365 he was prominent enough to take a lease of the three London taverns selling sweet wines. He was still principally a vintner in 1376, when he was owed £518 for wine supplied. Like most successful merchants, he extended his interests into other areas: in 1376 he owned a ship, iron valued at £198, cloth worth £649, lead worth £103, stocks of timber, and was lending to both the crown and private individuals (like the Duke of Brittany) on security. To redeem his loans to the crown he was appointed farmer of the petty customs and subsidy throughout England, which inevitably involved him in other areas of royal finance. He was sheriff of London in 1374 and alderman from then until dismissed in 1376, following his impeachment and forfeiture. He was back in business as a royal lender in 1379 and may have been richer at death than in 1376. He was knight of the shire for Essex in 1380.

Lyons' rapid increase in wealth is illustrated by his purchase of property in London from 1359, of the manor of Overhall-in-Leiston in Essex in 1365, and many other properties from 1375. At his death in 1381 he held thirty houses, sixty shops, twelve cellars, and six gardens in London and its suburbs north of the Thames, two shops and seven gardens in Southwark, three manors and other land in Essex and Kent. Most apparently escaped forfeiture in 1376 because held in trust. Moveables worth £2,443 had then been discovered in London alone, much of it in stock, but much comprising the contents of his house in the parish of St James Garlickhithe. Although he had been divorced in 1363, he was childless and presumably lived only with servants, his house contained a hall, parlour, five chambers, chapel, wardrobe and little wardrobe, pantry, buttery, kitchen and stable. These rooms were richly furnished with tapestries, chandeliers, and elaborate beds. The wardrobe and little wardrobe contained £87 worth of armour, linen and clothes, including a long list of colourful and furred gowns. Much of this was secured by the Duke of Gloucester on Lyons' fall. Lyons was probably not one of the richest aldermen and fell far short of the capital resources of the high nobility, yet his lifestyle was remarkably opulent.

It was Lyons' financial dealings with the crown that justified his impeachment in 1376 and his consequent unpopularity that led to his murder. Yet the charges are not particularly convincing. Lyons lent money to the crown at interest and may well have bought up old royal debts for less than their face value, but neither of these activities was illegal. No doubt, of course, he secured preferential terms for repayment, but all royal creditors sought to insist on that. 'Ambitious Lyons certainly was, and unscrupulous he may have been, but the evidence does not seem to justify the description of him as an "arch-thief"'. Some charges were apparently made maliciously by smugglers to divert attention from themselves, but the main reason for Lyons' impeachment seems to be political — because he was too intimately connected with the unpopular and unsuccessful policies of Lord Latimer and Alice Perrers in the mid 1370s. Like Gilbert Maghfield somewhat later he found trade and politics did not mix.

A. R. Myers, 'The Wealth of Richard Lyons', *Essays in Medieval History presented to Bertie Wilkinson*, ed. T. A. Sandquist and M. R. Powicke, 1969.

S. Thrupp, *The Merchant Class of Medieval London*, 1962.

MASTER JOHN WYCLIF (*c.* 1330–84), the 'evangelical doctor', was a heretic and the inspiration of England's only late medieval heretical sect: Lollardy. Except that he was a Yorkshireman, almost nothing is known of his early life, and he first occurs in 1356 as a bachelor of arts and fellow of Merton College. From there he moved to be Master of Balliol in 1360–1 and Warden of Canterbury College from 1365, whence he was ousted, when it became a monastic college in 1371. He entered royal service, but even moderate preferment obstinately refused to come. Thwarted ambition may have contributed to his increasing radicalism and ultimately heresy, although these were also logical extensions of his more orthodox beliefs. Although some of his doctrines were condemned, Wyclif himself never was — his friends were too powerful — and he was allowed to live out his last years in peace and to die naturally at his Leicestershire rectory, where he continued to write to the last and to reject the authority of the Church establishment. He did not found the Lollard movement, which was the work of his pupils.

Wyclif has been called the 'Morning Star of the Reformation', but those conclusions he shared with the sixteenth-century Protestant reformers were reached from quite a different direction. Where Luther condemned medieval scholasticism, Wyclif was a scholastic theologian — a product of the medieval academic system. He was a speculative philosopher before he was a theologian and his theology arose from his philosophy. Whereas Ockham had argued that only things that could be observed or experienced were real, Wyclif thought concepts — such as predestination — were just as real. From this emerged his belief that all being, all ideas and all matter were eternal. They came of God and were indestructible and unchanging. Hence he believed that all the Bible, even contradictions within it, were literally true. Hence too his doctrine of predestination: what God knew now must always have been. It was the pursuit of such theories to their logical extremes that made Wyclif's thought so dangerous.

Wyclif was always an extremist: an extremist philosopher before he became an extremist theologian. Utterly self-confident and convinced of his own rightness, he argued vigorously and at great length in treatises and disputations alike, sweeping aside the tentative replies of contemporaries, who were uncertain and intellectually less distinguished. Such qualities were valued by the crown, which wanted him to frighten the clergy into paying more taxes for fear of losing their endowments. Wyclif's *On Civil Dominion* (c. 1376) extended FitzRalph's argument that sinners could not exercise authority to argue that sinful clergy could be deprived of their lands. This theory was later applied by Lollards to tithes and to rents due to lay lords. About 1379, like Bradwardine, he claimed that God had settled in advance who was saved and who was damned. The Church of God, wrote Wyclif, thus consisted only of the saved, who were known only to God: the clergy and church establishment, even the pope, did not know if they were saved or 'the limb of the fiend'. They deserved respect only if saved and their functions, such as celebrating mass, were strictly useless as salvation had been settled beforehand. That was in theory: in practice Wyclif continued to write about the mass and died hearing it. His thought did not constitute a coherent system, but a series of interlocking and mutually contradictory ideas developed in the last decade of his life. All of it, however, threatened the Church as it was and carried dangerous implications for state and society as well.

K. B. McFarlane, *John Wycliffe and the Beginnings of English Nonconformity*, 1952.

J. Robson, *John Wyclif and the Oxford Schools*, 1961.

SIR THOMAS HUNGERFORD (*c.*1325–97) is the best-known instance of a speaker of the House of Commons who acted in a particular noble interest. He also established a future baronial family by acquiring Heytesbury from 1352, Farleigh Hungerford from 1369, and other properties on the Wiltshire/Somerset border. His success was sealed by a grant of hunting rights, by his construction of the inner ward of Farleigh castle, and by his benefactions to Lesnes Abbey and Edington Priory — rare Arrouasian and Bonhommes foundations, that suggest unusual religious discrimination. He returned himself to parliament on the first two occasions, but his later elections for Wiltshire and Somerset — ultimately fourteen in all — reflect his growing stature in the counties. Although sheriff of Wiltshire from 1355–60 and twice escheator, he was only an occasional commissioner until the late 1370s, when he occurs far more commonly, not just in Wiltshire, but further afield.

It is not clear how Hungerford acquired the resources to buy so much land. He can have inherited relatively little from his father William or uncle Sir Robert (d. 1352) and the inheritance of his second wife came relatively late in life. Apparently he never fought abroad. Perhaps some came from his shrievalty and much from his service to lords. Evidently very able and administratively expert, he was much in demand as estate official, councillor, feoffee and executor. An estate officer of the bishops of Salisbury (like his father and uncle) by 1354, he served Queen Philippa from 1354, Lord Burghersh by 1362, the Earl of Salisbury from 1365, and William Edington, Bishop of Winchester. Such pluralism was commonplace among administrators. Each position carried a fee and conferred local authority. He exploited inside information to acquire land, partly by purchase, partly by chicanery or force. At least one patron lost out because of 'the great maintenance of the said Thomas in the said county'. Whichever connections took priority with Thomas, 'at least he made the fortune of his house and that was probably his first concern'.

The outstanding contemporary nobleman was John of Gaunt, Duke of Lancaster, whose lands, income and retinue were all in a class of their own. About 1380 Gaunt had 202 extraordinary retainers, including 7 bannerets, 83 knights and 102 esquires. Some belonged to families that traditionally served the house of Lancaster, others lived near his principal estates, but many had no such connections. To all of them he offered exceptional opportunities — larger fees, better offices, better access to royal patronage. 'It is doubtful whether other affinities were as alluring as his — and they were certainly less prosperous'. Hungerford was one of the 66 knights and esquires attracted in 1371-6, initially as steward of his southern estates (1372), later as constable of Monmouth and steward elsewhere. It was apparently Gaunt who knighted him and he acted as speaker at the Bad Parliament of 1377. It was probably service to Gaunt that transformed his political and administrative career, as henceforth he sat frequently in parliament, served often on royal and ducal commissions not just in Wiltshire but everywhere — in Lincolnshire, Wales and Norfolk, for example. He had suddenly become a figure of national significance. If his 'Lancastrian connexion now became and henceforward remained the central, focal one of his career', yet Gaunt did not 'recruit his affinity for use as a political force in national affairs' (Goodman). Retainer by Gaunt thus did not conflict either with Hungerford's other loyalties or his own self-advancement, but instead made him a more attractive retainer and more formidable to oppose in his own affairs.

K. B. McFarlane, *England in the Fifteenth Century: Collected Essays*, 1981.
J. S. Roskell, *Parliament and Politics in Late Medieval England*, ii, 1981.

RICHARD II (1367-99) who ascended the throne in 1377, was the son of Edward the Black Prince and Joan of Kent. Few kings have been held more directly responsible for the disasters of their reigns and for their own depositions. A man of mercurial temperament, highly emotional and hot-tempered, Richard was inclined to outbursts of rage, impulsive actions, and violent quarrels with those about him. His lack of self-control helps explain his failure to establish his ascendancy over greater subjects, but it does not explain his deposition, nor does it detract from such good qualities as his loyalty to his servants and his intelligence. If Richard was indeed 'temperamentally unsuited for kingship', it was because he departed from the accepted pattern of kingship, because of his arbitrary autocracy, and because of his inability to understand where power in England really lay.

It was unfortunate that there was no regency on Richard's accession in 1377 at nine years of age. The only credible regent was John of Gaunt, Duke of Lancaster, eldest surviving son of Edward III, but his controversial role in the crises of 1376–7 ruled him out. Richard therefore had to be allowed the attributes of an adult king, such as a personal seal (signet), whilst government was conducted *at first* on his behalf by his council, ministers and household and he himself remained in the care of his mother. No formal decision was ever made about the date when Richard would take over in person. This proved an unfortunate mistake, for Richard was precocious, assertive and impatient to exercise his own prerogatives. He was still only fourteen in 1382, when his wishes were already an important ingredient in policy and when he dismissed his chancellor for failing to implement his commands. He was still only sixteen when he told parliament that the choice of his councillors was his business alone, and still only nineteen when he refused to dismiss even a scullion from his kitchens at parliament's request! The crises of 1386 and 1388 arose from the misgovernment of a teenager, who should not have been in charge so early. They would not have happened had his authority been postponed to his formal majority in 1389. His early mistakes soured his reign, creating the mutual distrust and resentment that surfaced so dangerously in the last years. His subjects found his assertion of his kingly dignity and prerogatives difficult to stomach in a child and therefore little easier when he was grown.

Richard's exalted sense of royal dignity as a teenager continued into adult life. He consistently regarded his government, policies, choice and conduct of officers and councillors as exclusively his business. To criticise any of these was intolerable: it was not just opposition but treason. The impeachment of his chancellor in 1386 was followed in 1387 by Richard's questions to the judges, who declared the acts of opposition and parliament to be illegal and treasonable. Criticism of household finances in 1397 was also condemned as treason. Opposition could not be brooked and must be destroyed with overwhelming force, as it was in 1397, but the cards were seldom stacked so strongly in Richard's favour. When parliament rejected his objections in 1386, Richard could only prevaricate obstinately and was given an uncomfortable lesson in mixed monarchy. He should have learnt that he must co-operate with his greater subjects and must rule by consent if he wanted to retain his crown. What he learnt, apparently, was that his subjects did not approve of autocracy. Hence his defensive preoccupation in his last years with his own personal security, which by itself was not enough to keep his throne.

To be an effective medieval king was to take on an arduous office carrying awesome responsibilities for the good of one's subjects. Richard was not a hardworking administrator and did not consistently seek the benefit of his people. Admittedly he was on occasion genuinely compassionate to his lesser subjects, but he was less conscious of his duties and responsibilities towards them than of the rights, prerogatives and personal advantages that kingship held for himself. Such defects were muted in his peaceful middle years, but from 1396 he treated his subjects' property with contempt. Not only did he take loans that he did not repay, not only did he force his subjects to buy pardons, but he compelled individuals and communities to seal so-called 'blank charters' that placed their goods and bodies at his mercy. This was rule by terror. In the last resort Richard preferred to coerce and frighten rather than cultivate support and rule by consent.

Nobody's consent and support was more important to a medieval English crown than that of the nobility, for no king could withstand their concentrated resources. Hence their accustomed role as friends and natural councillors of kings. Richard, however, never seems to have cultivated the nobility as a class or to have appreciated the enormous resources dispersed in their provincial estates. His council did not consistently contain the greatest and most experienced magnates, even though Richard was a man of uncertain judgement and limited experience, who needed the best advice he could get. He did not like honest councillors, who told him the truth about his government, and preferred those who said what he wanted to hear and deferred to his wishes. He relied on intimates like Vere and Aumarle, who were short on power, experience and competence, but agreeable to him personally. He was the prey of flatterers, who pandered to his wishes rather than speaking out and thus secured immediate access to his patronage. If Richard's councillors were insubstantial and indeed corrupt, his distribution of favours was indefensible, because it favoured the unworthy over the deserving. Contemporaries, for example, objected to the endowment of Vere and Suffolk in preference to his uncle Gloucester and considered that his creation of five dukes in 1397 devalued the title itself. He surrounded himself with rich courtiers with grand titles without realising that their promotion counted for little in the provinces. The *duketti* of 1397 could not rival John of Gaunt.

Just as Richard deliberately departed from contemporary expectations as a ruler, so too he shrugged off the military responsibilities of kingship. Richard's father and grandfather were both great soldiers, Richard succeeded to their titanic struggle with France, and the unsuccessful war dominated his reign, yet Richard was no soldier. He must have been trained in arms like all young aristocrats, but displayed no prowess or strategic sense. Richard led expeditions only to Ireland, where there were no serious enemies, and to Scotland, where he relied heavily on the experience and advice of others. He never led an army to France, as many thought to be his duty, and left this tougher and more important assignment to his great nobles. He was not without courage, but lacked the inclination — and perhaps the aptitude — to acquire the military competence or fulfil the military role expected of a king.

If Richard failed to conform to the normal pattern of kingship, it was because he arrogated to himself exceptional status and dignity. Probably not a carefully considered policy, it was a habit of mind that set him at odds with his subjects, whom he knew would disapprove. A mixture of injured pride, vengeance, and a desire to vindicate past conduct and assert himself in future help explain his actions in his second tyranny of 1397–99. His political and military incapacity and the unpopularity of himself and his agents explain why it all ended so disastrously. In the last resort Richard was not clever enough to make a success of the unconventional style of kingship that he chose for himself.

C. Barron, 'Tyranny of Richard II', *Bulletin of the Institute of Historical Research*, xli, 1968.
C. Given-Wilson, *The Royal Household and the King's Affinity: Service, Politics and Finance in England 1360–1413*, 1986.

A. Goodman, *The Loyal Conspiracy: The Lords Appellant under Richard II*, 1971.
R. H. Jones, *The Royal Policy of Richard II: Absolutism in the Later Middle Ages*, 1968.
A. B. Steel, *Richard II*, 1941.
J. A. Tuck, *Richard II and the English Nobility*, 1973.

JOHN BALL (*d.* 1381), chaplain, was the ideologist of the Peasants Revolt. Contemporaries made him its symbol. To some he was a foolish fanatic, wrongly supposed to be a follower of Wyclif, but to others he was a prophet, 'a true and worthy man, prophesying things useful to the commons of the kingdom and telling of woes and oppressions done to the people by the king and his aforesaid ministers'. Ironically it is the accounts of his foes that appeal most today, so that Froissart's account of Ball's Blackheath sermon 'becomes the most moving plea for social equality in the history of the English language'. Too dangerous to let live, Ball was executed at St Albans.

Alone among the rebel leaders, Ball was already notorious before 1381: 'an evilly disposed priest', he was 'held a most famous preacher to the laity', and had long 'sowed the word of God in a foolish manner, mixing tares with the wheat'. He claimed to have been 'St Mary priest' at York, presumably a chantry chaplain, but his recorded history is confined to Essex. By 1364 he had been excommunicated by Simon Sudbury, Bishop of London, whose diocese included Essex, and by 1367 he had taken refuge from him at Bocking (Essex), part of the diocese of Canterbury, where he preached 'many errors and scandals to the danger of his soul and to the manifest scandal of the church' and in particular Archbishop Langham. It was probably near Braintree that he was misbehaving in 1376, but next year he was chaplain at St James' Church, Colchester, where the rector was his namesake and perhaps a kinsman. After each imprisonment he reverted to his old ways:

> Like the fox that evades the hunter, he had slunk back to our diocese, and feared not to preach and argue both in churches and in churchyards (without the leave or against the will of the parochial authorities) and also in markets and other profane places.

Ultimately he 'was tried and lawfully convicted by the clergy, who committed him to perpetual imprisonment' at Maidstone, whence the rebels rescued him. He was one of the ecclesiastical proletariat, who ran the parishes. Poorly paid, without security of tenure or responsibility, they were the most numerous and most obscure branch of the clergy. Ball, however, was hardly typical, for he had a social message that he felt compelled to preach and which laymen wished to hear.

Before 1381 we know only that Ball spread scandals about pope, archbishop, prelates and other clergy. To denounce clerical abuses was unexceptional and even respectable, but Ball overstepped what was permissible, probably encouraging non-payment of tithes and denigrating celibacy. However that may be, once he had joined Wat Tyler's Kentish rebels, he presented his ideals in sermons and cryptic letters to a large and sympathetic audience. Equality was his keynote:

> When Adam delved and Eve span
> Who was then a gentleman?

Lords, lawyers, and bishops were to be killed, their property shared out, and Ball himself was to be archbishop. The rebels responded rapturously. Hence perhaps the deliberate elimination of opponents (including Sudbury) and hence perhaps also the greater radicalism of Tyler's Kentish men, who rejected the terms accepted by their Essex counterparts and stayed at arms after they had left. Ball, however, 'was a visionary and a prophet rather than an organiser' and could not keep the rebels together after Tyler's death. His intellectual heirs were the humbler Lollards of the next century.

P. Bird and D. Stephenson, 'Who was John Ball?', *Transactions of the Essex Archaeological Society* vii, 1976.

R. B. Dobson, *The Peasants Revolt of 1381*, 2nd ed. 1983.

W. H. Liddell & R. G. E. Wood, *Essex and the Great Revolt of 1381*, Essex Record Office, 1982.

R. H. Hilton, *Bond Men Made Free: Medieval Peasant Movements and the English Rising of 1381*, 1973.

WAT TYLER (*d*.1381), leader of the Peasants' Revolt, is one of the most famous and yet most obscure figures in late medieval England. He first appears as leader of the Kentish rebels. Contemporaries described him variously as a tiler, highwayman, or discharged soldier; from Kent or Essex; and a pseudonym for Jack Straw. None of these claims can be confirmed.

By drastically reducing English population the Black Death of 1348–9 should have improved the prospects of working people, who should have received more pay and paid less rents than before. Their lords, however, strove to maintain their incomes by fixing wages and by using serfdom to prevent free movement of labour and to keep up rents. To these underlying grievances should be added the appalling cost of the unsuccessful war against France. Ministers could not even protect the Kent coast and were denounced by the rebels as traitors. The final straw was the third poll-tax, which was exceptionally heavy and touched even the poorest. These grievances were widely felt, so that the revolt was led by prosperous peasants and craftsmen, the leaders of their local communities.

Inquiries into tax evasion were rudely rebuffed at Fobbing in Essex and a judge sent to punish the culprits was even more roughly treated. The offenders appealed for support, provoking rebellion in Essex. Peasants and townsmen in Kent, East Anglia, and further afield followed suit. Tyler took command of the Kentish men at Maidstone about 7 June and led them to Canterbury and on 12 June to Blackheath, where he was recognized as overall leader of the uprising. His men entered the city of London, thus permitting attacks on John of Gaunt's palace of the Savoy and the Clerkenwell headquarters of the current treasurer of England. Tyler and Ball may have been principal draughtsmen of the peasants' manifesto, which made general demands much more radical than the freedom and pardons offered at Mile End by the king on 14 June. These offers satisfied the men of Essex, who went home, but not Tyler, who may not have been present. Later that day he seized the Tower, murdering the chancellor Archbishop Sudbury and the treasurer, and next day presented his own more extreme demands at Smithfield, where he was killed. The young King Richard memorably averted catastrophe, and the mob dispersed homewards, where they were pursued and punished.

Tyler lacked refinement. He drank 'villainously', swore frequently, and spoke coarsely. He was quick to anger, impulsive, violent, bloodthirsty, and vengeful. He was also a capable organiser. He determined the objectives, imposed his will on others, instilled them with urgency, and enforced discipline. It may have been to keep the disparate groups together that the manifesto was couched in general terms and that a distinction acceptable to all was made between the lawyers, royal ministers, leading nobles and bishops, who were to be killed, and the king, for whom they protested their loyalty. 'With whom hold you?' asked the peasants. 'With King Richard and with the true commons' was the password. Tyler negotiated in person, thrice rejecting draft charters, and refusing to be hurried: 'I will come when it pleases me so do', he said. He treated the king as a near equal. Maybe he became over-confident, vowing he would shave the heads (behead) of those who opposed him, declaring that in four months all law would come from his own mouth, and demanding the instant execution of an enemy at Smithfield. Perhaps, as the chronicler Walsingham says, he 'was beside himself in the insolent pride of success.' His meteoric political career ended in his death after one week.

T. H. Aston and R. H. Hilton, *The English Rising of 1381*, 1984.
R. B. Dobson, *The Peasants' Revolt of 1381*, 2nd edn. 1983.
E. B. Fryde, *The Great Revolt of 1381*, Historical Association Pamphlet, 1981.
R. H. Hilton, *Bond Men Made Free: Medieval Peasant Movements and the English Rising of 1381*, 1973.

WILLIAM GRINDCOBBE (*d.* 1381) was a townsman involved in the Peasants Revolt. The rebellion was not confined to peasants and included many townsmen, who remedied their local grievances by force. Grindcobbe came from St Albans, a substantial town kept in subjection by its lord, St Albans Abbey. Lords who refused self-government to their towns were usually churchmen: Bury Abbey at Bury St Edmunds, which also rose in 1381, and the bishop at Salisbury. The events of 1381 at Bury and St Albans

typify the conscious alliance of the townsmen with rural rebellion in pursuit of their own sectional aims. The reason for the leadership of the rebellion by the urban upper strata in these two towns was that in both cases the administrative and judicial control over the town by the monastic overlord had been preserved intact.

Thomas Walsingham, the hostile St Albans Abbey chronicler, says that Grindcobbe had been brought up, educated and nourished by the abbey, where relatives were monks. He was otherwise obscure.

St Albans Abbey was the main landlord in Hertfordshire. Its exactions from its villeins were not particularly heavy, but had long been resented. 'The court book of every manor tells the same story. Difficulty about labour services begins almost as far back as the court books', since about 1250 in fact. Its townsmen were allowed no more privileges and their subjection was symbolised by denial to them of private hand-mills. Many clashes and a major crisis in 1327 had all ended with reassertion of the abbey's authority. No concessions were made in response to changed conditions after the Black Death. The monks felt that they were performing their pious duty in maintaining the rights of St Alban. Their tenants, if not economically miserable, felt oppressed. Their rebellion was thus 'a genuine uprising of villeins against their lord, against seigneurial oppression'.

News of rebellion elsewhere prompted rebellion in the towns, which invoked support in the surrounding villages. Some extremists wished to destroy the abbey and kill the monks, but Grindcobbe was more moderate. He wrongly supposed that charters of liberties had been made to the tenants by Henry I and even King Offa and therefore only restoration of rights was required. He preferred threats to actual violence. He won Wat Tyler's support and secured a royal writ instructing the abbot to restore the tenants' rights. Grindcobbe sanctioned the breaking of the abbey's parks and warrens, demolition of a house in St Albans market-place, breaking the abbey gaol and executing one prisoner, but not violence against monks or officials. The abbot had to surrender bonds extorted from tenants in 1332 and records of their subjection, which were burnt, and conceded charters of liberties. The men of St Albans secured rights of pasture, hunting and fishing, permission for private hand-mills, and self-government, all of which were cancelled after the rebellion. It was to Grindcobbe's credit that 'the men of St Albans put forward their specific objectives in an articulate, moderate and constitutional form' and for 'the restraint with which the rebels pursued their quest', yet he was subsequently condemned and executed. Reasonable and dignified to the last, 'the talented and articulate William Grindcobbe' was 'a man whose courageous bearing and evident disinterestedness might have moved a sentiment of pity and admiration in any one but the monastic chronicler who has told this tale'.

R. B. Dobson, *The Peasants Revolt of 1381*, 2nd ed. 1983.
R. H. Hilton, *Bond Men Made Free: Medieval Peasant Movements and the English Rising of 1381*, 1973.
A. E. Levett, *Studies in Manorial History*, 1938.
C. Oman, *Great Revolt of 1381*, 1906.

WILLIAM COURTENAY (1342–96), Bishop of Hereford (1369–75), London (1375–81) and Archbishop of Canterbury (1381–96), was one of the ablest English primates in the later middle ages. Born at Exminster into the highest nobility, the fourth son of an Earl of Devon, grandson of an Earl of Hereford, and great-grandson of Edward I, he was early destined for high office in the Church. His relatives promoted him to his first benefice in 1355 when only thirteen, to others worth 100 marks (£66.66) by 1366, and in 1369 he secured his first bishopric, whilst still under the canonical age. Yet he was not without other qualifications. By 1366 he was a doctor of both laws and the following year chancellor of Oxford University, his progress admittedly eased by his exalted station. Supposedly his rank also fortified him as bishop, both in 1373 and in 1377 in a famous quarrel in St Paul's cathedral with John of Gaunt, Duke of Lancaster:

John of Gaunt: You trust in your parents, who will not be able to assist you, for they will have enough to do defending themselves.
Courtenay: I do not put my trust in my parents, nor in you, nor in any man, but in God.
John of Gaunt: Rather than endure this, I should take him by the hair and drag him out of the church.

Neither of Gaunt's threats were fulfilled and he was lucky to escape unscathed from the ensuing riot.

Certainly this exchange reveals Courtenay's hot-temper and self-confidence with his fellow aristocrats, but it also shows him to be a churchman first. He was conscientious in performance of such episcopal duties as visitation and ordination, implemented the pope's interdict against Florentines in 1375 and supported his crusade against Flanders in 1383, and led the attack on Wyclif and the Lollards. Early attacks on Wyclif were thwarted by the heretic's powerful friends, notably John of Gaunt and Joan of Kent, and by the ineffectiveness of Archbishop Sudbury, but once archbishop Courtenay took decisive action. Leaving Wyclif himself unmolested, he secured the condemnation of 24 of his propositions at the Earthquake Council at Blackfriars, London in 1382, purged Oxford University of its academic Lollards, and ended open teaching of heresy there. Covert heresy, however, persisted. 'And the combination of firmness and moderation with which he attacked the problem augured well for the endurance of his work'. He was a sympathetic pastor, who allowed offenders like John Ball time for reflection, forgave those who repented their errors, treated defaulters with understanding, and avoided making martyrs through undue rigour. Gradually middle-aged prudence supplanted the intemperate enthusiasms of youth.

Courtenay was always independent, subservient to neither king nor pope, and uncompromising on points of principle. In 1373 he publicly refused to pay papal taxation until grievances had been remedied; twice in 1376-7 he clashed with Gaunt over Wyclif, but nevertheless intervened to save the duke's life and property; and in 1385 he condemned King Richard for plotting Gaunt's death and warned him to mend his ways and sack his evil councillors. Understandably this enraged the king, who overstepped convention by trying to kill Courtenay with his sword. Yet at the Merciless Parliament of 1388, when those same councillors were on trial for their lives, Courtenay withdrew from activities incompatible with his ecclesiastical duty not to shed human blood. Unlike most aristocratic bishops, Courtenay was no politician, serving only for two months as an interim chancellor, and left politics to others. Instead, like Archbishop Winchelsey, he defended what he saw as the rights and doctrines of the Church, marshalling his connections in support of the Church rather than subordinating his position to his aristocratic lifestyle. He 'aspired to be a churchman, not an agent of the crown'.

J. Dahmus, *William Courtenay, Archbishop of Canterbury 1381–1396*, 1966.

WILLIAM SWINDERBY is representative of the humble missionaries, who spread a popular form of Lollardy among ordinary people. Little is known about Swinderby's early life. It cannot even be demonstrated that he was ordained, although he claimed to have been, and certainly he had no licence to preach. Like John Ball, he was an unbeneficed and non-conforming chaplain before Lollardy began, but unlike Ball he advocated moral rather than social reform. He was evidently intelligent and literate, an impressive preacher, and possessed of a pragmatic but not foolhardy courage. He occurs first at Leicester, where he denounced the pride and wantonness of women and subsequently the trade and wealth by which the townsmen lived. Understandably such teachings made him unpopular, so he became a hermit in the woods, perhaps supported by John of Gaunt, lord of Leicester. Meantime Lollardy was introduced, perhaps by Philip Repingdon, a canon of Leicester Abbey, and a Lollard congregation was formed by the layman William Smith and another chaplain in a disused chapel. There Swinderby joined them, helped them to organise Lollard services and schools, and from thence he embarked on teaching tours to neighbouring towns and villages. Thus Leicester became one of the strongest centres of Lollardy.

Inevitably such activities came to the attention of the bishop of Lincoln, who followed up Archbishop Courtenay's Earthquake Council and attack on academic Lollardy by citing Swinderby to appear before him in 1382. Swinderby was contumacious but eventually appeared, probably under coercion. He was examined, found guilty of heresy, recanted and did penance. His recantation however was insincere and he resumed preaching as soon as he was at liberty, proceeding westwards to Coventry, to the dioceses of Worcester (1387) and Hereford (1390). All the time he was winning influential friends, so that in 1392 local gentry insisted on a safeconduct for him before his examination by Bishop Trefnant. The bishop found him a relapsed heretic, but Swinderby escaped into Wales, where he disappeared from history.

Such men spread Lollardy too widely to be eradicated when the church authorities organised their counterattack. Swinderby's career demonstrates the scope for a determined subversive to exploit diocesan boundaries, the slow and formal procedures of ecclesiastical justice, and the lack of an ecclesiastical police force at parish level. Although Swinderby feared burning as a heretic, deprivation or lack of promotion could not deter him. Penance and prison were the only penalties available against him. The act of 1401 that permitted heretics to be burnt was thus an important deterrent even though seldom invoked, for Swinderby was typical in his distaste for martyrdom. The thirty years up to 1414 were crucial in establishing Lollardy before it was driven underground.

Swinderby is typical also in the debased form of Lollardy that he preached. Here is none of the profundity, complexity, or subtlety of Wyclif's theology, which emerges in only a few crude simplifications — for example, that the communion bread remained bread after consecration. Other beliefs, such as the right to withhold tithes from a lecherous priest and the nullity of sacraments performed by a sinful one, may have been Wycliffite in origin, but need not have been. They were directly relevant to contemporary laymen and came to distinguish popular Lollards from the orthodox, right up to the Reformation. They were dangerous to the church because they made obvious sense and appealed to the prejudices and interests of those humble laymen with whom Swinderby was genuinely concerned.

K.B. McFarlane, *John Wycliffe and the Beginnings of English Nonconformity*, 1952.

P. McNiven, *Heresy and Politics in the Reign of Henry IV. The Burning of John Badby*, 1987.

PHILIP REPINGDON (*c.*1340–1424), Bishop of Lincoln from 1404 until 1420, was the only Lollard to become a bishop in late medieval England. He entered the Augustinian abbey of St Mary-in-the Meadows at Leicester by 1369, when he was ordained a priest. The Austin canons were not an enclosed order and could act as parish priests: Repingdon had considerable pastoral gifts and became an able preacher. Before then, however, he was despatched to Oxford University, where he distinguished himself, becoming in 1382 a doctor of theology and being selected by Robert Rigg, chancellor of the university, to preach on the feast of Corpus Christi in the Austin priory of St Frideswide's (now Christchurch Cathedral). It was apparently at this point that Repingdon joined other young scholars convinced by the theology of John Wyclif, notably Nicholas Hereford, John Aston, and Laurence Steven *alias* Bedman. Whereas Wyclif wrote abstrusely and was content to be read only by academics, his disciples propagated his message openly, both at Oxford and on preaching tours in the provinces. They have been credited with making Lollardy into a movement. Repingdon may have made Leicester into a Lollard centre; certainly he preached heretically on the Holy Communion both at Brackley (Northants.) and at Oxford, where his sermon was applauded by the chancellor and university authorities. In 1382, however, Archbishop Courtenay's Earthquake Council struck at the Oxford Lollards: Rigg was humiliated into submission, the errors of Repingdon and his associates were condemned, and they were required to submit. At first all refused, Repingdon and Hereford appealing both to John of Gaunt and to Rome, and were excommunicated. Repingdon then submitted, abjured his errors, and was absolved, thus reopening the promising career that he had apparently thrown away. He became abbot of Leicester in 1393, chancellor of Oxford University in 1400, bishop of Lincoln in 1404 — exceptional for an Austin canon — and in 1408 was created cardinal — but not generally recognized as such — by the anti-pope Gregory XII. His conversion was complete. No bishop, according to Archbishop Arundel, was more vigorous in his attacks on heresy.

Repingdon was indeed an excellent bishop, who 'strove for order, reform and unity within the church' and whose 'work as diocesan surely entitles him to rank high among the churchmen of the later middle ages'. He administered his see efficiently, can be shown to have visited much of his vast diocese three times, and sought to settle differences between the cathedral dean and chapter. He promoted orthodoxy and sought to root out the heresy that he may have founded at Leicester in his visitation there in 1413. His concern for ecclesiastical standards and discipline, for example by encouraging university education and fulfilment of parish duties, was motivated by pastoral concern for the spiritual well-being of ordinary Christians. Hence, too, his encouragement of preaching. Such conduct suggests that his recantation in 1382 involved only Wyclif's theology and that his dissatisfaction with clerical abuses and commitment to improved pastoral provision for the laity remained. His career thus confirms that Lollard strictures against the church were widely shared and that it was their speculative theology that overstepped the bounds of orthodoxy. Unlike those other bishops, like Orleton and Wykeham, whose last years of physical incapacity were spent still clinging to office and income, Repingdon resigned in 1420 in a final expression of missionary idealism.

M. Archer, 'Philip Repingdon, Bishop of Lincoln and his Cathedral Chapter', *University of Birmingham Historical Journal* iv, 1953–4.

K.B. McFarlane, *John Wycliffe and the Beginnings of English Nonconformity*, 1952.

MASTER JOHN TREVISA (*d.*1402) is 'notable as an early translator of Latin works into English'. He was a Cornishman by birth and retained his Cornish contacts and interest in Cornwall whilst making his career elsewhere. He attended Oxford University, where he graduated as a Master of Arts. As a west-countryman he was a fellow of Exeter College from about 1361 until 1369, when he became a fellow of Queen's College, and was ordained in 1370. In 1379 he was expelled from Queen's College as unworthy with the provost and other fellows. It was perhaps then that he entered the service of his patron Lord Berkeley, 'who may be called Thomas the Magnificent'. It was he, who by 1387 had made Trevisa vicar of Berkeley. About 1389 Trevisa also became a canon of the college of Westbury-upon-Trym. Although normally resident at Berkeley and the confidant of Lord Berkeley, whose castle was a stone's throw from his parish church, Trevisa was apparently absent for prolonged periods. He was presumably at Oxford in 1382–6 and 1394–6, when he rented rooms at Queen's College, probably to facilitate access to the works he was translating. Again about 1390 he travelled abroad, visiting Aachen and 'Ayges in Savoy', perhaps Aix-en-Provence.

Until the late 14th century Latin was the language of the Church, learning and formal documents, and French was the language of the court and aristocracy. The first use of the English language in these contexts dates from the 1370s and 1380s and coincides with the poetic achievements of Chaucer, Langland, Gower and the Gawain-poet. About 1385 Trevisa records that aristocrats were beginning to speak Engish to their children and that pupils at grammar schools were speaking English rather than French. These developments implied that educated people would be unable to read French in future and foreshadowed the enormous expansion of English usage in the next century. Encouraged and perhaps even persuaded by Lord Berkeley, Trevisa therefore set out to make 'famous works available to those who knew no Latin' (Gransden). His principal achievements were his translations of Higden's *Polychronicon* and Bartholomew Glanville's *De Proprietatibus Rerum,* 'the biggest encyclopaedia and the biggest history he could find'. The *Polychronicon* of Ranulph Higden, monk of Chester, was a vast universal chronicle from the Creation to 1360. Trevisa's continuation of it, though highly derivative and of little independent value, foreshadows 'the rise of the vernacular chronicle ... the most remarkable historiographical development in the fifteenth century' (Gransden). These enormous projects were achievements enough for any translator, but Trevisa certainly tackled other works and yet more have been attributed to him. He did translate the apocryphal gospel of Nicodemus and was associated with the Lollard translation of the Bible at a time before bible translation was condemned as heretical. He also favoured preaching in English and translated an anti-mendicant sermon by Archbishop FitzRalph, a choice which suggests a commitment to church reform that fell short of heresy.

Trevisa's original work was slight. His translations had no stylistic pretensions, but were clear, workmanlike and readable. They were also marred by frequent errors. His works were not widely read, far fewer copies surviving of his translation of the *Polychronicon* than of the Latin original, so his campaign of popularisation achieved limited success. His significance does not rest however either in his popularity or the quality of his works, 'but in their interest as early examples of English prose' (Kingsford).

B. Cottle, *Triumph of English 1350–1400,* 1969.

GEOFFREY CHAUCER (*c.*1343–1400), esquire, was the first great English poet to write in English and 'whose work is not religious in purpose and content' (Saul). He thus pioneered the use of *southern* English as a literary language and of secular literature and

Geoffrey Chaucer
(Artist: Thomas Hoccleve)

has been called, with some justice, 'the father of English poetry'. He was merely the son of a London vintner, who by 1357 had entered the household of the Countess of Ulster, wife of Edward III's son Lionel, Duke of Clarence. He served in France in 1359–60, where he was captured, and became esquire of the king's household by 1367. By 1366 he had married Philippa Roet, daughter of a herald from Hainault and damsel of Queen Philippa of Hainault. Following the deaths of Blanche Duchess of Lancaster in 1368 and the queen in 1369, Philippa Chaucer became attendant to Constance Duchess of Lancaster and her sister Katherine Swynford became governess of Constance's stepchildren, mistress of her husband John of Gaunt, and eventually his third duchess. Chaucer was controller of the London customs from 1374 and went on frequent missions to France, Spain and Italy. Given that his inheritance cannot have sufficed for court life, Chaucer probably depended on the annuities of himself and his wife, which grew to the substantial sum of £63 from 1378. In 1385–6 he was J.P. and M.P. for Kent. His replacement as controller (1386), Philippa's death in 1387, and the assignment of his annuities may have financially embarrassed him and caused him to become clerk of works in 1389. His income recovered to £66 at death. Chaucer was thus a trusted, competent and not undistinguished royal servant. He remained a Londoner, residing in leasehold premises over Aldgate and at Westminster. He lacked the rural estates normal for his rank.

Chaucer's formal education covered both arms and letters. He liked nothing better than to read in solitude and was indeed amazingly widely read. His knowledge and experience stretched from bawdy tales, through love and religion, to philosophy and science. Ultimately he could read English, French, Latin and Italian. His education was appropriate for a gentleman and courtier. He understood and shared their values, for instance the knightly ideal, read courtly literature, and wrote for a courtly audience. His earliest love poems as 'poet of Venus' are now lost and his first major surviving work is his *Book of the Duchess* of 1368–9, which laments the dead Duchess Blanche and consoles her husband, 'the man in black'. It is deeply influenced by French poetry and as an English poem is quite unique for its time. Later works draw on the Italians Dante and Boccaccio, particularly *Troilus and Criseyde*. He translated Boethius' *Consolations* into English prose, wrote other major poems such as the *House of Fame* (c. 1380), *Parliament of Fowles*, and from 1387 his masterpiece *The Canterbury Tales*.

The general prologue of *The Canterbury Tales* is 'an exquisitely satirical comedy of manners' and the tales themselves, though only a fraction of those intended, include an amazing range of genres, learning, and characters. 'We will never get closer to ordinary fourteenth century lives than in these amazingly dramatic and interesting episodes'. But Chaucer is not merely a storyteller and a master of different moods. He has ideals, a conventional one in the Knight and an unusual one in the Parson, and his other characters are satirised and their motives exposed in a penetrating, but humane and understanding way. Chaucer may once have accepted uncritically the standards of his time, but he had developed an independent judgement, profundity of thought, and a critical incisiveness all his own. It is sad that ultimately, conventionally enough, he wished to retract all his worldly poetry.

D. Brewer, *Chaucer and his world*, 1978.
Chaucer's Life-Records, ed. M. Crow and C. C. Olson, 1966.
G. Kane, *Chaucer*, 1984.
Works of Geoffrey Chaucer, ed. F. N. Robinson, 2nd ed. 1957.

SIR JOHN CLANVOWE (*c.*1341–91), poet and Lollard, belonged to a close-knit group of knights with literary interests at Richard II's court. Others were Sir Richard Sturry and Sir John Montagu. The Clanvowes were minor Radnorshire gentry of Welsh extraction. His father and namesake, an esquire of the king's household, was dead by 1362, when Clanvowe himself was of age. He is not known to have married, but Sir Thomas Clanvowe may be his son. Given his domicile, it is not surprising that he was a retainer of Humphrey, last Bohun Earl of Hereford, and progressed directly after the earl's death in 1373 into royal service, where his existing fee was more than doubled. By 1381 he was a knight of the chamber paid £66 a year, constable and steward of Haverfordwest in Pembrokeshire, and keeper of the forests of Snowdon and Merioneth. He served in Brittany in 1364, presumably under Lord Latimer, in France in 1370 and, under John of Gaunt, in 1373–4 and 1378, and as a diplomat. As a courtier he was surety to Latimer in 1376 and wisely lay low during the crises of 1386–9. In 1390 he joined in

Louis de Bourbon's unsuccessful crusade to Tunis and he died in Greece in 1391, perhaps on pilgrimage, together with another Lollard knight, Sir William Neville.

Clanvowe's moderately successful and conventional career acquires extra importance when his cultural interests are considered. He was a writer of some ability both of English prose and verse. His poem *The Boke of Cupide* is a dream vision containing a debate about the nature of love between a cuckoo and a nightingale. It is influenced by *The Parliament of Fowls, The Knight's Tale,* and perhaps also *The Legend of Good Women* of Geoffrey Chaucer, with whom Clanvowe was personally acquainted, and was probably written no earlier than 1386. Also to his last years belongs *The Two Ways*, a moral treatise advocating the narrow way to heaven rather than the broad way to hell. Although unoriginal in its mixture of pulpit commonplaces and biblical quotations, it is a remarkable work for a layman both in its serious reading and reflection and its skilful composition. Clanvowe's narrow way was a life based on biblical precept, rejecting secular values like those military and courtly standards he had hitherto accepted. No reference is made to the official Church and its contribution, nor indeed to any specifically Lollard heresies. Yet he admitted to being accused of Lollardy:

> Such folk the world scorneth and holdeth them lollers and losels [good-for-nothings] fools and shameful wretches. But surely God holdeth them most wise and most worshipful ... And therefore take we savour in those things ... and reck we never though the world scorn us or hold us wretches. For the world scorned Christ and held him a fool ... And therefore follow we his tracks and suffer we patiently the scorns of the world as he did.

On this evidence Clanvowe's sympathy with Lollardy arose from a shared personal morality and devotional piety, not from doctrines he cannot be shown to have accepted. Indeed his departure on crusade and pilgrimage, activities condemned by Wyclif, suggest ignorance of details of doctrine by himself and Neville too, yet it is compatible with the actual contents of *The Two Ways*.

Did Clanvowe in practice reject the military, courtly and secular values of his earlier career and *The Boke of Cupide* when he wrote *The Two Ways*? Or did all the contradictory facets of his character exist side by side, a possibility suggested by the alleged role of Lollard knights *at court* in protecting heretics? Did his final travels stem from chivalric, courtly and pious convention or did they mark a new religious direction to his life? Such questions cannot now be answered, but that they have to be asked indicates the cultural depth and complexity of the group to which Clanvowe belonged.

K.B. McFarlane, *Lancastrian Kings and Lollard Knights*, 1971.
V.J. Scattergood, *Works of Sir John Clanvowe*, 1975.

SIR RICHARD STURRY (*c.*1330–95) rose from the bottom rungs of the royal household at a time when promotion of any kind was rare, let alone elevation from obscurity to high favour. He was only a valet in the 1340s, still only king's yeoman in 1353, an esquire of the chamber in 1359, and a knight of the body from 1365 until death. He became a trusted councillor both of Edward III and his grandson Richard II. By the 1370s 'he was clearly a favourite of the old king's', his 'familiar servant', and continuously in his company. He has recently been identified with the chamberlain Lord Latimer and mistress Alice Perrers as one of the five individuals most influential with Edward III in his last years. He shared in the defeat and disgrace of this group in the Good Parliament of 1376, when he was dismissed from the council but not impeached, yet remained powerful at court and returned from 1389 as a royal councillor, attending council on 159 days in 1392–3 alone.

No layman could rise in this way without sharing the king's aristocratic and military outlook. Sturry must have been of gentle birth and upbringing, although his origins are obscure. Any connection with the Kentish knight Sir William Sturry, marshal of the household, must be distant. His military career lasted from at least 1347, when he displayed great courage in a sea battle, to 1378. He was companion at arms both to the king and Black Prince. He was captured in 1359–60 and received £50 from Edward towards his ransom. His real forte proved to be diplomacy, however, and he became an expert in treating with the French. He was engaged in negotiations almost every year from 1368 to 1394. This 'ancient and valiant knight' owned a *Romance of the Rose*, knew both Froissart and Chaucer, and is one of the circle of reputed Lollard knights supposed — like Clanvowe and Montagu — to have used his position at court to protect heretics from persecution. This Sturry could certainly have done. The precise nature of his Lollardy and indeed his literary interests remain obscure.

Sturry's lack of inherited wealth made him particularly dependent on royal bounty. The most important expression of this was apparently his marriage in middle age c.1374 to Alice Blount, an heiress in her own right, widow of an heir to a barony, and a connection through the Staffords with the royal house itself. His fee of a mere 10 marks (£6.66) increased tenfold by 1370; a further £60 came from John IV of Brittany from Richmond honour, probably from 1372 following a mission to Brittany in 1371; in 1384 he received a further £66 from the king's mother Joan of Kent; and he was paid 10s. a day as royal councillor from 1389. Besides these he received a series of other rewards, particularly — and probably deliberately — in Wales. Most important perhaps was the custody of the great marcher lordship of Glamorgan in the minority of its lord from 1376–94 with a fee of £66 with full power of administration and appointment to offices. He was keeper of Aberystwyth from 1385, justice of Cardigan in 1387, and justice of the whole of South Wales in 1391. He showed a sharp eye for profit, securing grants of the escheatorship of Ireland both in 1363 and 1372, only to swop them for opportunities elsewhere, exchanging both his custody of Bamburgh castle and his annuities for lands, and in 1373 and 1388 acquiring custody of two Kentish alien priories. Certainly he used his influence at court to advance himself and presumably enrich himself. Equally he has left more concrete evidence of calculated self-advancement than his associate, the more notorious Lord Latimer.

C. Given-Wilson, *The Royal Household and the King's Affinity: Service, Politics and Finance in England 1360–1413*, 1986.

K. B. McFarlane, *Lancastrian Kings and Lollard Knights*, 1971.

JOHN NORTHAMPTON alias COMBERTON (*d.* 1397–8), draper of London, led the attack on the victualling monopolies and on the political dominance of the great merchants within the City during the 1380s. His origins are uncertain, for we know only the Christian names of his parents James and Mariota, although they were probably residents of London where he had many relatives.

John himself was a tradesman prominent enough to be one of four upholders of his guild (livery company), but he owned no ship, did not trade abroad, and lacked foreign contacts. His brothers William and Robert, respectively skinner and esquire, were of little account. John's career was transformed in 1371–5 by his second marriage to Petronilla, a wealthy heiress and widow, who brought him extensive urban property yielding rents of £120 a year and the substance to qualify as an alderman. It was probably this marriage, in short, that gave him the means to champion the smaller masters and retailers with whom he properly belonged. He had become 'a man of position and of considerable, though not of great wealth. His supporters were insignificant in both respects'.

Like all corporate towns, London was ruled by a self-perpetuating oligarchy of the richest merchants. Their power was attacked by two changes to the City constitution in 1376 that introduced annual election of aldermen and transferred election of common councillors from the wards to the guilds. These reforms widened the group of officeholders without breaking the dominance of the plutocrats. Northampton, who first became alderman in 1375, may have initiated these changes and certainly exploited them. When elected mayor in 1381 in the aftermath of the Peasants Revolt, he employed his authority first to break the power of the fishmongers, whose monopoly over fish-sales and virtual independence of the corporation were universally unpopular. His attacks on immorality and on the level of ecclesiastical fees also enjoyed widespread support. Hence his re-election in 1382. When he abandoned caution to attack the other victualling trades, however, he overstretched himself, alienating the most powerful guilds and the greatest merchants. The 1383 election was disfigured by violence and Northampton lost to Nicholas Brembre. Northampton admitted defeat only reluctantly, spurned reconciliation, and sought to recover power by seeking to have the election annulled, by plots, and by a mass demonstration of lesser guildsmen. He became associated with threats to the peace and social revolution. The crown intervened, he was tried and imprisoned at Tintagel, his patron John of Gaunt securing his restoration only in 1390. By then, however, Northampton's cause was lost. The old constitution had been restored and the oligarchs had recovered their monopoly of power. Northampton's only lasting achievement was to curb the independence of the fishmongers, although he himself, unlike his rival Brembre, died peacefully in his bed.

Evidently Northampton was something of a demagogue, who drew the lesser masters and trades into London's politics to secure lower food prices and a greater say in City affairs. Shrewd and clear about his objectives, he was resolute and inflexible in their pursuit and did not flinch from the use of force. Contemporaries were uncertain whether he sought personal power or whether he was motivated by abstract principle. While he inspired considerable loyalty among his partisans, he never enjoyed the united support of the non-victuallers, of the lesser crafts, or among their aldermen. In other ways, he appears a conventional merchant-capitalist, founding a chantry in Elsingspital and patronising both the Benedictine nuns of Cheshunt and the newer and more other-worldly Carthusians.

R. Bird, *The Turbulent London of Richard II*, 1949.
S. Thrupp, *The Merchant Class of Medieval London*, 1962.

HENRY DESPENSER (*c.*1341–1406), Bishop of Norwich from 1370 until his death, commander of a notorious crusade in 1383, was one of those younger sons of the medieval nobility, who made his career in the Church and achieved rapid promotion at an early age. This was due rather to his birth than his conventional qualifications, for he was not particularly learned, discreet, or spiritual. He did however bring administrative ability and energy to his office and is reported to have been the only vigorous persecutor of the Lollards among the bishops in 1389. He remained an impulsive nobleman, sensitive about his honour and rights, and with a marked taste for warfare. England was not used to such warrior-churchmen as Cardinals Albornoz and Scarampo, who were relatively common in contemporary Italy. Indeed it was in Italy that Henry Despenser first made his mark, serving with his brother in the campaigns of Pope Urban V in 1369–70 and securing as reward the bishopric of Norwich, whilst still under the canonical age of thirty. Merely to administer his diocese peacefully did not satisfy him and helps explain his other adventures.

The bishop of Norwich was a great landowner and peer of the realm and Bishop Despenser appears in parliament, on committees, and in the royal council. He quarrelled with King's Lynn in 1377, when he sought to have a mace carried before him in the town and was attacked and wounded by the townsmen; with the 'men of Norfolk', who plotted his death in 1382; and with St Albans Abbey. Clad in helmet and chain mail, sword in hand, he attacked the camp of rebellious peasants at North Walsham in 1381, stormed it, and executed the ringleader. In 1385 he accompanied Richard II to Scotland and in 1386-7 shared in a naval expedition to Flanders. His political support for Richard II and the rebellious earls explains his imprisonment both in 1399 and 1400.

The Crusade of the Bishop of Norwich against Flanders in 1383 was thus thoroughly in character with the man. The Great Schism of 1378-1415 meant that there were two rival popes: Urban VI, the Roman pope backed by the English, and Clement VII, the pope at Avignon supported by the French. Each strove for mastery, if necessary by force, declaring to be crusades the wars fought by their adherents against the schismatics. As early as 1381 Despenser had secured papal bulls to raise money against the Clementists and in 1382 he took the cross at St Paul's. Despenser thus had authority for a crusade, which he proposed should regain Flanders for Urban VI. This conformed to the English government's strategy of keeping Flanders out of the hands of the French prince Philip the Bold, Duke of Burgundy. The Flemings had been in revolt against Philip since 1379 and Bishop Despenser was able to secure official and parliamentary backing for his crusade in support of them. Parliament voted him taxes, he contracted to raise a substantial army, invaded Flanders in May, and returned discomfited in September. The expedition was too late as the Flemings had been decisively defeated in 1382 at Rosebeke, but Despenser was also at fault for several breaches of his contract with the government. He took less men than agreed, changed his destination, took command himself rather than employing a nobleman as king's lieutenant, and disbanded his forces, which could have been employed in another theatre of war. Evidently his martial tastes were not matched by military capacity. Impeached in parliament in October 1383 and convicted, he was sentenced to imprisonment and seizure of his lands, and never took the political or military lead again.

M. Aston, 'The Impeachment of Bishop Despenser', *Bulletin of the Institute of Historical Research* xxxviii, 1965.

MICHAEL DE LA POLE, EARL OF SUFFOLK (*c.*1330–89), was the first son of a merchant to become an earl. His father William was the great Hull merchant and financier and Michael kept up his local roots, building a fine house and founding a Carthusian monastery there. Michael was brought up as an aristocrat and developed a taste for chivalry and warfare, which his own inheritance and that of his wife supported during thirty years of service to the crown 'without shame or reproach'. From 1355 he frequently campaigned in France and Scotland and was thrice captured. He was captain of Calais and an admiral. He was the ambassador who negotiated King Richard's marriage to Anne of Bohemia. Appointed to Richard II's first council, he was nominated by parliament to be continually about the king, and from 1383 was chancellor and in effect chief minister. Such experience and distinction justified his promotion first to a barony in 1366, for which he had land enough, and then in 1385 to an earldom, for which the king provided the endowment. His service, if not his birth, befitted his new rank.

Yet the Wonderful Parliament of 1386 insisted on his dismissal and impeached him on seven charges, three of corruption and four of negligence. He had derived undue advantage from office both through formal grants and by deceit. Thus he had exchanged uncertain annuities (including one of doubtful legality) for stable income of greater value in preference to the king's ducal uncles, which he could hardly have done had he not been chancellor. Whilst such deals were commonly sought by recipients of royal bounty, Suffolk was culpable because he abused his office, because his office bound him to pursue the king's advantage, and because he acted at a time of appalling financial difficulty. His self-interest and hypocritical concern for royal solvency was already notorious: 'If thou hast so much concern for the king's profit, why hast thou so covetously taken from him a thousand marks per annum since thou wast made an earl?' The context was crucial, for unsuccessful war and near bankruptcy accompanied enrichment of the councillors responsible. The Commons thought the government and hence Suffolk to be incompetent and negligent, particularly by failing to implement their proposals for retrenchment, appropriation of funds for defence of the seas, and for supporting the rebels of Ghent. Suffolk disagreed with these policies and had indeed failed to fulfil them, but he claimed successfully that responsibility was shared by other councillors. This did not mean that the government as a whole was acquitted, for Suffolk's impeachment was, 'in effect, an attack upon the whole scheme of government'. Richard II asserted his authority, but he was only a boy, who needed the sound guidance and advice which Suffolk could well have provided. Instead the earl saw more advantage in humouring the boy, accepting warrants under his signet, monopolising his confidence, accroaching his royal power, estranging him from the nobility, and benefiting personally himself: the charges justifiably made in 1388.

Suffolk's offences were so commonplace as not normally to cause the raising of an eyebrow, but they were not therefore trivial. Contemporaries saw them as symptoms of a deeper corruption and the Lords convicted him. The same attitude prompted his encouragement to the king next year to overthrow parliament's acts and break with the Duke of Gloucester. 'Hold thy peace, Michael', said Bishop Braybrooke, 'it becometh thee right evil to say such words, thou that art damned for thy falsehood both by the lords and by parliament'. Military victory by the Lords Appellant brought sentence of death and forfeiture for Suffolk in the Merciless Parliament (1388), which he evaded only by flight abroad.

J. S. Roskell, *The Impeachment of Michael de la Pole, Earl of Suffolk in 1386, in the context of the reign of Richard II*, 1984.
A. B. Steel, *Richard II*, 1941.

GILBERT MAGHFIELD (*c.*1340–97), ironmonger and alderman of London, is representative of the lesser trades of the city. He had presumably completed his apprenticeship by 1367, when he was acting for another merchant at Danzig in modern Poland, and he established himself as a leading merchant during the next decade. He concentrated on the iron trade to the Basque port of Bilbao in northern Spain and to Bayonne in south-west France. Relatively little of his imports were sold directly to blacksmiths, as he dealt mainly with other wholesalers. He normally bought and sold on credit and by about 1390 had an annual turnover of about £1,150, compatible with total capital of £1,000-£1,500 and comparable to members of the city's ruling oligarchy. His standing was recognized by his election as alderman in 1381 and as sheriff and alderman in

1392. He also entered royal service, acting as custodian of the seas along the east coast in 1383 and from 1385 as collector of customs at Southampton and Boston. Royal favour and involvement in politics distracted his attention from business and/or damaged his trade and his credit collapsed. Without credit, he was forced to curtail his foreign trade, he was driven into moneylending, got behind with his customs payments, and ran into debt. His fortune was eroded, his goods and a surviving account book were seized by the crown as security, and at death he can have been worth no more than £500. Medieval trade was a speculative and uncertain activity. It was as easy to lose everything as to make a fortune and there must have been many failures like Maghfield, few of whom can be studied as he can be. Despite his misfortunes, 'this early ironmonger must at one time have been typical of the outstanding group of London merchants who together created the immense prosperity of the city at the end of the 14th century'. He has also been considered, somewhat implausibly, as the model for Chaucer's Merchant in the *Canterbury Tales*.

The ships that imported Maghfield's iron also carried his cargoes of grain and woollen cloth, the latter being overwhelmingly the most important English export. Iron was Maghfield's main import, but woad and alum — ingredients in clothmaking — were of secondary importance. He sold them mainly to country clothiers and to a lesser extent to London grocers. Other minor imports were beaver, saffron, licorice, wax, copper, millstones, greenginger and canvas. He also dealt in fish, as befitted a resident of Billingsgate, the city of London's fishmarket. His varied business shows him to be representative of 'a large group of merchants who, while specialising to some extent in one trade, also dealt in a wide range of miscellaneous merchandise'.

By 1390–5 Maghfield no longer ventured overseas, but directed operations from his London home, where he maintained a substantial household including butler, cook, and two maids. The house was leased in 1372, lay between Thames Street and the river, and possessed a private quay. By 1386 he had also acquired a neighbouring wharf and six shops at Billingsgate. Other property in London and lands in Woolwich, Middlesex, Kent and Buckinghamshire completed his estate: a clerk and three valets were needed to administer it for him. Like so many successful city businessmen he had obviously invested the profits of trade in real estate, which was more secure and which offered an income, albeit a relatively low one. Rents bulked larger in his finances in his last years, although unable to avert his decline. Even if his misfortunes disqualified him from the London aldermanry, his eventual estate compared very favourably with those of leaders of the less prosperous provincial towns.

M. K. James, *Studies in the Medieval Wine Trade*, ed. E. M. Veale, 1972.

E. Rickert, 'Extracts from a fourteenth-century account book', *Modern Philology* xxiv, 1926-7.

THOMAS OF WOODSTOCK, EARL OF BUCKINGHAM AND DUKE OF GLOUCESTER (1355–97), youngest son of Edward III, was a leading opponent of Richard II in 1386–9. His marriage to the heiress Eleanor Bohun, his creation as earl and duke, and his endowment by Richard II gave him the rank and wealth — perhaps £2,500 a year — commensurate with his royal birth. Hence the princely lifestyle represented by his armour, tapestries, jewels and books. Like his father and brothers, he jousted and fought abroad: at sea in 1377–8, as commander of the last great chevauchée from Calais to Brittany in 1380–1, in Scotland in 1385, and in Ireland in 1395. He took seriously his duties as Constable of England, presiding over several *causes célèbres* in the court of chivalry and codifying the law of arms. His veneration of St Thomas Becket, his foundation of Pleshey College, and his patronage of the Minoresses and other orders prove him a man of more than conventional piety. Both interests merge in his concern for the crusade: his own abortive campaign in Prussia in 1391 and his support for exiles from the middle east. He had been well-educated and was perhaps unusually cultured. As a politician, he was positive and practical, assertive and decisive, frank and persuasive. His public outbursts of temper, sometimes a liability and sometimes assets, demonstrated how sincere and committed he always was to the cause at issue.

Thomas thus represented what contemporaries admired most in a great nobleman. Hence his popularity and the devotion he inspired in dependants. Yet compared with his brothers he should have been disappointed: 'a man of choleric temper and militant tastes whose misfortune it was to have been born too late' (McKisack). He was forced to share the Bohun inheritance and his royal endowment comprised annuities that were irregularly paid and scarcely converted into land. His hopes for an independent sphere of activity in Ireland were dashed and he failed to secure what military commands there were. In the mid 1380s he was offended by a king, who governed by a clique of intimates rather than his natural councillors — the princes of the blood and the nobility. The French war was prosecuted ineffectively: royal finances were mismanaged, so that his own annuities went unpaid; favours were heaped on unworthy favourites in preference to more deserving cases like his own; accusations of treason and murder plots were hatched against his brother Gaunt; and his honour was touched by the rejection of his niece Philippa Coucy by Robert Vere. Private and public grievances fused, so that he took the lead in the continuing criticisms of royal government by the House of Commons. In 1386 threats of deposition by Bishop Arundel and himself forced Richard II to attend parliament, dismiss his ministers, allow Suffolk's impeachment, and accept the appointment of a commission of reform. King Richard responded in 1387 by ignoring the commission and by securing judicial opinions that the acts of the Wonderful Parliament were invalid and indeed treasonable. Thomas and the Earls of Arundel, Warwick, Nottingham, and Derby — the five Lords Appellant — then accused the royal favourites of treason, defeated Vere at Radcot Bridge, and forced the king to comply. Richard *may* indeed have been temporarily deposed and Gloucester *may* have hoped briefly to succeed him. However that may be, the destruction of the king's favourites at the Merciless Parliament of 1388 was very largely Thomas's achievement. He it was who held together the disparate parts of the opposition and used the Commons to override the qualms of the Lords.

In 1386–9 Thomas restored what he saw as constitutional normality without ever departing from his obligation of allegiance to the crown. Yet he paid a high price for his achievement. Once of age in 1389, Richard did not employ his uncle as his birth demanded and then, in 1397, destroyed him in revenge for 1388. He was murdered because Richard could not risk his public trial in parliament.

A. Goodman, *The Loyal Conspiracy. The Lords Appellant under Richard II*, 1971.
A. Tuck, *Richard II and the English Nobility*, 1973.

ROBERT VERE, EARL OF OXFORD (1362–92), (created Marquis of Dublin in 1385, and Duke of Ireland the following year), was the most important of Richard II's favourites. Succeeding as a child to his father's modest earldom, he became a royal kinsman by his marriage to Edward III's granddaughter Philippa Coucy and thus an intimate of his younger contemporary Richard II. Precisely what Richard saw in him is uncertain — although Vere was handsome, a homosexual relationship appears unlikely — but the king became quite besotted with him. Young though he was and indeed still technically a minor, Richard exercised considerable influence over policy in the early 1380s and distributed his own patronage, dismissing the veteran Lord Scrope of Bolton as chancellor, when he sought to restrain his generosity. Richard's favours were largely confined to a narrow group of courtiers headed by Vere. Whilst inevitably Vere channelled royal patronage to his dependants, he was himself the principal beneficiary of it, becoming among other things custodian of Colchester castle, sheriff of Rutland for life, lord of Queenborough, guardian of Lord Roos, and the dominant figure in Cheshire and North Wales.

Such favours, however, pale beside Vere's remarkable promotion in rank. In 1386 the new rank of marquis was created for his benefit to give him precedence over the other earls and in 1386 he became Duke of Ireland, second only to John of Gaunt. He was allowed to quarter his arms with those of Edward the Confessor and was given palatine powers in Ireland, where Richard reserved only homage and gave him resources to undertake complete conquest. In fact, Vere never went to Ireland — probably he never intended to — and Richard even condoned his divorce from his royal wife and remarriage to his mistress Agnes Lancecrona, a German or Czech attendant of his queen Anne of Bohemia.

Vere did not earn these favours by ability or good service. He was still only 26 years of age at his fall and had little experience to his credit. Indeed he seems to have been incompetent both as a soldier and administrator. He was arrogant, frivolous, immoral and empty-headed. His excessive promotion caused great offence, particularly as his birth and resources in no way surpassed those over whom he claimed precedence. His divorce offended the royal family and his grants often infringed the rights of others, notably the Duke of Gloucester and the king's half-brother John Holland. Hence his unpopularity at the time. Modern historians have been even more scathing. For Miss McKisack he was 'a man of neither talent nor judgement. Though not wanting in personal courage, Vere was foolish and irresponsible, rather than sinister and dangerous'. Certainly he seems to have had no distinctive policies to offer.

Opponents of the court did not accept that he was harmless. They wanted him destroyed. Suffolk's impeachment in 1386 had failed to curb Richard and his favourites and it was in anticipation of further trouble that Vere became justice of Chester and North Wales in September/October 1387. Later the same year Vere exploited their potential for military recruitment for the campaign that ended in his defeat at Radcot Bridge in Oxfordshire and confirmed the Lords Appellant in control. Vere himself swam the Thames to safety and fled abroad, thus escaping the sentence of death passed on him in his absence at the Merciless Parliament of 1388. Although the king wished to recall him, his magnates did not, and Vere died in poverty, still in exile, after a hunting accident in 1392. His formal reinterment at Earls Colne by the king in 1395 was poorly attended by the nobility, who remembered their ill-will towards him. Absence had not caused their hearts to grow fonder.

C. Given-Wilson, *The Royal Household and the King's Affinity: Service, Politics and Finance in England 1360–1413*, 1986.
A. B. Steel, *Richard II*, 1941.
J. A. Tuck, *Richard II and the English Nobility*, 1973.

THOMAS MOWBRAY, EARL OF NOTTINGHAM AND DUKE OF NORFOLK (c. 1366–99), was 'an intensely ambitious young man with a taste for intrigue'. A younger son, he succeeded in 1383 to his father's modest barony and became heir apparent to the Segrave and Norfolk estates of his grandmother Margaret Marshall. Her longevity kept him relatively poor and dependent on royal favour. He was brought up with the king, who immediately made him an earl, a knight of the Garter, and married him to a shortlived heiress. Mowbray had a private apartment at King's Langley palace and shared in Richard's plot to murder John of Gaunt in 1385. He served with the king as Earl Marshal in Scotland and shared a naval command with Arundel in 1387. The advance of Robert Vere as dominant favourite apparently involved the eclipse of Mowbray, whose victory off Margate and unlicensed marriage were both ill-regarded by the king. Rivalry with Vere may explain why late in 1387 he joined the three original Lords Appellant: Gloucester, Warwick, and his father-in-law Arundel. Factional strife rather than constitutional principle probably impelled him into opposition and rapid reconciliation with the king followed the ruin of his rival Vere.

Whereas Gloucester, Arundel and Warwick were dismissed on Richard's majority in 1389, Mowbray returned to favour. He was appointed warden of the East March and captain of Berwick and Roxburgh in 1389. He exchanged these posts for the captaincy of Calais in 1390, supplanted Gloucester as justice of Chester and North Wales in 1394, and in 1397, with royal help, wrested Gower from Warwick, another fellow Appellant. As a diplomat he negotiated Richard's second marriage. As a former Appellant of 1388, he had a key role as one of the king's own Lords Appellant in 1397. It was Mowbray who arrested Gloucester, imprisoned and murdered him at Calais; who as Earl Marshal supervised the execution of his father-in-law Arundel; and who was rewarded by a dukedom (Margaret Marshall became Duchess), recognition as Earl Marshal, and by the grant of large parts of the estates of Arundel and Warwick. He was now a magnate of the front rank.

Yet his fall was abrupt. Exiled for life in 1398, he died at Venice next year, still only 33 years old. Behind his fall lay the conversation with Hereford that prompted each to accuse the other of treason. Mowbray had been the proudest and most presumptuous of courtiers of the 1390s, the most deserving and best rewarded of Richard's Appellants, yet he never enjoyed Vere's proximity to the king and never knew Richard's innermost thoughts and ultimate intentions. Apparently he still feared vengeance for his actions in 1388 and invoked it to excuse Gloucester's murder. 'And he swore great oaths swearing that he would answer before God that it was never his will that he should be killed but only for dread of the king and eschewing of his own death'. Whether indeed Mowbray plotted further treason, his exile shows that he was not indispensable and perhaps even an embarrassment to Richard, who seized the chance to be rid of him. He thus lost a formidable adherent and further fuelled the dangerous uncertainty of his last years.

Yet Mowbray was more than a 'self-seeking renegade'. He was literate, probably appreciated music, and was pious. His patronage of monasticism included the foundation of a Carthusian house at Axholme. Reputedly a chivalrous knight, he patronised a new crusading order in 1395, planned a pilgrimage to Jerusalem in 1399, and heard three masses at the Coventry Charterhouse before his abortive duel with Hereford. To gauge his complex personality accurately requires a precise assessment of the boundary between his sincerity and commitment and his ambition, self-interest, and devious subtlety.

A. Goodman, *The Loyal Conspiracy: The Lords Appellant under Richard II*, 1971.
J. A. Tuck, *Richard II and the English Nobility*, 1973.

RICHARD EARL OF ARUNDEL AND SURREY (1346–97) was one of the Lords Appellant of 1388 and was executed in 1397 in Richard II's revenge. Yet the career of his father and namesake had been characterised by distinguished military service, which the son wished to emulate. He served in the royal household in 1368; in France in 1369 and 1380; at sea in 1371, 1377–8, when he took Cherbourg, in 1383, and in 1387, when he won a major victory off Margate; in Scotland in 1385; on the councils of Edward III and Richard II from 1376; on a commission to reform the royal household in 1380; and as one of two trusted councillors about the king in 1381. As councillor and commander he was well-placed to criticise the government's management of the war in France in the 1380s and his actions as Lord Appellant were probably intended to ensure its more effective prosecution. Certainly he did not act to enrich himself or from disloyalty, but used the temporary predominance of the Lords Appellant to command a successful naval raid on the Isle of Oleron, to become captain of Brest, and to secure his re-appointment as admiral for a further five years.

King Richard's majority in 1389, however, ended all that. Arundel was supplanted as admiral and received no further commands. A man of action forced into inactivity, hot-tempered and tactless, honest to a fault and lacking in finesse, he was ill-suited for political survival under a hostile king anxious to humiliate him: his unlicensed second marriage resulted in a heavy fine; his charges against Gaunt in parliament in 1394 were dangerously near to the truth, but resulted only in an enforced public apology; probably innocent of involvement in the Cheshire revolt, he was blamed nevertheless; and his disrespect at Queen Anne's funeral, if such it was, resulted in a blow from the king, imprisonment, and binding over to keep the peace on massive sureties — surely a disproportionate punishment for such an offence. Understandably, perhaps, 'Of the former appellants, only Arundel maintained his old attitudes of defiance and suspicion', fuelled Richard's hostility, and thus led directly to his own trial and execution.

Arundel has received a bad press from historians. They have disparaged his weapons and martial pursuits as an obsession with violence and his involvement in the political murders of 1388 as an extension of it. 'Opposition was in his blood' (Steel). Yet it was not. Up to 1387 he was 'devotedly loyal' and his opposition thereafter was compatible with his allegiance and can indeed be seen as public spirited. His criticism of government in 1384, of Gaunt in 1394, and his actions in 1388 all aimed at more effective use of royal resources for prosecution of the war. They were constructive, not destructive. Historians have generally accepted the deficiencies of the government of the 1380s and hence, by implication, that the Lords Appellant were justified in their actions.

Arundel was not merely a soldier and politician. He was certainly literate. He was genuinely affectionate to his brother the archbishop, to his second wife Philippa Dowager-Countess of Pembroke, after whom he renamed Shrawardine Castle as Castle Philip, and was committed to the advancement by marriage of his children. His father, who did not die until 1376, intended to establish a hospital at Arundel, a project that Arundel fulfilled and indeed expanded, setting up and endowing Holy Trinity College there. His piety emerges also in other benefactions, his will, and his proposed trips abroad on pilgrimage or crusade in 1383 and 1389 that were overtaken by events. To accept him as 'a typical product of late fourteenth chivalry' (McKisack) does not make him unintelligent, inhuman or narrow-minded.

A. Goodman, *The Loyal Conspiracy: The Lords Appellant under Richard II*, 1971.
M. McKisack, *The Fourteenth Century*, 1959.
A. Tuck, *Richard II and the English Nobility*, 1973.

SIR SIMON BURLEY was impeached at the Merciless Parliament of 1388 and executed for his part in Richard II's first tyranny. Related only distantly if at all to the famous academic Walter Burley, Simon Burley was a penniless Herefordshire squire, who joined the service of the Black Prince, serving in his campaigns (he was captured in 1369), building up a reputation for chivalry, and becoming the ailing prince's chamberlain. On the deaths of his master in 1376 and of Edward III next year, he was one of the Black Prince's knights, who transferred to the chamber of Richard II. Burley became vice-chamberlain at a time when there was no effective chamberlain and thus head of the king's upper household. Always a key position — witness the careers of the Younger Despenser and William Lord Hastings — the chamberlainship was particularly important when the king was a minor without a regent. Burley in practice dealt with suitors, initially determining suits himself, then enabling Richard to assert himself prematurely: refusal to carry out a command under Richard's signet caused the dismissal of Chancellor Scrope in 1382. Unlike Scrope but like his successor Pole, Burley assisted the king rather than checking him. If 'the brains of the new court party are to be found in the immediate circle of the king' among the chamber knights, then Burley was 'undoubtedly in this period the real power behind the throne'. Lower in rank than Vere or Pole, Burley was not initially appealed of treason by the Lords Appellant, but was impeached later. Some charges were shared with other defendants, others accused him of personal abuse of office, but his main fault was too close involvement with Richard's autocracy and counter-attack against his opponents. It is illustrative of the respect in which he was held and the importance that both the king and his opponents attached to him, that his sentence provoked one public quarrel between the royal dukes Gloucester and York, who claimed Burley to be faithful to king and realm, and another between the five Appellants themselves, and involved overriding the pleas for mercy of both Richard II and

Queen Anne, who knelt for three hours before Arundel pleading for Burley's life.

Burley was a brave and distinguished soldier, a competent administrator, and a man of some culture, who owned 21 romances at his death. Most modern historians have found him an attractive and sympathetic character. It would be wrong, however, to accept him as a disinterested man, who did not enrich himself, since a contemporary reports that 'no equal of his rank was more glorious in outward apparel', his ostentatious lifestyle caused some offence, and he was capable of haughty and high-handed treatment. Beginning with no more than 20 marks (£13.66) a year, Burley ended with an estimated 2,000 marks (£1,333.66), the endowment of a duke. He secured all this from royal service at a time of financial stringency, when the king had little to give and other more deserving cases, such as his uncles, went without. The obvious parallel is William Montagu, Earl of Salisbury a generation earlier, but Salisbury's service enabled Edward III to fulfil contemporary expectations, while Burley helped Richard II to flout them. Apart from his lands, some of them given by the king and others bought, Burley aquired the key offices in key areas of constable of Windsor in 1378, Chief Justice of South Wales in 1382, Constable of Dover and Warden of the Cinque Ports in 1384. Burley's wealth was the reward of royal service, but it was also the result of exploitation of his proximity to the impressionable king. He even secured outright ownership of lands intended by Edward III to endow his religious foundations and placed a brother and nephews within the royal chamber. If not illegal, Burley's activities were nevertheless resented. Richard might well have restored him to favour had he been spared. Thus he had to die.

N.B. Lewis, 'Simon Burley and Baldwin de Raddington', *English Historical Review* lii, 1937.
A.B. Steel, *Richard II*, 1941.
J.A. Tuck, *Richard II and the English Nobility*, 1973.

SIR NICHOLAS BREMBRE (*d.*1388), grocer of London, has two claims to lasting significance. Firstly, he represents the merchant capitalists, who defeated John Northampton's attack on their monopoly of power during the 1380s. Secondly, he was one of the allies of Richard II eliminated by the Lords Appellant in 1388. He epitomised those Londoners, who unwisely dabbled in the politics of the nation normally monopolised by the high nobility. Brembre's origins are obscure. He was apparently only a first generation Londoner, but married one of the four daughters of the staggeringly rich John Stodey (d. 1376). This brought him valuable plate, extensive real property, and probably the resources for an international business of the front rank. Described alternatively as a merchant, grocer and pepperer, he dealt in iron, wines and woad, and had contacts with Flemings, Italians, Spaniards, and Portuguese. He was also a considerable creditor of the crown and personally advanced £2,970 to Richard II on one occasion. First and foremost, however, he was a dealer in wool, exporting 288 sacks in 1384–5, a total exceeded by only three others, all of them Londoners. From at least 1373 he lived luxuriously in the mansion of La Ryole in the Vintry and held city property worth £60 a year and nine manors in Kent and Middlesex at his death. He had no children.

Brembre's marriage also brought him three wealthy brothers-in-law, one, John Philpot being the richest merchant of his day, and also admission to the city elite. He and Philpot were appointed aldermen and sheriffs together in 1372, both acting frequently as aldermen thereafter. Brembre was first mayor in 1377 and twice more mayor in 1383–5. These were the years of constitutional experiment designed to end the power monopoly of men like Philpot and Brembre. It was Brembre whose victory at the mayoral election of 1383 defeated the experiment, rebuffed John Northampton, and led in 1384 to the revision of the city constitution to perpetuate their own dominance. To achieve this result Brembre capitalised on his connections at court, lending the king money both as an individual and in his corporate capacity. Subsequently he became a royal councillor and even attended the fatal council at Nottingham in 1387, where the questions were posed to judges. He tried — and failed — to exclude the Lords Appellant from the City later the same year. Thus he was one of the five Ricardians that they initially appealed of treason and the only one in custody. He stood trial in person. He could not be proved guilty of treason, but once his fellow oligarchs abandoned him and even declared him probably guilty, he was condemned and duly executed.

Brembre was a man of ability, ruthlessness and courage, who did not lose his nerve or shrink from conflict and harsh decisions. Thus he temporarily deposed a sheriff disrespectful of him as mayor and sought trial by battle in 1388. He was a partisan, who made many enemies — for example, by depriving crafts of their charters in his first mayoralty — and was depicted by his enemies as 'a monster of cruelty, injustice and violence', who was not averse to force and had a reputation for personal vengeance. A burgess aggrieved by his first mayoralty, who visited his home, had to be bought off in 1381. Such stories probably exaggerate his toughness and his unpopularity. He was agreeable enough to his fellow oligarchs, with whom he habitually dined, and to the king, who interceded, unavailingly, for his life.

R. Bird, *The Turbulent London of Richard II*, 1949.
S. Thrupp, *The Merchant Class of Medieval London*, 1962.

JOHN HOLLAND, EARL OF HUNTINGDON AND DUKE OF EXETER (c. 1352–1400), was half-brother of King Richard II. This was the basis of his successful career, for as a younger son he inherited nothing from his parents the Earl and Countess of Kent. He was not without merit: 'a man of great strength and master of his weapon' (Armitage-Smith), he became 'famous for knightly prowess'. Froissart was much impressed by his achievements on the battlefield and in tournaments in Spain in 1386–7 and he distinguished himself in further jousts in 1390. His internationalism emerges in his pilgrimage to Palestine in 1394, his abortive support of the Hungarians against the Turks, and in his proposed crusade against schismatics in 1397 as Gonfaloniere (standard-bearer) of the Church. His military talents were not in doubt, but his self-discipline certainly was. Had he not been the king's brother, his promotion would have been thwarted by his offences. He tortured and apparently killed an insane friar in 1384, murdered the Earl of Stafford's son near York in 1385, and seduced Elizabeth of Lancaster, who was already betrothed to another. His first escapade excited only criticism. Sir Ralph Stafford's death infuriated the king, who seized Holland's lands, threatened him with death as a common murderer, and drove him into sanctuary at Beverley, whence he emerged later only on pain of founding three chantries for his victim's soul. His relations with Elizabeth resulted in a shotgun wedding in 1386 and earned him the immensely valuable patronage of John of Gaunt.

Less precocious than Montagu and Scrope, his immediate contemporaries in age, Holland first appears as recipient of grants in 1380 and first fought in 1381, when he became a knight of the Garter and justice of Chester. Further promotion was impeded by his youthful escapades, which caused him to lose ground to Robert Vere and 'various persons ill-disposed to the said John who were about the king'. It may be as an Appellant supporter that he was created Earl of Huntingdon (and endowed with £1,333 a year) in 1387. Alternatively his promotion may have been designed to please John of Gaunt, who gave his unintended son-in-law the chance to distinguish himself as constable of his expedition to Spain in 1386-7. However that may be, Holland benefited at once from the king's majority in 1389, becoming great chamberlain of England for life, admiral of the west, captain of Brest, constable of Tintagel, and a royal councillor. Other employment and grants followed. His proximity to the king ensured his support as Lord Appellant in 1397. In reward he was created Duke of Exeter — one of five *duketti* (little dukes) Richard elevated at that time; he became warden of the West March and in 1398 captain of Calais; Arundel honour, Reigate and Lewes castles were among the forfeitures he received; he was custodian of the Mortimer lands in South Wales; and he served as royal commissioner in eleven counties.

All these lands, honours and offices were held *in absentia* whilst he served on Richard's invasion of Ireland in 1399 and there was thus nothing Holland could do to prevent Richard's defeat and deposition. Indeed, he himself was in danger and was charged with his fellow Appellants with Thomas of Woodstock's death. Denying knowledge and complicity, he was condemned with them to lose titles and grants granted since 1397. He thus lost his duchy, 'the worship and dignity thereof', and became mere Earl of Huntingdon once more. Although he supported the 1400 rebellion, he was not at Cirencester but in London. Fleeing eastwards he was taken at Prittlewell in Essex and was executed at Pleshey Castle by Gloucester's mother-in-law in the presence of Arundel's son. Good service to the Lancastrians eventually recovered even his duchy for his son.

A.B. Steel, *Richard II*, 1941.

JOHN MONTAGU, EARL OF SALISBURY (1351–1400) was 'one of the few genuine friends that (King) Richard had' in 1399 and is supposedly the only one motivated by 'love rather than self-interest'. Six generations of Montagus gave loyal service to the crown. The third generation had been represented by the first Earl of Salisbury, John's grandfather; the fourth generation by the second earl — a soldier of distinction — and by John's father John Lord Montagu, soldier and steward of Richard II's household; John himself was the fifth; and his son Thomas, the great earl, the sixth. The younger John distinguished himself militarily in France in 1369 when only eighteen, securing several ransomable captives, went on crusade to Prussia against the Slavs in 1391–2, and succeeded his uncle as knight of the Garter in 1397–8. He was a member of the royal household — a king's knight — by 1383, during his father's stewardship, but he was not yet important enough to be appealed at the Merciless Parliament of 1388. More influential later, he was then one of the so-called Lollard knights who protected heretics from persecution, associated with other Lollard knights like Clanvowe and Sturry, and wrote highly-regarded poetry — 'ballads, songs, rondels, and lays' — all of which are now apparently lost. Although only once a diplomat, sent in 1398–9 to thwart Bolingbroke's second marriage, he 'seems to have had unusually close relations with the French court'. Soldier, courtier, crusader, and poet, he 'belonged to the international chivalrous class and spoke its *lingua franca*'.

Yet Salisbury was an earl only for the last three years of his life. His father was a younger son, whose barony and offices were earned by arduous service to the Black Prince, Edward III and Richard II. Unable to endow his son generously, he doubtless gave him access to military and courtly circles, whilst overshadowing him for many years. How much the younger John needed independent means is suggested by his marriage to the twice-widowed daughter of a London mayor: Maud, daughter (but not heiress) of Adam Francis (d.1375), widow of the grocer John Aubrey and Sir Alan Buxhull K.G. His chosen residence was her manor of Shenley in Hertfordshire. He was the first earl to marry into mercantile stock, though he was not then an earl. His cousin's death in 1382 made him heir presumptive, but not until 1397 did he succeed his uncle as third earl. No longer the vast inheritance of 1337, shorn of Denbigh and the Isle of Man, the earldom of Salisbury nevertheless remained an outstanding West Country estate sufficient to transform Montagu's status, prosperity and political career.

Montagu first came to the forefront of the political stage in 1397, when he was one of eight noblemen who appealed Gloucester, Arundel, and Warwick of treason. He was not one of the *duketti* — little dukes — selected for further promotion, but the king did back his claims to the great lordship of Denbigh, though significantly not to the point of success: Earl Roger Mortimer's death in 1398 reduced the value to the king of Montagu's rival claim. Montagu accompanied King Richard II on his second expedition to Ireland in 1399 and was sent back on Bolingbroke's invasion to recruit in North Wales. He failed. The Welsh would not join him, even the forces he brought deserted, believing the king to be dead, and he withdrew with only a small force to the security of Conway Castle, where King Richard joined him and where he surrendered to his enemies. Montagu was briefly imprisoned but released in time to join Exeter in the abortive rebellion of 1400 against Henry IV, which resulted in his lynching at Cirencester and the forfeiture in parliament of his estates. Montagu's heir, however, was allowed to succeed in 1409 and lived up to the family tradition of good service, this time to the Lancastrian dynasty.

K.B. McFarlane, *Lancastrian Kings and Lollard Knights*, 1971.
A.B. Steel, *Richard II*, 1941.
J.A. Tuck, *Richard II and the English Nobility*, 1973.

WILLIAM SCROPE OF BOLTON, EARL OF WILTSHIRE (*c.*1351–99) was the brains behind Richard II's second tyranny of 1397–9. He was the eldest son of Richard Lord Scrope of Bolton (*d.*1403) and his early career rivalled his father's for military and administrative distinction. He served in France with John of Gaunt in 1369 and 1373, assisted in a Neapolitan blockade of Venice, and went crusading in Prussia. From 1383–92 he was seneschal of Gascony, in 1386–9 captain of Cherbourg, and from 1389 captain of Brest. National recognition came in the 1390s with his election as knight of the Garter (1394) and appointments in turn as chamberlain of the royal household (1393–8) and treasurer of England (1398–9), his brother Stephen succeeding as chamberlain. He was nominated executor by the king in 1399. His creation as Earl of Wiltshire completed his family's rise from obscurity to comital rank in only three generations.

Scrope's personal promotion was not exceptionally rapid. Like Montagu, he was already in his forties when he became chamberlain of the household, the key political position that brought him, like Latimer and Burley somewhat earlier, the dominance of the royal household, control of access to the king, and the king's friendship and trust. He became Richard's indispensable agent everywhere. Constable of Beaumaris in 1394 and of Caernarvon and Pembroke in 1395, he became justice of Chester and North Wales, and in 1397 was granted the 'whole county and lordship of Anglesey'. He accompanied Richard to Ireland in 1394 and became justiciar there from 1395. He commanded the important castle of Queenborough. He was a Lord Appellant in 1397. His councillorship led ultimately to his dominance of the council, of which he was an assiduous attender with a wide brief. Of all Richard's favourites, only the Duke of Aumarle received more honours and rewards, but he lacked the ability, industry, and willingness to shoulder the daily routine of government that enabled Scrope to dominate the central administration. It was Scrope, not the Duke of York as figurehead, who was really in charge in England during Richard's second invasion of Ireland. 'Modern historians have not fully recognized the pervasiveness of his powers, but it was all too apparent to his contemporaries', who regarded him, Bushy and Green as 'the king's most evil councillors and the fosterers of his malice'.

Scrope, like Montagu, was long denied his baronial inheritance by the longevity of his father and provided for himself by marrying an heiress. His wealth emerges from his purchase of lands in Wiltshire and the Isle of Man, whose arms he quartered with his own. He was greedy for wealth and prestige and was not scrupulous how he acquired it. Royal favour was exploited to accumulate offices, which he exercised by deputy and thus less effectively than Richard hoped. Each office brought a salary and from 1397 he secured a stream of outright grants: in 1397 Anglesey and Warwick's lordships of Barnard Castle, County Durham, and Pains Castle in Wales; in 1398 the Lancaster honour of Pickering in Yorkshire; and in 1399, so it was rumoured, he planned the ruin of further magnates to secure their lands. Already he was great in Wales, Wiltshire and the North: what would satisfy him? Acquisitive and underhand, socially inferior to the other *duketti,* he was detested, despised, but also feared as the ablest and most dangerous of Richard's favourites. Hence his summary execution with Bushy and Green at Bristol in 1399: the only one of Richard's favourites of noble birth to be executed, whilst Surrey, Salisbury, and even Exeter and Aumarle, were spared. He died childless and his earldom died with him, but his brother was allowed to keep their father's barony.

C. Given-Wilson, *The Royal Household and the King's Affinity: Service, Politics and Finance in England 1360–1413,* 1986.
J. A. Tuck, *Richard II and the Nobility,* 1973.

JOHN GOWER, (*c.* 1325–1408), esquire, was one of four great poets in late 14th century England. Two, the writer of *Gawain and the Green Knight* and William Langland, author of *Piers Plowman,* are too shadowy for the biographer, but Gower, like Chaucer, is a little better known. He first occurs in 1365, when it is generally assumed that he was already middle aged. He may indeed be the legal counsel and judge of 1355–6, which tallies with his interest in the law. He probably belonged to a Yorkshire branch of the Kentish family, whose arms he bore. Presumably a younger son, somehow he found the means to acquire manors in Kent and Suffolk and was an esquire when retained by Henry Earl of Derby, later Henry IV, in 1392–3. From the mid 1370s he settled at the priory of St Mary Overy, Southwark, where he concentrated on writing and whose canons probably wrote multiple presentation copies of his books. His interest in personal morality led to concern about the quality of government and hence to increasing involvement in politics. Gower regarded himself as spokesman for all:

> I cry out what the voice of the people cries out. Nothing I write is my own opinion. Rather I shall speak out what the voice of the people has reported to me. I intend my words of good to bring evil to light.

High hopes of the young Richard II were first dispelled and then transferred to Henry IV, whose panegyrist he eventually became in 1399. By then he was old, decrepit and half-blind.

French courtly poetry influenced Gower much less than Chaucer.

John Gower
(From his effigy in Southwark Cathedral)

It is unlikely that he was ever a court poet. From the mid 1370s he embarked on his three major poems, which ultimately totalled 80,000 lines. His French *Mirrour de l'Omme (Speculum Meditantis)* was probably completed by the Peasants Revolt; his Latin *Vox Clamantis* was started before it and finished afterwards; and his English *Confessio Amantis* was completed by 1390. Each was subsequently revised at least once and made compatible with his *Cronica Tripatita*, which celebrated the Lancastrian usurpation of 1399.

Like most contemporaries, Gower was conventional in his religious, social and political beliefs. He accepted the doctrinal teachings of the Church and patronised monasticism, respected the social hierarchy and royal authority, saw the king as fount of justice and supported his claim to France, and yet also attacked the abuses of churchmen, lawyers and aristocrats, denounced bad government and bad kings, and longed for peace at home and abroad. Like so many contemporaries, he looked forward to each estate performing its duties properly as in some mythical golden age in the past. All this was completely conventional, for Gower was not an original thinker. He employed the characteristic contemporary medium of complaint. He brought together the scattered social criticisms of others, welded them into a single unified whole, and presented them clearly and coherently throughout his vast works. His single-minded consistency is most impressive. Behind all the social evils of his day Gower saw faults in government. What was needed was a good king, who took his responsibilities seriously, and thus provided the conditions for moral regeneration and social order. Bad kings, like Richard II, and evil-counsel, like that of Richard's flatterers, were recipes for sin and chaos. He voiced the ideas of his generation. 'Of all the Ricardian poets', it is Gower who is

> most representative of the middle and 'professional' stratum of free society, which in the late fourteenth century had become alienated from royal government and impotently voiced its grievances and remedies in a wide range of surviving literature (Harriss).

Obviously a lesser poet than Chaucer, he was coupled with him in his day and is indeed more typical of contemporary concerns.

J. H. Fisher, *John Gower: Moral Philosopher and Friend of Chaucer,* 1965.

THOMAS WALSINGHAM (*c.*1345–1422) was 'the last of the great medieval chroniclers' (Emden). Presumably from Walsingham in Norfolk, he became a monk of St Albans — the premier English Benedictine house — about 1364. He was therefore already quite senior when he became precentor and head of the scriptorium about 1380 and started writing his chronicles. He was appointed prior of the cell of Wymondham (Norfolk) in 1394, but retired in 1396 at his own request, 'weary of worldly cares'. Thereafter he was a cloister monk at the mother-house without administrative responsibilities. While he continued to write history in his last years, he was no longer head of the scriptorium and devoted much attention to study of the classics. His commentary on Ovid's *Metamorphoses* and his works on the ancient gods, Trojan War, and Alexander the Great probably took up more of his time than his chronicles.

Walsingham's early life was dominated by the great Abbot Thomas De La Mare, who built a new scriptorium, revived intellectual activity, and presumably encouraged Walsingham to restore St Albans' flagging tradition of historical writing. Starting apparently with modest intentions as historian of his own monastery and his own day from 1376, he ultimately produced a 'formidable body of writing and one unequalled by any other chronicler working in 14th-century England'. Like his predecessor and model Matthew Paris, he produced a *Great Chronicle* from 1272–1420, a *Short Chronicle*, and continued the *Deeds of the Abbots* to 1393. He also produced a *Book of Benefactors* and a history of Normandy (*Ypodigma Neustriae*). The relationship of these works is complex, partly because Walsingham treated the years before 1376 last, partly because he was no longer in charge of the scriptorium after 1394, and probably also because of successive revisions to rehabilitate John of Gaunt and take account of the Lancastrian succession to the English crown. His works overlap in coverage and all have original contributions to make.

His principal achievement as historian was his

full-scale coverage of English history of nearly half a century. Walsingham's great gift was as a reporter of current events. He was excellently informed and wrote close in time to the events he recorded — and thus reflects the opinions of at least some of his contemporaries. He often wrote in considerable detail in clear expressive prose ...

He used a wide-range of oral and written sources and 'believed in stating even opponents' views'. On the debit side, like most medieval chroniclers, he loved prodigies and marvels and believed that History records God's rewards and punishments on good and evil. He was a Benedictine monk of St Albans, loyal to his house and order, and hence hostile to the Peasants Revolt, moral failings, and Wyclif, whom he denounced as 'angel of Satan and forerunner of Antichrist'. He was patriotic and anti-French, admired courage and chivalry, and feared that knightly standards were declining. Emotional, even hysterical and unrestrained in his denunciations, his early work virulently attacked John of Gaunt and was deservedly nicknamed the *Scandalous Chronicle*. Walsingham was not consistently anti-court or indeed politically or constitutionally principled in his stance, becoming increasingly pro-Lancastrian and praising Henry V in particular for his bravery and piety. He lacked the depth and range of Matthew Paris, 'operating entirely within the chronicle conventions of his time', but was nevertheless 'a not entirely unworthy successor'.

A. Gransden, *Historical Writing in England*, ii, 1982.
J. Taylor, *English Historical Literature in the Fourteenth Century*, 1987.

ADAM USK (*c*. 1352–1430), the chronicler, was born in the Welsh marcher lordship of Usk and was sent by its lord Edmund Earl of March (*d*. 1381) to Oxford University. He became a notary public in 1381, bachelor of canon law in 1387, principal of the civil law school, and by 1393 a doctor of civil law. He held a succession of rectories from 1383 and was advocate at the court of Canterbury up to 1399, when his support for Henry IV transformed his fortunes. He visited Richard II in prison, advised on his deposition, was employed in royal diplomacy and legal business, and attracted the patronage of Archbishop Arundel. Perhaps because of the theft of a horse, perhaps because he wanted papal preferment, he left England for Rome in 1402, becoming a papal chaplain and auditor of the sacred palace. His hopes of a bishopric were disappointed, but he was promoted to archdeaconries, canonries, and other livings that should have brought an income of about £250. This phase of his career ended with the pope's expulsion from Rome and Usk's humiliation by the Romans, which prompted him in 1406 to return home. Henry IV, however, refused him a pardon, so he languished abroad until 1411, when, now about sixty years of age, he proceeded secretly to Wales, briefly joined Glendower, and spent two years as a poor chantry priest at Pontypool. Pardoned at last, he resumed his legal practice and secured two rectories, which he occupied until 1428-9, when he was pensioned off.

Usk's *Chronicon* continues Higden's *Polychronicon*. Up to 1394 and from 1404 it is meagre, but in between it is full, detailed, and of primary importance for the exciting events of his turbulent life, especially the Lancastrian revolution, the papal Curia, and Glendower's rebellion. Usk was an acute eyewitness and his chronicle, although biased, is an independent account, which owes nothing to any other source.

Usk's *Chronicon* is also revealing about its author, who 'happily had enough vanity to think his personal experience not unworthy of a place among the general events of his time'. Personal reminiscences are interspersed with national and international events and indeed it is Usk's own career that shaped what he wrote. Inevitably he justified his own actions and condemned his opponents, but he supplies ample information for a more balanced — and not altogether favourable — judgement to be reached. His Welsh origins coloured his whole life: witness his riot against the northern scholars at Oxford in 1388-9, his repeated returns to Wales, his patronage of his home town, and his interest in the Mortimers and their relatives Archbishop Arundel and the Earl of Arundel. Whilst undoubtedly a learned man whose legal counsel was widely valued, he made excessive parade of his expertise — he 'certainly missed no opportunity for airing his knowledge' — and was once silenced by a bishop for an untimely display of learning. Vain and boastful, he probably exaggerated the eminence of his friends, the quality of his advice, and his influence on decisions and events, for he revealed himself to be a man without tact, sense of timing, discretion or judgement. Even by the standards of his time he was unduly credulous about signs and miracles and claimed to experience both visions and dreams, which he included as serious portents in his chronicle. Impulsive, passionate, and lacking a capacity for self-criticism, he blamed on others the misfortunes that he brought on himself. His naked pursuit of promotion and profit, which did not stop short at looting, accompanied generosity to friends and his native town. Whilst undoubtedly ill-suited for the bishopric he sought, he deserved more than the obscurity in which he died.

A. Gransden, *Historical Writing in England*, ii, 1982.
E. M. Thompson, *Chronicon Adae de Usk AD 1377–1421*, 1904.

HENRY IV (*c.*1366–1413) who ascended the throne in 1399, was born at Bolingbroke in Lincolnshire. He was the eldest son of John of Gaunt, Duke of Lancaster (*d.*1399), third surviving son of Edward III, and his first wife Blanche, daughter and heiress of Henry Duke of Lancaster (*d.*1361). From birth he was destined to become the greatest of subjects but not to become king. Moreover his chances of succeeding to the English throne diminished with time and his accession cannot have been planned for or expected. When he acceded his character was already formed, yet his reign did not offer his talents greater scope, but called for quite different qualities. From 1399–1406 he was beset by rebellions, financial problems, and parliamentary opposition, and thereafter incapacitating illness made him a caretaker, whose demise was impatiently awaited. 'Grim and careworn', he came to regret his seizure of the crown, was troubled by guilt about that and his execution of Archbishop Scrope, and probably considered his malady to be God's punishment for the latter's death. He was still only about 47 when he died.

Yet in 1399 he had possessed all the qualities hoped for in a king. He was a distinguished soldier and 'something of a European celebrity'. He first jousted in 1381–2, when only sixteen, by 1386 he was winning tournaments, and in 1390 he established a European reputation for himself at the jousts of St Inglevert at Calais. The logical sequel was a crusade, perhaps to the Barbary Coast — but that was abandoned — and in practice to Prussia in 1390 and 1392. The first campaign included storming the outworks of Vilnya in Lithuania, the second became instead a pilgrimage across central

Henry IV
(From his effigy in Canterbury Cathedral)

Europe and Italy to the Holy Land. Gaunt prevented him from campaigning in Hainault and from joining the Nicopolis crusade. Such expeditions acquainted him with most European powers and made him known to them. His hosts were impressed by his handsome appearance, prowess, courtesy, chivalry and affability. He was 'an amiable knight, courteous and pleasant to all' (Froissart). He was thus the favourite to win his duel with the Duke of Norfolk in 1398.

Apart from his expectations, Henry possessed extensive lands by his marriage to the coheiress of the Bohun earldoms of Essex, Hereford and Northampton. By 1397 his share brought him £900 a year — more than enough for an earl — and gave him experience in landownership, particularly in Brecon in Wales, where he featured as a grasping landlord. It gave him the means to dress richly and live splendidly. For exceptional expenditure, such as his crusades, he drew on the almost bottomless purse of his father. By his thirtieth year he was a widower with four sons and the dynastic future of his house was assured. Created Earl of Derby in 1377 and Duke of Hereford in 1397, he was not impatient to succeed to his father, for whom he felt a genuine affection and whose death he sincerely regretted.

As the son of Gaunt's first marriage, he could not share Gaunt's ambitions for the throne of Castile arising from his second marriage and did not accompany him on his crusade in 1386. Remaining at home, he joined Gloucester, Arundel, Warwick, and Nottingham as Lords Appellant, fought at Radcot Bridge, and participated in the destruction of King Richard's favourites. Though very much a junior partner, Henry made his mark in two ways, first of all, it appears, by opposing Richard's deposition in favour of his uncle of Gloucester, and, secondly, by intervening unsuccessfully to save the life of Sir Simon Burley. Again in 1397 he shared in the appeals of his erstwhile colleagues, being perhaps lucky to escape unscathed himself. All this time he was accumulating experience without apparently raising any suspicion that he was aiming for the crown.

Conventional in arms, politics, and as a landowner, Henry was also more than conventionally pious. His various journeys and jousts were interspersed with crusades — not to be regarded as purely military expeditions — and pilgrimages to holy shrines. His European hosts were impressed by his conspicuous piety and industrious visits to churches, though somewhat critical of his superstitions. As king, he was to prove unfailingly orthodox, yet he had a sense of proportion and refused to treat irreverence with the gravity attached to heresy and preferred converting heretics to burning them. He may indeed have been touched by the reforming puritanism that coloured the thought of Bishop Brinton, Langland and even the Lollards. Certainly his references to himself in his will as a sinful wretch, to his sinful soul, and to the life he had 'mispended' point to a sense of unworthiness and self-abasement that they could all have shared.

Yet Henry had not imbibed purely conventional values. He had undergone an unusually literary education and provided a more rigorous intellectual training for his children than was normal for the nobility. He himself was literate in both English and French and perhaps also Latin, able at least to quote a Latin maxim. The books he kept in his study at Eltham when king and his visits to the tombs of St Augustine and Boethius all point both to wide reading and genuine intellectual tastes. He was patron to the poet Gower, an enthusiastic listener to music and an instrumentalist himself, perhaps even a composer. He has a better claim to be regarded as a patron of the arts than his cousin Richard II. 'Henry, in fact, was that comparatively rare combination, the man of action who was also an intellectual'.

This, then, was the man who became king in 1399. It is not clear when he decided to do so. Was he prepared to content himself with his duchy, as he apparently swore publicly at Doncaster, and to risk the vengeance of the unforgiving Richard II? Or was he after the crown from the start, counting on his own popularity, Richard's unpopularity, his Lancastrian connection, and the power-vacuum that Richard had left in England to achieve it? His systematic elimination of Richard's favourites could fit either scenario, but Richard's arrest was only achieved by promises that he would remain king that Henry cannot have meant even if his representatives were sincere. He was thus at least twice perjured before he secured Richard's forced abdication and took the crown by conquest, election, and a hereditary claim — from Edmund Crouchback — that he knew to be fraudulent. The end justified the means. In pursuit of the crown, truth and honour could be sacrificed. Perhaps he had no choice but to depose Richard, no alternative but to take the throne himself, but the manner of his accession and his perjury justified opposition in the Commons and the rebellions that an undoubtedly legitimate king might have escaped.

Henry was subjected to a series of assassination plots, some quite ludicrous, and dynastically motivated rebellions designed to replace him by Richard II and, later, Edmund Earl of March (d. 1425). The first of these, by Richard's *duketti*, resulted in the rapid death of the culprits and noticeably strengthened Henry's hold on the throne. The Percy revolts of 1403, 1405, and 1408 were more serious, but fortunately the Percies were never able to concentrate their resources and Henry's Lancastrian retinue held firm. The prolonged Welsh revolt led by Owen Glendower was not only formidable but lengthy and ruinously expensive. It was a great strain and victory significantly relieved the crown's financial problems. To internal threats were added external ones — Scotland, Aquitaine, and the south coast — which Henry had to ignore in favour of more pressing internal problems, but which were dispelled only gradually as he became safer on his throne. Only then could he intervene in the struggles for power in neighbouring France. Only then did Henry become the king by consensus, everyone's king rather than the leader of a faction, and only then did control of government become worth contesting for the rival groups within the royal family.

Henry IV became king at a time of falling revenues, notably the customs, and therefore had less money to meet commitments than Richard II. Internal and external threats were among the reasons that increased his expenditure and necessitated the maintenance of his Lancastrian retinue. He therefore needed extraordinary taxation, which the Commons were reluctant to grant and made conditional on economies, resumption of grants, and reform of his council which they considered, wrongly, to be the cause of his financial difficulties. Henry fought a series of rearguard actions against them as he sought to maintain his prerogative intact. Several times he suffered humiliating reverses and had to make concessions, but ultimately these were all retrieved and his prestige was restored. From 1406 his ill-health prevented him from effective rule. Power was delegated first to Archbishop Arundel as chancellor and then from 1409 to a ministry imposed by Prince Henry and the Beauforts against the king's better judgement. A proposal that he should be deposed in favour of his son enabled the king and Arundel to reassert control for the last two years of his reign. A violent power struggle was a distinct possibility, but instead Prince Henry submitted and was reconciled with his father before his death.

'For most people he (Henry IV) is only a rather dreary, if ambitious fumbler' and 'was never able to secure that position of unquestioned dominance in the kingdom' that kings normally possessed. Yet his achievements were considerable. He did retain his throne and maintain his prerogative intact. He did succeed in passing them on to his son, who was his unquestioned successor. Despite all his problems and difficulties, therefore, 'by contemporary standards he proved a capable king'.

A. Goodman, *The Loyal Conspiracy: The Lords Appellant under Richard II,* 1971.

J. L. Kirby, *Reign of Henry IV,* 1970.

K. B. McFarlane, *Lancastrian Kings and Lollard Knights,* 1971.

P. McNiven, *Heresy and Politics in the Reign of Henry IV: The Burning of John Badby,* 1987.

J. A. Tuck, *Richard II and the English Nobility,* 1973.

THOMAS ARUNDEL (1353–1414), Bishop of Ely (1373–88), Archbishop of York (1388–96) and Canterbury (1396–7 and 1399–1414) was the youngest son of the Earl of Arundel and thus destined for a career in the church. He attended Oxford University and had already accumulated benefices 'fit for a young lord' before becoming bishop of Ely at the age of 20. With his brother Earl Richard from 1386 he became the 'most uncompromising advocate of baronial opposition to the king's government ... politically and morally the sixth appellant'. Hence his promotion to archbishop and chancellor in 1388. Dismissed from office in 1389, he was again chancellor in 1391, resigning following translation to Canterbury in 1396. Included in Richard II's revenge on the Appellants in 1397, Thomas was nominally moved to the see of St Andrews and sent abroad, where he joined in Henry IV's invasion and facilitated his usurpation. Arundel was again appointed to Canterbury. He became the dominant councillor, especially after Henry's health collapsed, served twice more as chancellor (1407–9, 1412–13), and decisively defeated the constitutional pretensions of the Commons in 1407. In return King Henry backed Arundel in ecclesiastical matters.

Whilst Thomas' promotion to bishop was 'one of the most

Thomas Arundel as Bishop of Ely
(From the Book of Benefactors of St Alban's Abbey)

notorious examples of the combined power of aristocratic influence
and papal patronage', he was no negligent prelate. He was conscientious, 'came to his diocese to work', and spent as much time there as
possible. His visitations, his defence of episcopal rights, and the
buildings, plate and jewels that he gave to his dioceses and cathedrals
were conventional behaviour but exceptional in scale. As primate,
however, he decisively crushed parliamentary moves to deprive the
Church of its lands and forced the Lollards underground. He banned

heretical preaching and heretical books, purged Oxford of heresy and thus finally destroyed Lollardy's academic wing, and secured the death penalty for heresy (1401). Burning was used mainly as a deterrent, for Arundel preferred to save souls. He examined Lollards in person, seeking patiently and sympathetically to win their recantations and save their lives, revealing himself to be humane and well-versed in theology and canon law. Royal support on such matters received priority over revenge for the execution of Archbishop Scrope, whose life he sought to save, and he accepted the stifling of academic speculation as a necessary price of orthodoxy.

Arundel was independent and courageous, thoughtful and sagacious, principled but never impractical. His birth emerges in his noble life-style, his circle of friends, and in his autocratic dismissal of the Commons' attempts to fetter their betters. There was an 'uneasy balance between his authoritarian correctness, his naturally aggressive impatience, and his attempts to demonstrate the humane side of his Christianity'. He was a munificent benefactor, a loyal friend and ally, a lover of music, and deeply pious. He was genuinely shocked by disrespect to the sacrament and to individual clerics and his will reveals a streak of puritan self-denial worthy of the Lollards themselves in his self-image as 'a most miserable and unworthy sinner' and 'most useless and lukewarm servant of the holy church of Canterbury'. The chronicler Walsingham more appropriately acknowledged him to be 'the most eminent bulwark of the English church and invincible champion'.

M. Aston, *Thomas Arundel: A Study in Church Life in the Reign of Richard II*, 1967.

R. G. Davies, 'Thomas Arundel as Archbishop of Canterbury 1396–1414', *Journal of Ecclesiastical History*, xxiv, 1973.

P. McNiven, *Heresy and Politics in the Reign of Henry IV. The Burning of John Badby*, 1987.

RICHARD SCROPE (*c.*1346–1405), Bishop of Lichfield (1386–98) and Archbishop of York (1398–1405), was the only English archbishop to be executed for treason in the middle ages. Up till then, he was 'an obscure and colourless figure' with no distinguishable political affiliations and was indeed the 'very antithesis of the ambitious, worldly prelate'. Although a younger son of Henry Lord

Scrope of Masham, he did not rise with the rapidity of such aristocratic clergymen as Courtenay and Arundel. He studied at both Oxford and Cambridge Universities. By 1375 he was a bachelor of arts reading civil law and was the official principal (judge) of the bishop of Ely and by 1379 he was doctor of both laws. He had received his first benefice in 1368 and was ordained in 1377. Birth and education did not lead however to administrative service to the crown, but to the Papacy: he was a papal chaplain and auditor of the sacred palace in 1381 and an apostolic notary in 1386. Hence, apparently, his appointment as dean of Chichester in 1382, his abortive election as bishop there in 1385, and his appointment as Bishop of Coventry and Lichfield. He was consecrated by Pope Urban VI himself at Genoa in 1386. Returning home, he may have become an unusually conscientious bishop and was certainly regarded by the chroniclers as 'primarily a churchman and a scholar'. He became a royal councillor and served on diplomatic missions to Scotland and the Curia. In 1398 he was rewarded by elevation to the archbishopric of York.

No archbishop could entirely escape involvement in politics and inevitably Scrope was involved in the formalities of Henry IV's succession to Richard II in 1399. Neither then nor in 1403, however, did Scrope reveal clear political loyalties and he does not seem to have taken a distinctive line in convocation either. It was therefore probably as great a surprise to Henry IV as to modern historians that Scrope should have rebelled in 1405. His immediate accomplice was the young Earl Marshal, with whom he raised the city of York, but he must have been in league with the Earl of Northumberland as well. Northumberland certainly hoped to depose Henry IV and this may also have been Scrope's aim, for he denounced Henry IV's perjury in taking the crown. His other charges, however, concerned misgovernment that could have been remedied: excessive taxation of clergy and laity — which had some justification — and evil counsel and other abuses, which may not have done. Whatever his intentions, Scrope was unable to join forces with Northumberland and was forced to negotiate. Promised that his grievances would be remedied, he disbanded his forces — the alternative being certain defeat — and once defenceless was arrested. In spite of the desperate intervention of Archbishop Arundel, the king organised his summary and illegal trial, in which Chief Justice Gascoigne refused to participate, and he was executed in his own cathedral city of York.

He died as a dignified spiritual leader. Conveyed to execution in humiliating style on a 'collier's sorry mare ... bareback with a halter for a bridle', he sang psalms as he went, and was beheaded with five blows in commemoration of the five wounds of Christ. His claim to have rebelled for the liberties of the Church, his illegal execution, his local popularity, and the manner of his death all enabled him to be presented as a martyr and help explain his immediate veneration as such. In 1070 Becket's violent death forced Henry II into humiliating penance, but times had changed. Archbishop Scrope's death gave Henry IV a guilty conscience that lasted until his own death, but no immediate political repercussions — such as papal hostility — counterbalanced the deterrent effect on other potential rebels. It is highly debatable whether Scrope's execution was indeed King Henry's 'biggest mistake' (Kirby).

P. McNiven, 'The Betrayal of Archbishop Scrope', *Bulletin of the John Rylands Library* liv, 1971.

HENRY PERCY, 1st EARL OF NORTHUMBERLAND, (1341–1408), raised the Percies into 'the most powerful magnates on the Scottish border', made Henry IV king, and died in rebellion against him. The Percies of Alnwick already had large estates in Yorkshire and Northumberland before his second marriage brought much more in Cumberland and Northumberland. Initially he rose as a Lancastrian retainer, serving in France under successive dukes in 1359–60, 1369 and 1373, but his interests focused on the borders, where he was repeatedly diplomat and warden of the marches. The warden system enhanced the Percies' local authority and financed an inflated private army of retainers. 'During the reign of Richard II it is clear that they aimed to control Border politics and administration through securing the Wardenships of both the East and West Marches towards Scotland'. His son Hotspur was defeated at Otterburn in 1388, they were victorious at Homildon Hill in 1402, and their exploits against the Scots were celebrated by the border ballads. They jealously protected their monopoly of power against John of Gaunt and Richard II's termination of their tenure of both wardenships in 1396 may explain their rebellion in 1399. Henry IV restored both offices and authorised them to conquer much of southern Scotland, but he would not finance their conquests. As these could only be realised with royal finance, they tried to replace King Henry by the young Earl of March in 1403.

Percy's career was not confined to the north. He campaigned and negotiated abroad, was marshal of England in 1376–7 and constable in 1399. He was created Knight of the Garter in 1366 — Hotspur became one in 1388 — and earl in 1377. Hotspur (1364–1403) fought in Scotland, Prussia, and Flanders, was marcher warden and lieutenant of Aquitaine, justice of Chester and North Wales, and from 1402 commander against the Welsh revolt of Owen Glendower. Northumberland was an astute politician and a moderating influence under Richard II. He served on commissions of reform, declined to attack Arundel and told Richard that the Appellants were loyal subjects with whom he should negotiate in 1387, found Brembre not deserving of death in 1388, and yet interceded for Gloucester and Arundel with the royal council in 1389. He was 'one of the honest brokers of politics in 1388 and 1389'.

Richard II purged many noblemen, took others to Ireland, and several were killed in 1400. Together these circumstances enabled the Percies to play a bigger political role than their actual power justified. Their support in 1399 ensured the success of Bolingbroke's invasion, they captured Richard II, and they immediately received lavish rewards, which make it hard to believe their claim that they did not intend to make Henry king. He made them completely dominant on the borders and north Wales, gave priority to their salaries as far as his straitened finances permitted, and allayed other sources of friction. Yet in 1403 Hotspur launched a rebellion from Cheshire. He was defeated at Shrewsbury before Glendower or Northumberland could assist, he and his uncle Worcester were killed, but Northumberland himself was acquitted. Rebelling again in 1405, Northumberland was frustrated by Westmorland and fled into exile. Now a convicted traitor and fugitive, Northumberland rebelled again in 1408, but was easily defeated by the sheriff of Yorkshire at Bramham Moor. The family was restored in 1416, but never again were the Percies the national arbiters of power that they *appeared* in 1399–1408.

J. M. W. Bean, 'Henry IV and the Percies', *History*, xliv, 1959.

P. McNiven, 'The Betrayal of Archbishop Scrope', *Bulletin of the John Rylands Library,* liv, 1971.

P. M. McNiven, 'The Scottish Policy of the Percies and the Strategy of the Shrewsbury Campaign', *Bulletin of the John Rylands Library* lxii, 1980.

J. A. Tuck, *Richard II and the English Nobility,* 1973.

JOHN NORBURY (c. 1350–1414), esquire, was one of those Lancastrian retainers, whose career was transformed by Henry Duke of Lancaster's accession as King Henry IV in 1399. Though of gentle birth from Nantwich in Cheshire, he was merely the younger son of a younger son. Lacking his own inheritance, he had to make his own way, initially as a soldier of fortune and latterly, perhaps, as an administrator. He was already experienced militarily by 1385, when he was a mercenary captain in the decisive Portuguese victory over Castile at Aljubarrotta. He crusaded with Henry Earl of Derby (later Henry IV) in Lithuania in 1390. Norbury also became one of the many members of the great retinue of Henry's father John of Gaunt, Duke of Lancaster and married his daughter to the treasurer of the ducal household. This points to no more than respectable affluence, for Norbury was still merely a minor middle-aged Hertfordshire squire in 1399. He joined Henry IV before his formal accession and immediately afterwards the new king appointed him Lord Treasurer, keeper of the privy wardrobe, captain of Guines, and a permanent councillor. A wide variety of administrative tasks were crowded on him, so that he went on diplomatic missions, received custody of royal lands, was Henry's creditor and commissioner. He married again, this time to the sister and widow of the peerage, sired sons, and built up estates in the shires. This 'stern round of new duties' and opportunities lasted only a decade, for by 1409 Norbury had effectively retired from public life.

It must have been prior personal service that had earned Norbury the complete confidence of Henry IV by 1399. From then on he was constantly with the king, receiving his commands by word of mouth and undertaking the most secret business. King Henry even stood godfather to Norbury's son and gave him his name. Yet the man so honoured remained no more than an esquire. His case illustrates in an extreme form the medieval king's right to seek advice where he chose and to favour his own servants over his greatest subjects. An insecure king rated personal loyalty to himself higher than the mere allegiance due to him as king and Henry relied heavily for support and service on the great Lancastrian affinity built up by his father. 'Henry IV's position as king was strengthened by the local service of many who had served him and his family before 1399'. Norbury's transition from ducal to royal servant made his fortune and defeat for the House of Lancaster would have entailed his fall. Such considerations made him 'at every turn the king's man. Thus the king's cause was his own and the king's profit his own profit'. He was far from alone. No wonder Henry IV resisted so firmly all the Commons' efforts to cut the cost of his Lancastrian connection.

In 1399 Norbury was a widower with one married daughter and no obvious incentive to marry again. It was the rewards of royal service that gave him the means and desire to father a second family. Similarly it was royal service that made him a man of account at court. Hence, perhaps, the rapidly accumulated wealth that he was able to lend to the king and to invest conventionally in substantial country estates that made his heirs into a county family of standing. Hence also his rapid acceptance 'into the highly interdependent society of local landowners' in Hertfordshire. Norbury was a commisioner both there and in Kent and served his gentry neighbours as a valued trustee. Whilst royal patronage came too late to lift him into the peerage, it carried him far indeed from his unpromising origins and even from the position he had attained in 1399.

M. Barber, 'John Norbuty (c.1350–1414): An Esquire of Henry IV', *English Historical Review*, lxviii, 1953.

RALPH NEVILLE OF RABY, EARL OF WESTMORLAND (1354–1425), defeated the Percy rebels under Henry IV and made himself 'supreme everywhere north of the Humber'. A series of successful marriages had built up estates extensive enough for an earl before Ralph's succession as 6th Lord Neville of Raby in 1388. These included the four castles of Raby and Brancepeth in County Durham and Middleham and Sheriff Hutton in Yorkshire. By then he had already served in France in 1380, on diplomatic missions to and campaigns against the Scots, and had been warden of the West March in 1385. He deputised as constable of England both in 1391 and 1497. All this time he was a trusted retainer of John of

Gaunt, Duke of Lancaster, and in 1397 he married as second wife Gaunt's bastard daughter Joan Beaufort, who was legitimated with her brothers that same year. This marriage transformed Neville's career. He was created Earl of Westmorland and in 1399 he supported the usurpation of Gaunt's eldest son as Henry IV. Joan was in turn half-sister, aunt and great-aunt of the three Lancastrian kings and Ralph, who was generally called the king's brother under Henry IV, was councillor to all three. The connection bore imme-diate fruit in his grant for life of the marshalcy of England and honour of Richmond. His brother Thomas Lord Furnivall became treasurer of England in 1404–7. A string of other grants followed. More important, Westmorland established the Nevilles as natural wardens of the West March and secured a string of wardships that largely explains the remarkable series of marriages that he arranged for his twenty-two offspring — many of them while they were still children. The matches contracted for Ralph and Joan's sons made them Earl of Salisbury, Lords Fauconberg and Abergavenny res-pectively, while daughters became Duchess of Buckingham, Norfolk and York. By the 1450s the Nevilles were related to almost the whole peerage and one line was powerful enough to act as king-makers. That not all Nevilles co-operated was also largely West-morland's fault, for he transferred his principal lands from his eldest son's Westmorland line to Joan's eldest son Richard Neville, Earl of Salisbury. His heir was left with less land as earl than his father had inherited as a baron and a violent feud ensured. Ralph's new-found eminence was marked by the new college he established at Stain-drop, where he was buried.

John of Gaunt's vast estates had supported the most powerful retinue in medieval England. Henry IV and Henry V succeeded both to the Duchy of Lancaster and the Lancastrian retinue, which they assiduously cultivated as essential buttresses to their throne in spite of repeated criticisms of its cost by the House of Commons. The careers of John Norbury and Thomas Chaucer illustrate their reliance as kings on family retainers. Only during Henry VI's minority was the Lancastrian connection allowed to decay. No-where were the Duchy estates more concentrated and the retinue stronger than in northern England, where John of Gaunt had overshadowed both the Percies and Nevilles. It was this connection — which included Westmorland — that enabled Henry IV to take the crown and subsequently defeated the Percy rebellions in 1405 and 1408. Numerous and important though the Yorkshire followers of the Percies were, they were not so many or so powerful as the Lancastrian retainers in the same county. Westmorland was the Percies' principal rival in the north and his appointment as constable of Roxburgh in 1401 may have been a factor in the Percy rebellions. It was Cheshiremen whom Hotspur led to defeat at Shrewsbury in 1403, but subsequent risings were centred in Yorkshire. It was essential for Northumberland to eliminate Westmorland in 1405, but the latter evaded capture, organised resistance, quickly contrived the capture of Archbishop Scrope and the dispersal of his forces, and drove Northumberland northwards into exile. Similarly Westmorland held the north for Henry IV in 1408. His loyalty was crucial in the survival of the Lancastrian dynasty.

J. L. Kirby, *Reign of Henry IV*, 1970.
J. A. Tuck, *Richard II and the English Nobility*, 1973.

MASTER PETER PAYNE (c. 1380–1455) was the last of the academic Lollards at Oxford and was a vital link between the English Lollards and the Hussite heretics of Bohemia (modern Czechoslovakia). He was born at Hough-on-the-Hill near Grantham in Lincolnshire to a French father and English mother and was educated at Oxford University, where he became a master of arts but never apparently qualified in theology. In 1408 he was renting White Hall and from 1411 he was principal of St Edmund's Hall, one of the fifty private hostels for students at the university. Payne fled abroad in 1413 and spent the rest of his life in Bohemia.

Wyclif was an Oxford academic before he became a heretic and his early followers were concentrated in Oxford. Archbishop Courtenay tried to purge the university of heretics in the 1380s and many of Wyclif's theological tenets had been condemned. Such efforts, however, failed to eradicate heresy from Oxford. Wyclif's philosophical works, which contained the seeds of his theology, remained uncondemned; copies of his theological works survived; and there were still academic Lollards to prepare further Lollard tracts and to convert new generations of heretics. Peter Payne presumably encountered Wyclif's philosophy on the arts course before he was converted by the Lollard Peter Patrich. According to Thomas Netter, he then became the worst of the Oxford Wycliffites. Translation of the Bible from Latin into English, which Payne defended in 1405, was a respectable view not yet confined to heretics, but in 1406 it was apparently he who used the university seal to commend the life and teachings of Wyclif. This letter was carried by two Czech scholars, who had visited Oxford to secure Wycliffite literature, and marks Payne's first contacts with the Hussites. He failed to appear for a public disputation on Lollard theology with Thomas Netter of Walden and in 1410 was acquitted of heretical opinions about the sacrament of communion. By then, however, control of Oxford's heresy was moving from the university to Archbishop Arundel, who secured the condemnation of 267 errors of Wyclif and thoroughly purged the university. Wisely Payne declined to stand trial and fled abroad, reaching Bohemia by 1415.

Payne brought to Bohemia a thorough knowledge of Wyclif's writings, both philosophical and theological, and of later Lollard literature. He is supposed to have taken further books there, but there is no direct evidence of this. His distinctive handwriting shows that he annotated many surviving Wycliffite books in Bohemia and he has been credited with indexing some for easier use. Almost at once Jan Hus was burned by the Council of Constance, the Hussite revolution followed, and Payne was thrust into the theological and diplomatic limelight. In 1421 he was engaged in mediating between the moderate Ultraquists, who wanted communion in both kinds (bread *and* wine), and the more radical Taborites and was engaged in offering the crown of Bohemia to the King of Poland. He was one of the Hussite delegation to the Council of Basle in 1432, he became vicar-general of Archbishop John of Rokycana, and in 1451 he was sent on a mission to Constantinople. Even by Bohemian standards, however, he was a theological radical, who associated himself with the Taborites, and his safety was far from assured. He was a fugitive in 1437–9, when he was captured and could have been deported to certain death in England, but was instead ransomed by the Taborites. He shared in the decisive defeat of the Taborites in 1452, but was allowed to live at peace in Prague until his death three years later.

R.R. Betts, *Essays in Czech History*, 1969.

S. H. Thomson, 'A Note on Peter Payne and Wyclif', *Medievalia and Humanistica*, xvi, 1964.

HENRY V (1387–1422), Henry of Monmouth, who ascended the throne in 1413, was the eldest son of Henry IV and his first wife Mary Bohun (d. 1394). Few kings have been the subject of more extravagant praise: 'Take him all round and he was, I think, the greatest man that ever ruled England' (McFarlane); 'the simple record of Henry V's achievement is sufficient to establish him as a great king' (Harriss). Sadly, however, he died with all his work unfinished and is thus one of history's most intriguing might-have-beens. Could he — and he alone — have completed the conquest of France or was he saved from disappointing failure only by his premature death? Such questions cannot readily be settled and must always colour our interpretations of Henry V and his reign. Perhaps the closest parallel among English kings is Edward I up to 1290.

As befitted the son of Henry IV, Henry V was unusually well-educated. He learnt to read and write not just English and French but Latin too, and read from choice *inter alia* both law and theology. English, however, was his first tongue, preferred both for business and pleasure, and he is the first king to have left behind state papers in his own hand. Similarly his tastes in religion were traditional, and orthodox, but based on genuine knowledge and understanding. The monasteries he chose to patronise, the Bridgettines at Syon and Carthusians at Sheen, were not merely fashionable but particularly austere. As king, he not only burnt heretics — after allowing them ample time to recant — but publicly upbraided abbots and priors about abuses in their monasteries and urged them towards reform. Conventionally enough he hoped, after conquering France, to go on crusade and free the Holy Places: a heroic and perhaps impracticable venture that he was unable to attempt.

Crusading is merely one aspect of the way in which Henry came to exemplify chivalry. He was of course proficient in arms both as a warrior and a general from a young age. He was still in his teens when he took charge of operations against Owen Glendower and still in his early twenties when he brought his protracted struggle to a triumphant conclusion. There too he learnt personnel management and identified those lieutenants on whom he was to rely in France. He was economic in his use of force, first luring the French army to

*Henry V as Prince of Wales is presented by the poet
Thomas Hoccleve with his* Regement of Princes
(Artist: Thomas Hoccleve)

self-destruction at Agincourt (1415) and then steadily occupying Normandy. He was certainly fortunate to build on the divisions and uncertain leadership of the French, but what he achieved in seven years took thirty more to dismantle. His armies were particularly well-organised and disciplined, his noblemen were partners rewarded with the spoils of victory, and his troops became devoted to him. His enemies respected him as an honourable foe.

Henry also began his political career at an early age, seizing power in 1409 in something very like a coup d'état, ruling with little reference to the king in 1410–11, and threatening rebellion when dismissed. He was impatient of his father's weaknesses, anxious to start his own reign, and confident that he could improve on his father's rule. Recent assessments of his financial and other policies have been favourable, but at this time he lacked the authority of a king and contrived to alienate even close relatives. Once king, however, and the legitimate wielder of authority, Henry ruled with an imperious hand and kept a personal eye on details of government. His financial reforms, his promise of good justice, and his efficient management were all subordinated to his prime end — the conquest of France. Diplomacy was designed initially only to discredit his opponents by putting them in the wrong, so that he could adopt a high moral tone in pursuit of his just cause. Later his skilful drafting of the Treaty of Troyes (1420) enabled him to claim France as the heir of Charles VI and protector of French liberties rather than as a foreign conqueror! How realistic this was is another matter. The French were surely bound to resist his claims, however ostensibly legitimate. Similarly his judicial activity, if impressive, was symbolic rather than decisive, his arbitration of noble disputes proved impermanent and was not untinged by selfish motives. It is not enough to describe his more oppressive settlements as 'trifling' compared with those of other kings. Whether indeed 'A king who ruled his magnates as Henry V did had nothing to fear from them or anyone else', he appeared to his contemporaries the model of good government and justice. He was a king raised far above his subjects by regal dignity, prerogatives and simple force of character. Time again was too short for a more balanced assessment to be struck.

What is clear is that Henry V was a man of remarkable vigour and energy, who knew what he wanted to do, how to do it, and who achieved his aims with rapidity and efficiency. He was intensely businesslike, wasting no time on fancy speeches or phrases, proceeding directly to the point. Thus his letters are terse and autocratic, his parliaments brief and hardworking, his punishments inexorable, and his anger terrible to behold. Yet Henry was not without friends and devoted followers. He played musical instruments, frequently played games of chance, and was himself a trustworthy and loyal friend. Wild and dissolute as prince, he deliberately reformed his conduct on his accession, devoting himself to a life of simple self-denial in pursuit of his self-imposed mission. It was this dedication that impelled him to his triumphs. It was also the reason that he married late and that his heir was too young to build on his achievement. No wonder that 'His last hours were embittered by a sense of work unfinished, of the dangers of his infant heir, of the infidel in the Holy Places'. Nobody is immortal, not even Henry V and the mad Charles VI of France, who also died in 1422, and it was perhaps Henry V's greatest error to suppose he had plenty of time.

Henry V: The Practice of Kingship, G. L. Harriss, ed., 1985.
K. B. McFarlane, *Lancastrian Kings and Lollard Knights*, 1971.
E. Powell, *Kingship, Law and Society*, 1989.
T. B. Pugh, *Henry V and the Southampton Plot of 1415*, 1988.

RICHARD WHITTINGTON (d. 1423), was the outstanding London merchant of his day. He was the third son of Sir William Whittington of Pauntley (Gloucs.), an aristocrat of moderate means, and was apprenticed to a London mercer. He can never have been poor. Richard was already established in the city by 1379 and rapidly built up a successful business as a mercer dealing in bulk luxury fabrics, such as embroidered velvet, taffeta and cloth of gold. Particularly important customers were Richard II's favourite, the Earl of Oxford, the Earl of Derby (later Henry IV), and from 1389 Richard II himself, to whom Whittington supplied £3,474-worth in 1392–4, when he had five apprentices. This was the peak of Whittington's career as mercer: no new apprentices were enrolled after 1402, Henry IV proved a less valuable customer, and Whittington transferred his interest and capital to other areas. Trading with the crown drew him into the speculative field of royal finance, which increasingly absorbed his energy and capital. Repayment of debts by the crown was often by instalments from particular royal revenues (assignment), such as the customs, or by licences to ship wool free of custom, so Whittington was also involved in customs administration and the wool trade, in which he became a leading exporter. Finance and the wool trade were probably not particularly profitable, but they brought with them public office and status.

Whittington was three times master of the Mercer's Company, in 1395-6, 1401-2 and 1408-9, after which he abstained from company business. He was elected a common councillor of the City by 1384, sheriff in 1393, and alderman continuously from 1393. He was first appointed Lord Mayor in 1397 by Richard II, perhaps because the king wanted a compliant agent. It is striking that Whittington's nomination coincided with a large royal loan from the city and the repayment of royal debts due to Whittington himself. He was M.P. for the City in 1416. Two more terms as Lord Mayor in 1406 and 1419 singled Whittington out from his fellow aldermen, but he was never a knight, his knighthood — like his cat — being a later addition to his legend.

The legend of Whittington's stupendous wealth arises from the lavish charities established by his executors after his death and from his display of wealth during his life. In fact both employed the same resources. Whittington's lifetime loans ran into hundreds rather than thousands of pounds and his total capital was probably only about £6,000, an exceptional sum for a townsman, but not comparable with that of the nobility. The wealth of the aristocracy and most merchants was tied up in land or merchandise, but Whittington exceptionally kept his fortune in cash and thus had unusual liquid sums available for use at any time. The prior death of his wife, his lack of heirs, and the apparent absence of close friends or relatives meant that Whittington did not need to provide for any dependants in his will and could devote his whole fortune to the charities founded for the good of his soul. Such conduct conforms both to his cold egotism and to his conventionally orthodox piety. He left it to his executors to dispose of his wealth, often in ways of which he had no prior knowledge, and they did their work well: Whittington's almshouse, Whittington College, the foundation of the Guildhall Library, and the rebuilding of Newgate Prison earned him renown and indeed Whittington Hospital, Highgate remains today. £6,000 for charity made a big splash in fifteenth-century London. Hence Whittington's fame and hence the development of his legend.

C. M. Barron, 'Richard Whittington: The Man behind the Myth', *Studies in London History* ed. A. E. J. Hollaender and W. Kellaway, 1969.

THOMAS CHAUCER (c. 1367–1434) of Ewelme (Oxon.), esquire, was five times Speaker of the House of Commons — a record not to be emulated for three centuries. He was the son of Geoffrey Chaucer the poet. More important for his own career, he was son of Philippa Roet, sister of Katherine Swynford, mistress and ultimately third duchess of John of Gaunt, Duke of Lancaster, and mother of the Beauforts. Probably Gaunt took Thomas to Spain in 1386 and certainly it was at Bayonne in 1389 that he granted him an annuity. He also made him constable of Knaresborough castle. Only this connection accounts for Chaucer's marriage about 1395 to the wealthy heiress who financed his career. Yet more valuable patronage was offered after 1399 by Gaunt's sons Henry IV and Cardinal Beaufort and by his grandson Henry V. All helped their cousin Thomas on his way.

The Lancastrian kings were usurpers and consequently insecure on their throne. They therefore maintained Gaunt's vast retinue for their own protection. As 'life-long servant of the house of Lancaster' Chaucer was guaranteed continued employment, but as kinsman, he was assured also of advancement. This factor alone sufficiently explains his earliest appointments to estate offices in 1399 and even as Chief Butler of England (1402). What followed depended not on who Chaucer was but what he did — on the services he performed and the confidence he inspired. He worked mainly in England, as a local administrator and parliamentarian, but he also served abroad (1402), against Glendower (1403), as diplomat (1413), soldier (1413, 1417–20), and eventually councillor (1424). To be Speaker of the Commons was no sinecure, not a reward but a responsibility, a duty of delicacy indeed. That Chaucer discharged it five times demonstrates an unusual capacity to satisfy both king and Commons. Just as sensitive surely was the dispute between Henry V and Bishop Beaufort in 1420, which he handled to the satisfaction of both cousins. He was no political neuter, however, identifying himself firmly with his Beaufort cousins under Henry IV and again against the Duke of Gloucester in the 1420s, yet he was 'circumspect, politic and *affairé*, well-versed in all his branches of administration and diplomacy, a practised chairman and envoy, influential and respected'.

Thomas declined knighthood and remained an esquire. He inherited little from his parents, but his marriage brought estates throughout southern England, which he augmented by purchase and less permanent means. His principal seat was at Ewelme in Oxfordshire in the middle Thames Valley, which he dominated from Wallingford castle and as steward of Wallingford, St Valery, and the Chiltern Hundreds from 1399. He strengthened his position with wardships of leading local families and offices and leases from the king, queen and others. Local government office duly followed: he was sheriff of Oxfordshire and Berkshire in 1400 and 1403, escheator in 1406, J.P. 1403–34, and M.P. for Oxfordshire fourteen times in all. He mattered outside Oxfordshire too, notably in the south-west, thanks to appointments by cardinal and king, and in Hampshire where he had lands, where he was royal forester of Woolmer and Alice Holt (1413) and sheriff, and where he may sometimes have resided. By his death 'there can have been few knights in England richer than he'. Hence the marriages of his daughter Alice successively to a baron and then to two earls, the great Thomas Montagu, Earl of Salisbury (d. 1428) and William de la Pole, Earl of Suffolk (d. 1450), who made her a duchess and turned her Ewelme into his principal seat. It was all a far cry from Alice Chaucer's grandfather the poet and her great-grandfather the London vintner.

K. B. McFarlane, *England in the Fifteenth Century*, 1981.
J. S. Roskell, *Parliament and Politics in Later Medieval England*, iii, 1983.

THOMAS HOCCLEVE (c. 1370–1430) was a poet who could not live from his pen alone. Like Chaucer, he wrote poetry as a pastime, pursued in spare time from his employment. An autobiographical element in his verse enables us to glimpse the lifestyle of the minor medieval civil servant. Perhaps from Hockliffe in Bedfordshire, Hoccleve must have attended grammar school. He was probably about eighteen when he entered the privy seal office. By 1395 he was a clerk, one of the office elite, and remained one for thirty-five years. Promotion was rare in the royal administration. But the crown was an indulgent employer, tolerating ill-health, lateness to work, afternoons off, and drunkenness. In his *Bad Rule of Thomas Hoccleve* the poet boasted of being the worst offender on all counts. That Hoccleve was proficient at his job is suggested by the formulary of precedents he wrote for his office. Like other bachelor clerks, he lived at the town house of the Bishop of Lichfield until his marriage after 1412, a love match contracted after he had given up hope of a snug rectory somewhere. He was not badly off. Besides fees and odd rewards, he received £10 a year from 1395, more than most parsons, and £23.66 a year after 20 years. Although irregularly paid, he supported a life of extravagance, frequenting pubs and snack bars — 'Excess at table has laid his knife in me' — boating in office hours, and entertaining harlots:

Had I a kiss I was content full well
Better than I would have been with the deed.

Yet lewd talk made him blush and he was too timorous to risk involvement in brawls. By generous tipping he persuaded boatmen and other menials to treat him as a gentleman. Hence the debts he later regretted so much, when he had reformed, that forced him to curtail his tipping and to live with his wife in straitened circumstances. It was self-indulgence in his youth as much as the boring and exhausting drudgery of the office that sped the physical decline of his later years. Bending and concentration strained back, stomach and eyes, for he was too vain to wear glasses. He had a nervous breakdown before 1422, from which he recovered physically, but without his friends. Only in 1424 was he pensioned off with a corrody at Southwick Priory in Hampshire, where presumably he died about 1430. There must have been many such self-important, and slightly inadequate, clerks in royal service.

But Hoccleve was also a poet, whose verses brought him into contact with dukes and countesses, his employers and those with influence on them. What an opportunity! Thus his poems frequently sought prompt payment of his annuities. He wrote much less than Lydgate but infinitely more readably. He eschewed flowery elaboration, but was better able to arrest attention with the striking phrase. His admiration for Chaucer did not lead him into plagiarism. But it is the personal and autobiographical element that most distinguishes his work. He wrote with immediacy, colloquialism, and a wry sense of humour. Over twenty years his moods ranged from earthy coarseness to sensitive piety and compassion, as when exploring the humanity of the Virgin and lamenting the misfortunes of old soldiers. He was interested in topical issues — such as Lollardy, of which he strongly disapproved — and his verse is indeed 'a store-house of information on fifteenth-century society and politics'. His principal work, the highly popular *Regement of Princes*, is a manual of instruction for a prince or mirror for princes, as they were called. There were many continental examples of this genre, some of them used by Hoccleve, but this is the first in English and the precursor of many others. It is one of many firsts in English that Hoccleve registered.

H. S. Bennett, *Six Medieval Men and Women*, 1955.
J. Mitchell, *Thomas Hoccleve: A Study in Early Fifteenth Century Poetic*, 1968.
B. O'Donaghue, *Thomas Hoccleve: Selected Poems*, 1982.

SIR JOHN OLDCASTLE, Lord Cobham (c. 1378–1417), led the first Lollard revolt in 1414 and was burnt as a heretic in 1417. Yet his origins were quite conventional. The Oldcastles were substantial gentry in Herefordshire and John was not the first to be a knight, sheriff or M.P. That marcher gentry were remote from central government is shown by his presence in the Scottish campaign in 1400 in the retinue of a minor nobleman Lord Grey of Codnor. The Welsh revolt of Owen Glendower made such men strategically important. Oldcastle knew Wales: his seat at Almeley was on the western edge of Herefordshire, his wife had a Welsh name, and so he could probably speak Welsh too. A succession of campaigns, cus-todies of castles, and commissions brought Oldcastle the favour and friendship of the future Henry V and a European chivalric reputa-tion. Hence his part in jousts at Lille in 1410 and in the Burgundian victory at St Cloud next year. Hence also his choice as fourth husband of the great heiress Joan de la Pole and his acquisition in her right of the title Lord Cobham and extensive Kentish properties including the new castle of Cooling. No longer an obscure Here-fordshire squire, Oldcastle was an important magnate. A dazzling military career with Henry V beckoned.

Presumably already a Lollard in Herefordshire, Oldcastle was certainly one in Kent. He was literate and acquainted with Lollard doctrine, which he could expound at length; he owned and read Lollard tracts; he harboured Lollards in his household; and he condoned attempts to convert his tenants and neighbours. He was thus a late example of the Lollard knights so important under Richard II and it was apparently 'His social position rather than any peculiar fitness (that) made him the leader of the Lollard party'. He had apparently attained this position by 1409, when he was corresponding with the Hussites in Bohemia. When his Lollard connections came out in 1413 and the clergy wished to try him, Henry V offered him time to reconsider. Oldcastle, however, was adamant and scorned to recant. Although given every chance to withdraw, Archbishop Arundel found in Oldcastle a Lollard of principle and foolhardy courage, whose temper several times betrayed him into heretical outbursts. Repeatedly pressed, he denounced the pope as the head of antichrist, the archbishops and bishops as his limbs, and the friars as his tail. Even after his condemnation, Henry V postponed his execution, hoping for recantation. Instead Oldcastle was rescued from the Tower, hid in London, and organised his rebellion. This was designed to capture the king. What else was intended is unknown: the authorities thought that it aimed to kill the royal family, the nobility, and clergy, and divide England into smaller principalities. The plot was exposed, the few hundred insurgents were easily defeated, but Oldcastle himself escaped. His last years were spent in hiding: in the West Midlands in 1415 and in 1417 near Welshpool. There he was overpowered and thence he was taken to London for execution.

That Lollardy was a sect with an organisation and structure is suggested by what we know of Lollard texts. These were systematically researched and written, apparently at Oxford, mass-produced and distributed to Lollard congregations, all of which thus shared the same beliefs. By purging Oxford, Archbishop Arundel destroyed academic Lollardy and ended Lollard book production. Oldcastle apparently used the Lollard communication network to enlist support in many cells and exposed them to persecution. He revealed them to be few and humble, nothing for the king to fear, and by identifying them with treason he discredited them with the propertied elite. After Oldcastle and his friends, no noblemen nor gentry are known to have been Lollards. The movement degenerated into isolated cells, secret and humble, often out of touch with one another. Its organisation was destroyed.

K. B. McFarlane, *John Wycliffe and the Beginnings of English Nonconformity*, 1952.

W. T. Waugh, 'Sir John Oldcastle', *English Historical Review* lv, 1940.

THOMAS LANGLEY (c. 1360–1437), Bishop of Durham from 1406, was propelled to high ministerial office by the Lancastrian usurpation of the crown. Apparently a younger son of a cadet branch of a gentry family from Langley near Manchester, he proceeded via the service of the Radcliffes of Radcliffe into that of John of Gaunt and the Lancastrian kings. 'To no one of these Duchy servants was the triumph of Henry of Derby to bring greater success than to Thomas Langley'. Appointed his secretary, he became keeper of the privy seal — third of the great ministers of state — in 1401, and chancellor of England and principal royal diplomat in 1405–7. He had accompanied Henry to Scotland in 1400 and to the battle of Shrewsbury in 1403. He was again the leading diplomat in 1412–17, served again as chancellor in 1417–24 — an exceptionally long term distinguished by the marked expansion of the court of chancery — and was a royal councillor until finally allowed to retire in 1433. Diplomatic duties on the northern border continued until death. Essentially an administrator devoted to the house of Lancaster, he avoided taking sides in the crises of 1410–12 and 1426 and was rightly trusted by each master in turn. He was executor of John of Gaunt, Henry IV and Henry V, and continued settling their affairs until at least 1436, 1429, and 1435 respectively.

Langley was bearded and had an aristocratic love of the chase and splendour rather than the noble connections and university education increasingly expected of a bishop. Obviously he was not illiterate. He acquired a collection of books useful to his position and patronised schooling for others. His first rectory at Radcliffe in 1385 was followed by two prebends, thanks to John of Gaunt, but it was only after 1399 that his ecclesiastical career really took off. Chief among his new positions were the archdeaconry of Norfolk and deanery of York, which he seems, unusually, to have treated as more than sinecures, but he had to wait for his bishopric. Pope

Innocent VII thwarted him at London and York before he secured the important and valuable bishopric of Durham in 1406. This was obviously a reward for administrative services, but he took his responsibilities more seriously than most, for he went to Durham twice a year even when chancellor, spent long periods there at other times, and showed close and continual interest in its management. He overhauled the administration of his see, enjoyed good relations with his cathedral priory and contributed generously to its building operations. In his last years he rebuffed Sir William Eure's attack on his regalian rights as count palatine of Durham. 'The most outstanding feature of Langley's episcopate was his work to reform the secular foundations'. This was designed to adapt outdated institutions for modern needs. Earlier he had helped Lord Delawarr to found Manchester College and Henry V to found Syon Abbey and he himself established chantries and schools both at Durham and Middleton (Lancs.). He even shone on the international ecclesiastical scene, for he attended the council of Pisa in 1409 as representative of the northern province and attorney for 14 bishops and 103 abbots and priors, and he was offered the cardinalate in 1411, which Henry IV declined on his behalf. He was a civil servant who proved a thoroughly worthy bishop.

Langley was conscientious and meticulous over every detail. He possessed great physical and mental energy and enjoyed good health until the very end. He was trustworthy and thus a frequent choice as executor. Rigid on principles and harsh with the unrepentant, he possessed the flexibility necessary for a diplomat and the patience required of a pastor. He remained loyal to Lancashire, liked to have Lancashiremen about him, and genuinely cared what happened to old friends and to members of his household on his death. In a lifetime in politics he made no personal enemies.

R.L. Storey, *Thomas Langley and the Bishopric of Durham 1406–1437*, 1961.

WILLIAM BRUGES (c. 1370–1450), herald, was the first Garter King at Arms. During the age of chivalry it was the heralds who supervised the law of arms, courts of chivalry, and tournaments, and it was they who were the collective memory of coats of arms and ceremonial. They knew how to stage knightings, creations of peers

William Bruges, first Garter King of Arms,
kneels before St George
(Artist: William Bruges)

and coronations, they administered truces, and hence they were useful for negotiating ransoms and in diplomacy generally. There were three grades: pursuivants, heralds, and kings of arms. Only at the very end of the middle ages, as their original function disappeared, did they acquire more formal organisation. The English heralds were incorporated as the College of Arms by Richard III and only in the 16th century did they become primarily concerned with granting new coats of arms, their main function today. They represented one of the class of professional experts that was emerging at the end of the middle ages.

William Bruges was born into this profession. His father Richard Bruges (d. c. 1415) had been first Lancaster herald and then king of arms to John of Gaunt, Duke of Lancaster (d. 1399) and Henry IV. He was the senior herald and died in very comfortable circumstances. His son William may have been Chester pursuivant as early as 1391. He was certainly Chester herald from 1398, when Chester became a principality, and from 1399 to Henry Prince of Wales as Earl of Chester, the future Henry V. Understandably, perhaps, it was Bruges that Henry V appointed Guyenne King of Arms at his coronation and he who in 1415 was chosen as the first Garter King of Arms, attached to the most noble order of the Garter itself. Bruges petitioned to have his rights defined, unsuccessfully, but he did secure general recognition as sovereign of all arms in England. He officiated at the coronation of Queen Katherine and Henry V's funeral. He made the first known grant of arms to the Drapers Company of London in 1439, basing his grants on his own personal recollection that no similar arms existed. His roll of arms was 'the earliest known armorial of an order of the chivalry and the prototype of the whole series of armorials with men of arms'. He served on innumerable diplomatic missions, which carried him all over Europe, the last in 1449. Twice he took the insignia of the Garter to new Iberian knights. Many times he officiated at knightings, creations and tournaments. It was a full and busy, if poorly documented, career.

Bruges was paid nothing as Garter until 1423, when the knights agreed a tariff of payments to him temporarily pending proper provision, which never happened. This should have brought him £35 a year. Presumably it was his robes and diet from the crown and his fees, uncertain but substantial, that enabled him to serve unpaid for so long. Probably he did not profit from his expenses. In 1429 he was awarded an annuity of £20 and in 1439 £40. Bruges owned a fine house at Kentish Town with 130-yards frontage on the Great North Road. It contained a well-equipped chapel and was where he entertained the Emperor Sigismund in 1416. He possessed another house in the Fleet Street area. A further six houses in Stamford

(Lincs.) were bequeathed to St George's Church there, together with the elaborate furniture from his household chapel. It was also there that he paid for windows depicting knights of the Garter. He seems to have possessed no more lands. His bequests and an opulent lifestyle impressed contemporaries, but it is comparable with that of many successful townsmen rather than the nobility or gentry. Heralds were a professional group who were allowed to marry. Bruges made his wife Agnes his principal executor and had three daughters, one of whom married a future Garter king at arms.

H. S. London, *The Life of William Bruges the First Garter King of Arms*, Harleian Society, 1970.

WILLIAM SOPER (d. 1459), keeper of the king's ships, was already an established merchant of Southampton, when first recorded in 1410. What he was trading in then is not known, but later he had commercial contacts in Spain and dealt in wool with Italy, which he may even have visited. He owned at least one ship and was engaged in piracy or privateering. From the mid 1420s his trading activities declined, perhaps because he became a financier: certainly he employed sophisticated Italian banking techniques and mixed freely with the Italians. He also dealt extensively in property, driving a particularly shrewd bargain with the Southampton Franciscans, and improved his sites by building. He even leased the Southampton Watergate. However he made his money, he certainly became rich, acquiring lands in and around Southampton and leaving hundreds of pounds in cash in his will. Perhaps second in wealth among citizens of Southampton, he became a member of the ruling oligarchy, becoming steward (1410), twelve times M.P. from 1413–49, and mayor in 1416 and 1424.

In 1413 Soper was appointed collector of both the customs and subsidy and held office for thirty years. From 1418 he was surveyor, from 1420 keeper, and from 1441 controller of the king's ships. Soper's keepership coincided with Henry V's massive naval build up and Henry VI's shameful neglect. As the chief royal agent in Southampton, Soper served on commissions of all kinds and was appointed a verderer of the New Forest. Already old and unable to ride, Soper relinquished his offices in the 1440s and spent his last years in comfortable retirement.

If the extent of Soper's royal service was unusual, his financial expertise and head for business were not, yet he was no merchant stereotype. He may have married Isabel for convenience, but before her death he was lover of her kinswoman Joan Chamberlain, whom he married on Isabel's death. Although their marriage was technically null, their adultery and its invalidity were not generally known. Soper's conscience, however, was troubled and he went to the considerable trouble and expense of securing papal absolution and a dispensation to remain married. Not surprisingly he provided carefully for his widow. He also sought the salvation of his soul. Before his death he built a marble tomb in Southampton Friary, re-roofed and adorned the friary, and endowed a chantry and obit there. While his benefactions to the poor were unusually extensive, he was quite conventional in his desire that his obit should be marked by sounding Southampton's assembly bell and by the attendance of friars, mayor and other city fathers. His concern for status in death is paralleled by his lifestyle. 'Soper certainly seems to have used his wealth in what might be called the classic English manner — to build up his social position by obtaining the status that attached at the time to the ownership of land'.

He resided from choice at his country house at Newton Bery, where he maintained a substantial staff, a private chapel and chaplain, and horses and hounds for hunting in the New Forest. It was there in 1430 that he entertained the captain of the Florentine galleys so courteously that he did not wish to leave and there apparently that Soper retired, dying an esquire: a remarkable distinction at a time when it was normally businessmen's sons, not businessmen themselves, who achieved acceptance as gentlemen.

C. Platt, *Medieval Southampton: The Port and the Trading Community AD 1000–1600*, 1973.
S. Rose (ed.), *The Navy of the Lancastrian Kings: Accounts and Inventories of William Soper, Keeper of the King's Ships 1422–27*, Navy Records Society 123, 1972.

HENRY VI (1421–71), born at Windsor, King of England (1422–61, 1470–71), was the only son of Henry V and Katherine of France. He was still in his cradle when he became king both of England, by inheritance, and France, under the Treaty of Troyes

(1420), thus exemplifying the Dual Monarchy for which his father had yearned. Both kingdoms were lost while he was still a young man. Defeated abroad, the English lost not just the conquests of Henry V, but Gascony too. At home faction and corruption were unrestrained, effective government and justice were suspended, and the personal and political differences of the great were conducted by assassination and private warfare. His reign 'has strong claims to be considered the most calamitous in the whole of English history'. For all this King Henry VI himself bears a heavy responsibility. Great though the difficulties were and dubious the integrity of his agents, it was the king who provided not firm leadership but well-meaning incompetence and then, following his breakdown, who almost ceased to interest himself in government. Ultimately he became a cipher, a mere symbol of allegiance, who ensured his custodians — whoever they were — the acquiescence of the majority and the moral authority to rule. This pathetic puppet, however, was potent enough as a symbol to prolong the conflict for ten hopeless years after he had lost his throne in 1461, not — of course — for the benefit of either Henry or his subjects.

The first stage of his reign was his long minority. The disaster of Henry V's death was compounded by the existence of his son, an infant whose right to succeed unquestionably took precedence over the able adult male — the Duke of Bedford — that the critical situation so obviously demanded. For fifteen years government in both his kingdoms was conducted in his name without his active participation except in the most ceremonial and symbolic guise, such as his adminstration of the Maundy money and knighting of others at the age of six and his two coronations at Westminster (1429) and Paris (1431). Neither in England nor France could there be any permanent decisions, concessions or diminution of royal rights, which had to be maintained undiminished for the day when Henry himself could decide. Both the English and French governments — separate and independent — triumphantly met this challenge and indeed provided the period of most effective government in the whole reign. England was ruled collectively by a council made up mainly of loyal and experienced servants of earlier Lancastrian kings, such as Archbishop Kemp, Bishop Langley, Lords Hungerford and Cromwell, and Thomas Chaucer. As chairman, without any independent power or initiative, was the king's younger uncle

The young Henry VI borne by his guardian Richard Beauchamp,
Earl of Warwick (left)
(Artist: John Rous)

Humphrey, Duke of Gloucester, initially as Protector (1422–5, 1427–9), then as King's Lieutenant (1429–31), and Chief Councillor (1432–3, 1434–7). Together they kept the system going, keeping business ticking over and tackling problems as they arose, but they were no substitute for an adult king. Solutions were temporary, pending royal confirmation, and tensions among themselves, particularly between Gloucester and Cardinal Beaufort, could be solved only by the intervention as *deus ex machina* of Henry's eldest uncle Bedford, who took precedence over Gloucester, whose power superseded Gloucester's, and who alone could impose a decision as an adult king should have done. In France, on the other hand, Bedford had a much freer hand as Regent, extending Henry V's conquests, making alliances, and providing effective rule by Frenchmen in the spirit of Henry's status as rightful King of France rather than alien conqueror. More might have been achieved had there been a king to determine overall priorities and to harness English resources to further conquests, for substantial resources were made available only after the first major English setbacks at the hands of Joan of Arc from 1429. As stabilised, however, the English held more in 1437 than in 1422 and such obvious problems as overall command, growing financial stringency, and diplomatic isolation were perfectly soluble for an adult monarch able to take a determined lead in the war. Henry VI, lamentably, was not such a man.

Henry was given as normal an upbringing as any infant king could receive. Other noble boys were brought up with him. He was trained in arms, horsemanship and hunting, dressed and ate well, and was introduced to conventional aristocratic values. He learnt to speak French fluently and to read Latin. He was punished when he skimped his lessons. By 1432 he expected the respect and authority due to a king and had to be persuaded not to begin his personal rule in 1434, when still only twelve. Physically fit and intellectually able, he wanted to take up the reins, attended council from 1435, and ended his majority in 1437. Eton College was a thank-offering for a potentially glorious reign.

In retrospect his upbringing must have been somehow deficient. He did not lack intelligence or application but a proper sense of priorities. All kings were expected to practise virtue, avoid sin and be pious, as Henry V indeed was, but Henry VI was exceptional in putting piety first. He was obsessively religious. Once king, he never travelled on Sundays and feast days, attending instead all the canonical hours (church services) and even acting as server. He studied his Bible and discussed theology. He so revered the Blessed Virgin and Christ's Real Presence in the sacrament that he even had visions. Not content with his own soul, he sought to reform those about him, denouncing irreverence in church, swearing, naked bathing, immodest female fashions, and sexual immorality. Virtue was urged on children and bishops alike. He was 'a diligent exhorter and adviser, counselling the young, and admonishing men of mature years'. Inevitably this spilled over into government.

It was not that in these early years Henry VI ignored his function as king. He was enthusiastic, active, and even dictatorial about what interested him and rode roughshod over opposition. 'Henry VI, in fact, allowed no-one, not even Suffolk, any real initiative'. But if 'to fight and to judge are the office of a king', Henry did not see himself that way. He never fought in France, gave inconsistent support to his agents, let judicial abuse flourish, and left the great uncurbed. What concerned him most were his two foundations of Eton College and King's College, Cambridge, into which he poured time and money, personally planning the buildings, drawing up statutes, selecting staff and pupils, lobbying for privileges, and diverting money away from more urgent purposes. Compassion for war victims perhaps explains his interest in peace, which he explained in detail to Gloucester in 1440. When crossed, he could be unnecessarily vindictive. Even more ominous, twice he pardoned those condemned on the scaffold in gratitude for the grant of papal privileges. The Christian virtues of morality prompted unwise compassion and generosity — the pardoning of criminals and alienation of his patrimony.

Henry could not be crossed on matters that concerned him. No aspiring minister or favourite, even in 1460, could oppose his peace policy or his religious foundations. But he could be managed. To Bishop Waynflete must be attributed the modification of his plans for Eton and King's along the lines of Wykeham's Winchester and New Colleges. The suggestion that Gloucester was a traitor, certainly untrue, prompted the duke's fall. Suitors could persuade the king to give them titles, land, offices, leases, money, pardons etc without consideration of merit, previous grants, or repercussions. Sob stories and the desire to please played a part, but so too did straightforward indifference: importunate suitors distracted Henry from his prayers. About 1444 the council sought unsuccessfully to halt the flow but it was brought under control instead by limiting access to his person. This was not public spirited, for those about him confined his favour to themselves, but it was done with the consent of the king, who frankly preferred the company of those he liked. A monopoly of patronage and justice enabled Suffolk and his friends to dominate the localities. Their enemies could have no justice or remedy from the king. Therefore they impeached the duke or rebelled with Cade. Cocooned from reality, Henry did not understand the causes or strength of the opposition. He equated the court with power and did not understand the physical force available to the great in the localities. Hence his admission of responsibility for most of the errors in foreign policy, his bold defence of Suffolk, his aggression towards Cade, his obstruction of resumption, and his return to factional rule.

As king, Henry could not be criticised. Attacks were levelled in 1450 against his evil councillors, but he soon found others, led by the Duke of Somerset. The Duke of York's coup of 1452 failed. He was forced to submit and Henry punished his supporters. The succession problem that had existed since at least 1447 — was Henry's heir York or Exeter or Somerset? — was solved by the birth of Henry's son Prince Edward in 1453. Henry had never been stronger politically. At this point, unfortunately, heredity asserted itself: Henry's grandfather Charles VI had been mad and the king had his first breakdown. Henry may have had another, less severe, attack in 1455. He was physically and mentally prostrate, unable to understand anything let alone rule, and he emerged from it a changed man, whose religious obsession was now overpowering. Henceforth he was a recluse. He dressed simply, spent much time in prayer, ate in silence, and said little at other times. He said nothing to York's proposals either in 1455 or 1460, when the duke proposed his deposition. He could take his place in decisions, but was no longer interested in making them himself, even delegating responsibility for his colleges to others. Henceforth he was the tool of other people. Initially Henry's breakdown gave a chance to York, who became Protector. His protectorate and his victory at St Albans in 1455, when the king's favourites were killed, enabled him to build a party. Most noblemen, in 1456 and 1460, gave priority to their allegiance to the king. A third failed coup by York in 1459, which resulted in his condemnation for treason, was followed by his invasion in 1460, when he again eliminated his foes, and laid claim to the crown. The compromise agreed by York and the uncommitted lords, that Henry should remain king but York should succeed, was rejected by Queen Margaret's supporters. The first war of 1460-1 was fought between York's faction and a much larger number of Lancastrian peers. It was the Yorkists who won and Henry VI lost his throne.

That was not quite the end of the story, for resistance continued. Henry himself was captured in 1465, but his life was spared because his son was still at large. Henry's Readeption or second reign in 1470-1 was the result of an alliance between rebel Yorkists led by Warwick the Kingmaker and Henry's former supporters. Henry was merely a puppet, whose decisions were confined to minor and ecclesiastical matters. Had he been more effective, he might perhaps have brought the unity of purpose to his mutually suspicious supporters that could have kept him on his throne. Instead, Edward IV defeated rebel Yorkists and Lancastrians in turn and then, with Prince Edward safely dead, arranged Henry's murder. Even the symbol had gone.

R. A. Griffiths, *The Reign of King Henry VI 1422-61*, 1981.

R. Lovatt, 'John Blacman: biographer of Henry VI', *The Writing of History in the Middle Ages*, R. H. C. Davis and J. M. Wallace-Hadrill, ed., 1981.

R. Lovatt, 'A Collector of Apocryphal Anecdotes: John Blacman Revisited', *Property and Politics: Essays in Later Medieval English History*, A. J. Pollard, ed., 1984.

B. P. Wolffe, *Henry VI*, 1981.

THOMAS NETTER (c. 1370-1430) of Walden was 'perhaps the most distinguished friar of any order between the age of Ockham and the Dissolution'. He was born to humble parents at Saffron Walden in Essex, probably about 1370, and became a Carmelite friar. Of the four principal orders of friars in England — Franciscans (Friars Minor), Dominicans (Friars Preachers), Augustinians and Carmelites — the Carmelites were the smallest. He was in the London convent in 1396 when ordained priest. It was probably before this that he met the Franciscan William Woodford, who contributed to his theological orthodoxy, and subsequently he attended Oxford University, becoming a bachelor of theology (1409) and a doctor somewhat later. He was a theologian of great learning and skill. He attended the General Councils of the Church at

Pisa (1409) and Constance (1414–17). From 1414 until death he was provincial of the English Carmelites, exercising office efficiently and justly and devoting himself to the improvement of discipline and observance. He preached at the funerals of both Henry IV and Henry V and was confessor of Henry V from 1414 and Henry VI, accompanying him to France in 1430 and dying there.

The friars, especially the Carmelites and above all the East Anglian Carmelites, were the principal bulwarks of orthodoxy against heresy in late medieval England. Among them Netter stands out 'as the theologian who gave a full and final answer to the Lollards'. This was in his *Doctrine of the Catholic Faith against the Lollards and the Hussites (Doctrinale)*, the Hussites being heretics from Bohemia (now Czechoslovakia) who were strongly influenced by Wyclif's teachings. Netter was too young to have been taught by Wyclif himself, but he attended Oxford when the heretic's works were still in current use and some of his followers were still teaching. When he first encountered Wyclif's logic and speculative philosophy, he was most impressed:

> Whilst at first I thought of this in silence, afterwards in my early years I lent credulous ears to his logical teaching. I was quite astounded by his sweeping assertions, by the authorities cited and by the vehemence of his reasoning.

Moving on to the study of theology, Netter found Wyclif to be 'an open counterfeiter of Scripture' and devoted himself to the destruction of Lollardy. Whilst still at Oxford he discomfited the future Hussite Peter Payne, and he participated in a succession of trials of leading Lollards. As preacher at St Paul's Cross and as royal confessor he urged stronger measures against Lollardy and in 1419 went on a mission to Eastern Europe to drum up Polish and Lithuanian support for the Emperor Sigismund's crusade against the Hussites. It was King Henry V who encouraged him to write his *Doctrinale*, which he presented in 1426–7 to Pope Martin V, who received it with enthusiasm.

Netter brought an excellent knowledge of Lollardy to his task. He read most if not all of Wyclif's philosophical and theological works, he was familiar with much of the literature compiled by his followers including items since lost, and he had participated in many heresy trials and had access to records of them. In Book I of his

Doctrinale he laid bare the roots of Wyclif's philosophy as preliminary to its comprehensive refutation and in Books II and III
firmly rebutted Wyclif's deductions from his philosophy, reasserting
a whole range of traditional Catholic doctrines in the process. He
wrote clearly and directly, eschewing scholastic jargon, and his book
may well have discouraged new recruits to Lollardy among academics. No Lollard replied: perhaps no reply was possible.

J. Robson, *John Wyclif and the Oxford Schools*, 1966.

JOHN LYDGATE (c. 1370–1449), monk of Bury St Edmunds,
was one of the most prolific of poets. He came from Lidgate near
Bury in Suffolk, became a monk of the great Benedictine abbey there
by 1382, and attended Gloucester College, Oxford about 1406–8.
He read widely but less than has often been supposed: he was no
humanist and knew the classics mainly through French translations.
Contemporary appreciation of his poetry gave him a highly unusual
career for a monk, for without apparently holding high office at
Bury he spent much of his lifetime outside the cloister. He lived some
years in London and in Lancastrian France. He was absentee prior of
the alien priory of Hatfield Broadoak in Essex from 1423 until
1434, when he returned to Bury for his old age. His principal works
were his *Troy Book*, commissioned by Prince Henry in 1412 and
completed in 1420, his *Siege of Thebes* (1421–2), and the *Fall of
Princes* (1431–8) commissioned by Humphrey Duke of Gloucester.
There is also a mass of poetry relating to particular occasions — for
Lydgate acted like a poet laureate — and much love and religious
poetry, most of it commissioned by his patrons. These included King
Henry VI, Queen Katherine, the Earls of Salisbury and Warwick, the
Countesses of March, Shrewsbury, Stafford, Suffolk and Warwick,
St Paul's cathedral chapter and several London companies. He was
unrivalled in his own day and was considered the equal of Chaucer, a
judgement no longer accepted.

Lydgate may have known Chaucer, certainly admired him, and
constantly borrowed from him. 'From him he took his style, his
verse-forms, his metre, and many of the genres in which he wrote'.
He imitated and tried to improve on the master, tackling the same
topics and seeking to surpass him. By our standards he failed, but our
standards are not Lydgate's. Lydgate and his age did not admire

Chaucer's originality, freshness and realism as much as we do, but commended instead his moralisation and rhetoric. Lydgate constantly moralised and amplified, writing at inordinate length in ornate language. He was the equivalent in verse of the prose-writer Abbot Whetehamstede. He was the master of saying nothing at excessive length and showed no fear of repetition when drawing a moral. A 'profusion of surface decoration' takes priority over any meaning. Plot, realism, narrative flow, and drama are lost in a mass of words. Thus his *Troy Book* is 'homily first, an encyclopaedia second, and an epic nowhere'. It makes Lydgate's poetry too longwinded, dull and tedious for us, but it was what contemporaries admired.

No doubt the appalling amount he was required to write largely explains occasional technical deficiencies, such as loose syntax and lame metre. Yet most of his work is competent — he had remarkable facility in versifying — and little falls disastrously short. Moreover his best work contains good lines, near-flawless craftsmanship, high rhetorical flights, genuine eloquence and feeling. He was never an innovator. 'He can never, even at his best, rivet us with the uniqueness of his language or enrich our awareness of words'. His verbosity, his inability to select, and his tendency to make everything seem the same are the marks of a profoundly unoriginal mind. They indicate in him:

> total acquiescence in the conventions and demands of his age. Like any competent professional, he did what was asked of him, and working within an established literary tradition he had neither the desire, nor the incentive, nor the creative power to make things new.

This makes him typical of his age, not untypical. It is no disgrace to fall short of the standards of Chaucer, particularly when the character of Chaucer's genius was still imperfectly understood.

D. Pearsall, *John Lydgate*, 1970.

MARGERY KEMPE (c. 1373–c. 1438) is the subject of 'the first biography in English'. This is because she was a highly exceptional woman, but her early life was commonplace enough. Her father, John Brunham, may have been the richest man in Kings Lynn, where he was mayor five times, alderman and M.P. He married her about 1394 to John Kempe, another member of the oligarchy, who was chamberlain of the town, but never achieved the same eminence. Margery criticised him for this and had to pay his debts, but his difficult wife may be behind his failure. Margery bore her husband several children. Like other wives, she pursued her own trade as well, operating for a while as the principal brewer in the town and also as a miller. She wanted to outshine other women by her gaudy and trendy clothes. Her difficult first labour induced a breakdown, from which she recovered. The failure of her businesses, which she interpreted as God's judgement, contributed to her decision to devote herself to religion.

Margery's autobiography records her retrospective account of her experiences as set down much by a not uncritical priest long after most of the events recounted. That it was written at all shows that he at least believed Margery's religious experiences to be genuine and sufficiently important to be recorded. This was open to question, for Margery's vow of chastity during her husband's lifetime, her visions, her wildly fluctuating moods, and above all her anti-social fits of 'plenteous and continual weeping', which occurred as often as fourteen times a day, could be evidence of mental derangement. Her scribe and the local religious houses were aware of this possibility and, after due consideration, rejected it. In the same way those bishops, who examined her for heresy, satisfied themselves about her orthodoxy and let her go. They put up with her denunciations of the conduct of themselves and their servants very well. She was forever condemning immoral and improper behaviour, disrupting church services, or depressing people at mealtimes. We can sympathise with them.

> No English writer, hitherto, had committed to writing so intimate, revealing, and human an account of his life and thoughts. The self-portrait of a minor mystic remains, however, the more credible for its merciless honesty and its fidelity to life.

There were not many Margery Kempes. Her autobiography exists because she was unique and thus worthy of commemoration. Her first breakdown, after the birth of her child, lasted for seven months and involved hallucinations, attempted suicide, and self-mutilation. A period of worldly social climbing was followed by a permanent conversion. Lengthy prayer, fasting, mortification of the flesh, weeping, and — from 1413 — celibacy characterised the rest of her life. She now wished to wear a white dress and the ring of Christ, which Bishop Repingdon — recognizing her instability — initially denied her. In 1413–14 she went on pilgrimage to Jerusalem; subsequently in 1417 to Compostella. She spent all her wealth and survived only by the alms of those she convinced. She suffered terribly, because her companionship — especially her weeping — was intolerable to her fellow pilgrims. Back in England, the townsmen of Bristol, Leicester and elsewhere referred her as a suspected heretic to their bishops. For most of her last years she lived at Lynn, where she was admired and respected by local monks and friars and by the theologians who came to visit her, but where she was hated and reviled by many of the layfolk. Was she inspired by God or was she mad?

H. S. Bennett, 'Margery Kempe', *Six Medieval Men and Women*, 1955.
A. Goodman, 'The Piety of John Brunham's daughter, of Lynn', *Medieval Women*, ed. D. Baker, Studies in Church History, Subsidia, 1, 1978.
The Book of Margery Kempe, ed. S. B. Meech, Early English Text Society ccvii, 1940.

MARGERY BAXTER was one of the leaders of the East Anglian Lollards in 1428. Bereft of its educated leadership after 1414, lay Lollardy could have degenerated into local cells, each with its own debased version of Wyclif's teaching. That this did not happen and that Lollardy remained a recognizable movement was largely because Lollard literature had been widely distributed and thus taught each group the same doctrines. Texts were read, studied, and learnt by rote in Lollard schools. Lollard missionaries admittedly added their own slant to the beliefs that were generally accepted. Whilst recognizably part of the main movement, the East Anglian Lollards were strongly influenced by the Kentish priest William White, who was active in East Anglia from 1425 and burnt at Norwich in 1428. This was part of a concerted campaign against heresy initiated by the Canterbury convocation, which feared Lollardy was increasing. Margery Baxter was one of a hundred Lollards tried by William

Alnwick, Bishop of Norwich in 1428-31.

Women have played an important part in many radical religious movements. By minimising the role of the sacraments and the ordained priesthood, Wyclif allowed more scope to lay people. Perhaps there were no Lollard women-priests, though the possibility was certainly considered, but there were plenty of forceful female Lollards, among them the East Anglian housewives **Margery Baxter** and **Hawisia Moon**.

Margery was the wife of William Baxter, a wright from Martham in East Norfolk, whom Margery considered was the best teacher of Christianity. The Baxters had harboured White and hid his books. To Margery he was 'a great saint in heaven and a holy doctor ordained by God'. The Baxters were not secretive. Margery boiled bacon in a bronze pot during Lent, not an unobtrusive activity, corrected erroneous beliefs, and helped her husband teach potential converts by night in their home. Her doctrines were commonplace, but her justifications for them were unusual, for example her defence of meat-eating on Fridays on economic grounds and her denunciation of St Thomas Becket for fleeing from his assailants. She urged Joanna Calfland not to swear:

> Dame, beware of the bee, for every bee will sting, and therefore look that you swear neither by God nor by Our Lady nor by none other saint, and if you do the contrary, the bee will sting your tongue and venom your soul.

Don't adore 'stocks and stones and dead men's bones', she said. 'Lewd wrights hew and form stocks into crosses and images and after that lewd painters glorify them with colours'. You might as well worship a gallows or Margery's own arm in your own home as images in a church. The holy communion bread could not be the true body of Christ, for if it was a thousand priests made gods a thousand times, ate them and excreted them, and these gods were therefore to be found in their excrement. She said that St Thomas was not blessed, but cursed, as were the pope, cardinals, archbishops and bishops, especially her Bishop of Norwich, whom she called Caiaphas! Self-confident and self-righteous, eloquent and persuasive, Margery exercised a powerful influence on those about her. The charter of salvation in her womb gave her immunity from prosecution, she said.

However Margery abjured. Clad only in a kirtle and bearing a wax taper, she was sentenced to four floggings around Martham church on Sundays, to two more around Ocle market-place on market-days, and to two penitential visits to Norwich cathedral. To offend again spelt death, but we do not know if she did. Lollardy was not a heroic creed: most Lollards recanted rather than face the flames and relatively few relapsed. Lollardy's survival after 1431 stemmed partly from problems of detection and partly from local communities's reluctance to convict. Hence perhaps the end of the Norwich heresy trials.

M. Aston, *Lollards and Reformers: Images and Literacy in Late Medieval Religion*, 1984.
Heresy Trials in the Diocese of Norwich 1428–31, ed. N. P. Tanner, Camden 4th Series xx, 1977.

WALTER LORD HUNGERFORD (*c.*1378–1449) combined business and piety to a remarkable degree. His father, the Lancastrian retainer and former speaker, had built up a major estate in Wiltshire, Somerset and Berkshire, to which Walter succeeded in 1398. At once he backed the Lancastrian revolution, but spoilt the effect next year by his dubious role in the rebellion of Richard II's *duketti*. The new king used him only as the chamberlain escorting Princess Philippa to Denmark in 1406, although Walter acted also as sheriff of Wiltshire, Somerset, and Dorset, sat repeatedly in parliament, and attended Great Councils. Certainly Henry IV was not remembered in Walter's chantry foundations, unlike Henry V, whose biography Walter commissioned and whose accession brought immediate employment and promotion. Walter was at Agincourt in 1415 and campaigned subsequently both on land and, as admiral, at sea. Henry sent him on embassies to the Emperor Sigismund, to the General Council of the Church at Constance, and to the French. He was speaker of the Commons in 1414, a councillor from 1417, and from 1415 was steward of the household and constantly in the company of the king, who made him knight of the Garter, appointed him as executor, and charged him with the care of the infant Henry VI. Walter remained as steward until 1424 and as councillor, campaigned abroad and negotiated, and in 1426 was created Lord Hungerford and appointed Lord Treasurer, which he remained until 1432. Advancing years prompted his retirement from public life in the late 1430s but he remained in touch and influential at court.

Walter's political services made his fortune. Apart from his barony and ministerial positions, he held a host of English offices, such as chief steward of the South Parts from 1413–37 and chamberlain (1425) of the Duchy of Lancaster, chief forester of Dartmoor (1425), and constable of Windsor. In France Henry V gave him Homet and other lordships and the captaincies of Cherbourg and Château Gaillard. He also raised large ransoms from his captives. His English offices carried salaries that rose to £500 a year from 1426 and scope for other profits too. He bought about 30 manors, raised his lifetime income to £1,800 and his heirs' expectations to over £1,000 a year: more than many an earl. The marriages he arranged for his eldest son and grandson promised to add further estates of equivalent value and to make the Hungerfords into the foremost West Country family. He spent his income on building, adding a second ward to Farleigh Castle and undertaking extensive works at Heytesbury, on founding an almshouse and five chantries, and on ransoming two sons, all of which he managed without apparent strain. He lived nobly and was accepted by the old nobility, many of whom nominated him among their executors or feoffees. They trusted him.

For Walter was much more than a clever and ambitious administrator. The expert jouster and pilgrim to Jerusalem was also a skilled Latinist with broad cultural interests. He read poetry and theology, commissioned a life of Henry V, patronised Merton College, Oxford, and founded a school. Similarly his almshouse continued a family tradition of charity. Certainly his chantries served temporal as well as spiritual ends, but the statutes he drafted testify to his lifelong devotion to the Annunciation and to his clearcut religious preferences. The chantry, almshouse and school he created at Heytesbury was one of only five triple foundations in England and show him in touch with the latest religious fashions right to the end. Vows, pilgrimages, and gifts to the Church regularly took priority over the advancement of his career and family fortunes.

J. S. Roskell, *Parliament and Politics in Late Medieval England* ii 1981.

M. A. Hicks, 'Chantries, Obits and Almshouses: The Hungerford Foundations 1325–1478', in *The Church in Pre-Reformation Society*, C. Barron and C. Harper-Bill, eds., 1985.

M. A. Hicks, 'St. Katherine's Hospital, Heytesbury: Prehistory, Foundation, and Re-foundation 1408–72', *Wiltshire Archaeological Magazine* lxxviii, 1984.

HENRY BEAUFORT (*c.*1376–1447), Cardinal-Bishop of Winchester, was the greatest royal creditor of the fifteenth century. Born perhaps at Beaufort in Anjou, he was the second son of John of Gaunt, Duke of Lancaster by Katherine Swynford and was legitimated in 1397 after their marriage. He attended both Cambridge and Oxford universities from 1388 and accumulated livings from 1389, receiving the inevitable bishopric — Lincoln — in 1398 and moving to Winchester, richest of all, in 1404. He held the see for 43 years, was chancellor three times, and was politically active for half a century. All this resembles the pattern set by earlier noble bishops, but Beaufort's career also anticipates future developments. He was the first English cardinal to retain his diocese and reside in England, he identified himself politically with the royal house, and he fathered a bastard. If leadership of the English church was not his top priority, he was nevertheless not an unworthy churchman. He ran his diocese competently, crusaded against heresy, refounded the great almshouse of St Cross at Winchester, attended General Councils of the Church, and visited both Jerusalem and Santiago. He even considered renouncing his worldly wealth and he righted wrongs troubling his conscience on his deathbed. Twice, in 1417 and 1429, his support for the pope created problems for him in England, but the houses of Lancaster and Beaufort came first.

Of course Beaufort was also an able administrator, diplomat and councillor of great value to the Lancastrian dynasty. Following his first term as chancellor in 1403–5 he supported Prince Henry, perhaps even favouring Henry IV's abdication. Henry V made him chancellor again in 1413–17, when he was 'a veritable *eminence grise*', and he committed himself to the king's French cause. 'The myth of Agincourt as the divine signal of a greater destiny for England was born and it would seem that Henry Beaufort was probably its author and was certainly the first to formulate it'. At the Council of Constance he secured the election of a sympathetic

Cardinal Beaufort
(From the Book of Benefactors of St Albans Abbey)

pope and his own nomination as cardinal and legate. Henry V, however, forced him to renounce it, humiliated him, and restored him to favour only in 1421.

The minority of Henry VI offered Beaufort greater scope. Both he and Gloucester wanted the same end, Lancastrian victory, but they were personally incompatible. Certainly Beaufort thought himself the best man to achieve this result and led those councillors opposed to Gloucester's ambitions. For long periods Beaufort was abroad, but his chancellorship of 1424–6 provoked a crisis and in 1429 and 1431–2 he was vigorously attacked by Gloucester. His services were valued by Bedford, by other councillors who recognized his loans to be indispensable, and from the late 1430s by Henry VI, who found in him a minister prepared to treat for peace. Probably only then did Beaufort's aims diverge from Gloucester's. The cardinal's loans totalling £212,303, representing the same money lent repeatedly, were secured like those of other lenders. No interest was charged. To hazard his capital assisted the Lancastrian cause in which he believed, but it also carried political benefits, 'enabling him to contest, and intermittently to usurp, the leadership in council claimed by Humphrey Duke of Gloucester'. They also bought royal favours, most notably the right to buy royal lands to endow his Beaufort nephews and his almshouse, advancing both his soul and his family.

G. L. Harriss, *Cardinal Beaufort: A Study of Lancastrian Ascendancy and Decline*, 1988.

JOHN DUKE OF BEDFORD (1389–1435), third son of Henry IV, ruled Lancastrian France for his nephew Henry VI from 1422 to 1435. A thickset man of great strength and a capable soldier, he was also a statesman and diplomat and ranks second in ability among Henry IV's sons. Well-educated like his brothers, he was a man of some culture. He purchased the great library of Charles VI, which he housed in his mansion of Joyous Repose at Rouen, read Latin and Greek classics in French translation, and commissioned illuminated books of his own. His piety emerges from the two monasteries he founded at Rouen, one belonging to the distinctively French order of the Celestines: a choice that shows how French his tastes became during his prolonged sojourn abroad and his contented marriage to Anne of Burgundy. He possessed all the pride and hauteur of his rank, yet was also affectionate, sensitive, and genuinely compassionate to the unfortunate. So successfully did he curb his naturally hot temper that he was considered remarkable for his caution and prudence.

Bedford's political employment long antedated his creation as duke in 1414. He had administrative, diplomatic, military, and even naval experience as warden of the East March against Scotland in 1403–14 and Guardian of England almost continuously from 1415–21. He thus missed Agincourt. Following the deaths of Henry V and Charles VI in 1422, he became Regent of France for Henry VI, and remained in charge, though not as regent, after Henry's coronation in 1431. Although he was Henry V's eldest surviving brother and heir presumptive to Henry VI, he left England to his brother

The Regent Bedford kneels before St George
(From the Bedford Hours)

Humphrey Duke of Gloucester, asserting his priority of birth only twice — in 1425–6 as Protector and in 1433–34 as Chief Councillor. On both occasions he restored harmony and harnessed English resources for his French wars. He accumulated many honours, acquiring two French duchies and six counties, but he had no heir by either marriage. He served his nephew's interests better than his own.

The Treaty of Troyes of 1420 had recognized Henry V as heir to Charles VI in preference to his own son the Dauphin, the future Charles VII. As Charles VI also died in 1422, Henry VI was legitimate King of France and not a conqueror. It was Bedford's responsibility to retain those areas controlled by Henry V, to extend control over the remainder, and to rule the whole on behalf of Henry VI's French subjects. Victories at Cravant and Verneuil in 1423–4 were high points in a steady extension of the conquered area up to the siege of Orleans in 1429, when he was thwarted by 'a disciple and limb of the Fiend, called the Pucelle, that used enchantments and sorcery' (Joan of Arc). He then suffered his first serious reverses, but nevertheless stabilised the position, retaining in 1435 more territory than Henry V had held. He was then deserted by the Duke of Burgundy, whose alliance he had consistently sought to maintain. Bedford lived like a French nobleman, imposed strict discipline on his troops and combated brigands, used French officials and Norman institutions, and — as the war zone shifted southwards — brought peace and prosperity to Normandy. His rule was not just acceptable but even popular to the Normans, whose taxes financed the war. He was a successful ruler, even if he understandably failed to complete his brother's conquests. Clearsighted, singleminded and consistent, he was loyal to his subordinates and earned their confidence. If he lacked Henry V's remarkable personal magnetism, he nevertheless possessed all the qualities needed in a king and was respected by all those whom he encountered. At his death he could not be replaced.

C. T. Allmand, *Lancastrian Normandy 1415–1450: The History of a Medieval Occupation,* 1983.
R. A. Griffiths, *The Reign of King Henry VI 1422–61,* 1981.
E. C. Williams, *My Lord of Bedford 1389–1435,* 1963.

HUMPHREY DUKE OF GLOUCESTER (1390–1447), youngest son of Henry IV, had many attractive qualities. He was handsome and well-mannered, affable and genial, kind and generous, fluent and persuasive, brave and pious. Unfortunately he was also impatient, reckless, inflexible and arrogant and was thus unfitted both for military command and for diplomacy. Henry V was therefore right to confide France to the prudent Duke of Bedford during Henry VI's minority. For England he nominated Gloucester, who claimed the regency that 'belongeth unto him by right as well by the mean of birth as by the last will of the king that was'. Instead, however, council and parliament merely gave him precedence,

Humphrey Duke of Gloucester and his duchess Eleanor Cobham
(From the Book of Benefactors of St Albans Abbey)

patronage and a salary, and made him Protector with 'a personal duty to attend to the actual defence of the land but no name of tutor, lieutenant, governor or regent, nor any name that shall import governance of the land'. Bedford became Protector when in England. Gloucester resented these limitations, which he saw as the devices of his enemies, especially his uncle Beaufort. Hence, perhaps, his unwise wedding to Jacqueline of Bavaria, heiress of Hainault, Holland and Zeeland, who was already married. Hence too his feud with Beaufort. They nearly came to blows in 1425–6, when Bedford's intervention forced Beaufort to retire abroad. Gloucester tried to use Beaufort's cardinalate to exclude him from council (1429) and from his bishopric (1431–2). The duke was strongest after he had purged government and household in 1432–3. Although Duke Humphrey was heir apparent from 1435, Henry VI preferred Beaufort's faction. The duke's attacks on them and their diplomacy, though unavailing, were embarrassing, and led to his arrest and premature death. His line ended with him: his marriages were childless and his offspring bastards.

Humphrey's campaigns with Henry V 'explain his nostalgic, not to say outdated, and certainly unrealistic attitude towards the conflict with France'. He underestimated the Duke of Burgundy, flouting him by invading Hainault in 1424–5 and thus diverting much needed support from Bedford. He responded to English setbacks after 1429 by ill-informed criticism, unrealistic counter-proposals, and by rejecting all peace terms. More measured criticism might have averted the disasters of the 1440s.

Yet Gloucester was not a fool. He was clever, ingenious, and cultured. He read French and Latin well enough to master such complex texts as Aristotle's *Ethics* and Plato's *Republic*. He had 'no real pleasure but the reading of books' and did 'not think that anything can give us more pleasure than that which relates to learning and the cult of letters'. He quoted precisely from memory to support his points. His interests were broad and he sought out learned men not just in England but also leading Italian humanists like Bruni, Decembrio, and Tito Livio Frulovisii. He commissioned translations from Greek into Latin and had works dedicated to him. Although mean and unreliable in paying his protegés, he spent lavishly on his library, which remarkably contained many ancient classics imported from Italy. At least 280 books were given to

Oxford University: 'a more splendid donation than any prince or king had given since the foundation of the university' and one vital to the advancement of English Renaissance scholarship. As the first great figure in the English Renaissance, Humphrey secured the fame he sought. 'No man has left a greater mark on the progress of English thought than this Duke Humphrey and in the realm of ideas he did the good work that he failed to do in the realm of action'.

C. T. Allmand, *Lancastrian Normandy 1415–50: The History of a Medieval Occupation*, 1983.
R. A. Griffiths, *The Reign of King Henry VI 1422–61*, 1981.
K. H. Vickers, *Humphrey, Duke of Gloucester*, 1907.
R. Weiss, *Humanism in England during the fifteenth century*, 1967.

THOMAS MONTAGU, EARL OF SALISBURY (1388–1428) and Count of Perche, was *the* great earl of Salisbury. He was the outstanding English commander in France in the 1420s. He alone was undefeated and he alone could rival the prestige of King Henry V. As a contemporary wrote, 'he was accounted in his time throughout France and England the most expert, subtle and successful in arms of all the commanders, who have been talked about in the past hundred years'. Relatively few noblemen were professional soldiers like Salisbury, who served almost continuously in France from 1415 to his death. In 1415 he fought both at Agincourt and in the Duke of Bedford's naval victory over the Genoese. He returned with Henry V to Normandy in 1418, serving both with the king and on detached missions, and in 1419 was singled out to be lieutenant-governor of Normandy. He emerged with credit from the Duke of Clarence's unnecessary defeat at Baugé in 1421. From being one of the Regent Bedford's commanders, he became his principal field commander. When the English took the initiative and advanced southwards in 1423, Salisbury took the lead. In that year he defeated a Franco-Scottish force at Cravant, next year he participated in Bedford's even greater victory at Verneuil, he helped conquer Maine in 1425, when he captured both Le Mans and Mayenne, and was commander of Upper Normandy in 1427. He was 'a sound strategist, an excellent tactician, and an expert in the use of artillery. Like all great commanders, he had the gift of inspiring confidence in his men and filling them with the confidence of victory'. But his career was tragically cut short and what he could have achieved is forever hidden from us. It was almost certainly his strategy that led to the siege of Orleans, which it is clear he knew how to undertake and that his successors did not. His death right at the start of the siege deprived the English of their direction even before the intervention of Joan of Arc, exposed them to defeat, and marked the military turning point. He proved to be an 'irreplaceable loss'.

Yet Salisbury was a most unlikely Lancastrian devotee. His father Earl John had been Richard II's friend and died in rebellion against Henry IV. John had suffered forfeiture, but in 1409 his son Thomas was allowed to recover his earldom and those lands that were entailed. Only in 1421 did he secure the full restoration, which he had earned by outstanding service. Long before then, however, he had become a model of Henry V's well-attested willingness to win over potential troublemakers by friendship and trust. Thus Salisbury was elected a knight of the Garter as early as 1414, became a royal councillor in 1417, was employed as diplomat, and received military responsibilities. During the 1420s he was one of Bedford's councillors in France and one of Henry VI's minority council in England. He was rewarded with a French county, lordships and garrison-captaincies in France, and was appointed warden of the New Forest and to other offices in England. Even when restored, however, his inheritance was modest for an earl and was supplemented by his marriage to two heiresses. The first, Eleanor Holland, coheiress of the Earl of Kent, bore him only a daughter, so he remarried to Alice Chaucer. She was a connection of the Beauforts and the royal family and so too was his son-in-law Richard Neville, so Thomas was integrated with the house of Lancaster and identified with its interests by kinship as well as service. Since neither marriage brought Salisbury a legitimate son — he already had a bastard son John — his augmented inheritance passed to the Nevilles and his widow to his less fortunate colleague-in-arms the Earl of Suffolk. Despite his sense of dynasty, Thomas was thus to be the last Montagu Earl of Salisbury.

E. C. Williams, *My Lord of Bedford 1389-1435,* 1963.

RICHARD BEAUCHAMP, EARL OF WARWICK (1382-1439) and Count of Aumale, was a medieval hero and *the* great Earl of Warwick. The Beauchamps had dominated the West Midlands since 1268, when they inherited the earldom created in 1088, and they traced their descent back to the legendary giant Guy of Warwick. With the death of a cousin in 1421, Richard became the last male of his line. His first wife, the heiress Elizabeth Berkeley, had borne him only daughters. To let the lineage expire was unthinkable for Earl Richard. Remarrying to another heiress, the widowed Isabel Despenser, he founded at the prompting of a York anchoress a chantry at Guys Cliff near Warwick — the legendary lair of Guy of Warwick — 'that God would send him heirs male'. His prayers were answered and a son, Henry Beauchamp, was born, whom the earl charged never to change his title from Warwick however much promoted. Henry obeyed this command, becoming Duke of Warwick, but ironically his premature death ended the line and conveyed the earldom to his brother-in-law Richard Neville, 'Warwick the Kingmaker'. Earl Richard Beauchamp lived in state at Warwick, maintained a great household and retinue, and strove to develop Warwick's economy by founding fairs and making the Avon navigable. Like his father, he chose to be buried in his college of St Mary at Warwick, where a great new chapel — the Beauchamp Chapel — was erected by his executors under the provisions of his will. The lands that he inherited and those of the two heiresses he married gave him an income of over £5,000 a year in his last years, more than any previous earl and any contemporary English noble-man. He arranged splendid marriages for his daughters. The name that had been dishonoured by the tearful cowardice of his father Earl Thomas II (d. 1401) in parliament in 1397 received new lustre from Earl Richard.

He was certainly one of the outstanding soldiers of his day. He distinguished himself many times in tournaments against inter-national opposition. His military experience stretched through many campaigns from the battle of Shrewsbury in 1403 until his death. He exercised many subordinate commands with credit, acting as captain of Calais from 1423, and from 1437 as king's lieutenant (i.e. commander-in-chief) in France. Yet he was much more than a warrior. As pilgrim and knight errant in 1408–10 he had journeyed to the Holy Sepulchre, Italy, Russia and Germany. He was a knight of the Garter, councillor to both Henry V and Henry VI in England and to the Regent Bedford in France, and a skilled diplomat employed at the Council of Constance and the Treaty of Troyes. He was a moderating influence in politics and acceptable to all parties in 1437, when he took on the lieutenantcy against his will, despite ill-health, from a profound sense of duty. He was literate, cultured, and the centre of a minor literary circle. Earl Richard was, in short, exactly what contemporaries admired in 'a noble knight'. The Emperor Sigismund, it was reported, 'called him the father of courtesy, for if all courtesy were lost he said it might have been found in his person'. No better mentor could be found for the young Henry VI, thought the minority council. This charge was exercised by Earl Richard for eight troubled years, for the young Henry VI was assertive and wilful and corporal punishment was required to correct him. Earl Richard became a legend, commemorated in glowing terms not only by John Rous — who knew him — but also in the unique *Pageant* recounting his life. What the Black Prince and Henry of Grosmont were in the fourteenth century, so Henry V and Earl Richard Beauchamp were in the fifteenth.

M. A. Hicks, 'The Beauchamp Trust, 1439–87', *Bulletin of the Institute of Historical Research* liv, 1981.

Viscount Dillon and W. H. St. John Hope, ed., *Pageant of the Birth, Life and Death of Richard Beauchamp, Earl of Warwick, K.G.*, 1914.

C. D. Ross, *Estates and Finances of Richard Beauchamp, Earl of Warwick*, Dugdale Society, Occasional Paper 12, 1956.

J. Rous, *The Rous Roll*, W. H. Courthope, ed., 2nd ed. 1980.

SIR JOHN FASTOLF (*c.* 1378–1459) is the classic instance of a professional soldier enriched by the Hundred Years War. By 1401 Fastolf had entered the services of Henry IV's second son Thomas (later Duke of Clarence), accompanying him to Ireland and then in 1412 to France, where he became deputy-constable of Bordeaux. He was still only an esquire at Harfleur and Agincourt (1415), served in the Harfleur garrison and then from 1417 in the conquest of Normandy, was knighted and appointed constable of Fécamp and of the Paris Bastille. The deaths of Clarence in 1421 and Henry V in 1422 resulted in the appointment of Bedford as Regent of France and transformed Fastolf's career. From being a distinguished subordinate he became an important commander. Bedford made him master of his household (1422), councillor of France, and governor of Anjou and Maine (1423). He fought at Verneuil, where he captured the Duke of Alençon, subdued Maine in 1425, and in 1429 won the battle of the Herrings and escaped unscathed from Pataye. He was at the Congress of Arras in 1435, when he reported on the future of the war, and retired from active service about 1440 in time to avoid the final defeat of the English.

Fastolf was not alone in profiting from the wars in France, but only in his case is it 'possible to plot with fair accuracy the stages by which a military adventurer of modest fortune and family rose to be a great landowner'. Fastolf's genteel inheritance of three Norfolk manors worth £46 a year took second place to the £240 a year of his wife's dower and was dwarfed by the £775 income from the lands he bought. The purchase prices came from the profits of war: estate revenues of £401, ransoms, pillage, and wages. He had twice the minimum income for an earl and indeed lived like one. Apart from £13,855 that he paid for land, he spent £9,495 on building, at least £2,500 on plate, and an incalculable amount on tapestries and other luxuries, including at least twenty books. He aspired to be a patron of the arts, gave generously to the Abbey of St Benet Holme, and planned to found a new monastery/college beside his new castle at Caister, his birthplace. Since he owed his fortune to the French war, his bitter complaints that £11,000 remained due to him are surprising. His resentment at the military mismanagement that lost him his valuable French estates is more understandable and perhaps more representative of other war veterans.

Fastolf's military successes were not enough by themselves to make his fortune. He needed a head for business too. Whilst he was above all an unsentimental and ruthless soldier committed to an English victory, he also exploited to the full the opportunities for personal profit. Where others squandered their winnings in high-living, Fastolf regularly remitted his profits home, invested them at interest in the short-term, and selected land for purchase with great care. He knew his evidences at first hand, made his titles as watertight as possible, forgot no injuries or debts, sued any who offended him, manipulated the legal process as required, and managed his estates with a view to maximising his profits. In the process he trampled on those in his way, such as the stepson whom he disinherited, and was an exacting and ungrateful lord, who did not reward faithful service as he should. He became worse as he became older, lapsing into 'querulous and unmanageable senility', but, as a servant remarked, 'cruel and vengeful he hath *ever* been and for the most part without pity and mercy'. Although a childless, widowed, septuagenarian, he did not stop to consider why he acted as he did or who would benefit from his parsimony, litigation, and rigour. He was the complete egotist to the end.

H.S. Bennett, 'Sir John Fastolf', *Six Medieval Men and Women*, 1955.

K.B. McFarlane, 'The Investment of Sir John Fastolf's Profits of War', in *England in the Fifteenth Century*, G.L. Harriss, ed., 1981.

A. Smith, 'Litigation and Politics: Sir John Fastolf's defence of his English Property', in *Politics and Property: Essays in Later Medieval English History*, A.J. Pollard, ed., 1984.

MASTER JOHN SOMERSET (*c.*1395–*c.*1455) was one of the most successful doctors in late medieval England. Having studied in the arts faculty at Oxford University, he migrated to Cambridge to escape the plague and was fellow of Pembroke Hall from 1416. He was Master of Arts and grammar by 1418, when he was schoolmaster at Bury St Edmunds grammar school and was already skilled in medicine. In 1423 he was practising medicine and surgery in London and by 1428 had graduated as doctor of medicine, probably at Cambridge. Before then he served Thomas Beaufort Duke of Exeter (*d.*1426), whose executor he was, and it was probably as nominee of Humphrey Duke of Gloucester that he became physician to Henry VI in 1427, accompanying him to France in 1430 and remaining with him until at least 1451. Somerset's other skills were quickly pressed into use as one of King Henry's teachers and he was sometimes described as the king's master from 1429, becoming one of the formative influences on the young monarch. Their intimacy outlasted the royal minority. In 1440 he was trustee of lands that King Henry intended for his new colleges at Eton and King's, Cambridge. He supervised the building operations for Henry VI's new foundations of Eton and King's colleges and may indeed have helped shape them. In 1450 he was one of twenty-nine individuals that Cade's rebels wanted removed as a harmful influence from the royal entourage. He was alive in 1453 but dead by 1455.

Somerset's influence emerges in his rewards, which were quite exceptional for a royal physician and teacher. As he was married twice and not ordained, he could not be rewarded at no direct cost to the crown with benefices or even a bishopric like William Wayn-flete, but received instead annuities and offices. His original annuity of £40 in 1428 was increased by £60 in 1432 and by £40 in 1439, making a total of £140 a year, but this was not all. He was appointed chancellor of the exchequer in 1434, warden of the king's exchange and mint in the Tower in 1439, and in 1442 surveyor of the king's works at Sheen and Westminster palaces, the Tower, and Eton College. From 1439 he received £40 a year from Bury Abbey, from 1441 a pension from Merton Priory, and no doubt other sums from other bodies. Not surprisingly, he became rich — his pleas of poverty in 1449 lack conviction — and he acquired a house at Osterley in Isleworth and sufficient land nearby to qualify as J.P. for Middlesex from 1439 and M.P. in 1442. He built up a considerable library, had a reputation for charity, and founded a hospital for 9 poor men, chapel, and gild of St Raphael, St Gabriel, St Michael, and All Angels at Brentford End, Middlesex, for which he was licensed to grant endowments in 1446. There were no children from his two marriages.

Somerset was 'immensely learned and a polymath of his day' with interests embracing medicine, the arts, and grammar. He reputedly wrote medical treatises, though none can certainly be identified today. His closeness to the king made him an obvious intercessor for learned people and individuals seeking royal favours. Hence, per-haps, the dedication to him in 1428/32 of a historical work, the second recension of the pseudo-Elmham, and hence too the fees paid him by ecclesiastical corporations. He was an executor of Duke Humphrey and was asked by Oxford University to secure the books promised by the duke. If he did anything about this, he was unsuccessful, but he gave the university a book and vestments on his own behalf. He gave substantial collections of books both to Peterhouse and Pembroke College, Cambridge. His was a unique career.

A. Gransden, *Historical Writing in England* ii, 1982.

R. A. Griffiths, *The Reign of King Henry VI 1422–61*, 1981.

JOHN TALBOT, EARL OF SHREWSBURY and Waterford (*c.*1387–1453) and Count of Clermont, was the outstanding English commander in France after 1429. His death marks the end of the Hundred Years War. His name of Talbot spread terror among the French and children were scared into obedience for fear that 'the Talbot cometh'. To celebrate his death the church of Notre-Dame-de-Talbot marks where he fell. In 1421 he added his niece's two Shropshire baronies of Talbot of Goodrich Castle and Strange of Blackmere to that of Furnivall, lord of Sheffield and Hallamshire, which he had held by his first marriage since 1409. John was thus no parvenu, but a nobleman of long lineage and extensive property both in England and Ireland. His income of £1,205 in 1436 was itself more than sufficient endowment for the earldom he received in 1442. 'A deep and genuine commitment to the code of chivalry as he understood it offers the most convincing key to Talbot's character and career'. He was conventionally pious, hearing mass before battle, founding a chantry, and going on pilgrimage to Rome. His commitment to the advancement of the Talbots, the dictates of honour and prestige, and above all his hot temper and ready resort to force explain the many quarrels in which he became embroiled: his quarrel with the Earl of Arundel in 1413, which earned him a spell in the Tower; the thirty-year Talbot-Ormond feud in Ireland, which parliament tried — unavailingly — to end in 1423; his disputes with a former estate officer in Herefordshire, with Joan Lady Abergavenny, and, over parliamentary precedence, with Lord Grey of Ruthin; his unfounded charge of cowardice at Pataye against Sir John Fastolf; his involvement in the Berkeley-Lisle dispute on behalf of his second wife Margaret, and the Talbot-Lisle feud he created by diverting property from his heir to Margaret's own son. As lieutenant of Ireland he was charged with misgovernment and abuse of power. He was an aggressive and combative nobleman, whose energies were best employed abroad if domestic peace was to be preserved.

Talbot's first campaign was against Glendower in Wales in 1404 and he fought in Ireland as lieutenant in 1414–19, missing the Agincourt and first Norman campaigns. He was lieutenant of Ireland twice more. He first served in France in 1419, but returned continuously, sharing in almost every campaign and battle. The ransom he paid in 1429–33 probably prevented any financial profit, but he gained greatly in prestige. Surprise attacks repeatedly captured what he could not formally besiege. He regularly appeared where least expected and his vengeance was fearsome and immediate. Intrepid and dashing, he was the 'most strenuous and most audacious leader of all the battles'. Hard and cruel, 'there was not from the time of Herod anyone so wicked'. For most of his career he was in retreat, suppressing revolts, repeatedly resisting attacks and relieving sieges. One of several generals before Salisbury's death in 1428, he was the favoured field commander of successive lieutenants and accumulated many town captaincies. It was largely due to him that the English remained fifteen years after the Congress of Arras (1435). He was not responsible for the loss of Normandy and was the obvious choice to recover Aquitaine. 'Selfless service in a dying cause' earned promotion as K. G. (1425), count (1434), marshal of France (1436), constable of France (1442) and Ireland (1446).

Except in 1441, under York, and in Aquitaine in 1452–3 Talbot was never commander-in-chief. He 'was primarily an executant, not a planner, of military operations'. This was his appropriate role. He was not a strategist and was defeated in both his battles. Neither should have been fought. His suicidal frontal assault made Châtillon the first battle decided by artillery. He was not the great general suggested by his legend, but the best of those who remained.

A. J. Pollard, *John Talbot and the War in France 1427–1453*, 1983.
E. C. Williams, *My Lord of Bedford 1389–1435*, 1963.

ELEANOR COBHAM, DUCHESS OF GLOUCESTER (*c.* 1400 –1454) was the central figure in the most celebrated sorcery case of late medieval England. She was the daughter of Sir Reginald Cobham of Sterborough in Kent, titular lord Cobham, who was one of the captains in Humphrey Duke of Gloucester's Côtentin expedition of 1418. A lady of great beauty and some charm, Eleanor was an attendant of Gloucester's first duchess Jacqueline of Hainault in 1425 and was perhaps already his mistress. She was the probable mother of his two bastards Arthur and Antigone. Following his divorce, he married Eleanor in 1428. There was criticism of the match, whence (we are told) 'arose shame and more disgrace and inconvenience to the whole kingdom than can be expressed'. Eleanor's relatively humble birth and soiled reputation were considered to disqualify her from marriage to a royal prince second in line and, from 1435, heir presumptive to the thrones of both England and France. She added to her unpopularity by her ostentatious display, arrogant high-handedness, constant exaltation of her husband, and her open aspiration to be queen. There was thus little sympathy for her in her fall and she did not share in the posthumous popularity of Good Duke Humphrey.

Contemporaries believed in sorcery, which involved the exercise of black magic in collaboration with the devil. All sorcery was condemned by the Church as evil and heretical, but public opinion was more lenient. Eleanor was certainly interested in sorcery, owning at least one relevant book and employing an expert — the canon Master Roger Bolingbroke — in her household. She admitted consulting sorcerers long before to make Gloucester love her and marry her and again in 1441 that she might bear her husband a legitimate heir. Her accomplices were Bolingbroke and another clergyman Thomas Southwell, who celebrated a black mass one Sunday night in St Paul's churchyard, and Margery Jordan, the witch of Eye (Ebury). Their worst offence was to communicate with the dead (necromancy) to predict the date of the king's death, which constituted treason. Eleanor denied this particular charge, although it seems likely that she did want to know when the king would die and her husband and herself would succeed him. She was tried both by the Church, who condemned all sorcery as evil, and by the State. Her accomplices were sentenced to death, Bolingbroke being hanged and Jordan burnt, but Eleanor herself was *only* required to perform humiliating public penances in London, was divorced, and consigned to perpetual imprisonment until her death in 1454, seven years after Gloucester, who did not marry again.

There were a series of celebrated sorcery cases in the fifteenth century involving the Dowager-Queen Joan of Navarre in 1419, Jacquetta of Luxemburg, Duchess of Bedford in 1469, and servants of the Duke of Clarence in 1477. It was evidently commonplace for high society to dabble in the black arts with the assistance of respectable academic sorcerers. Each of these cases also had political overtones, as enemies sought to eliminate those involved. Eleanor's own activities offered the grounds for her trial, but it was the alienation of her husband from court that gave her foes the motive and opportunity to attack him through her. He could do nothing to save her and indeed her conviction damaged his standing and contributed to his own fall in 1447.

R. A. Griffiths, 'The Trial of Eleanor Cobham: An episode in the fall of Humphrey of Gloucester', *Bulletin of the John Rylands Library* li, 1968–9.
K. H. Vickers, *Humphrey Duke of Gloucester,* 1907.

JOHN KEMP (*c.*1375–1454), Cardinal-Archbishop of Canterbury, is the most remarkable instance of a royal civil servant promoted to high office in the English Church. The son of Thomas and Beatrix Kemp of Wye in Kent, he proceeded to Oxford University, where he was already fellow of Merton College in 1395, and graduated as doctor of canon law in 1414. Before then he entered the service of Archbishop Chichele, participating in the trial of Sir John Oldcastle in 1413, and from 1414 he was dean of the court of arches. Already a rector and canon, in 1417 he became an archdeacon, and in 1418 was licensed to perform his duties by deputy. Now middle-aged, Kemp could look forward to a career of moderate distinction in ecclesiastical administration, comparable perhaps with that of William Lyndwood.

Already, however, he had attracted the attention of Henry V. Negotiations with Aragon in 1415–16 were followed in 1417 by appointment as chancellor of Normandy and in 1418 as keeper of the privy seal. He joined Henry VI's minority council in 1422 and sat on the council of France from 1423–5. Following the Gloucester-Beaufort quarrel, Bedford appointed Kemp as chancellor of England in 1426, where he remained until dismissed by Gloucester in 1432. Meanwhile Kemp's diplomatic career continued. His firm stance was counterproductive at the Congress of Arras in 1435, but thereafter he was converted to Cardinal Beaufort's peace policy. Gloucester initially persuaded Henry VI to reject conciliatory terms proposed by Kemp, but next year peace became the official policy and Kemp was linked with Beaufort in Gloucester's fruitless denunciations. As Beaufort aged, so Kemp became the dominant force in government, but he too was ageing and by the late 1440s had been supplanted and indeed alienated by Suffolk. The duke's opposition to the promotion of Kemp's nephew as Bishop of London in 1448–50 fostered and may have caused the rift. The murders of Suffolk, Saye, Moleyns and Aiscough in 1450 were accompanied by the resignation as chancellor of Archbishop Stafford. Kemp, his predecessor in 1426–32, succeeded him. An elder statesman enjoying general confidence, Kemp was a force for stability when Henry VI went mad in 1453, but his death early in 1454 precipitated the Duke of York's first Protectorate.

Kemp's political services brought meteoric promotion. He was appointed Bishop of Rochester in 1419 and of Chichester and London in turn in 1421, making him the classic instance of the mercenary churchman skipping to progressively richer sees. In 1425 he became archbishop of York, in 1439 cardinal, and in 1452 he succeeded Stafford as archbishop of Canterbury. Whilst Kemp's political commitments restricted the time he spent in his dioceses, Thomas Gascoigne unduly minimises his periods of residence. To the Yorkshireman Gascoigne, Kemp was an outsider and his officers were foreigners, but there was nothing unusual in bringing in new men and they were certainly competent at their jobs. For long periods all medieval English bishoprics were run perfectly adequately by their permanent officials. Moreover Kemp's concern to defend and extend archiepiscopal rights would normally have been applauded. He persuaded Henry VI in 1441 to extend his franchises, asserted the rights of his fairs at Otley and Ripon to take tolls, and in 1445 threatened excommunication on all those infringing his privileges and franchises. He thus infuriated the Percies. The ensuing riots were not appeased by Kemp's use of royal authority to imprison Northumberland in the Tower and to convict his sons. Conciliation of his most powerful neighbour was to be preferred. A man of conventional piety, Kemp's sense of roots and family emerges both from his foundation of Wye College and his advancement of his kinsfolk. His cardinal's hat was a particular source of simple pride.

R. A. Griffiths, *The Reign of King Henry VI 1422–61*, 1981.

WILLIAM LYNDWOOD (*c.*1375–1446), Bishop of St Davids from 1442, was a great canon lawyer and 'stood head and shoulders above the rest of fifteenth-century English and Welsh bishops'. The son of a woolman from Linwood near Market Rasen in Lincolnshire, he attended Gonville Hall and perhaps Pembroke Hall, Cambridge University, and graduated as doctor of canon law in 1407. A career in ecclesiastical justice and administration duly followed. He must have had some such experience before 1414, when he became chancellor to Henry Chichele, Archbishop of Canterbury and auditor of causes. From 1417 to 1431 he was official principal (chief judge) of the court of Canterbury, and in 1419–26 he was prolocutor (speaker) of the Canterbury convocation. He thus presided over all litigation at the provincial court for fourteen years, including several important heresy trials. He was 'a notable heretic-hunter'. In 1433 he represented the English at the General Council of the Church at Basle. By the end of his term nobody can have known more about the canon law of the province of Canterbury and certainly nobody was better able to codify it than Lyndwood, whose great *Provinciale* digests and explains in five books the decrees of the province of Canterbury from the time of King John to Archbishop Chichele. It was and is the main source for English medieval canon law.

As early as 1402 William Lyndwood had been described as a king's clerk and he was regularly employed on diplomatic missions from 1417 to 1441. Only in 1431, however, did he transfer formally from the archbishop's service to that of the king. Due to the chancellor's indisposition, Lyndwood preached his sermon at the opening of parliament. He then joined the young King Henry VI in France, where he was a councillor and acted as clerk of the privy seal. On their return to England in 1432 he was appointed by Gloucester as keeper of the privy seal — the third minister of state. He remained in office until 1443, probably only resigning in order to devote himself to his distant diocese. His exceptionally long appointment demonstrates both that he was acceptable to all and also how well he filled his office. So belated a promotion to such a poor, remote and generally unattractive see indicates, however, how limited was his political stature. Lyndwood, in short, was a highly efficient bureaucrat, but not a political figure of the front rank.

Lyndwood's long and valued service for a variety of masters brought him many different livings from 1397 on culminating in the archdeaconry of Stow in 1434. He may have taken a drop in income on his promotion as bishop. Generally, no doubt, he was non-resident, but that he had some pastoral experience and concerns is suggested by a licence to preach in 1417. His educational interests were expressed also through the king's foundations at Eton and King's College, Cambridge, whose statutes he helped to draft, and through the benefactions to Gonville and Pembroke halls in his will. Such legal erudition and such experience and capacity for ecclesiastical administration surely fitted him ideally for a bishopric, but this came only late in life for political services. Bishoprics were no longer allocated primarily for spirituality or services to the Church. What ranked highest in Lyndwood's own estimation and what he wished to be remembered for was his *Provinciale*, a chained copy of which he directed to be available at the chantry founded for him by his executors in the crypt of St Stephen's Chapel, Westminster. His wish was granted. This is his claim to fame.

R. A. Griffiths, *The Reign of King Henry VI 1422–61*, 1981.

   JOHN WHETEHAMSTEDE (*c.*1390–1465), Abbot of St. Albans (1420–40 and 1452–65), was one of the leading literary figures in fifteenth-century England. The son of Hugh and Margaret Bostock of Wheathampstead (Herts.), he followed an uncle into the great Benedictine abbey and was sent to Oxford University, where he became prior of Gloucester College 1414–17 and doctor of divinity. He was abbot from 1420 until 1440, when he resigned from ill-health — apparently he was subject to uncontrollable blushing — but was re-elected in 1452 on the death of his allegedly laxer successor. As befitted the senior English Benedictine, he was on the English delegations to the General Councils of Pavia and Siena in 1423. In his last years his sight and hearing failed and he was crippled with arthritis.

   Whetehamstede was shy and bashful in public, yet egotistical and boastful in his writings. He could be a harsh disciplinarian to his monks, yet could also be humane and win their affection. He placed a brass on his parents' tomb and sought fame for himself. He was utterly committed to his profession and to St. Albans in particular. Like his predecessors he defended the abbey against its rivals and was therefore litigious; he sought extra privileges from Rome and adorned the buildings; he defended monasticism against attacks in General Council; and he sought to combat that 'ignorance of letters and neglect of study (that) relegates monks to obscurity'. He was himself a considerable scholar and patronised learning. He read extensively not just commonplace medieval texts, but Latin classics, Greek classics in translation, and even modern works by Italian humanists, many of which must have been in his own library. He contributed generously towards a library for Gloucester College and quadrupled the number of St. Albans monks studying there. He gave his books to others, notably Humphrey Duke of Gloucester, and included Italian humanists among his extensive scholarly correspondence. He was fascinated by the Renaissance and particularly admired the works of Boccaccio and Petrarch. He wrote history, dictionaries of classical mythology, about heroes etc, and was regarded in England as an outstanding Latin stylist. He is an important figure in the transmission of the Italian Renaissance to England, but his own humanism was merely a superficial veneer on an essentially medieval outlook. His historiography, encyclopaedism, and Latin style all fit into medieval traditions and are not of high quality. His history is designed to present the most favourable view and consists mainly of anecdotes of purely local importance. His encyclopaedias display formidable learning without original thought. His flowery Latin is exuberantly stuffed with allusions of all kinds and is

> almost a caricature of late medieval finery. His sentences are inflated and contorted, his metaphors often so extravagant, that it is not easy to grasp the meanings he intended to convey.

No humanist could have written in this way, for Whetehamstede was quite unable to emulate the clarity and economy of their prose. Even his mastery of Latin grammar was not complete. He is thus 'one of the last English medieval polymaths rather than one of the early English humanists'. If his writings are thus less original and polished than he himself and many contemporaries supposed, he was nevertheless influential in his day and helped create conditions more propitious for the English humanists that followed.

A. Gransden, *Historical Writing in England* ii, 1982.

E. F. Jacob, 'Verborum Florida Venustas', *Essays in the Conciliar Epoch*, 3rd edn., 1963.

R. Weiss, *Humanism in England during the Fifteenth Century*, 3rd edn. 1967.

DR THOMAS GASCOIGNE (*c.*1403–58) was the conscience of the fifteenth-century Church. Of gentle birth, he was the son of Richard and Beatrix Gascoigne of Hunslet near Leeds in Yorkshire and inherited their estate at an early age. Proceeding to Oxford University about 1416, he had qualified as doctor of divinity by 1434, yet remained in residence for the rest of his life. He was three times elected chancellor of the university, served twice, and deputised on two other occasions. His private income enabled him to study for unusually long without any need to seek lucrative preferment within the church. He did indeed secure livings — he was a canon of Wells Cathedral from 1449 and held two rectories — but he did not depend on them. Thus he surrendered the chancellorship of York Minster in 1432 because he disapproved of its endowment with two rectories and resigned again in 1445 as rector of St. Peter, Cornhill because of ill-health. He could afford his scruples and was in no danger of sharing the abuses of the wordly clergy he criticised because, unlike them, he had no financial worries.

Such principles did, however, earn him great respect in his own day. Gascoigne was certainly a learned man, well-versed in scholastic theology and in the works of the Fathers. Like the humanists, he studied Hebrew, but unlike them wrote barbarous Latin untouched by classical example. His library was substantial. He wrote a life of St. Jerome and translated a life of St. Bridget, but his principal work has been best described as a theological dictionary: Gascoigne researched it and prepared the entries in 1434–57, which were written up as a book after his death under the terms of his will. It is a massive work comprising entries arranged alphabetically, which refer not only to authorities but to topical events and Gascoigne's own views. Much of it is repetitive, for Gascoigne had many hobbyhorses and constantly returned to the same themes. He was forthright in his condemnation of all kinds of ecclesiastical abuses and churchmen. Non-resident parish priests and bishops who did not preach were particular bugbears, especially Bishop Pecock, whom he thought arrogant and heretical. Gascoigne himself was utterly orthodox and the sworn enemy of Lollardy, yet was also critical of Archbishop Arundel's curbs on intellectual debate. He belongs to the tradition of moral criticism and pulpit oratory represented by Archbishop FitzRalph, Bishop Brinton, and the heretic John Wyclif. His denunciations embraced excesses of dress, the chicanery of lawyers and the sophistry of the university. Nothing escaped his critical attention. He cared passionately, lamented the ills of his own day, and feared that worse was to come. Such attacks were perfectly acceptable at the time. Gascoigne was highly respected, though he never secured the bishopric for which he probably hoped. He was entitled 'Catholic Doctor' by the university in 1436, was allowed to live at Oriel College rent free in his last years, and received the unusual privilege of burial in New College Chapel. His interest to modern historians lies not in his morality, however, but as commentator on his contemporary scene. His observations:

> are singularly illustrative of the darkest period in the social and political history of England. In Gascoigne we have an estimate of English society, made by a contemporary who had considerable opportunities for forming a judgement, and possessed sufficient fearlessness in dealing with men and facts.

These need to be considered cautiously, however, for Gascoigne's accuracy is much more debatable than his piety and zeal.

G. R. Owst, *Preaching in Medieval England: An Introduction to the sermon manuscripts of the period c.1350-1450*, 1926.

W. A. Pronger, 'Thomas Gascoigne', *English Historical Review*, liii, 1938.

J. E. T. Rogers ed., *Loci e Libro Veritatem: Passages selected from Gascoigne's Theological Dictionary illustrating the condition of Church and State 1403-48*, 1881.

MASTER JOHN BLACMAN (*b.*1408?) biographer of King Henry VI, was born in Somerset about 1408. He proceeded to Oxford University, where he was a fellow of Merton College from 1436, and eventually qualified as Bachelor of Theology and notary public. Henry VI recruited him as fellow of his new college at Eton in 1443, whence he moved in 1452-8 to become warden of King's Hall, Cambridge, another royal foundation. During these years he was well-acquainted both with the king and his ecclesiastical advisers, such as Bishop Carpenter, who made him dean of his remodelled college at Westbury-on-Trym. In 1457-8, however, Blacman decided his salvation depended on turning his back on this world. Resigning his livings, he entered the most austere of monastic orders, the Carthusians. Though never apparently a fully-fledged monk, he seems to have lived first at the London Charterhouse and then from at least 1463 to 1474 at the Witham Charterhouse in Somerset. It is not known when or where he died. At Witham he followed the monastic rule, read and meditated. The 44 books that he gave Witham Priory, some of them copied by himself, constitute

> the most remarkable private library of devotional literature which is known to have existed in fifteenth-century England. It was a strikingly wide-ranging collection containing books representative of many different schools of spirituality and texts written as recently as about 1461. No other English contemporary can be shown to have such an extensive knowledge of recent devotional literature.

Blacman was clearly a practitioner of the new, private, inner spirituality of the middle ages. He was a 'paradigm of late medieval spirituality'.

Blacman's concerns were thus wholly spiritual and educational, moral and other worldly. He was ignorant of politics and diplomacy, 'oblivious to the political implications of his subject', and quite uninterested in Henry VI as a king or ruler. Why then did he choose to write a biography about him? Actually the term biography misrepresents the *Collectarium* (compilation) that Blacman wrote. It is very short, only twenty pages long. It unsystematically assembles anecdotes unevenly distributed across three decades from his personal reminiscences and from oral testimony of others. It was probably compiled over many years, some items certainly before 1471 and some after. It was certainly not written or revised for publication. It is simply entitled *A Compilation of the Meekness and Good Life of Henry VI*. It thus illustrates the character of the man that Blacman served and admired as 'a model of that form of lay piety which has come to be seen as characteristic of late medieval England' and which Blacman, as we have seen, sought to emulate. No doubt he hoped his record would inspire others to behave likewise. To illustrate Henry's piety was his principle of selection: he was frankly uninterested in Henry's political strengths and failings. He reports factually, without distortion, and his work cannot be dismissed as stereotyped hagiography (biography of saints). Based entirely on reminiscences and hearsay, it is sometimes

demonstrably inaccurate, frequently gullible and definitely unso-
phisticated, but his sources were good and so it is full of insights and
information, many of which can be confirmed elsewhere. Idealised
and biased though it undoubtedly is, the portrait of Henry VI is
consistent, immediate, convincing, and ultimately damning. No
wonder Henry VI was unfit to be king!

R. Lovatt, 'John Blacman: biographer of Henry VI', *The Writing of
History in the Middle Ages,* R. H. C. Davis and J. M. Wallace-
Hadrill, ed., 1981.
R. Lovatt, 'A Collector of Apocryphal Anecdotes: John Blacman
Revisited', in *Property and Politics: Essays in Later Medieval
English History,* A. J. Pollard, ed., 1984.
B. P. Wolffe, *Henry VI,* 1981.

JOHN BROME (*c.*1410–1468) of Baddesley Clinton (War-
wicks.) gentleman is a rare example of a small landowner who can be
studied. Historians' knowledge of medieval agriculture derives
overwhelmingly from the records of the great estates — royal, noble,
and ecclesiastical — but these covered only a fraction of English
land. Much more numerous was the land farmed by small landowners, ranging from the county gentry to the poorest peasants.
Unfortunately medieval peasants did not need records and the
references to them in the records of others enables us to study only
parts of their activities as a class and not as distinct individuals. As
the examples of Howard, Hopton and Stonor show, the gentry were
landowners who took an active interest in the farming of their
estates but did not sully their hands themselves. To keep track of
their affairs, therefore, they required their bailiffs to keep accounts,
but very few of these have survived. Hence the importance of John
Brome, perhaps as small a landowner as can be studied. Even he
probably enjoyed an income of £50 a year, lived in some state in a
multi-roomed house where he drank wine, and had a significant
political career as J.P., three times M.P., and undertreasurer of the
exchequer. He even made himself unpopular with the Yorkist
government and his murder was probably politically motivated. But
smaller than him we probably cannot get.

The Bromes were originally tradesmen in Warwick, where John
inherited a house, Bromesplace, and house property that he rented

out. From his mother he inherited the manor of Baddesley Clinton, comprising a manor house which he rebuilt, about 300 acres of land in enclosed fields and 200 acres of woodland, which he consolidated by piecemeal purchase. It was a compact estate, much more like a modern farm than the scattered open-field strips of many other demesnes. Brome lived on site in his manor house surrounded by fields, animals, bucolic smells and sounds. He also had land at Lapworth and bought two other substantial properties, almost all within eight miles of Warwick. We only know about the Baddesley Clinton estate. Previous owners had leased it out, thus avoiding the burden and risks of management and securing a guaranteed income that left a margin of profit in the farmer's (lessee's) pocket. Brome took over the direct management himself and showed himself willing to invest quite heavily in improving the hedges and ditches, restoring a tilekiln, building fishponds, and upgrading the buildings. He bought cattle (probably Welsh) from local markets, fattened them for a year, and then sold them for consumption in the royal household and to local butchers, selling at 30% above his purchase price. As the beasts grazed in enclosed pastures and there were minimal overheads, the farming was easy, the marketing perhaps more difficult. He employed four full-time farm staff and as many as 24 others did work for him from time to time. Direct management of the farm, quarry and kiln involved considerable capital, a turnover of about £70, and profits of about £20 in cash. Total profits were actually larger than this, for grain, fish, beef, hay, timber, and stone were taken for household consumption and to build Brome's new manor house. Brome appears as an innovative landlord, prepared to give his time to the business, to plough in money for future profit and with his eyes open for commercial opportunities. Even so, it seems that he could not make as much out of the estate as lessees were willing to pay, presumably over and above their own profit, and therefore gave up his direct operation and leased the estate out. His example cannot tell us how lessees like the grazier Benet Lee, who bought fattened beasts from Brome, could make enough to lend £178 to the Duke of Clarence. But it does show how large an income even the smallest gentry could enjoy.

C. Dyer, 'A Small Landowner in the Fifteenth-Century' *Midland History* i, 1972.

RALPH 3rd LORD CROMWELL (c.1394–1456), 'the longest serving treasurer for almost a century', was a trusted royal councillor for most of Henry VI's reign. His public career began somewhat earlier in France. Henry V had knighted him at Agincourt and he served in Normandy from 1417, becoming captain of several towns. From 1422 he sat on the English minority council, apparently backing Cardinal Beaufort in 1425–6 and in 1431–2, when he was appointed chamberlain of the household whilst Henry VI was abroad and was abruptly dismissed by Gloucester on their return to England. Next year, however, Bedford had him appointed treasurer of England. He remained in office in 1443, when he resigned ostensibly on health grounds, but perhaps because of political differences with his colleagues. However that may be, by the late 1440s he was opposed to Suffolk, whose henchman William Tailbois attempted to kill him in Westminster Palace in 1449 and was protected from justice by the duke. Cromwell had the duke's maintenance of Tailbois included in the charges against him. Although harassed by Tailbois until 1453, Cromwell was satisfied with Suffolk's fall and avoided military commitment to the Duke of York, whose councillor he was. His quarrels with the Duke of Exeter over his lordship of Ampthill (Beds.) and with the Percies over the marriage of a coheiress to one of their Neville rivals had national implications that Cromwell had overlooked. He was briefly imprisoned in 1454 and in 1455 was accused, not wholly unfairly, with responsibility for creating the divisions expressed in the first battle of St. Albans.

As Lord Treasurer, Cromwell demonstrated 'a rare combination of clear-sightedness, realism, and determination to manage the king's financial affairs in a particularly difficult era'. He began by taking parliament into his confidence with a detailed statement of the royal finances in 1433. Although serious, the position was not yet desperate. Accumulated debts of £168,000 — three years ordinary revenue — and an annual deficit of £22,000 could be covered by regular taxation. Unfortunately his economies and attempts to prevent new expenditure coincided with the greater demands of the French war and the irresponsible extravagances of the young Henry VI. In 1449, when Bishop Lumley's determined retrenchment ended, debts had risen to £372,000. Exasperation may have contributed to Cromwell's resignation.

Cromwell has been dubbed a rare example of 'integrity in high office', but the profits of office surely contributed to the transformation of his financial position. His own modest inheritance was greatly augmented by the possessions of his wife, in her own right Lady Deincourt and Grey of Rotherfield, which in 1429–30 brought in £1,020, more than many an earl. This was more than doubled to £2,263 by his death, when his moveables were worth £21,456, he had built extensively at Tattersall Castle, South Wingfield and Collyweston, and he had founded the almshouse, school and chantry of Tattershall College. Not all his purchases were legally watertight — hence his quarrel with Exeter over Ampthill — and his executors restored lands that he had seized wrongfully, 'as full greatly it moved the conscience of the said executors'. The ability that he displayed in public service also enabled him to advance himself, most probably through abuse of royal authority and perhaps also through private profit from his treasureship. How different was his conduct from that of those who were disgraced, like Suffolk? Genuine and extravagant piety was compatible with dubious political and business morality.

R. A. Griffiths, *The Reign of King Henry VI 1422–61*, 1981.
J. L. Kirby, 'The Issues of the Lancastrian Exchequer and Lord Cromwell's Estimates of 1433', *Bulletin of the Institute of Historical Research* xxiv, 1951.
K. B. McFarlane, in *England in the Fifteenth Century*, G. L. Harriss, ed., 1981.
K. B. McFarlane, *The Nobility of Later Medieval England*, 1973.
S. J. Payling, 'The Ampthill Dispute: A study in aristocratic lawlessness and the breakdown of Lancastrian government, *English Historical Review* civ, 1989.

WILLIAM DE LA POLE (1396–1450), Earl (1415), Marquis (1446), and Duke of Suffolk (1450), was the hated favourite of Henry VI. Impeached in 1450 for defeat in France and corrupt government at home, he was murdered on his way into exile. His end, however, contrasts sharply with his earlier character and career. A poet, reputedly 'the embodiment of chivalry', and genuinely pious, his life was spent in service to the crown. His military career began in 1415, when the deaths of father and brother made him Earl

of Suffolk. Continuous campaigning from 1417 won the approval
of Henry V, who made him admiral of Normandy (1419) and
knight of the Garter (1421). Second only to Salisbury as field
commander of the Regent Bedford, he took over in 1429, when the
division of his forces led to Talbot's defeat at Pataye and his own
capture at Jargeau. Ransomed, he fought on briefly and returned in
1436, but he served mainly in England from 1433, when he became
steward of the royal household. Although Bedford's nominee, he
was highly acceptable to Cardinal Beaufort, whose kinswoman
Alice Chaucer he had married and whose policies he came to share.
Beaufort's faction became the government in the 1440s and Suffolk
emerged as its leader. He held no ministerial office after 1446, yet
dominated through his personal influence on the king. Decisions
were made outside council, which became thinly attended and was
purged of critics and rivals. Patronage was confined to Suffolk's
adherents, who were placed about the king and in key positions in
the localities. Henry VI was 'enveloped by an impenetrable self-
perpetuating oligarchy that (admittedly) protected him, but yet also
isolated him from alternative sources of council'. Single-faction
rule, the ideal of all favourites, had been achieved. Now Suffolk's
tool, the king became dangerously identified with a narrow clique
that proved to be incompetent.

Suffolk stood for a policy of peace with France, which went
disastrously wrong. He already wanted peace by 1433 and inevitably
supported it when it was taken on by Beaufort and became royal
policy in 1440. Albeit reluctantly, it was he who negotiated the
king's marriage and a truce in 1444, which gave the much weakened
English a respite. Not Suffolk but Henry VI himself agreed to give
up Maine, yet the duke was certainly responsible for the disastrous
attack on Fougères, that enabled the war to resume, and for running
down Norman defences, that gave the French quick victory. He was
no traitor, merely inept.

The poor earl of 1415 became a rich duke by 1450. Whatever his
profits of war, they can hardly have matched his £20,000 ransom, so
his wealth must have come from his marriage and his political career
in England. He was granted the county of Pembroke (1447) and
other property, such important wardships as those of the Duke of
Warwick (1446) and Margaret Beaufort (1444), and many offices:
chief steward of the Duchy of Lancaster (1437); chief justice of

Wales and Chester (1440); great chamberlain (1446) and admiral of England; and warden of the Cinque Ports (1447). Such grants to himself and his supporters were legitimate, if expensive for a bankrupt government, but Suffolk and his adherents also enjoyed profits of extortion, coercion and manipulation of justice. Suffolk himself dominated East Anglia, where 'no man dare do or say anything against my lord of Suffolk or his servants and those that have so done or said shall sore repent'. His local agents relied on his maintenance and Suffolk counted on Henry VI, who duly warded off his conviction in 1450. The duke's murder solved nothing, for King Henry transferred his confidence to other members of the faction, and allowed tensions to develop into the Wars of the Roses. However idealistic and public-spirited they might be, medieval favourites like Suffolk regarded their exploitation of office as legitimate reward for their service.

R. A. Griffiths, *The Reign of King Henry VI 1422–61,* 1981.
C. L. Kingsford, *Prejudice and Promise in Fifteenth Century England,* 1925.

WILLIAM WAYNFLETE (*c.* 1394–1486), Bishop of Winchester from 1447 until his death, was the only schoolmaster to become a bishop in late medieval England. He was the son of Richard Patyn *alias* Barber of Wainfleet (Lincs.) by the daughter of a Cheshire knight. In 1416, when only an acolyte, he was already a Lincolnshire rector and was at a university, probably Oxford, graduating sometime as Bachelor of Theology. Experience in teaching, perhaps in Oxford, may have filled the period up to 1430, when he became headmaster of Winchester College, then the greatest English school. Twelve years later Henry VI poached him as second provost of Eton College. Waynflete probably moulded Henry's initial conception of a triple foundation of chantry, almshouse and school at Eton along the lines of Winchester College and modelled its link with King's College, Cambridge, Henry's other new venture, along the lines of Winchester College and New College, Oxford. That his inclination as well as his experience ran this way is suggested by his own subsequent foundations. His 'great discretion, high trust and fervent zeal' led in 1447 to appointment as Bishop of Winchester, the richest

William Waynflete, Bishop of Winchester
(Artist unknown)

English see: a remarkable testimony to Henry's sense of priorities
and his valuation of Waynflete's services. Waynflete was very close
to the king. He was his confessor, baptised his son, and attended him
both in 1455, when he recovered his sanity, and in 1470, when he
recovered his throne. Hence perhaps the sacking of his palace in

1450, when other favoured bishops were murdered, and his term as chancellor of England in 1456–60. His relations with Edward IV were generally good, but he was implicated in Cook's conspiracy in 1468 and supported the Readeption in 1470–1, when he escaped punishment for his misjudged loyalty.

Waynflete's long life enabled him to outlast rival claimants and to complete other people's projects, although not always as they wished: Eton and King's, Tattershall and Caister Colleges, and St. Cross Hospital, Winchester. Many bishops patronised education, but none placed his stress on 'the practical side of teaching and schoolmastering' and none possessed the exceptional resources that made him 'the most prolific and influential founder in the fifteenth century episcopate'. As early as 1448 he had founded Magdalen Hall, Oxford, later Magdalen College, whose seventy scholars ultimately matched Wykeham's New College and Henry VI's King's College. He lavishly endowed it with lands worth £675 a year. His feeder schools, Magdalen College and Wainfleet schools, were less grand than Winchester and Eton Colleges, but they were just as educationally innovative. Though no humanist himself, Waynflete was receptive to new ideas and new technology. Magdalen College School spear-headed a 'revolution in grammar teaching' along Renaissance lines, used new *printed* textbooks devised by its master John Anwykyll, and thus foreshadowed John Colet's more famous St. Paul's School. Thus trained humanists went on to Magdalen College itself, where Waynflete's lectureships were a novelty copied in all future institutions. Such achievements explain the attribution to him of 'an outstanding role in the promotion of the educational revolution in England'.

Yet Waynflete was also a churchman. Though ordained late and non-resident as a rector, he was trained in theology and was an active and resident bishop. He wanted his students to become pastors and parsons, not lawyers and administrators. Hence his preference for theology as their course of study and his requirements that they should take out priest's orders within a year of their M.A. degree and that they should preach and say mass regularly. Moreover Magdalen College and Wainfleet School were chantries and a third one was founded in his cathedral. It was there among his fellow bishops that Waynflete chose burial.

V. Davis, 'William Waynflete and the Wars of the Roses'. *Southern History* xi, 1989.

V. Davis, 'William Waynflete and the Educational Revolution of the Fifteenth Century', in *People, Politics and the Community in the Later Middle Ages,* J. Rosenthal and C. Richmond, eds., 1987.

R. A. Griffiths, *The Reign of King Henry VI 1422-61,* 1981.

ADAM MOLEYNS (*c.* 1400–50), Bishop of Chichester from 1445, distinguished himself both as a politician and as a Renaissance humanist. The younger son of a Lancashire knight, he prepared for a career in the Church by studying at Oxford University, where he graduated as doctor of civil law in 1435. Long before then, in 1429, he was at the papal Curia in Italy, where he not only ingratiated himself with the pope, but mixed with Poggio and other Renaissance humanists. He was appointed papal chamberlain and clerk of the apostolic chamber in 1435, when he acted as royal proctor at the Curia. He visited the Council of Basle on his way home to pursue an administrative career in England. He was clerk to the royal council from 1436–42 and was employed on frequent diplomatic missions from 1438. His appointment as king's secretary in 1441 involved close contact with Henry VI. Moleyns won his trust — witness his involvement in the foundation of Eton College — and established considerable influence over the impressionable monarch. In 1444 he achieved ministerial rank as keeper of the privy seal. Capable and diligent, he made himself indispensable to the Duke of Suffolk by the late 1440s, becoming intimately and emotionally involved with his policies. Hence his rash accusations of financial maladministration and favouritism against the Duke of York as lieutenant of France in 1446. The fall of Rouen in 1449 and the Crown's virtual bankruptcy represented complete failure and discredited him politically, as Moleyns recognized. To escape the inevitable storm, he resigned his ministry in December 1449 and planned to go on pilgrimage abroad. Before going, however, he went to Portsmouth to pay the troops, was accused of treachery for losing Normandy, and was murdered on 9 January 1450. Suffolk's impeachment followed.

Moleyns's aristocratic connection contributed to his lightning promotion, but his ability and literary accomplishments mattered more. He

> successfully cultivated an elegant Latin style free from the conventions of Latin prose as taught during the Middle Ages. Moleyns appears to have been on the same level as most Italian humanists of the time and by far superior to any of his English contemporaries, Beckyngton included.

Since such skills had become essential for diplomacy, they brought Moleyns rapid ecclesiastical promotion. His first rectories in the 1420s presumably came through family connections, but those that followed were the rewards of papal and royal service. Altogether he enjoyed fourteen rectories and twelve canonries, archdeaconries and deaneries, not all at once. He duly became Bishop of Chichester in 1445.

As Chichester was a poor bishopric, Moleyns, who was certainly ambitious and reputedly covetous, could expect promotion to a better see in due course. Suffolk indeed proposed him unsuccessfully for the bishopric of London. In the meantime Moleyns applied himself to improving Chichester's rights and amenities. He secured royal exemption from the court of admiralty on his lands and in 1447 was licensed to include 12,000 acres of land in his parks and to crenellate twelve manor houses. Even after returning to England, he maintained his classical interests, corresponding with the noted humanist Aeneas Sylvius Piccolomini (later Pope Pius II 1458–64), but he was far too eminent and busy to teach or write. Like other early English humanists he found that his intellectual accomplishments were worth more in politics than education and brought rapid promotion to positions of responsibility that prevented further study.

R. A. Griffiths, *The Reign of King Henry VI 1422–61*, 1981.
R. Weiss, *Humanism in England during the Fifteenth Century*, 3rd edn., 1967.

JACK CADE, leader of the Kentish rebellion of 1450, is almost totally obscure. The revolt occurred in the spring, soon after Suffolk's impeachment, and for some of the same causes. From the Ashford area in late May the rebels made a fortified camp at

Blackheath on 11 June, just as Robert Kett was to 'inkennell' himself in 1549, and waited for the king's return from the Leicester parliament. Negotiations were fruitless and the rebels withdrew rather than face the king in battle. An easy victory over their pursuers brought them back to Blackheath and caused the king's men to mutiny and demand action against Lord Saye and other evil councillors. The king placed them in protective custody in the Tower before withdrawing to the Midlands. The rebels entered London, executed Saye, ostensibly legally, and some insurgents for indiscipline, broke sanctuary and prison, looted and burnt. Driven out on 5 July, Cade retired to Kent, where his men melted away. He was mortally wounded resisting arrest at Heathfield in Sussex. Other risings occurred in Essex, Sussex, Wiltshire and elsewhere. There were further disturbances in 1451. A 'harvest of heads' followed.

Jack Cade himself first emerged from obscurity during the rebellion. He *may* have been an Irishman or from Kent or from Sussex, where he *may* have served in Sir Thomas Dacre's household. He *may* have been Dr. John Aylmer, a physician, and he *may* have formerly served Charles VII of France. His pseudonyms of John Amend-All and John Mortimer, the latter suggesting kinship with the Duke of York, were chosen 'for to have the more favour of the people'. Like his splendid armour and the sword he had carried before him, the name Mortimer fuelled his prestige and helped to 'advance his pride and display his victory'. Presumably it was Cade who arranged rebel grievances in manifestoes appropriate for different audiences: 'Cade's rising was the first popular rising in English history to produce a coherent programme of grievances, requests, and remedies in the form of written, publicised manifestoes'. He did well to hold his forces together for so long and to maintain discipline. He did not shrink from violence and private vengeance, but used the forms of law when they served his purpose.

In many ways Cade's rebellion was a typical popular uprising. Participants were not just poor rustics, but well-to-do farmers, tradesmen, Londoners and even some gentry. They pleaded loyalty to the king, claiming to be petitioners rather than rebels, and sought the remedy of their grievances. Some were purely Kentish in origin, such as corrupt parliamentary elections and oppressive Cinque Port officials; others, such as abuses of purveyance and justice, had wider appeal; and the rest denounced the 'false traitors about his highness'

— the king's ministers — for their deceit and mismanagement, for monopolising patronage and perverting justice. Henry VI

> had false counsel, for his lands are lost, his merchandise lost, his commons destroyed, the sea lost, France lost, himself so poor that he may not pay for his meat nor drink, he owes more than ever did king of England, and yet daily his traitors that be about him wait for anything that should come to him by law and they ask for it from him.

They wanted such men punished. They did not seek revolutionary change, but to make the existing system work better. They wanted a more substantial, aristocratic council. It was thus typically conservative in its objectives. York was a proposed councillor and was seen as a reformer, but he was abroad and was not behind the revolt. Weakness made Henry VI negotiate with Cade, but as he conceded nothing of substance the rebellion was fruitless.

R. A. Griffiths, *The Reign of King Henry VI 1422–61*, 1981.
H. M. Lyle, *The Rebellion of Jack Cade 1450*, Historical Association, 1950.

WILLIAM SAVERNAKE (c. 1380–1460) illustrates the lifestyle of the lower clergy and perhaps also of the urban tradesman of the later middle ages. Presumably a Wiltshireman, he was ordained in 1409, was appointed vicar of Ibberton (Dorset) in 1441, and in 1452 became chaplain of Munden's chantry, Bridport. This was a less arduous post than that of vicar for an old man, for cantarists had no parochial responsibilities and had only to celebrate mass (Holy Communion) and hold other services daily for the good of the soul of the founder. Most founders of chantries provided for only one priest, who held services at an altar or chapel within an existing church. The chantry founded by John Munden in 1349, somewhat unusually, employed two chaplains, used a separate building for services (St. Michael's Chapel), and paid them £5 each, which was quite a generous salary and was actually exceeded in practice. Many chantries failed, sometimes through lack of income, but often because the chaplains neglected or embezzled the endowment. It was to prevent this and to ensure that masses were said for their benefit forever that founders often made monasteries or town corporations responsible for supervision of their chantries. Bridport corporation took its responsibilities seriously, inspecting the accounts and property each year. It was probably for this reason that Savernake as warden compiled accounts in 1453–60, though he certainly kept them in much more detail than was needed. It is this detail that is of such value, as such relatively poor and small households normally could not keep accounts and had no need for them anyway.

John Munden had been a wealthy and important man — M.P. and J.P. for Dorset — and his house, in which the chaplains lived, was a substantial structure containing hall, kitchen, pantry, separate bedrooms, and probably other rooms too. It was quite well-furnished with tables, chairs, pots and pans, and even silver spoons. There was a walled garden, a dovecot, which provided fresh meat, and an orchard, where the chaplains grew fruit. It must have been one of the better residences in Bridport. The chaplains were responsible for keeping up these premises, the chapel, and the properties that formed the endowment, all of which were repaired from time to time by workmen, who took lunch with them. They also provided candles, wine etc for the chapel. They were able to afford a servant paid not more than £1 10s. a year and a laundress at 4d. a quarter, and were also able to entertain guests, mainly ecclesiastics and some for weeks at a time. Evidently they were quite comfortably off, though life for two old priests was extremely quiet.

The accounts are most valuable for what they tell us about the diet of ordinary people in the later middle ages. The basic foodstuffs were bread and second-best ale, though best ale or wine was consumed on occasion. They ate a lot of meat; normally beef, pork *and* mutton each week, sometimes veal, lamb or chickens, once each woodcock and goose. The fish and other seafood they ate one day each week and daily in Lent was often fresh rather than salted and was surprisingly varied: stockfish, mackerel, oysters, ling, haddock, cod, whiting, conger eel, hake, herrings, mussels, whelks and cockles. They made the Lenten diet slightly more interesting with almonds, figs and raisins. After Lent, understandably fed up with fish and figs, they cut them to the minimum and instead ate more eggs and butter. Like most medieval people, they consumed a lot of peas, spices like pepper, ginger and cinnamon, and used honey as a sweetener. They bought only a little fruit, perhaps because they grew it themselves. It is surprising how varied their diet was and that they could buy fresh meat and fish in such small quantities throughout the year. It is also amazing how well the two of them could live on a combined income of about £12.

K.L. Wood-Legh ed., *A Small Household in the XVth Century*, 1956.

WILLIAM WORCESTER alias BOTONER (1415–*c.*1483), the antiquary, was one of the new gentlemen-bureaucrats of late medieval England. He was born in Bristol and was educated at Oxford University in 1432–8. He was financed there by the distinguished soldier Sir John Fastolf, whom he served from 1439–59 in many different capacities. His only official office was steward of Castle Combe (Wilts.), but he wrote Fastolf's letters and was sometimes called his secretary; he organised his extensive land-purchases, researching titles and defending them in the courts; he supervised his building operations; he toured his estates; and he was his doctor in his last years. As Fastolf's executor he realised his assets, lobbied the great, and litigated in church and secular courts. Prevented from fulfilling Fastolf's wishes, he compromised in 1472 with Bishop Waynflete, who diverted endowments from Caister College to Magdalen College, Oxford. Fastolf's affairs were finally settled about 1477. Worcester was thus one of the expert administrators so indispensable in late medieval England. A century earlier he would have been a cleric, but Worcester, though pious enough, remained a layman and married. His service did not make his fortune, for Fastolf was a particularly mean employer. Only in the 1470s did Worcester achieve financial security and time for the leisure interests crowded out by his professional career.

Worcester's inquiries were wide-ranging and miscellaneous. He was interested in zoology and botany, medicine, geography and topography, heraldry and genealogy, architecture and antiquities, history and legend, classical literature, the Greek and Hebrew languages. He used them in his work, for example when valuing properties and tracing titles, and his work informed his studies with expert knowledge of land law, surveying and building costs. Manuscript books, documents, buildings and monuments, and oral history were all grist to his mill. He recorded his discoveries and sources in notebooks organised thematically with a view to eventual publication. Some have been published as they stand. Of his finished works, we have his *Survey of Bristol,* his *Book of Noblesse,* and his translation of Cicero's *Of Old Age,* and the works of others that he corrected. Much more has been lost.

Worcester was an indefatigable researcher, who consulted his sources for the information they contained. He was untouched by Renaissance notions of style or history. His Latin was pedestrian and workaday; he did not discriminate between history and legend, oral history and folklore; and his historical work was rough and incoherent. Such criticisms, however, are misdirected. Worcester did not aspire to be a humanist and even those fifteenth-century Englishmen who did shared his emphasis on matter over manner. We should appreciate his documentary expertise, his criticism of modern stories, and his awareness of historical change. What we have are not finished histories, but his notes.

> Few of us would care to be judged posthumously by the evidence of our notebooks alone, let alone our prose style. If all he had done was to fill a handful of notebooks, that would still be remarkable on more than one count, of which the least weighty perhaps is the value of their contents to us; yet that is great indeed.

He was instead an antiquary, founder of a great tradition, and the anticipator of many later developments. His *Itineraries* precede by fifty years those of Leland and are inferior only in quantity, not quality; his *Survey of Bristol* foreshadows those of Stow and Hooker on London and Exeter a century later; his lost *Ancient Families of Norfolk* was the first county history; and his lost *Acts of Sir John Fastolf* was a pioneering biography. We should regret what is lost, not what remains.

A. Gransden, *Historical Writing in England* ii, 1982.
K.B. McFarlane, 'William Worcester: A Preliminary Survey', in *England in the Fifteenth Century*, G.L. Harriss, ed., 1981.

RICHARD, DUKE OF YORK (1411–1460) turned the crisis of the 1450s into the dynastic contest of Lancaster and York. The son of Richard Earl of Cambridge by Anne Mortimer, he was descended from Edward III through two lines: via Cambridge's father Edmund

Duke of York (*d.* 1402) and via Anne's great-grandfather Lionel Duke of Clarence (*d.*1368). Lionel was the elder brother of John of Gaunt, ancestor of the Lancastrian kings. Cambridge was executed for treason in 1415 but his brother's death a few weeks later made his son Duke of York. When Anne's brother died in 1425, Richard became Earl of March and Ulster. Though not quite in the class of John of Gaunt, Richard's income of about £6,500 made him the richest nobleman of his age. He was particularly strong in Wales and Ireland. His marriage to a daughter of Ralph Neville, Earl of Westmorland and Joan Beaufort gave him wide family connections and proved a priceless political asset.

York was a knight of the Garter as early as 1433 and king's lieutenant in France (commander-in-chief) in 1436. His terms of reappointment in 1440 withheld only the title of regent, and he was given two counties and three vicomtés in 1444. Like his Mortimer predecessors, he became lieutenant of Ireland in 1446 and 1454. About 1445 his two sons were created earls and he benefited as much as anyone from the fall of the Duke of Gloucester. He was thus treated exceptionally favourably. But York was not satisfied to be the greatest of subjects. The regal scale of his spending outran even his income. He planned to wed his son to a French princess, dreamed of the crown of Castile, and saw himself as heir to Henry VI in 1447–53. Supreme command was merely his due. He was unduly bitter about arrears in his salary, was insulted by the independent command of one Beaufort in 1443 and his succession in France by another in 1446, and he may even have resented the creation of new dukes. He felt he had not received his due and was being victimised. It was thus a mixture of pride, ambition, and paranoia that prompted him, like Gloucester earlier, to insist that government required his approval.

Yet York was not outstandingly able. Extravagance forced disagreeable expedients on him which, characteristically, he blamed on the government. In France he delegated military operations to others and barring some minor reforms appears inactive. There and in Ireland the support he won may stem partly from misapplication of royal patronage, as he was charged in 1446. Certainly his protectorates won him new partisans. Ten years spent continually abroad preceded his identification in 1450 as the remedy for evil rule, an image he assiduously fostered. He posed as a reformer and presented

Somerset as an obstacle to be removed by any means. He would not accept even the king's veto. Most lords initially supported neither duke and gave priority to their loyalty to the king. They thwarted York's coup in 1452, but by preventing his punishment enabled him, more ruthlessly, to eliminate his foes in 1455. Because King Henry could not curb him, York repeated his protests, obstruction, and coups and made effective government impossible. Once acceptable to all, York evolved into a factional leader, forcing a choice first between himself and royal favourites, and then in 1460 between himself and the king, repudiating his allegiance and claiming the crown by hereditary right. His recognition instead as Henry's heir solved nothing, but precipitated the Wars of the Roses and his own death at the battle of Wakefield in the last day of 1460.

J. M. W. Bean, 'The Financial Position of Richard, Duke of York', in *War and Government in the Middle Ages*, J. Gillingham and J. C. Holt, ed., 1984.

R. A. Griffiths, *The Reign of King Henry VI 1422–61*, 1981.

P. A. Johnson, *Duke Richard of York 1411–60*, 1988.

M. K. Jones, 'Somerset, York and the Wars of the Roses', *English Historical Review* civ, 1989.

T. B. Pugh, 'Richard Plantagenet (1411–60), Duke of York, as the King's Lieutenant in France and Ireland' in *Aspects of Late Medieval Government and Society*, J. G. Rowe, ed., 1986.

R. L. Storey, *The End of the House of Lancaster*, 2nd edn., 1986.

EDMUND BEAUFORT, DUKE OF SOMERSET (*c.*1406–1455) was blamed for Henry VI's loss of France. His father was the eldest legitimated bastard of John of Gaunt (*d.*1399). As a younger son, Edmund depended for his support on a good marriage and royal favour. Service in France brought him the counties of Mortain (1427) and Maine, other lands and offices, all lost by 1450, whilst his uncle Cardinal Beaufort left him some lands and secured him command of royal castles in England and Wales. In 1442 he became Earl and in 1443 Marquis of Dorset. His elder brother the Duke of Somerset died in 1444. Edmund became Duke of Somerset himself in 1448, constable of England (1450), captain of Calais (1451), and justice of the forests south of Trent (1453). He must have cherished hopes of succession to the crown. If profitable at all, his offices were held only for life. So too were his wife's lands. His own main resource comprised royal annuities inherited from his brother and others granted on his various promotions, but the crown could not pay them regularly. Edmund was almost landless. He lacked those great estates that gave other noblemen independent power in the provinces. He could not rival the Dukes of York and Buckingham.

Edmund's military career began with capture and defeat at Baugé in 1421. He served repeatedly in France from 1427, particularly distinguishing himself by the recapture of Harfleur in 1440, and was thus well-qualified militarily for appointment in 1446 as lieutenant-general and governor of France and Normandy (commander-in-chief). 1446-9 was a time of truce, when English defences withered, whilst the French prepared their decisive assault. Probably nothing could have averted their victory in 1449-50, but Somerset did not prepare for determined defence or counter declining morale. The biggest errors of these years, the surrender of Maine and attack on Fougères, were decided at Westminster, but Somerset's obstruction of the former and recalcitrance over the latter merely postponed the inevitable, heightened tensions, and offended Charles VII. English resistance collapsed at once. Somerset quickly surrendered Rouen on unnecessarily humiliating conditions that placed his own well-being first and capitulated again at Caen next year. Whatever other factors contributed, Somerset's conduct made matters worse and he deservedly received much of the blame.

His defeat destroyed his reputation everywhere but in the immediate circle of the king. Appointed a councillor in 1443 as ally of Cardinal Beaufort, he remained to support Suffolk, and became the leader of Suffolk's faction, which remained in power in the face of the Commons' hostility. Cade's men did not include Somerset in their projected council and the duke was nearly lynched by his defeated soldiers on his return to England. The Duke of York focused his attack on him, presenting him as an obstacle to reform and seeking to try him for treason for losing France. York distinguished between allegiance to the king and hostility to Somerset. Successive appeals to King Henry in 1450 and 1452 failed to upset Somerset's favour with the king. When Henry VI went mad in 1453, however, York's ally the Duke of Norfolk appealed Somerset of treason and had him imprisoned in the Tower. No trial had taken place when Henry VI recovered his senses. Immediately Somerset was freed, acquitted of the charges, and restored to favour. He may have planned York's destruction. York's resort to force aimed to counter this and to destroy Somerset, whose surrender he demanded. Both ends were achieved by the first battle of St. Albans, where Somerset was killed fighting heroically, at which point, a Yorkist chronicler revealingly remarked, 'the battle was ceased'. York recovered power over Somerset's dead body, but his death proved not to be the end of factional struggles, but merely a stage in their escalation.

C. T. Allmand, *Lancastrian Normandy 1415–50: The History of a Medieval Occupation,* 1983.

R. A. Griffiths, *The Reign of King Henry VI 1422–61,* 1981.

M. K. Jones, 'Somerset, York and the Wars of the Roses', *English Historical Review* civ (1989).

HUMPHREY STAFFORD, DUKE OF BUCKINGHAM (1402–60) strove to moderate the personal antagonisms that escalated into the Wars of the Roses. He was only a baby when he succeeded his father Edmund Earl of Stafford (*d.*1403), a Midland magnate with a long tradition of service to the crown. His mother Anne (*d.*1438), daughter of Thomas of Woodstock (*d.*1397) and grand-daughter of Edward III, brought him half the great Bohun inheritance mainly in Wales, the earldoms of Buckingham, Hereford and Northampton, and four Bourchier half-brothers. He was a prince of the blood royal and with £6,000 a year 'among the richest and most powerful landowners in England', scarcely second to Richard Duke of York. He married Anne daughter of Ralph Earl of Westmorland and Joan Beaufort, legitimated bastard of John of Gaunt and half-sister of Henry IV. Such wealth, power and connections explain his election as K.G. in 1429 and his creation in 1444 as Duke of Buckingham with precedence over all future dukes not the sons of kings. Charles VII of France seriously considered a match between his daughter and Buckingham's son.

The duke's exceptional services during the 1450s built on those of preceding decades. Already in France in 1420, he accompanied Henry VI there in 1430, contributing to English consolidation as lieutenant-general of Normandy, governor of Paris, and constable of

France. He went on embassies and was captain of Calais in 1442–51. He was a royal councillor in England from 1424 and attended fairly assiduously. In reward for such services he was created Count of Perche in 1431, controlled Tutbury honour from 1435, was granted Penshurst from 1447 and was appointed warden of the Cinque Ports from 1450. Perche brought in an estimated £533.66 'in time of peace', but he was owed £19,395 for Calais in 1449, a time when his Welsh income was declining. Unlike the Duke of York, who faced similar problems, Buckingham surmounted them without resort to crisis measures. His high regard amongst contemporaries reflects the industry and capacity he brought to his military and administrative responsibilities, even if he did lack the 'necessary qualities ever to become a great statesman and leader'. If he avoided commitment to Beaufort or Gloucester in the 1420s and '30s, he shared in the trials of Joan of Arc and Eleanor Cobham and the arrest of Gloucester. He quarrelled with other noblemen and arbitrarily imprisoned and despoiled the Montford family. His reputation was not without blemish.

Buckingham was related to all important parties in the 1450s — the king and queen, York and Somerset, the Nevilles and Bourchiers — but refused to join any faction. In 1455, on the eve of the first battle of St. Albans, he gave priority to his allegiance and the maintenance of royal authority:

> We wish the whole world to know that we have not come here to support any one person or for any other cause but only to be in company with the king our sovereign lord, as by right we are bound to do.

His refusal to surrender the Duke of Somerset did not mean he thought him right. He stood by the king during Cade's rebellion and the Dartford fiasco, but he sought to prevent extreme measures against York. When the king was mad, Buckingham backed York and his Bourchier half-brothers held ministerial office. He acted as surety for both parties. Loyalty and even-handedness, however, became ever more difficult. In 1459 he stood by the court both at Ludford and the ensuing Coventry parliament, when York was defeated and condemned. In 1460 he was one of those deliberately eliminated by the Yorkists at the battle of Northampton. The time for principled moderation and reconciliation had passed.

R. A. Griffiths, *The Reign of King Henry VI 1422–61*, 1981.
C. Rawcliffe, *The Staffords, Earls of Stafford and Dukes of Buckingham 1394–1521*, 1978.

RICHARD NEVILLE, EARL OF SALISBURY (c. 1400–60), turned Richard Duke of York from an ineffectual protester into a realistic pretender for the crown. Salisbury was the eldest son of Ralph Neville, Earl of Westmorland (d.1425) by Joan Beaufort (d.1440), legitimated daughter of John of Gaunt. From his father he inherited the great northern lordships of Middleham, Sheriff Hutton (Yorks.) and Penrith (Cumbs.). Like him, he was warden of the West March towards Scotland in 1420–34 and from 1443. His mother's royal and Beaufort connections secured him his earldom in right of his wife in 1429 and his victory over his nephew, the second Earl of Westmorland. The claims of birth were supplemented by good service on the borders, in France (1431, 1436), and from 1437 as a councillor. To both parents he owed exceptionally wide connections: his brothers were the Bishop of Durham and three barons and his many brothers-in-law included the Duke of York. Outstandingly able, he capitalised fully on his financial and military resources, court connections, and the marriages of his siblings and children.

Salisbury was first and foremost a great northern nobleman. His wife's southern inheritance was a source of cash spent in the north. So too was his border wardenship, which he converted into 'a principal buttress of dynastic policy'. His own lands were concentrated in the West Riding, but he built on the wardenship, the promise of favour at court, his brother's bishopric, the custody/lease of Barnard Castle (Durh.), and his capacity to pay retainers to extend his power into Cumbria and County Durham, and throughout Yorkshire. Hence Westmorland's unwilling surrender in 1443 and the feud with the Percies provoked by trespassing on their preserves both in Cumbria and Yorkshire. Their quarrel was pursued not by Salisbury or Northumberland but by their sons. Beginning after 1450, the violent clashes culminated in a private battle at Stamford Bridge in 1454.

The Neville-Percy feud was the chief single factor which turned political rivalry into civil war. Richard of York could not have renewed his challenge to Somerset without the Neville alliance. The first battle of the St. Albans was the immediate outcome of the harnessing of this private quarrel to the central issue between the two royal dukes.

That had not been Salisbury's intention. He backed the king in 1452, whilst striving to temper York's punishment. He had too much to gain from his court connections. But these were strained by his son's dispute with Somerset over his Warwick inheritance and Henry VI failed to intervene on his behalf in the Percy feud. York did, however, during his first Protectorate. Salisbury was then a generally acceptable nominee as chancellor, but was replaced on Henry VI's recovery by a council that included, significantly, his rival Northumberland. Salisbury was therefore at York's side at the first battle of St. Albans, where significantly Northumberland as well as Somerset was eliminated. A twenty-year extension of his marcher wardenship and his son George's promotion to a bishopric during York's second protectorate showed York rather than the court to be best able to serve his interests. Salisbury and his son Warwick shared York's defeat, exile and forfeiture in 1459. They defeated their enemies at Northampton in 1460 and placed the king in protective custody. As in Buckingham's case a tension between allegiance and faction remained. It was the Nevilles who blocked York's usurpation late in 1460, substituting recognition as King Henry's heir, and Salisbury died with York when this unworkable compromise was decisively rejected by Margaret of Anjou at Wakefield. Without the Nevilles, York could achieve nothing, but at the crucial moment their support faltered. Consequently Salisbury's son saw York's son to the throne.

R. A. Griffiths, *The Reign of King Henry VI 1422–61*, 1981.
A. J. Pollard, *North-Eastern England during the Wars of the Roses*, 1990.
R. L. Storey, *The End of the House of Lancaster*, 2nd edn. 1986.

REGINALD PECOCK (*c.*1390–1460), Bishop of St. Asaph (1444–50) and Chichester (1450–8), was the only bishop convicted of heresy in late medieval England. A Welshman and Oxford graduate, Pecock held rectories in Gloucester (1424) and London, where he was also master of Whittington College (1431), before becoming in turn Bishop of St. Asaph in 1444 and Chichester in 1450. Convicted of heresy in 1457, he was forced to recant to escape the flames, his books were burnt, he had to resign his see (1458), and he was confined to Thorney Abbey, where he was allowed

> a secret close chamber (having a chimney) and convenience within the abbey, where he may have some sight to some altar to hear mass and that he pass not the said chamber. That he have no books to look on, but only a breviary, a mass book, a psalter, and a Bible. That he have nothing to write with; no stuff to write upon.

Pecock's loyalty to the Church explains both his submission and his life's work. Firstly, he defended the Church against criticism, as in his *Repressor of Overmuch Blaming of the Clergy* and his defence of non-preaching bishops, whose many essential duties, he argued, did not include preaching. Secondly, he wrote to improve lay understanding of Christianity and to convert heretics to orthodoxy. To reach such audiences, he wrote in English — the first theologian to do so — and relied overwhelmingly on logical reasoning. Lollards, he appreciated, rejected the authority of Catholic theology and tradition, interpreted the Bible for themselves, and therefore needed to be persuaded of the reasonableness of the official position. He was too serious about his subject and too respectful to his readers to simplify and wrote at whatever length was needed to make his meaning clear. The result was 'monumental, heavy, massive, dull and sometimes, but not always, wearisome and lacking in originality'. It was too excessively academic and technical for any but intellectuals. They, however, objected to his refusal to insist on unreasonable beliefs, such as Christ's descent into hell, and his determination to prove by logic what was already supported by Scripture, the Early Christian Fathers, or tradition. In his recantation they forced Pecock to admit to 'presuming of mine own natural wit, and preferring the judgement of natural reason before the New and Old Testaments, and the authority and determination of our mother, Holy Church'. Apart from attributing to him certain doctrines that he never taught, his critics failed to realise that 'the authority of the Bible was for Pecock unquestionable' on matters of faith. As his arguments probably passed unnoticed by those for whom they were intended, Pecock's sufferings were in vain.

It was not what Pecock said, but how he said it that led to his downfall. He was handsome, dignified, and immensely vain. Although not particularly learned or original, he exaggerated the value of his work — never had Christianity been expounded 'so clearly, so feelingly and comprehensively' — and wrongly thought his arguments irrefutable. He was extremely critical and historically acute, rejecting the Donation of Constantine, parts of the Creed, and even the Ten Commandments for his own Four Tables! He was amazingly tactless and did not understand the strength of hostility to him or its source. Such grave personal defects obscured his utter sincerity, intellectual honesty, and ardent sense of mission. His English prose and sense of the past are more memorable than his theology.

C. W. Brockwell, *Bishop Reginald Pecock and the Lancastrian Church*, 1985.

V. H. H. Green, *Bishop Reginald Pecock*, 1945.

E. F. Jacob, 'Reginald Pecock, Bishop of Chichester', *Essays in Later Medieval History*, 1963.

JOHN PASTON (1421–66), esquire, is perhaps the best known late medieval gentleman and has often indeed been taken as representative of his whole class. This is due to the survival of the incomparable Paston letters. Approximately 1,100 items in all, these constitute by far the most extensive collection of contemporary letters, larger by far than those of the Celys, Stonors and Plumptons. They are also the most interesting and significant. They date mainly from the years 1450–80 and it was evidently John I who first systematically hoarded them.

It was John's father William (d. 1444), a royal justice, who first raised the family into the ranks of the gentry by the profits of law and by the marriage of his son to Margaret Maltby, an important local heiress. John too received a legal training at the Inner Temple and was a practising lawyer as well as a landowner. His most important client proved to be Sir John Fastolf (d. 1459) of Caister (Norf.), an old, childless and extremely rich ex-soldier, whose last, oral, will gave all his East Anglian lands to Paston on condition of the foundation of Caister College and a payment of 4,000 marks

(£2,667.33). This lifted the Pastons into the front rank of the Norfolk gentry, justifying John's appointment as sheriff and his repeated election as knight of the shire. It also precipitated a series of disputes, conducted at law and by force of arms, that lasted for the rest of John's life, perhaps precipitating his death, and even beyond. Fastolf's oral will was not universally accepted as valid: it may have been fabricated by John Paston or else resulted from undue pressure on the old knight. It certainly brought John endless trouble and expense, three terms in the Fleet prison, and ultimately secured for the family only part of the lands at issue. Rigid, resolute and calculating, Paston does not appear even through his own correspondence as the most attractive and sympathetic of the participants.

The Paston letters are full of information on many topics. They have been ransacked by historians for information on love and marriage, religion, relations of landlord and tenant, and many other topics. Their principal value, however, is as a source for the politics, local government, law and order in East Anglia. As a new family, the Pastons had to defend their status and possessions against rivals: thus John himself was accused, wrongly, of being a serf; his title to his father's lands was contested; and he was engaged in litigation in several courts over the Fastolf lands. A good title was not sufficient, for the legal system could be perverted by bribery, influence and threats; it could be circumvented by violence in the locality or by influence at court. John Paston had a good title to Gresham (Norf.) in 1448, when it was stormed by Lord Moleyns, who could not be prosecuted because he was backed by the Duke of Suffolk, who was supreme both locally and nationally. Later Suffolk's son demolished John's lodge and the Duke of Norfolk besieged Caister Castle. Political fluctuations, calculations and tactics are faithfully mirrored by the letters. The impression is of a society where might rather than right prospered, where local government and justice were corrupt, and where gentlemen had to engage in politics, had to find a lord to depend on, and had to fulfil his wishes however outrageous they might be. This, it is often supposed, was the pattern everywhere. It may well be, however, that East Anglia was exceptional or that Paston's abrasiveness made him the centre and the *cause* of the trouble the letters depict. Perhaps some contemporaries even in East Anglia, such as John Hopton, managed to live more peaceful and trouble-free lives. But in their vivid details and lively language the

Paston letters evoke the fifteenth century as no other surviving records do.

H. S. Bennett, *The Pastons and their England*, 1932; repr. 1968.
N. Davis ed., *Paston Letters and Papers of the Fifteenth Century*, 2 vols. 1971–6.
J. Gairdner ed., *The Paston Letters 1422–1509*, 1904; repr. 1986.
C. Richmond, *The Paston Family in the Fifteenth Century: The First Phase*, 1990.

MARGARET PASTON (*c.* 1420–82), wife of John Paston I (d. 1466), illuminates the world of the married woman. The legal subjection of women first to fathers and then to husbands meant that most cannot be studied by historians and that those women who are best known are predominantly rich widows, whose property and behaviour was no longer controlled by men. Margaret Paston is immortalised by the Paston letters. She was born Margaret Maltby of Mautby in Norfolk and was a considerable heiress. Hers was an arranged marriage, but one in which Margaret willingly accepted her husband's superiority and in which convenience blossomed into affectionate companionship between the two partners. She bore her husband John Paston seven children and instilled in them respect and obedience to their father even after they had grown up. She deferred to John's wishes, accepted his priorities, and sought to fulfil them even after his death, when she upbraided their eldest son for falling short. Yet even Margaret did not *wholly* identify herself with John. It is striking that in 1482, 42 years after her marriage, she chose to be buried not at Paston but in the parish church of Maltby, her original home, which she improved and beautified.

Margaret's 104 surviving letters and those to her and about her cast a flood of light on the life of the fifteenth-century gentlewoman. They illuminate the upbringing and education of her children, relations with them before and after marriage, the material considerations behind the arranged marriage, and the traumas attendant on romantic love. The fifteenth-century gentlewoman was above all a housewife, responsible for running a household of considerable and fluctuating size. She was responsible for catering and clothing. Much had to be bought outside, some at local markets, luxuries from further afield, and much — like fish in Lent and livery cloth —

requiring bulk orders in advance. She was responsible for the operation of the brewhouse and bakery, the home farm and dairy, for preserving what was perishable and for making cloth into garments for the whole household. It was no sinecure. Housewifery had to be learnt and called for considerable administrative ability and foresight on the part of gentlewomen everywhere.

But Margaret also had other responsibilities. The Paston letters exist because the family did not continually live together and therefore needed to correspond. Margaret's husband practised law in London and was frequently absent on his own business or in prison. In his absence, Margaret took responsibility, for example in estate management, and he sent her instructions on a wide variety of topics for her to act upon. She, in return, kept him informed about local developments. That was in normal times, but times were not normal. Margaret was also involved in Paston's political activities, his litigation, and his struggles with the local nobility. She was actually within Gresham manor house when it was stormed by Lord Moleyns and it was she in person who appealed to the local justices when nobody else dared. She showed herself to be a formidable operator, no less shrewd and resolute than her husband, and perfectly capable of filling his place. Margaret's experiences were exceptional, but she was probably far from unusual in her capacity to cope, which widows had to do as a matter of course.

H. S. Bennett, *The Pastons and their England*, 1932; repr. 1968.
H. S. Bennett, *Six Medieval Men and Women*, 1955.
N. Davis ed., *Paston Letters and Papers of the Fifteenth Century*, 2 vols. 1971–6.
J. Gairdner ed., *The Paston Letters 1422–1509*, 1904; repr. 1986.

JOHN HOPTON (*c.* 1407–78), esquire, has been presented as a gentleman who avoided involvement in politics. His father was the bastard of Sir Robert Swillington (*d.* 1391) and was lucky to have lands in Derbyshire, but John inherited the whole estate when Sir Robert's line died out. There were five manors in Yorkshire and fourteen, worth £250 a year, in East Anglia. 'There are about and in Suffolk', we are told, 'but few men of gentlemen and men of substance, but if it be in Blythburgh hundred, where Hopton is great'. A natural leader of county society, he certainly started better off than his younger contemporary John Howard.

Hopton's estate accounts reveal him as a landowner interested in his locality. His estates were well-run by long-serving officers and sensible improvements were made on their advice. A prudent rather than extravagant lifestyle enabled him to buy land, to found a chantry at Blythburgh (1451), and to provide for his children. His friends were longstanding and local, he hunted on his own estates, and he had windows in Blythburgh and Walberswick churches glazed. But he was no mere country bumpkin. He moved in the best local circles and employed the best lawyers, visited London and Yorkshire, and put his sons through university and the inns of courts. He was content with his considerable lot, did not want for more, and steered clear of unnecessary commitments and arduous voluntary work.

So, at least, it is argued. Historians expect a man of Hopton's substance to be like the Pastons, immersed in local government, politics, and litigation, and indeed they suppose that such a life was inescapable for men of this type. Hopton, we are told, was not like that.

> We have to place him, as it were, outside those groupings of patrons and clients which we have come to regard as the very stuff of which fifteenth century local society was composed. Hopton, let us repeat, was *not* an active man, on the government's or his friends' behalf; he was not a man of affairs; not only was he apolitical (or as nearly so as time and place allowed), he was also not very, or perhaps at all, social, in the sense of playing an accepted role in society, the role that society, as well as we, would have expected him to play. He knew these important, influential men and women, yet they were not important, nor did they patronise him.

Hopton's example demonstrates that gentlemen could stand aside from politics and be content as they were.

There is nothing inherently improbable in this, for there were too many gentry for lords to recruit and most lords retained few gentry. Besides Hopton did not need retaining fees. There are problems however in seeing Hopton in this role. His two terms as sheriff and twenty years as J.P. (1444–58, 1461–8) represent substantial service in local government, ending only after the onset of blindness, age and infirmity, which forced more business responsibility on his wife Thomasin. He certainly attended the shire elections in Suffolk and Yorkshire with unexpected frequency for an a-political man. It was obviously as protegé of Henry VI's favourite the Duke of Suffolk that he entered the royal household in the 1440s and he left it on Suffolk's fall. In East Anglia he may have looked to Suffolk's son, in Yorkshire to the Nevilles and their heir Richard Duke of Gloucester, and such ties could explain his omission from the commission of the peace. Historians would normally take such material as indicating political involvement, not the reverse, and would argue that only gaps in the evidence conceal Hopton's political loyalties. The a-political gentleman existed but Hopton was not one of them.

C. F. Richmond, *John Hopton: A Fifteenth Century Suffolk Gentleman*, 1981.
C. F. Richmond, 'When did John Hopton become blind?', *Historical Research* lx, 1987.

WILLIAM CANYNGES (1402–74) pursued consecutive careers in trade and the Church. Presumably originally from Wiltshire, the Canynges family was one of those unusual dynasties that stayed in urban trade after making its pile rather than setting up in the country as gentry. From the first reference in 1334 probably five generations of Canynges lived in Bristol. William's grandfather was five times mayor of Bristol and his father John was mayor twice. John had died prematurely in 1405, leaving small children, each of whom inherited £72, and a young wife, who married another Bristol oligarch. William Canynges, the younger son, stayed in Bristol; his elder brother and a half-brother became merchants, aldermen, and mayors of London. As a merchant, William probably conducted a miscellaneous trade mainly with Spain, Gascony and Iceland, though he also had contacts in the Baltic. Merchants generally shared ownership of ships, thus spreading the risk in a pre-insurance era, but Canynges owned ships from at least 1436. Probably, however, it was late in his career that he responded to trading difficulties by specialising in the carrying trade, building up a *Canynges Line* of ten ships that employed 800 men, which must have made him Bristol's main employer. Most were probably built at Bristol and one monster, *The Mary and John*, cost £2,666 to construct. No other comparable fleet is known at this time. Through troubled times Canynges built up a substantial fortune, buying lands valued at £100 a year and constructing a fine stone house with tower and chapel in Redcliffe Street. He lent money to Edward IV and was able to pay him a £2,000 fine for some forgotten offence. He married into another aldermanic family and duly joined Bristol council about 1430, becoming bailiff, alderman, sheriff, and five times mayor in 1441–67. 'Very rich and very wise', his wealth was legendary in Bristol, but probably did not compare with that of his richer London counterparts. Most was probably destined for his two sons, but both predeceased him.

Evidently Canynges was well enough educated to read Latin. As early as 1454 he kept a chaplain to say mass in the chapel in his house and as he grew older he became concerned for his soul. That was not unusual: Canynges' remedy was. He took holy orders himself. His change of career came abruptly, for he was still mayor of Bristol, when ordained acolyte immediately after his wife's death. Clearly some prior arrangement had been reached with John Carpenter, Bishop of Worcester, who first appointed him to a Worcester parish and then in turn as canon and dean of Westbury College, the incumbents being induced to resign. Carpenter, a former chaplain of Henry VI, had recast the old college into a triple foundation like Eton College. The deanery was a sinecure that Canynges doubtless earned by contributing generously to the works. A similar hard-nosed bargain occurred at St Mary Redcliffe, where he paid to put the church's property in order, so that it could support three chantry priests of his own in addition to the two curates. Normally £340 would have bought much less than that. He also contributed generously to the repair of the spire of St Mary Redcliffe, which had been struck by lightning. Such generosity in his own lifetime reduced the hereditary expectations of his heiress, who sued him in chancery. The premature deaths of his sons may explain why he dispersed his fortune by continuing the construction of Redcliffe spire after his death. It earned him in 1483 the description 'renewer and as it were in other respects founder and among others a very special benefactor of the church of Redcliffe'. It also brought lasting fame and the removal of his monument to Redcliffe at the dissolution of Westbury College.

J. W. Sherborne, *William Canynges 1402-74*, 1985.

MARGARET OF ANJOU (1430–82) exercised unusual political influence for an English queen. Part of the package that brought Henry VI a French truce, she also brought the exalted connections of one of the European nobility. She was the younger daughter of King René, Duke of Anjou, Bar and Lorraine, Marquis of Provence, and titular king or claimant to Sicily, Jerusalem, Hungary, Aragon and Majorca. Still in her teens, she was a good looking girl, vivacious and spirited, who loved romances and the chase. Her household account of 1452–3 reveals her fondness for splendid clothes and jewels and her extravagance. She also shared her new husband's interest in education, accepting the patronage of what became Queens' College, Cambridge. She quickly won a place in his affections and ensured he kept his foolish promise to Charles VII to surrender Maine, whose count was her uncle Charles. Her extravagant husband endowed Margaret more generously than he could afford and she enlarged her resources as opportunity permitted. The succession question, already acute at her marriage, was solved by Prince Edward's birth only in 1453, when her husband's breakdown put his succession in doubt.

This breakdown plunged Margaret into English politics. Her application for the regency was set aside in favour of the Duke of York as Protector in 1453–4 and 1455–6. Now a formidable politician, she saw York as a threat and determined to manage affairs herself. Since Henry was too easily influenced, he must be removed from Westminster and from the duke into her control. She settled at Kenilworth and Leicester castles, which she fortified and backed by a Cheshire-based retinue. Henry performed some ceremonial functions and indulged his religious obsession, much of it in monasteries, while Margaret presided over the court. She insisted that Coventry render her the honours properly due to the king. Virtually bankrupt, her government could do little. It cannot strictly be claimed that 'the queen and her affinity ruled the realm as she liked'. As parliament was avoided and access to the king restricted, national politics almost ceased until York's next coup in 1459. Margaret followed York's defeat by his condemnation, but next year the Nevilles won possession of King Henry. The compromise reached in parliament, which made York into Henry's heir and

Margaret of Anjou
(Sculptor unknown)

effective ruler, disinherited Prince Edward and was thus unacceptable to Margaret. She rallied opposition in the north, wreaked revenge on York at Wakefield, defeated Warwick in 1461, but suffered decisive defeat at Towton shortly afterwards.

Margaret escaped with her son, her hope for the future, and continued resistance for ten years. Initially she sought support abroad, willingly hazarding Calais and Berwick as diplomatic counters, but realised how hopeless it was by 1463. At that point she retired to St Michel in Bar with her son and other Lancastrians, where a shadowy and impoverished government in exile was maintained. They plotted continuously, spinning elaborate and impractical combinations of rebellion and invasion, even speculating on an alliance with Warwick the Kingmaker. Impossible when first devised in 1468, this became reality on the earl's exile in 1470, when Margaret married her son to his daughter Anne Neville. She herself did not reach England in time to celebrate Henry VI's second accession but only for the desperate pursuit that ended at Tewkesbury with defeat, her son's death, and her capture. Days later Henry VI was murdered and the Lancastrian cause died with him.

Premature mortality and Louis XI's designs on their inheritances meant that the house of Anjou had almost expired by 1475, when Margaret was returned to France under the treaty of Picquigny. Edward's condition was that she renounced her English rights, Louis XI's terms that she gave up her Angevin ones. Her father King René supported her in Reculeé Castle until his death in 1480, when she was thrown on the charity of a gentleman at Dampierre. Fortunately she soon died.

R. A. Griffiths, *The Reign of King Henry VI 1422–61*, 1981.
A. R. Myers, *Crown, Household and Parliament in the Fifteenth Century*, 1985.

JAMES BUTLER, EARL OF WILTSHIRE AND ORMOND

(c. 1420–1461), is probably the most unattractive of Henry VI's favourites in the 1450s. He was the son and heir of the Irish Earl of Ormond. He also became an extensive West Country landowner by inheriting the lands purchased by his grandmother Joan Lady Abergavenny (d. 1435) and by his marriage to the heiress Avice Stafford (d. 1456). These justified his creation as Earl of Wiltshire in 1449. The ambitions of Wiltshire and another parvenu peer Lord Bonville of Chewton disturbed the stability of the West Country and challenged the traditional hegemony of the Courtenay Earls of Devon, thus precipitating the violent Courtenay-Bonville dispute in the 1450s. Wiltshire spent almost all his career in England, even after he succeeded to his father's earldom in 1452 and when Lieutenant of Ireland.

James Butler was knighted in 1426 by the infant Henry VI and accompanied him to France in 1430. Thereafter he served several times in France, in 1441 in the retinue of Richard Duke of York. York appointed him steward of his Somerset and Dorset estates in

1446 and as his deputy of Ireland in 1449. By then Butler was also closely associated with the court. Thereafter his support for the king and his backing for his favourites made him into one of the duke's political foes. Wiltshire was involved in the judicial commissions that tried Cade's rebels in 1450 and York's followers in 1452. In 1453 he became a royal councillor and supplanted the duke as Lieutenant of Ireland. Next year, during York's first Protectorate, the duke again became Lieutenant of Ireland and Wiltshire was briefly imprisoned for his part in the Courtenay-Bonville dispute. When the king recovered his senses, it was Wiltshire who fetched Somerset from custody and he who became the new Lord Treasurer. Defeat at the first battle of St Albans and York's second Protectorate resulted in Wiltshire's dismissal as treasurer. His requests either to be restored to favour or allowed to retire to Ireland were both refused. When the king resumed control early in 1456, Wiltshire returned to favour. He became a councillor of the Prince of Wales in 1457 and about the same time married a sister of a committed Lancastrian, the new Beaufort Duke of Somerset. In 1459 he was elected knight of the Garter and again replaced York as Lieutenant of Ireland, although York, in practice, did not relinquish control. By then he was 'as loyal a supporter of the Lancastrian crown as could be found'.

Wiltshire certainly exploited royal favour to his own advantage and apparently amassed a substantial private fortune. He was committed and ambitious, determined to build up his local power and quite prepared to challenge the spheres of influence of other noblemen. As early as 1439 his attempt to influence the Cambridgeshire county election involved maintenance and violent clashes between his men and those of Lord Tiptoft. Yet Wiltshire was unsuccessful both in private and civil wars, perhaps because he was not prepared to risk his skin in a resolute drive for victory. This at least is suggested by the bald summary of his military exploits. In 1451 he fled from the Earl of Devon's private army, which sacked his house at Lackham; in 1455 he escaped in disguise from the Yorkists at the first battle of St Albans; in 1460 he took refuge abroad from the Yorkist invaders; and after his return to England in 1461 he escaped from defeat at both Mortimers Cross and Towton. Then his luck ran out. His capture at Cockermouth (Cumbs.) and execution at Newcastle ended his ignominious military career. He was child-

less and his earldom of Wiltshire died with him. That of Ormond
was revived for a brother.

R. A. Griffiths, *The Reign of King Henry VI 1422–61*, 1981.
R. L. Storey, *The End of the House of Lancaster*, 2nd edn. 1986.

**RICHARD NEVILLE, EARL OF WARWICK AND SALIS-
BURY** (1428–71), alias Warwick the Kingmaker, was the supreme
example of an overmighty subject. Ineligible to reign himself, he
made and unmade kings because none served his purpose. Of royal
and aristocratic descent, he was eldest son of Richard Neville, Earl of
Salisbury (*d.* 1460) and thus heir to the northern Neville estates and
the custody of the West March. He benefited most from the Neville
marriages, acquiring in 1449 the earldom of Warwick and lands
yielding £4,000 mainly in the West Midlands and South Wales. He
had to defend his title against Henry VI's favourite Somerset and
thus aligned himself with his father with the Duke of York. During
the 1450s father and son proved determined, decisive, and ruthless.
Somehow they found pre-emptive strikes and assassination compatible with their allegiance and self-interest with constitutional
principle. Initially deferring to his father, Warwick familiarised
himself with warfare on land and sea and was the more forceful by
1460. After thwarting York's usurpation in 1460, he engineered
Edward IV's accession next year.

King Edward depended on the military and political support of
the Neville brothers: George was chancellor, John military commander in the north, and Warwick was everywhere. Now Earl of
Salisbury too, he was by far the richest nobleman of the decade. He
kept a splendid household, retinue, fleet of ships, and train of
artillery. Edward gave him many confiscated estates and exalted
offices: great chamberlain and admiral of England, warden of the
Cinque Ports and captain of Calais, chief steward of the Duchy of
Lancaster, warden of the marches and king's lieutenant in the north.
He used royal favour to marry off his sisters to coming men. His
brothers were promoted. He appeared the arbiter of English policy.

Of course he was not. As the Lancastrians were defeated, so
Edward preferred his own men and ideas. He listened to Warwick's
advice, treated him indeed as his most trusted councillor, but did not
always do as he wished. Warwick thought this ingratitude. So

Warwick the Kingmaker
(From his Great Seal)

extensive were his interests, that to advance anyone anywhere anyhow appeared an attack upon him. He could not satisfy himself with what he had and was offended by Edward's veto of his marriage of his daughters to royal dukes and his pro-French foreign policy. He dropped neither. Self-confident and self-righteous, pained and angry, he denounced Rivers and Pembroke as evil councillors and resolved as in the 1450s to eliminate them and place the king under restraint. Always a risk policy even with Henry VI, it failed with Edward IV. Firmly excluded from power, Warwick then backed Edward IV's brother George Duke of Clarence for the crown — an unforgivable and unsuccessful step. Exiled again, he increased the stakes by placing Henry VI on the throne, an expedient already faltering before his defeat and death at Barnet in 1471.

Yet in many ways Warwick was a conventional enough aristocrat: in his piety and recreations, building and display, pride of lineage and arrogance to parvenus. His plans for Warwick involved improvements to Guy's Cave and the Beauchamp Chapel and a new almshouse for old retainers. Such aspirations help explain the undoubted popularity that he so assiduously cultivated. He was the most ambitious and daring of politicians, strategists and pirates, but his disastrous over-caution as a tactician lost him all his battles. Ultimately therefore his great estates, retinue and popularity were all for nought. But his real error was he forgot that prime duty of allegiance that he forced on the Duke of York in 1460.

M. A. Hicks, *False, Fleeting, Perjur'd Clarence*, 1980.

P. M. Kendall, *Warwick the Kingmaker*, 1957.

C. Oman, *Warwick the Kingmaker*, 1891.

C. D. Ross, *Edward IV*, 1974.

C. L. Scofield, *Edward IV* i, 1923.

R. L. Storey, *The End of the House of Lancaster*, 2nd edn, 1986.

JASPER TUDOR, DUKE OF BEDFORD AND EARL OF PEMBROKE

(*c.* 1431–95), outlasted the Yorkist dynasty that he had resisted for quarter of a century. Born at Hatfield in Hertfordshire, he was the second son of Katherine of France (*d.* 1437), youngest daughter of Charles VI of France and Dowager-Queen of Henry V, by Owen (ap Maredudd ap) Tudor (*d.* 1461), one of her Welsh servants. Their other children were Edmund, the eldest; Owen, who became a monk; and a daughter, who died in infancy. A statute of 1427–8 forbade the queen to marry, so her wedding was secret. Her children were discovered only on her premature death, when the Abbess of Barking took charge of them and their father was severely punished. They were half-brothers of King Henry VI, who had not many close relatives, and were abruptly called from obscurity in 1452, knighted, and created earls, Edmund Earl of Richmond and Jasper Earl of Pembroke. They were generously endowed with lands worth about £900 a year, which rose to £1,500 for Jasper when Edmund died in 1456. Edmund's child-bride, the great

Lancastrian heiress Margaret Beaufort, bore him one posthumous son in 1457: Henry Tudor, the future Henry VII. Jasper remained a bachelor until after his nephew's accession.

Although their elevation was designed to buttress the ailing Lancastrian dynasty, the Tudor brothers did not equate their obligation of allegiance with support for the king's favourites and backed the Duke of York as Protector in 1454. Although Jasper took the king's side at the battle of St Albans in 1455, it was apparently on York's authority that Edmund was sent to restore order in Wales later that year. When York was dismissed as Protector in 1456, his retainers seized Edmund at Carmarthen and briefly imprisoned him before he died. Jasper then took Edmund's place, restoring order and building up his own power in Wales, which he turned against the rebel Yorkists in 1459–61. His levies were defeated by the future Edward IV at Mortimers Cross and he was still in Wales when the decisive battle of Towton was fought.

During the 1460s Jasper was a leading figure in Queen Margaret of Anjou's continued resistance. From Wales he proceeded to Scotland, to France to conclude a treaty, back to Scotland and the garrison of Bamburgh Castle, which capitulated on terms late in 1462. As he could not secure Henry VI's restoration, Jasper returned to Scotland, visited France and the north again, and was in Brittany in 1464 and France thereafter. In 1468 King Louis XI, his first cousin, backed an invasion of Wales, which reached Denbigh before it was defeated. Harlech Castle fell and the Lancastrian cause was hopelessly lost.

In 1470 Edward IV's erstwhile supporter Warwick the King-maker rebelled, was expelled from England, and agreed to restore Henry VI to his crown. Jasper Tudor joined in the successful invasion, recovered his earldom and lands, and was recruiting in Wales in 1471, when the decisive battles were fought. Henry VI and his son were killed, Queen Margaret was a prisoner, and Jasper therefore resumed his interrupted exile, this time in Brittany and accompanied by his nephew Henry Tudor. The two Tudors repre-sented unfinished business for Edward IV, who schemed for their return, but represented no real threat until Richard III usurped the throne and the Princes in the Tower, his obvious rivals, disappeared. As in 1471, Henry VII's accession in 1485 owed more to the support of alienated Yorkists than erstwhile Lancastrians, among whom

Jasper Tudor was pre-eminent. Now in his mid-50s, the king's uncle and Duke of Bedford, Jasper stalwartly backed his nephew through his early crises. Married at last, he nevertheless failed to establish a dynasty of his own.

R. A. Griffiths, *The Reign of King Henry VI 1422–61*, 1981.
R. A. Griffiths and R. S. Thomas, *The Making of the Tudor Dynasty*, 1985.

JOHN FREE *alias* **PHREAS** (*c.* 1430–65) stands 'beyond all doubt above every fifteenth century English humanist before the time of Grocyn and Linacre'. He was not the first Englishman to study in Italy who developed a good style of written and spoken Latin. All his predecessors, however, like the two bishops Adam Moleyns and William Grey, had been rapidly promoted in Church and/or State and had become too busy to write original works of their own or to pass on their hard-won lore by teaching others. John Free thus marks a new departure. He was the first Englishman to take up humane studies as a career and the first to prove himself 'from every point of view the equal of his humanist friends'. Brilliant though his achievements were, they were cut short prematurely by his death in 1465.

John Free belonged to a family of Bristol tradesmen, but may have been born in London. He attended Oxford University from 1445, was a fellow of Balliol College, and graduated as M.A. in 1454. He was ordained acolyte in 1450 and priest in 1456. The humanist William Grey, Bishop of Ely then selected him to accompany a nephew to study in Italy and financed Free's trip alone when the nephew died. Free studied first at Ferrara under the great Guarino da Verona in 1456–8, from 1458–62 at Padua, where he graduated as doctor of medicine, and thereafter at Florence and Rome. Initially supported by Grey and subsequently by John Tiptoft, Earl of Worcester, he was an impoverished scholar who had to copy books for himself. From 1458, however, he held benefices of his own and may have been able to support himself. Allegedly he was offered the bishopric of Bath by the humanist Pope Paul II, but died before any action could have been taken. Perhaps, therefore, like Moleyns and Grey, he too might have been promoted too much to persevere with original scholarship.

Although already a graduate by his arrival in Italy, Free was only too aware of his limitations as a classical scholar by Italian humanist standards. Admitting to a 'jejeune and rustic style', he declared himself 'unashamed to lay bare my ignorance, for it is by this means only that I hope to become more learned'. His progress was certainly remarkable both in extent and speed. His Latin style in prose and verse was rapidly transformed, his knowledge of the Latin classics enormously expanded, and his use of his new learning rapidly matured. He learnt Greek, developing an expertise equivalent to that of any contemporary Italian, and dabbled both in Hebrew and civil law. Moreover he embarked on original work, writing verses and orations, now lost, and making two substantial translations from Latin into Greek. Both were by the Greek Synesius of Cyrene, one *In Praise of Baldness* dedicated to Tiptoft and another *Of Dreams* for Pope Paul II. Although selected because of the difficulties they posed, Free was able to convert each into accurate Latin versions that were faithful to the spirit of the original and yet stylistically elegant in their own right. They were to remain unsuperseded throughout the Renaissance. The next natural steps were more important publications and his return to England to pass on his expertise, but his early death postponed the emergence of home-bred English humanists until almost 1500.

R. J. Mitchell, *John Free: From Bristol to Rome in the Fifteenth Century*, 1955.
R. Weiss, *Humanism in England during the Fifteenth Century*, 3rd edn., 1967.

EDWARD IV (1442–83), born at Rouen, Earl of March (c.1445), Duke of York (1460) and King of England (1461–70, 1471–83), marks a reversion to conventional medieval expectations of monarchy. Tall, handsome, athletic and masculine, Edward looked and acted like a king. He demanded respect from his subjects and had an elevated notion of his royal dignity. Edward immediately made his brothers into dukes, endowed them more generously than any princes before them, and subsequently made his sisters-in-law into countesses. A new sumptuary law in 1483 set the royal family far above the ordinary nobility.

Edward IV
(From the Royal Window in Canterbury Cathedral)

No manner of person, of whatsoever estate, degree or condition he be, may wear any cloth of gold or silk of purple colour, but only the King, the Queen, my Lady the King's Mother, the King's Children, his Brothers and Sisters, upon penalty for every offence — £20.

As sovereign, Edward expected allegiance and obedience without prevarication. Neither devious nor cunning, but direct and straightforward, Edward was a king with whom one knew where one stood.

Of course, Edward had expected to become not a king, but the greatest of nobles. His upbringing made him one of the nobility, able (unlike Henry VI) to understand them and be understood. Though intelligent, Edward was no intellectual; though literary in his tastes, no patron of humanism; and though strict in his religious observances, no saint. Like most contemporary aristocrats, he could read, write and speak English, French, and a little Latin. He read from choice chivalric romances and history, regretted the English loss of France, and aspired, like Henry V, to make good his right. He was a dashing and daring general, whose seizure of the strategic and tactical initiative was too much for his over-cautious rivals. His splendid clothes, jewels and buildings, his jousting, hunting, hawking, feasting, and wenching were tastes that almost all aristocrats shared. He competed with the splendid court of Burgundy and made his court a source of patriotic pride.

King Edward wanted to be a good king. He wished to command his troops in battle, to restore good order and government, to do justice to all without fear and favour. Suppliants could count on his good intentions, appeal to his better nature, and were often rewarded by a considered decision: to confirm a cancelled grant, to send a key servant as sheriff, to appoint a commission of inquiry, or to come himself. He made his own decisions, overruling his council when necessary. Many grants are warranted 'By the King', for Edward did not complain of importunity of suitors, baulk at rudely rebuffing the unworthy, or fail to weigh their claims in the light of his remarkable knowledge of their positions and services. Four times he used acts of resumption to review his patronage. These were acts that cancelled all his grants, except those specifically excluded by provisos of exemption attached to the act. There are 817 of these provisos, each one initialled by the king, and each one granted, as we now know, only after the most careful consideration. Once parliament had passed the act, suitors wanting provisos would be interviewed by Edward personally, who heard what they had received from him and decided what they could keep. Some retained everything, others made sacrifices, others lost out altogether. Having agreed with the king, the lucky ones prepared provisos for the king to initial. He did not sign them unread, however, but corrected grammar and terminology, checked the scope against his records, and often modified his decision, striking out particular items or rejecting whole provisos. Others petitioned for what he had taken back. Taken with the reversal of sentences of forfeitures against traitors, it offered Edward the chance to update his patronage in the light of changing circumstances. It gave him the initiative in his relations with his subjects: even the greatest, like Warwick the Kingmaker, had to come to him as suppliants, lost grants, and were *expected* to be grateful for what they were allowed to keep. But it was immensely time consuming and taxing for the king and could not therefore be often repeated. That it happened at all is testimony to his diligence and determination.

Moreover Edward's achievements were considerable. Acceding at nineteen, made king by a minority faction, he died in his bed and the throne passed automatically to his eldest son. He was recognized by all the powers of Europe. He did restore order, quell private war, and give the crown an ascendancy over its nobility. By 1478 he had paid off the enormous debts of the Lancastrians and he died solvent, which can be said of very few medieval English monarchs. He has even been linked with Henry VII as the initiator of the New Monarchy, the creator of more efficient estate administration, chamber finance, and financial bureaucracy. Such claims are somewhat exaggerated, for he foreshadowed Henry VII rather than sharing his achievement. Chamber finance gave him control over his finances, but his estate administration was not systematically improved and the quantity of lands kept in hand was very small. In contradiction of legend, Edward died at best solvent and left no treasure behind him. Edward valued lands primarily as a source of political support, Henry VII as a source of income. It is not clear that either was right.

But piecemeal innovation, good intentions, and diligence are not everything. Medieval government was not about innovation, but was a matter of routine punctuated, erratically, by troubleshooting. Young and inexperienced at his accession, Edward had to learn his trade and made many mistakes in his opening years. He gave too freely, pardoned too easily, and delegated too much to his Neville cousins, who did know the ropes. Once he had learnt, he too often indulged himself, enjoying his kingship, and was unprepared for crises when they came. His judgement was often suspect and it is not difficult to find instances where the wrong course of action was pursued. His marriage, his priorities in foreign policy from 1475, and the Scottish war of his last years all seem seriously misconceived. His achievements, real though they were, did not stem from consistent pursuit of a coherent policy, but were rather piecemeal reactions to particular crises and circumstances. In between there were many hiccups. It was not without justice that in 1469 he was charged with evil government like the 1450s and lost his throne.

Edward was charged both in 1469 and 1483 with reliance on evil councillors and it is certainly obvious that those about him were able to exploit their positions at the expense of others, as all medieval noblemen, given the opportunity, were inclined to do. The problem was that, impressive though Edward appeared and conscientious though he was, he could be managed. At the very beginning of his reign, when he was young and inexperienced, he relied too heavily on the Nevilles and dispersed the vast fund of Lancastrian forfeitures, which he had honestly hoped to use for financial reconstruction. He was happy to recognize obligations to kinsfolk and friends, who returned repeatedly to enlarge and extend their grants. His awesome powers to review his patronage were exploited by his favourites to their own benefit. Even when he became avaricious late in his career, he was easily persuaded to make concessions that cost him nothing personally and turned a blind eye to the abuses committed by those who were close to him. It was in this way that Warwick and Herbert in the 1460s and Gloucester and the Wydevilles in the 1470s converted limited authority into regional hegemonies. He preferred not to cross them, to let things be. It was one thing to denounce liveries or to warn the Duke of Norfolk's principal councillor to beware, it was another to enforce legislation on the politically powerful or to say the same to Norfolk himself. On occasions Edward did steel himself to confront individuals, but the most famous example, the destruction of his brother Clarence in 1478, is best seen as an example of his manipulation by the Wydevilles. He regretted it at once, just as his grandson — that awesome puppet Henry VIII — regretted too late the fate of Thomas Cromwell. Clarence's death made Edward politically secure and enabled him to confront those who offended him to his face. This new-found power, however, was used not to strengthen the monarchy, but to advance the sectional interests of his sons, stepsons and in-laws. Edward, no doubt, saw no distinction, but those dispossessed or hostile to the Wydevilles certainly did. He cannot be blamed for what befell after his death, which was not predictable, but he can be blamed for leaving a regime so narrowly based that it could be overthrown, unlike the 1450s or 1460s, by a few overmighty subjects. If Edward's principal success was to secure his dynasty, it lasted for less than three months after his death.

M. A. Hicks, 'Attainder, Resumption and Coercion 1461–1529', *Parliamentary History* iii, 1984.
M. A. Hicks, *False, Fleeting, Perjur'd Clarence*, 1980.
J. R. Lander, *Crown and Nobility 1450–1509*, 1976.
C. D. Ross, *Edward IV*, 1974.
C. L. Scofield, *The Reign of Edward IV*, 2 vols. 1923.

HENRY BEAUFORT, DUKE OF SOMERSET (1436–64), illustrates the role of dynastic principle in the Wars of the Roses. He was bound to the house of Lancaster by birth, as a descendant of John of Gaunt, and by royal favour. He fought at the first battle of St Albans in 1455, where he was severely wounded and his father was deliberately assassinated. Vengeance therefore explains a skirmish in London with one of Salisbury's sons, an assassination plot against the Duke of York, and the failure of formal reconciliation. Somerset was skilled in arms, a proficient jouster who distinguished himself twice in 1458, and proved a competent, if not successful, commander. Under age at his father's death, he did not marry, but fathered one bastard — Charles Somerset, later Earl of Worcester — by one Joan Hill, spinster. Little else is known of his private life. Perhaps politics and warfare proved too engrossing.

He had succeeded his father in royal favour, becoming keeper of the Isle of Wight and receiving the reversion of the Cinque Ports. In 1459 he was appointed captain of Calais with the task of winkling out his immediate predecessor, the Yorkist Earl of Warwick. He secured a foothold by seizing Guines Castle, one of the outer defences, but was then bogged down, while Warwick's garrison invaded England and made York heir to the throne. Back in England, Somerset joined the disaffected Earl of Devon, collected their West Country retainers, and marched them north to support Queen Margaret. There they defeated and slew York and Salisbury, the victors at the first battle of St Albans (1455). Three months later Edward IV was victorious at Towton. Somerset escaped to Scotland, visited France, where he was imprisoned, Flanders and Scotland again, whence in 1462 he helped garrison three Northumberland castles. When his castle capitulated in December 1462, he made his peace with Edward IV. Somerset recovered his lands, hunted and slept with him, and became captain of his bodyguard. Late in 1463 he rejoined the Lancastrians in Northumberland. In command at the battle of Hexham in 1464, he was defeated, captured and executed.

Up to 1462 Somerset's career makes complete sense. Allegiance, kinship, favour, and vengeance pointed only one way. He did not consider recognizing York as heir in 1460 nor did he hesitate to continue the struggle after decisive defeat at Towton. If he did indeed attack York in 1460 under cover of a truce, he doubtless considered that such etiquette did not apply to traitors and that revenge on his father's killers justified his conduct. Probably Edward IV was unwilling to offer him anything worth serious consideration in 1461, but next year what was available was reconciliation that Somerset could honourably accept. That he did so probably reflects his realistic assessment of a hopeless military situation. But in that case why did he rebel again in 1463? It was not because of his treatment by the Yorkists, nor certainly on grounds of self-interest:

> the prospect was not the reconquest of England and complete vengeance on his enemies, but rather discomfort, ruin, and death. Surely no realistic assessment of personal advantage could have prompted Somerset to give up what he possessed in favour of future resistance.

Obviously he could not have defected had Lancastrian resistance wholly ceased, but his motive for defection was devotion to Henry VI's cause, which took priority over personal safety, self-interest, and subsequent forced agreements with the usurper. This is also why some Lancastrians continued the hopeless struggle and why others ostensibly reconciled with the new regime shared in plots, rebellions, and Henry VI's second reign. Similarly not all Yorkists did accept Bosworth field (1485) as decisive. Somerset's example shows that the dynastic principle did count in politics and civil war.

M. A. Hicks, 'Edward IV, the Duke of Somerset, and Lancastrian Loyalism in the North', *Northern History* xx, 1984.
M. K. Jones, 'Edward IV and the Beaufort Family: Conciliation in Early Yorkist Politics', *The Ricardian* 83, 1983.

GEORGE NEVILLE (*c.* 1432–76), Bishop of Exeter (1455–65) and Archbishop of York (1465–76), is the outstanding example of a political bishop of noble birth. As the son of Richard Earl of Salisbury and of royal blood, he was guaranteed high office in the church. A degree had become an essential qualification for a bishop, so he attended Oxford University, which pandered to his rank by shortening the courses leading to his B.A. and M.A. and his regent mastership and elected him as its chancellor in 1453, when he was only 21. From 1442 he rapidly accumulated benefices, including the 'golden prebend' of Masham in 1447, and a bishopric duly followed. It was his father, then chancellor of England, who persuaded the royal council in 1454 that George's 'blood, virtue and cunning' deserved the next see, and though under canonical age he became bishop of Exeter in 1455, his consecration being delayed until he was 27! Following their victory at Northampton in 1460, the Neville earls appointed George as chancellor of England, a post he held throughout Edward IV's critical early years. He was rewarded in 1465 with the archbishopric of York, which lay in his home area and complemented the local resources of his brothers. He aspired to become cardinal, but when the pope made his decision in 1467 it was the archbishop of Canterbury who was promoted. That same year he was dismissed as chancellor and his royal grants were taken back, as King Edward transferred his favour from the Nevilles. After initial mediation, George supported Warwick's resort to force in 1469. He had secretly obtained the licence for the marriage of Clarence to Warwick's daughter, he conducted the ceremony, his name appears on their manifesto, and it was he who actually arrested the king. After this scheme broke down and Warwick went into exile, George supported the return of Henry VI and was his chancellor during his Readeption. His failure to hold London in 1471 contributed substantially to the defeat and death of his brothers and the last Lancastrian claimants. Yet George continued plotting in 1472, apparently pointlessly, was indicted, and was imprisoned in Hammes Castle, Calais. Edward IV would have liked to deprive him of his see, but could not. Instead Richard Duke of Gloucester secured his release, so George, now sick and discredited, could die at liberty.

Clearly George Neville was an ambitious prelate with aristocratic tastes: his favourite residence at Ricksmansworth was his own and he had his own private estate; his enthronement was of legendary scale and splendour; and he reputedly possessed moveables worth £20,000 in 1472. He was a competent administrator and diplomat, and an astute politician and schemer. His political stance was unprincipled and was determined by his brother Warwick the Kingmaker: hence, perhaps, his confusion after Warwick's death. But he was not merely a noble politician in ecclesiastical garb. He could preach and had sufficient theological interest to be outraged by Pecock's contempt to the early Christian Fathers. He joined Warwick in founding St William's College for the chantry priests of York Minster in 1461. His intervention saved Lincoln College, Oxford from dissolution and he served four terms of seventeen years as chancellor of Oxford University. His own course of study, though confined to a curtailed arts course, brought him into contact with John Free at Balliol and introduced him to Renaissance scholarship. Though never as learned as his kinsman William Grey, George Neville was a patron of humanism and humanists, protecting a Greek Emanuel of Constantinople and selecting as secretaries men who could write letters in classical Latin. He himself read classical literature and acquired a basic knowledge of Greek. It was a mark of his depression in prison that he abandoned his literary studies.

M. A. Hicks, *False, Fleeting, Perjur'd Clarence*, 1980.

C. D. Ross, *Edward IV*, 1974.

R. Weiss, *Humanism in England during the Fifteenth Century*, 1967.

WILLIAM HERBERT, EARL OF PEMBROKE (*d.* 1469) ruled Wales for Edward IV and was therefore one of those eliminated by Warwick the Kingmaker in 1469. He was

the first Welshman since the Edwardian conquest to achieve a high position in English politics and to penetrate the upper ranks of the English aristocracy. He came to command a power in Wales never seen before and only briefly after. His employment as a virtual viceroy in Wales marks a departure from the policy of earlier English kings in relying on an alien and largely absentee English aristocracy for the government of that country. Not even Warwick enjoyed so complete a delegation of royal power in any one region.

His father, William ap Thomas of Raglan Castle, was a retainer of Richard Duke of York and so was his father-in-law Walter Devereux, who dominated the Welsh marches with Herbert for the duke during the 1450s. Herbert was York's constable and steward of Usk, Caerleon and Ewyas Lacy and Warwick's sheriff of Glamorgan. Violent and vengeful, Devereux and Herbert contributed to crime and disorder in the marcher shires. Occupying Hereford in 1456, they coerced an inquest and quarter sessions into convicting enemies, whom they then summarily executed. Apparently on York's behalf, they seized Carmarthen and Aberystwyth castles, imprisoning the king's half-brother in the process. The government treated Herbert leniently then and in 1459 in misconceived hope of reconciliation. He joined the future Edward IV at Mortimers Cross, drove Jasper Tudor out of Wales in 1461–2, and in 1468 finally took Harlech Castle, the last Lancastrian foothold in Wales.

As the counterpart of Warwick in the north, Herbert was made responsible for ruling Wales on Edward's behalf. Now Lord Herbert, he assembled an amazing collection of offices in the principality and marcher lordships in South Wales in spite of Warwick's ambitions in the same region. He steadily developed his position by converting titles from life to inheritance, by securing outright grants of land, by securing the creation of two new marcher lordships for himself, and by less legitimate means. Thus the Duke of Norfolk granted him Chepstow and Gower by *exchange* and over £200 a year was paid to him by those needing his favour. At first his authority was confined to South Wales but in 1468 it was extended into North

Wales and he was created Earl of Pembroke. In ten years his income rose to £2,400. He featured as a hero in contemporary Welsh poetry.

Grasping and ruthless, he did not restrict his ambitions to Wales. Having acquired the Dunster Castle estate in Somerset that Warwick coveted, he had his son created Lord Dunster on his marriage to the queen's sister Mary Wydeville. He also wanted to marry his other daughters into the nobility and secured the wardship of several young aristocrats. Among these were two, Henry Tudor and Henry Percy, whose inheritances had been bestowed on Clarence, Warwick and his brother. Herbert intended recovering their rights. He was not afraid of Warwick and did not shrink from clashes with wider political repercussions. However that may be, Warwick named Herbert among Edward's evil councillors in 1469 and Pembroke led a large Welsh contingent to defeat at Edgecote and his own execution by Warwick. He proved to be irreplaceable. His son lost Pembroke and Wales was governed by a council.

A. Herbert, 'Herefordshire 1413–61: Some Aspects of Society and Public Order', in *Patronage, the Crown and the Provinces in Later Medieval England*, ed. R. A. Griffiths, 1981.

M. A. Hicks, *False, Fleeting, Perjur'd Clarence*, 1980.

T. B. Pugh, 'The magnates, knights and gentry', in *Fifteenth-century England 1399–1509: Studies in politics and society*, ed. S. B. Chrimes, C. D. Ross and R. A. Griffiths, 1972.

C. D. Ross, *Edward IV*, 1974.

JOHN HALL (*c.* 1420–79) was an outstanding provincial merchant, who led Salisbury's attempts to emancipate itself from its bishop. So obscure were his origins that the Abbess of Amesbury could not prove that he was her serf, nor could he disprove it. Presumably a first generation immigrant, he became a Salisbury mercer and was probably still apprenticed in 1440, when no goods were carried for him from Southampton. By 1443–4 eighteen carts conveyed his alum and madder, used in cloth-making, his iron, tar and herrings from Southampton to Salisbury. He was also a retailer and in 1459 joint farmer of ulnage and subsidy of wool in Wiltshire. He owned ships at Poole in 1463 and traded in Gascon wine in 1478, when fish, tar, onions, garlic and fruit were brought to him from Southampton. He had sixteen tenements in Salisbury in 1455 and built a splendid hall for himself after 1467 by the canal opposite the wool market. His social ambition emerges in his coat of arms, his aliases as gentleman (1452) and esquire (1462), and his purchases of land in Wiltshire, where he was elector (1449), J.P. (1456), and escheator (1463), and in Hampshire, where he held three manors at death.

Wealth led inevitably to public office. He was collector of the subsidy in 1446 and constable in 1449, both for New Ward, a leading parishioner of St Thomas' Church in 1447, and in 1446 joined the Common Council. An alderman in 1448, he was four times mayor in 1450, 1456, and 1464–6, deputy mayor in 1471, and three times M.P. in 1453, 1460, and 1461.

Bishop Poore founded Salisbury when he moved his cathedral from Old Sarum and by 1450 it was one of the top ten English towns, though still subject (like St Albans and Bury) to the bishop. 'The city's dislike of the bishop's lordship and its desire to secure freedom and self-government were always latent'. Hall helped tension flare into conflict. When it was proposed in 1452 to appeal for borough status directly to the king, Hall was to present the petition, and when this was done in 1465 Hall led the delegation. Unfortunately he was imprisoned for disrespect and the king ordered election of a new mayor. The city refused and named Hall as its chief negotiator. The bishop again imprisoned him in 1471. 'Now at the height of its power and prosperity, the community was ready to seize every opportunity of contesting with its lord the right to govern', but the bishop had a watertight legal case and would not concede any of the sacred rights of St Osmund. Even when the king decided against the city, it continued to obstruct and prevaricate.

Hall's imprisonment by the king, bishop, and about 1468 by Amesbury Abbey point to a forceful personality. Unacceptable self-assertion and improper language caused Salisbury to regulate his conduct in 1457. In 1465 he allowed

> his old rancour and malice towards the said Reverend Father as it would seem contrary to his part and duty (and) broke out of the said matter concerning the said city into his own matters.

To Edward IV such 'riotous demeaning' showed him 'right seditious, hasty, wilful and of well unwitty disposition' and 'not of such sadness and ability as should serve necessarily for the good and politic guiding of the same city'. Hall sued Amesbury Abbey for wrongful arrest so vigorously that the arbiter had to protect *it* against *him*. Such an independent and uncompromising man was ideal to present Salisbury's case and to put citizens' interests first. Hence their complete confidence in him.

E. Duke, *Prolusiones Historicae or Essays Illustrative of the Halle of John Halle*, 1837.

F. Street, 'Relations of the Bishops and Citizens of Salisbury (New Sarum) between 1225 and 1612', *Wiltshire Archaeological Magazine* xxxix, 1915–17.

JOHN TIPTOFT, EARL OF WORCESTER (*c.*1427–70), 'Butcher of England', was 'the English nobleman of his age who came closest to the Italian prince of the Renaissance'. Although his father John (*d.*1443) was only the first Baron Tiptoft, he had established the estates and noble connections that enabled his son to advance himself to an earldom (1449) even before he displayed his outstanding ability. He was treasurer of England in 1452–4 and a royal councillor from 1453. Sent on embassy to Italy in 1458, Worcester delayed his return at least partly to avoid the Wars of the Roses until late in 1461, when it was safe to commit himself to the Yorkist cause. Edward IV advanced him at once. He became a councillor again, constable of England, chief justice of North Wales, constable of Portchester and the Tower, knight of the Garter (1462), treasurer of England again (1462–3), keeper of the seas (1463), diplomat and soldier. He sold his English offices in 1467 when sent as deputy to Ireland, where he unwisely (and perhaps unjustly) executed his predecessor the Earl of Desmond. Warwick's coup in 1469 caused Edward IV to recall Worcester and re-appoint him as Constable of England and (for the third time) Lord Treasurer. When Edward was deposed in 1470, Worcester was captured, and he alone was executed to great public rejoicing. He had exercised his responsibility as constable for trying traitors with great rigour. Minor offenders as well as ringleaders were executed and he impaled traitors as well as hanging, drawing and quartering them. At this 'the people of the land were greatly displeased and ever afterwards the Earl of Worcester was greatly hated among the people, for the disordinate death that he used'. He must die, they cried, 'for he had introduced the law of Padua' into England.

Whilst this claim was untrue, it shows how unusual Worcester was. He was fluent in Latin, studied at university — he was a lodger at University College, Oxford in 1440–2 — and developed a genuine understanding of Renaissance humanism. He sought to improve his Latin style even before 1458, when he studied at Padua, under the great Guarino da Verona at Ferrara, and then at Florence and Rome. His impressive library of classical and modern works showed a particular interest in Latin translations of Greek works. He patronised scholars, who dedicated their works to him, and even translated two Latin works into English himself. While he nearly purged his own Latin of barbarisms and errors, he cannot have penned the splendid oration that caused Pope Pius II to utter 'You alone of all the princes of this age are worthy to be compared in *virtu* and eloquence with the greatest Emperors of Greece and Rome'. His importance lay in his personal aspirations, in his patronage — only he and Bishop Grey genuinely assisted scholars — and in his wish to raise classical scholarship in England to Italian standards. Whilst the remedy he proposed to Oxford University may have been stillborn, he saw himself, not unjustly, as successor to Humphrey Duke of Gloucester.

Worcester was highly complex. A conventional chivalric upbringing enabled him to draft ordinances for jousts and umpire tournaments. He went on pilgrimage to Palestine and asked to be beheaded with three blows in honour of the Trinity. Though proud of his lineage, he allowed seventeen years to elapse between the childless death of his second wife and his third marriage at fifty-two. His certainty in his own rightness accompanied a marked sense of humour and a talent for friendship. He cared little for English public opinion, yet wanted respect from humanists not for his rank but as a scholar. Even in England, he could be remembered as 'a man most learned in all the liberal arts and skilled in the knowledge of letters both sacred and secular'.

R. J. Mitchell, *John Tiptoft 1427–70*, 1938.
R. Weiss, *Humanism in England during the Fifteenth Century*, 1967.

MARGARET LADY HUNGERFORD (*d.*1478) illustrates the capacity for business and politics of medieval women that is normally hidden from the historical record. She was daughter and heiress of William Lord Botreaux (*d.*1462) and wife of Robert Lord Hungerford (*d.*1459). Forty years of marriage and motherhood have left almost no record, but her husband's death exposed her as a historical individual. Like many widows, she wanted to prepare for salvation and depicted herself as kneeling in prayer with a book on her lap. What she 'desired above all things earthly' was to complete an almshouse at Heytesbury (Wilts.) and to found a chantry at Salisbury cathedral. Literate in English and French, she was up-to-date with the latest innovations in services, had clearly defined preferences — notably the chastity of the Virgin and Five Wounds of Christ — and devised services, furnishings and decoration to fit her taste. From these conventional materials, she produced something discriminating, coherent, sophisticated and highly individual. Determined not to spoil her chances by obstinacy and wilfulness, she cultivated humility and resignation at the same time as compiling statutes for her foundations that left nothing to chance. Her example shows the scope for religious individuality among even ordinary Christians unable to cultivate the mysticism of Cecily Duchess of York.

Margaret's achievement is the more remarkable in view of the enormous problems left her by her menfolk. Her husband left her responsible for the enormous ransom of their son Moleyns, whose Lancastrian politics led to increased debt and the confiscation of the family estates. Moleyns was executed in 1464, his son in 1469, and Margaret herself was imprisoned three times. These were not uncommon misfortunes for Lancastrian women under the Yorkists, some of whom were rendered almost destitute. Margaret, however, fought back with amazing resource and tenacity. She appealed to king and parliament, lobbied and bribed her way through the corridors of power, persuaded the great that her interests were theirs, played off opponents, argued her legal rights, and glossed over or faked weaknesses in title. She kept debt under control by selling land and plate, curtailing expenditure, and by closing an almshouse of her father's that represented a permanent drain on her income. Twice she rebuffed her opponents, once she drove a hard bargain with Richard Duke of Gloucester, and at the end almost the whole inheritance was saved for her heirs from the forfeiture that should properly have befallen it. She had also managed to liquidate the enormous burden of debt. But her hands could not be clean.

Margaret was actuated by two motives, her sense of inheritance and her piety, and it was the latter that took priority. She had chosen to pay off debts that could have been evaded rather than leave a stain of guilt on her husband's soul. That and her religious foundations had cost more money than her income could stand and so she had sold land that her heirs should have inherited, which they strongly resented and threatened to recover in the courts. Fearful for the repercussions for her soul, Margaret appealed to the next generation, her infant granddaughter, putting her own one-sided version of events. It is one of the first English autobiographies. Faced by a choice between responsibility to God and to her heirs, she had chosen God. Her rather colourless spouse cannot have dominated her as the law permitted during those forty unrecorded years.

M. A. Hicks, 'Counting the Cost of War: The Moleyns Ransom and the Hungerford Land Sales', *Southern History* viii, 1986.

M. A. Hicks, 'Piety and Lineage in the Wars of the Roses: The Hungerford Experience', in *Kings and Nobles in the Later Middle Ages,* R. A. Griffiths and J. W. Sherborne, ed., 1986.

M. A. Hicks, 'The Piety of Margaret, Lady Hungerford (*d.* 1478)', *Journal of Ecclesiastical History* xxxviii, 1987.

SIR JOHN FORTESCUE (*c.* 1390–1476), Chief Justice of King's Bench, was the outstanding constitutional theorist of late medieval England. He was the second son of a Devonshire knight and his elder brother was Chief Justice of Common Pleas of Ireland. John attended Lincoln's Inn, where he was repeatedly governor in the 1420s, and sat eight times in parliament from 1421, seven times for Devonshire boroughs. He became serjeant-at-law in 1430 and was Chief Justice in 1442–60. This brought him £160, two robes and two tuns of wine a year, sufficient to explain his additions to his wife's West Country estates. Fortescue joined Queen Margaret, shared her defeat and hence her exile in Scotland, Flanders, and from 1463 at St Michel in Bar. He was Henry VI's chancellor in exile. 'We be all in great poverty', he wrote, 'but yet the queen sustains us in meat and drink, so that we be not in extreme necessity. Her highness may do no more to us than she does. The bearer of this letter had from us no more than three crowns because we had no more money'. In 1470 he advocated the alliance with Warwick and the marriage of Warwick's daughter to Prince Edward, sought French support by offering a lasting peace, and even suggested, surely over-optimistically, that Edward IV might accept less than his throne. Not until 1471 did he accompany Queen Margaret to England and he shared her capture at Tewkesbury, where his life was spared. With nothing more to fight for, he made his peace and refuted his writings as the price of complete restoration. Despite his age, he even served on Edward IV's council.

But for his exile, Fortescue would have been merely a successful lawyer and would not have developed his capacity for constitutional thought. Exile gave him the leisure, incentive and responsibility to write. In Scotland in 1461-3 he wrote several pamphlets asserting the Lancastrian and refuting the Yorkist titles to the crown. From about the same time dates *On the Law of Nature,* which identified the English constitution as a mixed monarchy with features both of absolute monarchy and republicanism. It may have been written to familiarise Prince Edward with his future kingdom like Fortescue's vast *In Praise of the Laws of England (De Laudibus)* written at Bar, where he also penned advice for the Readeption government. Back in England he wrote his *Governance of England,* which summarised parts of the *De Laudibus* in English. It is 'the earliest constitutional treatise in the English language' and 'the first book about English law and the legal profession written by a lawyer specifically for the benefit of his unlearned brethren'.

Fortescue lacked systematic knowledge of civil or canon law and had read only standard works of political theory. His strength was his experience of English common law and statute, both of which, he considered, implemented natural and divine law. Pre-Roman custom was the origin of common law, which had survived only because it was good. If found wanting, it could be amended by statute in parliament, which declared natural law and which he probably realised could make new law. Statute was not the arbitrary decree of a prince, who was limited by law, but required the assent of subjects in parliament. He thought England's parliamentary monarchy far superior to what he had seen in France and Scotland in what is 'the first essay in comparative jurisprudence'. This patriotism even caused him to approve the high level of English crime. Many of England's ills were blamed on overmighty subjects, whom he wanted excluded from government, and his proposed reforms were generally conservative. He thus proposed conciliar control of patronage at the Readeption, but inconsistently placed executive authority directly in Warwick's hands in practice. He is the first writer of his type and the 'precursor of all the later lawyers who contributed to the literature of English constitutional institutions and laws'.

S. B. Chrimes, *English Constitutional Ideas in the Fifteenth Century*, 1936.
J. Fortescue, *De Laudibus Legum Angliae*, ed. S. B. Chrimes, 1942.
J. Fortescue, *The Governance of England*, ed. C. Plummer, 1885.

ELIZABETH WYDEVILLE (*c.* 1440–92), consort of Edward IV, was highly exceptional among English queens and hence highly controversial. She was the first English queen since King John's Isabella of Gloucester to be native born, she was of relatively humble rank, and she was already widowed with children when she married the king. Her marriage was clandestine, brought no diplomatic advantages, and was based purely on sex appeal. Unlike the foreign princesses who normally became queens, Elizabeth had both parents, two sons, five brothers, five sisters, and many cousins already living in England. King Edward felt obliged to provide generously for them all, mainly by marrying them into the peerage, and thus created a powerful political faction around the queen. All these circumstances were criticised at the time and contributed to those animosities within the government that contributed to the collapse of the Yorkist dynasty.

Elizabeth was the daughter of Jacquetta of Luxemberg, Dowager-Duchess of Bedford, by Richard Wydeville, created Lord Rivers in 1448. Whilst she was one of the European nobility on her mother's side, she belonged only to the county gentry through her father. Her first marriage was to Sir John Grey, heir to the Midlands barony of Ferrers of Groby. Following his death, her mother-in-law withheld her jointure, and it was to secure royal support that Elizabeth heavily bribed Lord Hastings for access to the king. Susceptible to her feminine wiles, Edward wanted to seduce her, but she virtuously

Elizabeth Wydeville
(Artist unknown)

declined any terms short of marriage. They married on May Day 1464. This romantic story of virtue rewarded rapidly attracted European renown. Three sons and eight daughters were its fruit.

Understandably the Wydevilles stressed their international connections, notably in the famous tournament with the Bastard of

Burgundy in 1467. They encouraged Edward to ally with Burgundy. This and the Wydeville-Herbert stranglehold on patronage precipitated Warwick's coup of 1469 and the death of the queen's father and brother. It was in sanctuary in 1471 that the queen bore the future Edward V, around whom the family built their hopes during Edward IV's second reign. Her brother Earl Rivers dominated the prince's household, supervised his education, and made his resources into a power-base for the family in preparation for when the prince would reign. The great Exeter and Norfolk inheritances were secured for her sons Prince Richard, Thomas Grey, Marquis of Dorset, and Lord Richard Grey. A potential threat, the king's elder brother Clarence, was eliminated in 1478. At court the queen's son Dorset and brother Sir Edward Wydeville competed for influence with Lord Hastings. Once Edward IV was dead, the queen intervened decisively to take control at Westminster and to organise the immediate majority of Edward V. This device was designed to prevent a protectorate and to move to Wydeville rule based on their influence of the king. It frightened too many people, however, generated opposition and unpopularity, and thus facilitated the succession of Richard III. Rivers and Lord Richard Grey were executed, the princes disappeared, and Elizabeth and her daughters took sanctuary.

Only when sure that the princes were dead and that Richard III had won did Elizabeth agree to a pension and a guaranteed future for her now bastardised daughters. She had miscalculated again, for Henry Tudor became Henry VII and married her eldest daughter Elizabeth of York. Elizabeth Wydeville was not rehabilitated. Alleged dabbling in treason enabled her to be deprived of her dower, to considerable royal profit, in 1487. She was almost without property at her death in Bermondsey Abbey.

C. Fahy, 'The Marriage of Edward IV and Elizabeth Woodville: A New Italian Source', *English Historical Review* lxxvi, 1961.

M. A. Hicks, 'The Changing Role of the Wydevilles in Yorkist Politics to 1483', in *Patronage, Pedigree and Power in Later Medieval England,* C. D. Ross, ed., 1979.

J. R. Lander, *Crown and Nobility 1450–1509,* 1976.

D. MacGibbon, *Elizabeth Woodville,* 1938.

C. D. Ross, *Edward IV,* 1974.

C. D. Ross, *Richard III*, 1981.
G. Smith, *The Coronation of Elizabeth Woodville*, 1935.

RICHARD WYDEVILLE, EARL RIVERS (*c.* 1410–69) made his fortune from two remarkable marriages. The Wydevilles of Grafton Regis were a minor Northamptonshire family with minimal estates. Richard's father distinguished himself in France in the service of Henry V and the Regent Bedford. Richard's career appeared likely to follow a similar course. Knighted in 1426, he too served in France, and like his sons was a successful jouster. Young, athletic, chivalric and French-speaking, he was presumably also handsome and charming in 1436, when he married Bedford's widow Jacquetta of Luxemberg (*d.* 1472). Herself a member of the European nobility, daughter of the Count of St Pol and descendant of Charlemagne, she was also Henry VI's aunt by marriage. As a *mésalliance* it ranks second only to Queen Katherine's marriage to Owen Tudor. With her connections and wealth, Richard's military and administrative career took off. He was created Lord Rivers in 1448, became a knight of the Garter and royal councillor in 1450, seneschal of Aquitaine and lieutenant of Calais. He married his three eldest children into the baronage. But he failed significantly to extend his estates to compensate for the loss of Jacquetta's dower on her death. Neither was he accepted as an equal by all the established nobility, such as Warwick the Kingmaker, who firmly reminded him in 1460 that:

> his father was but a squire and brought up with King Henry V and since himself made by marriage and also made lord and that it was not his part to have language of lords, being of the king's blood.

Perhaps, therefore, Rivers was fortunate that Edward IV accepted his submission after his usurpation and restored him to his council. He was not sufficiently in favour to intercede with Edward for his widowed daughter Elizabeth. She, however, secretly married the king: a *mésalliance* if anything more shocking than that of Rivers himself and even more profitable. Edward was obliged to endow his queen, who patronised her kinsmen, but he was certainly not obliged to provide for the whole family, still less on the scale that he did. Rivers himself was created an earl and was appointed treasurer and constable of England, posts that carried the massive income of £1,586 and offered further scope for patronage. Several of the grants to him and his sons were bought back for them by the king. Five heirs to peerages were bought to marry Elizabeth's sisters and another for her son by promotion in rank, grants of land, and gifts of cash from King Edward. Apparently fathers stated their terms to Rivers, who extracted the concessions from the king, who clearly considered that no sister-in-law should be less than a countess. The family also used its favour to extort concessions from third parties. The greed of the Wydevilles and especially Rivers became a byword — 'The Rivers are so high that I could hardly escape through them', it was joked — and they became extremely unpopular. Their rise was too great and too rapid.

More important, they made the king unpopular and were obvious targets as evil councillors in Warwick's manifesto in 1469. His rebellion demonstrated conclusively that the Wydevilles were merely courtiers, without the land or military resources to help the king through the crisis. Rivers was executed and the Duchess Jacquetta was charged with sorcery. High favour returned after 1471, but so too did the political penalties. Rivers' five sons died childless, three violently, and the marriages produced unity of interest for only a decade. The Wydevilles were a transient phenomenon in English politics.

M. A. Hicks, 'The Changing Role of the Wydevilles in Yorkist Politics to 1483', in *Patronage, Pedigree and Power in Later Medieval England*, ed. C. D. Ross, 1979.
J. R. Lander, *Crown and Nobility 1450–1509*, 1976.
C. D. Ross, *Edward IV*, 1974.

SIR THOMAS COOK (*c.*1410–78), richest Londoner of his generation, is best known for his celebrated treason trial. His parentage is not known. Apprenticed as a draper in 1425, he had £1,600-worth of cloth in stock in 1468, but also dabbled in other lines of business. In 1468 he lived in plutocratic style at his mansion in the parish of St Christopher Stock in Breadstreet ward, where his tapestries of religious and historical subjects were worth £984 and his plate valued at £397. He acquired extensive properties in and around London and a country seat at Gidea Park (Essex). By realising stock and selling land Cook paid off a fine of £5,333, equal to the whole estimated fortune of Richard Whittington, and yet remained in business. No doubt his wife's inheritance in 1469 helped. Support for the Readeption of Henry VI brought further loss, necessitating further sales, mortgages, and loans. Although obliged to move down-market, his new house was large enough to have its own chapel. Cook died in luxury and his estates endowed an important Tudor gentry family.

Great merchants inevitably joined the city's ruling oligarchy, marrying into aldermanic families, becoming aldermen and ultimately mayors themselves. So too with Cook. Inevitably they were drawn into royal finance: Cook was customer of Southampton for Queen Margaret of Anjou in the 1450s, leased property from Queen Elizabeth Wydeville in the 1460s, and lent money to Edward IV. Among his influential connections were King Edward's sister Margaret, who initially protected him in 1468 when he was financing her wedding to the Duke of Burgundy. He had ties too with his erstwhile patron Queen Margaret of Anjou, to whom he may have felt obliged. Certainly he was approached for financial help by Lancastrian agents in 1466. Perhaps unwilling to finance an invasion, he gave nothing, but neither did he expose her envoys as his allegiance to Edward IV demanded he should. So too did the confidence that Edward had reposed in him. Hence perhaps the king's anger, when Cook appeared among Lancastrian plotters and sympathisers exposed in 1468 and hence the exceptionally large fine (£5,333) Cook had to pay when convicted only of concealment, not treason. The size of the penalty was related to the degree of betrayal. Also, of course, Edward took the chance to improve his finances; so did his in-laws and the queen, who strove to secure an additional ten per cent for herself, without success.

Whatever Cook's prior loyalties, he certainly became a Lancastrian partisan after his trial. He backed Henry VI's Readeption with vigour and secured his re-appointment as alderman and election to parliament in 1470, where he pleaded his case eloquently and with considerable exaggeration. While the mayor 'sundry times feigned himself ill for fear of administering his office, the said Sir Thomas fearing no perils acted to the uttermost of his power to the hurt and damage of such as he knew bare any favour to King Edward', probably including his own brother-in-law. He tried to exclude King

Edward from London in 1471 and then, having overcommitted himself, he fled abroad. Brought back by Burgundian captors, his patron Margaret of York again saved him with only a brief term of imprisonment, a ransom to his captors, and another royal fine. If Cook was a bold politician and persuasive speaker, he was evidently also a considerable propagandist. His conviction for concealing a treason was recast as a court conspiracy against a wholly innocent victim. Hence his popularity at the Readeption and the favourable report that his apprentice and other Londoners included in their chronicles.

M. A. Hicks, 'The Case of Sir Thomas Cook, 1468', *English Historical Review* xciii, 1978.

P. Holland, 'Cook's case in history and myth', *Historical Research* lxi, 1988.

A. F. Sutton, 'Sir Thomas Cook and his "troubles": An Investigation', *Guildhall Studies in London History* iii, 1978.

GEORGE DUKE OF CLARENCE (1449–78), middle brother of Edward IV and Richard III, has given the late medieval nobility and the Wars of the Roses a bad name. Shakespeare's 'false, fleeting, perjur'd Clarence' says what contemporaries thought. Clarence's fall showed that 'perjury shall never have better end without great grace of God'. Execution by his brother Edward seemed just penalty for a life of disloyalty: rebellions against Edward IV in 1469 and 1470 (twice), against Henry VI in 1471, and more treason in 1473 and 1477. But he was untypical, not typical. He flouted the standard of behaviour expected even in civil war and to which others honourably conformed. All this, however, exaggerates his offences and misses the consistency present even in his career. His first rebellion stopped short at king-making, but its failure led him willy-nilly into those of 1470, when he tried to make first himself and then, in desperation, Henry VI, king. All three rebellions should therefore be lumped together as a single heinous act of treason. His betrayal of Henry VI in 1471 was at least a reversion to his original loyalty and was permanent. Rash talk in private, not treasonable conspiracy, seem the extent of any guilt thereafter. His trial was not fair, but rigged to get rid of him, and his condemnation is not therefore evidence of guilt.

George Duke of Clarence
(Artist: John Rous)

Treason among kings' brothers was all too common in fifteenth-century Europe. They had no role to match their rank and could not see themselves as subjects rather than siblings. Merely a younger son of Richard Duke of York, George found himself at only twelve a royal duke, knight of the Garter, and heir to the crown. The separation of royalty from the nobility, stressed by his brother, made Clarence arrogant and eager for power. He was sitting on judicial commissions and managing his great estates at seventeen. Great and unprecedented though Edward's grants to him were, they could not finance even the household of 399 people thought necessary for Clarence to be 'well and honourably served'. Clarence quickly found he could not decide policy or even choose his own marriage partner. Too hasty to wait and too susceptible to Warwick's flattery, he embarked on the wrong course and was too proud to draw back. Edward gave him several genuine grounds for grievance after 1471, but not for his fear that 'the King intended to consume him in like wise as a candle consumes in burning'. It was not the king but the Wydevilles who eliminated a dangerous future risk. Had Clarence survived, there could have been no Richard III.

Yet even Clarence possessed redeeming features. Every inch a prince, he was brave and athletic, intelligent and eloquent, loyal and generous. Earl of Warwick by his marriage to Warwick the King-maker's elder daughter, he fulfilled local expectations as a great builder and almsgiver, respecter of the legendary Guy and promoter of Warwick's prosperity. He was 'good lord' to his retainers, supporting them in their just and (sometimes) their unjust causes, arbitrating their disputes with apparent impartiality, bringing them to heel, and punishing poaching and rent arrears. He expressed his religion through chantries and his solemn vigil over his wife's coffin. 'Thanks be to God', wrote the dean of Salisbury, 'who has given such a benevolent and devout prince into the tutelage of the church'. He was never mightier than the crown. Twice he deferred unwillingly to Edward's authority. He knew he lacked the allies for a larger role. Shocking though the Ankarette Twynho affair was as an abuse of power, the proper penalty was imprisonment in the Tower, which he suffered, not drowning in malmsey wine.

M.A. Hicks, *False, Fleeting, Perjur'd Clarence: George, Duke of Clarence 1449-78*, 1980.

M.A. Hicks, 'The Middle Brother: "False, Fleeting, Perjur'd Clarence"', *The Ricardian* 72, 1981.

M.A. Hicks, 'Restraint, Mediation and Private Justice: George, Duke of Clarence as "Good Lord"', *Journal of Legal History* iv, 1983.

SIR THOMAS MALORY (*d.* 1471) was the author of the *Morte D'Arthur*, a literary masterpiece and a work of remarkable scale for any medieval layman to produce. Clearly the author was literate in

French and English, the language of his sources, but also unpractised in writing. His power of composition grew as the work progressed but his prose style remained simple, colloquial and direct, probably much like his speech. To Malory the romances contained 'unalterable historical fact' about a real Arthur and his court. It was thus history that Malory recast into chronicle, excluding verbiage and description in favour of sober narrative and moral significance. The *Morte* is a repository of chivalric and religious ideas that the author himself must have shared. It is concentrated, unified and powerful.

The identity of the author has been much disputed. He himself tells the reader that he was a knight prisoner, who completed it in custody in 1469-70. Almost certainly, therefore, he was the Sir Thomas Malory excluded from the 1468 general pardon with Lancastrian conspirators implicated in Cook's plot and probably also he was Sir Thomas Malory of Newbold Revel (Warw.). This has posed considerable problems to modern scholars, for this Malory's notoriety for violent crime conflicts wholly with the values of the *Morte* and he appears unexpectedly old to be the author. If he was indeed already campaigning in 1414, he could hardly have been less than his mid seventies and may have been much older, but this might have been some other Malory.

This Malory's continuous career begins only in 1439, perhaps when he returned from France following the death of Richard Beauchamp, Earl of Warwick and lieutenant of France, whose retainer he may have been. The *Morte* reveals him critical, appropriately for a veteran, of the loss of English possessions in France. The death of his father in 1433-4 had brought him a substantial estate in Warwickshire, which may have been unusually unstable during the 1440s due to the youth of Earl Richard's son Duke Henry (*d.*1446) and the latter's daughter Anne (*d.*1449). Malory was politically active, becoming M.P. for Warwickshire in 1445-6. He was feed from the Beauchamp estates, but we cannot be sure of all his affiliations or their priority. Local politics rather than criminal proclivities probably explain the crimes he committed from 1444, from his raid on the Peto lands to his attacks on the Duke of Buckingham and Combe Abbey, and his thefts in Essex in 1454. He was 'a rapist, church-robber, extortioner, and would-be murderer'. Although his indictments were made by his enemies and must be treated with caution, he does seem to have behaved quite without discretion and forfeited the confidence of all parties. Suggestions that he became unhinged or senile are surely disproved by the *Morte D'Arthur*. However that may be, this unlucky and incompetent politician was almost continually in prison throughout the 1450s, escaping briefly in 1459–60. Under such circumstances, it is hard indeed to identify his national political affiliations, but his pardon in October and military service in Northumbria in November 1462 has parallels among erstwhile Lancastrians who were allowed to buy their way back into favour. At peace with the government thereafter, he was perhaps embroiled in Cook's conspiracy in 1468, for which the circumstantial evidence is strong but the facts weak. Imprisoned again, like Sir Thomas Gray he turned to writing and earned undying renown.

M. C. Carpenter, 'Sir Thomas Malory and Fifteenth-Century Local Politics', *Bulletin of the Institute of Historical Research* liii, 1980.

P. J. C. Field, *Romance and Chronicle: A Study of Malory's Prose Style*, 1971.

P. J. C. Field, 'Sir Thomas Malory M.P.', *Bulletin of the Institute of Historical Research* xlvii, 1974.

P. J. C. Field, 'Thomas Malory: The Hutton Documents', *Medium Aevum* 48, 1979.

P. J. C. Field, 'The Last Years of Sir Thomas Malory', *Bulletin of the John Rylands Library*, 64, 1982.

JOHN VERE, EARL OF OXFORD (*c.*1443–1513), outlasted both the Yorkist dynasty he implacably opposed and the two kings whom he had helped to make. In 1462 his father and elder brother were executed for treason to Edward IV. John most likely succeeded because he married Warwick the Kingmaker's sister. Probably the government misinterpreted his continued disaffection as Lancastrian when it arrested him in 1468. A rumour that he had confessed 'much thing' is unsubstantiated. Once released, he attended Clarence's forbidden wedding to Warwick's daughter at Calais in May 1469 and rebelled with them against King Edward and his favourites. Oxford wisely joined Warwick in exile in 1470 and returned with him to make Henry VI king again. The earl became steward of the household and executed his father's own executioner. In 1471 he repelled Edward IV at Cromer, clashed with him at Newark, and was defeated with Warwick at Barnet. Although he fled abroad, Oxford was irreconcilable. He continued to resist Edward even without an alternative king. With French backing in 1473, he raided St Osyth in Essex and seized St Michael's Mount, which he defended vigorously until his garrison accepted terms. Imprisoned at Hammes Castle near Calais, he failed to escape in 1477, but suborned his keeper in 1484. He joined Henry Tudor, fought for him at Bosworth in 1485, and became a bulwark of his regime. He recovered his inheritances, was appointed great chamberlain and admiral of England and to many other offices. He held East Anglia, committing its levies to Henry's defence in 1487 and 1489. In 1499 as steward of England he even condemned Edward Earl of Warwick, son of Clarence and grandson of Warwick the Kingmaker.

Oxford was a poor earl up to 1471 and his income of $c.£1,900$ in the mid-'90s did not rank with the richest nobles. His will and inventory suggest a plutocratic lifestyle, but contain cash and chattels worth only £8,206, not a vast sum. It was not great estates and wealth that enabled him to dominate East Anglia in 1470–1 and from 1485, but a combination of the eclipse of the De La Poles and Dukes of Norfolk and Oxford's own favour with the crown, itself testimony to his ability. Like the Despensers in the 1320s, Suffolk in the 1450s and Hastings in the 1470s, Oxford's power was based on influence at court, not on the largest local estate. Norfolk possessed that, yet in 1470–1 he had to:

> sue to him as humbly as ever I did to them. In so much that my Lord of Oxford shall have the rule of them and theirs by their own desires and great means. I [John Paston] trust we shall soon have other offices suitable for us, for my Master the Earl of Oxford bids me ask and have.

Backed with royal patronage, Oxford secured 'the faithful guiding and disposition of the country, to my great comfort and pleasure'. Again, from 1485, he dominated the region, arraying its forces against outside threats, sitting on commissions, and arbitrating disputes. He attracted many gentry to his service, rewarding 56 in his will 'for such true and faithful service as they have done to me'. Perhaps there is truth in the unsubstantiated legend of his fine by Henry VII for illegal retaining. He does not seem to have abused his power, as all medieval nobles were prone to do. As late as 1509 he hoped for a son, but none arrived. Future earls descended from his nephew. None achieved his political stature.

M. A. Hicks, *False, Fleeting, Perjur'd Clarence,* 1980.

M. A. Hicks, 'The Last Days of Elizabeth Countess of Oxford', *English Historical Review* ciii, 1988.

C. L. Scofield, 'The Early Life of John de Vere, thirteenth Earl of Oxford', *English Historical Review* xxix, 1914.

R. Virgoe, 'The Recovery of the Howards in East Anglia, 1485–1529', in *Wealth and Power in Tudor England,* E. W. Ives, R. J. Knecht and J. J. Scarisbrick, ed., 1978.

JOHN HOWARD of Stoke-by-Nayland (Suff.), Lord Howard (1470) and Duke of Norfolk (1485), is a rare example of a public figure, whose private life can be studied. His grandfather had been Duke of Norfolk, but his father's estate made him only a country gentleman and servant of the great, initially the Dukes of Norfolk and York. He was apprenticed in war at Châtillon (1453), in administration as J.P. for Suffolk from 1455, and in politics as M.P. (1449, 1455). He was probably in Norfolk's retinue at Towton in 1461, when he was knighted, and it was therefore as his protegé that he became king's carver in 1461. Over the next decade he served on land and sea, was again M.P., and became a royal diplomat, councillor, and treasurer of the household. He remained Norfolk's councillor and was sheriff of Norfolk and Suffolk (1461), constable of Norwich and Colchester castles, and a constant local commissioner. His creation as Lord Howard in 1470 merely punctuated a hectic military, diplomatic and administrative career that culminated in command of the fleet against Scotland in 1481–2. It had made him a rich man.

His career illustrates the way in which personal service to the king might enrich a man and increase his influence, but it also shows how varied and continuous was the service demanded by his master. The successful Yorkist civil servant had to be a man of great energy and considerable ability.

But he owed his duchy not to service but to inheritance after his

John Howard, 1st Duke of Norfolk
(Artist unknown)

Mowbray kin died out. He then became the dominant personality in East Anglia.

Howard was never too great or too busy to attend to his own business. He watched carefully over his home farm and shipping and scrutinised every trivial household expense. He could thus live above his proper station. He had 100 servants at Tendring Hall in 1465, always dressed and ate well, and added further luxuries as he could afford them. His simple pleasures were those of the bluff soldier. Outdoors he practised archery, hunted and hawked, indoors he played chess, cards and backgammon, and always he bet on the result. Harper and minstrels played, players and fool entertained, and disguisings provided variety. In quieter mood he could always read French romances and tales of adventure. 'They form the sort of collection that a soldier of cultivated but unscholarly mind might have taken with him on a campaign for relaxation'. The chapel he built and staffed with organist and choristers conveys his genuine and simple piety less well than his impulsive charity to hermits, friars and those in need. He tipped his employees, cared for his offspring, and took his wife everywhere. A home-loving family man lies behind the admiral and grandee.

Howard's Norfolk inheritance materialised in 1481 on the death of the infant Anne Mowbray, wife of King Edward's younger son Richard. To provide cheaply for his son, Edward IV kept the Mowbray lands, thus disinheriting Howard. He 'would have been less than realistic if he had not felt a certain chagrin at the king's disregard of his rights'. A Wydeville regime offered no redress, but Richard of Gloucester did. Hence presumably Howard's backing for Richard III, which brought him his dukedom and an earldom for his son. On the eve of Bosworth he was too committed to heed his ominous warning:

Jock of Norfolk, be not too bold
For Dickon thy master is bought and sold.

He died for Richard on the field. The consequent ruin was brief and the Howard dukes are with us still.

A. Crawford, 'The Private Life of John Howard: A Study of a Yorkist Lord, his Family and Household', *Richard III: Loyalty, Lordship and Law*, P. W. Hammond ed., 1986.

CECILY NEVILLE, DUCHESS OF YORK (1415–95), the mother of Edward IV and Richard III, lived a life of such piety that it became a model for other noble ladies. This was during her last years. It had not always been so. What we know of her earlier career, like most noble ladies, is little more than a catalogue of birth, connections, and childbearing. Last of the twenty-three children of Ralph Neville, Earl of Westmorland (*d.*1425), she was married as a child to Richard Duke of York. She accompanied him as king's lieutenant to France and Ireland, bearing children both in Rouen and Dublin, and living in regal state. Perhaps to receive the new queen, Cecily commissioned a marvellous dress, mantle and hood of crimson velvet and ermine, for which 325 pearls and 8 oz. of gold were required. Hence expenditure on clothing in 1443–4 of £608, almost the income of an earl, and her husband's appointment of someone to watch over her spending. Whilst York engaged in English politics in the 1450s, his duchess lived mainly at Fothering-hay (Northants.) with her younger children. In 1459, when he fled abroad, she was placed in the custody of an elder sister, and in 1460 a brief triumph was followed by Richard's death. During her sons' reigns she lived mainly at Berkhamsted (Herts.) and Baynards Castle in London off her extensive dowerlands, apparently involving herself seldom in politics, but frequently in royal christenings and other family events. It seems clear that she objected to Edward IV's marriage to Elizabeth Wydeville, allegedly stating 'in a frenzy' that he was no son of hers and perhaps thus giving rise to the (presumably apocryphal) rumour repeated in 1469, 1477–8, and 1483–4 that 'the late King Edward was not begotten by Richard Duke of York but by some other, who privily and by stealth had knowledge of his mother'. Reputedly she indignantly denied the story after Richard III used it to justify his usurpation.

Cecily outlived all but two of her children. Her husband, three sons, four grandsons, and other kinsfolk died violently, but there remained many grandchildren in whom she interested herself. It was therefore not to escape from personal tragedies that she took to religion. Her piety was too active and positive for that. Her daughter Margaret of York could have learnt her own remarkable piety from her mother, but it is for Cecily's last decade that we are informed. 'I trust to our Lord's mercy that this noble princess thus divides the hours to his high pleasure', wrote someone describing the regime of these years. Between 7 a.m. and 8 p.m. she heard three services of matins, three low masses, and three evensongs, some in private and others in chapel. Arduous and extensive though such activities were, they are purely conventional. What distinguishes Cecily is the time given to private meditation and the spirit in which she undertook it.

The books of mysticism in her chamber — unusual in themselves — included advanced works of great depth and complexity, such as those by St Catherine of Siena and St Bridget of Sweden. For a laywoman like Cecily voluntarily to read them every day and extract enough to explain afterwards at table demonstrates both an advanced spirituality and a 'deep and personal love of mysticism'. Cecily's spiritual exercises, like those of Margaret Beaufort and Margaret Hungerford, did not conflict either with conventional observance, great wealth, or the demands of household, estate and family that she continued to fulfil. Only leisure made them possible, however, so such practices were probably confined to nuns and clergy, to dowagers without children to bring up like Cecily and the two Margarets, or to men who shirked their responsibilities, like Henry VI. The new piety could not be open to all.

C. A. J. Armstrong, *England, France and Burgundy in the Fifteenth Century*, 1983.

T. B. Pugh, 'Richard Plantagenet (1411–60), Duke of York, as the King's Lieutenant in France and Ireland', in *Aspects of Late Medieval Government and Society*, J. G. Rowe, ed., London 1986.

CHRISTOPHER AMBROSE (*c.* 1440–98), merchant of Southampton, illustrates the important role of foreign merchants in England and is himself one of their most remarkable success stories. Born in Florence as Cristoforo Ambruogi, trained in Italian trading methods, and despatched to Southampton as clerk to the Florentine agent in 1462, he became agent himself, was naturalised, and twice served as mayor of his adopted city.

Ambrose's presence in Southampton needs to be seen in the context of international trade dominated in the south by the Italians and in the north by the great cities of Flanders (Ghent and Bruges) and later Antwerp in Brabant. English traders lacked the sophisticated business techniques practised abroad, such as double-entry book-keeping and bills of exchange, and it was on Italian bankers that English kings normally relied for credit. All England had to offer was its high-quality wool and — from about 1350 — its unfinished woollen broadcloths, which were much in demand abroad. It was not only Englishmen who handled exports of such items, but foreigners, who carried them in their own ships and maintained resident agents to collect them and to organise the distribution of their imports. There were significant colonies of foreigners in several English towns, above all London. There lay the Steelyard, the factory of the Hanseatic League of north German and Baltic towns, and there too lived the representatives of Venice, Genoa, and Florence, the principal Italian trading states. Until the late thirteenth century the Italians had traded overland to the north, but once they established the sea-route Southampton became a minor staging post. At first Southampton saw more Catalans and Majorcans than Italians, who increased in number in the late-fourteenth-century only as the Cotswolds became the main source of high-quality wool. From then on Southampton featured both as an outport to London, Italian imports being transported by road to the capital, and as the distributive centre for the West Country. The relative importance of the Italians in the town also grew, for the Majorcans ceased coming in 1434, the Catalans in 1449, and the wine trade was disrupted by the loss of Gascony in 1453. South-ampton's prosperity came to depend principally on the Italians, even before riots against aliens in London in 1456 caused them to transfer all their operations there. At that point all the Italian trading fleets stopped off at Southampton. Unfortunately, however, Southamp-ton's new-found eminence came at a time when Italian trade with England was itself in decline. All three states sent less ships less regularly, the Florentines ceasing to come altogether in 1478, and much of what trade remained was handled from the English ships that sailed annually to Pisa from the late 1470s. The Venetian galleys alone continued their voyages into the sixteenth-century.

Ambrose's arrival in 1462 therefore coincided with the zenith of Italian activity in Southampton and immediately preceded its precipitate decline. His master soon left, leaving Ambrose as joint and then from 1470 sole Florentine agent, a post that scarcely occupied all his time or all his expertise. He was trading indepen-dently by 1464, when he was described as a Florentine merchant and householder, and was successful enough to become naturalised in 1472 and to take apprentices. He still traded in Mediterranean luxuries, principally wines, confectionary and textiles, which he distributed to merchants in London, Newbury, Oxford and Salis-bury, and to individual customers like the Earl of Arundel, to whom he supplied cloth of gold. His career demonstrates how friendly relations between English and aliens could be. So acclimatised did he become that local records do not distinguish between him and native Englishmen, whose faith in him emerges in his election as sheriff in 1484 and mayor in 1486 and 1497. He had become 'a man of great might within the same town'.

A. Ruddock, ed., *Italian Merchants and Shipping in Southampton 1270–1600,* Southampton Records Series, i, 1951.

HENRY PERCY, EARL OF NORTHUMBERLAND, (*c.* 1449–89) contributed to Richard III's usurpation and deposition, but his priority was to restore the Percies to a dominant position in northern England. From the 1450s the Percies were contesting Neville dominance in the region. Their private feud spilled over into civil war and led to total disaster. Henry's grandfather the second Earl was killed in 1455, his father the third Earl in 1461, the earldom and estates were confiscated and given to Clarence and the Nevilles, and finally in 1464 Warwick's brother John was created Earl of Northumberland. Henry's prospects were limited to his mother's lands. Respect for inheritance was such, however, that almost all heirs of Lancastrian traitors were ultimately restored and hopeful fathers made a speculative investment of marrying their daughters to them. Thus Lord Herbert secured Henry Percy for his daughter Maud. Weakness in the north revealed by Warwick's rebellions in 1469–70 prompted Edward IV to restore Percy to the earldom of Northumberland. He came through the revolutions of 1470–1 unexecuted and systematically reconstructed his retinue and authority throughout the 1470s and 1480s.

The Nevilles were dead, but their lands, retainers, and ambitions were inherited by Warwick's daughter Anne Neville, whose husband Richard Duke of Gloucester was more than a rival to Northumberland. As both reconstructed their shattered inheritances they clashed, Gloucester having a big advantage as the king's brother. To protect himself Northumberland became the duke's retainer. Gloucester thereafter left him in control in Northumberland and the East Riding, whilst he himself was supreme elsewhere. All the other northern nobles also took service under Gloucester, whose domination of the whole region was recognized in 1482 as king's lieutenant in the north. The relationship operated on a basis of mutual respect and warmth and worked well in practice. Percy served under Gloucester in the Scottish war of 1480–3 and in 1483 assisted Richard's usurpation as Richard III by executing Earl Rivers and by bringing a northern army south to overawe London.

Northumberland did well out of Richard III's accession, but not as well as he probably hoped. It did not mean the end of the Neville hegemony. Richard's power rested so heavily on his own dominance of the north that he was not prepared to delegate it to Northumberland. The earl sat on the new Council of the North as a simple member, not president, and his authority was restricted to what it was before. Such considerations disillusioned him and doubtless explain why he defaulted at Bosworth and assisted in Richard's defeat.

The new king, Henry Tudor, had known Percy as a boy and did not trust him. He needed him, however, to rule the north, but kept him under a tighter rein than earlier kings. The earl was able to expand into Cumbria, where he had large estates, to dominate Yorkshire, and to attract into his retinue many former supporters of Richard III. They, however, were jaundiced by his 'disappointing of King Richard at Bosworth field' and were unenthusiastic about suppressing rebellions raised by those former associates, who remained loyal to Richard's memory and sought to place his heir on the throne. Apart from crushing rebellions, the earl favoured a conciliatory policy to disarm the opposition and to encourage the north to accept Tudor rule. Henry VII, however, asserted his authority and insisted on tough action. In 1489, much against his better judgement, Northumberland was obliged to suppress a popular uprising against heavy and unprecedented taxation. The retainers he took with him agreed with the peasants, had no love for the earl, and left him to be lynched. This enabled Henry VII to impose an outsider on the north and led eventually to the Percies becoming the natural opponents to northern government rather than that government itself.

M. A. Hicks, 'Dynastic Change and Northern Society: The Career of the Fourth Earl of Northumberland, 1470–89', *Northern History* xiv, 1978.

WILLIAM LORD HASTINGS (*c.*1431–83) is best known for his execution immediately before Richard III's usurpation of the throne. So strong was Hastings' devotion to Edward V, it is usually argued, that he had to die before the usurpation could occur. He had served the boy king's grandfather and father continuously since 1458, shared their exiles in 1459–60 and 1470–1, and supported Edward IV through every crisis of his reign. The king was also his friend and went wenching with him. He was proud of the king's permission to be buried with him at Windsor. To permit Edward V's deposition would be a denial of his whole life.

Edward had raised Hastings to the peerage in 1461. He gave him the lands and offices to dominate the Leicestershire area, whence in 1471 he brought 3,000 men to the king's support. He gave him many other offices, notably the captaincy of Calais in 1471, which made him commander of the kingdom's only professional military force. Most important, however, was the chamberlainship of the household that Hastings held throughout the rein. It enabled him to control access to the king. Hastings' support was essential even for royal dukes seeking royal favour. People and institutions constantly sought his intercession and paid for it with gifts, annuities, and stewardships. While Hastings accrued royal favours and imposed hard terms for access, he escaped the conventional charge of rapacity and received several testimonials as an honourable man.

Hastings had 90 indentured retainers, more than anyone except John of Gaunt, in spite of offering not money but good lordship. Hence historians have mistakenly credited him with the dominance of the Midlands. Almost all his indentures are after 1473, when Clarence lost his great duchy of Lancaster estate in Derbyshire and Staffordshire and left Hastings as its steward. The first batch of indentures were made in the company with the king, who bestowed offices and leases on those retained. Edward approved the indentures, which linked the gentry to a reliable lord and stopped their retainder by Clarence or anyone else. They were rewarded with duchy offices and leases and Hastings' support at court. The indentures did not make Hastings dominant, which he did not seek. His famous retinue was thus a byproduct of his influence at court.

Even there Hastings' power fluctuated with court politics. Initially he rose with the support of Warwick, who secured him extra lands for marrying his sister. His authority suffered somewhat from the rise of the Wydevilles. Returning in 1471, he beat Anthony Earl Rivers to the captaincy of Calais, to Rivers' acute chagrin. Marriage of the queen's son Dorset and Hastings' stepdaughter did not improve relations. Both factions spread rumours to discredit one another with the king, not without success. The struggle for influence was sharpened by competition between Hastings and Dorset for the same mistress and by the queen blaming Hastings for leading Edward astray. Edward tried unsuccessfully to reconcile the factions before he died. His death ended Hastings' chamberlainship and seemed to give victory to the Wydevilles, causing Hastings, apprehensively, to turn to Richard. Richard is the only source for Hastings' supposed rapprochement with the Wydevilles, which may not have happened. It is not implausible, however, for their differences presumed their overriding allegiance to Edward V.

W. H. Dunham, 'Lord Hastings' Indentured Retainers 1461–83', *Transactions of the Connecticut Academy of Arts and Sciences* 39, 1955.

M. A. Hicks, 'Lord Hastings' Indentured Retainers?', *Richard III and his Rivals: Magnates and their Motives in the Wars of the Roses*, 1991.

I. Rowney, 'The Hastings Affinity in Staffordshire and the Honour of Tutbury', *Bulletin of the Institute of Historical Research* lvii, 1984.

I. Rowney, 'Resources and Retaining in Yorkist England: William, Lord Hastings and the Honour of Tutbury' in *Property and Politics: Essays in Later Medieval English History*, ed A. J. Pollard, 1984.

C. D. Ross, *Richard III*, 1981.

ANTHONY WYDEVILLE (*c.* 1442–83), Lord Scales (1460) and Earl Rivers (1469), was a man of many talents and enthusiasms. Like his father he was a proficient soldier and distinguished jouster. He served repeatedly on land and sea from 1459 and fought at Towton and Barnet, where he was wounded. His most famous tournament against the Bastard of Burgundy reveals not just skill at arms (and perhaps also his gamesmanship), but a knowledge of the chivalric code and courtly love conventions worthy of his Burgundian relatives. His pilgrimages to Santiago, Rome and Bury St.

Edmunds were conventional enough, but his proposed crusade against the Saracens of Portugal had become unusual by the fifteenth century and his hair shirt and religious reading mark him as a man of highly individual piety. Devotional and moral works were not just read, they were translated from the French, and they were published. That his *Dictes and Sayings of the Philosophers* (1477) was the first book printed in England marks him out as receptive to new ideas. The *Moral Proverbs* (1478) and *Cordyale* (1479) followed. It was his unique combination of military, moral, and literary qualities as much as his birth and connections that made him the obvious choice to be governor of Edward, Prince of Wales, the future Edward V. His literary interests above all may explain Mancini's unusual enconium: Rivers was, he wrote, 'a kind, serious and just man, and one tested by every vicissitude of life; whatever his prosperity, he had injured nobody, though benefiting many'. Mancini's tribute captures a certain lack of drive, that prompted him to go on pilgrimage or crusade, when administrative and military tasks remained undone. It infuriated Edward IV and perhaps explains why he deprived his brother-in-law so quickly of such frontline political appointments as constable of England and captain of Calais, for which Rivers seems otherwise so well-fitted. It may explain why Rivers failed to perceive Gloucester as his enemy in 1483. It has certainly caused modern historians to label him a dilettante and to ask 'what is the point' of his career. Such attitudes make the underlying assumption that competitive self-aggrandisement is normal. Those satisfied with what they have and without incentives to seek more may have been more common than we suppose.

Rivers, after all, had risen rapidly and effortlessly in the world. Raised to the baronage by his own marriage in 1460, his sister's marriage brought him to the limelight and made him rapidly governor of the Isle of Wight, Lord of Jersey, keeper of Portchester, and in 1469 an earl. He had no children, took his time in remarrying, and divided his property between his two unmarried brothers. If conscious of kinship, they were not dynasts. But his correspondence reveals a good grasp of affairs and awareness of financial implications, legal title, and government procedures. Royal favour, dubious titles, technicalities, speculation on forfeitures, and force if necessary all had their place. He was an effective diplomat and administrator. As governor of the Prince of Wales, he used the principality and duchy of Cornwall as a source of money, patronage, and manpower, moulding them into a power-base for himself and his family much more important than his own estates. He fixed parliamentary elections and negotiated his way into control of the Tower. In short, Rivers was as adept and formidable a politician as any other, but politics was not an obsession pursued to the exclusion of everything else. Had it been, had he distrusted even friends and put naked self-interest first, he would not have placed himself at Gloucester's mercy in 1483 and might therefore have survived.

M. A. Hicks, 'The Changing Role of the Wydevilles in Yorkist Politics' in *Patronage, Pedigree and Power in Later Medieval England*, C. D. Ross, ed., 1979.

E. W. Ives, 'Andrew Dymmock and the Papers of Antony, Earl Rivers, 1482–3', *Bulletin of the Institute of Historical Research* xli, 1968.

J. R. Lander, *Crown and Nobility 1450–1509*, 1976.

C. D. Ross, *Edward IV*, 1974.

C. D. Ross, *Richard III*, 1981.

JOHN ROUS (*c.*1411–91), antiquary of Warwick, was chantry chaplain of Guy's Cliff. He is thus one of the few members of the late medieval clerical proletariat to be more than a name. He took his M.A. at Oxford University by 1445 and worked the rest of his life at Guy's Cliff. That he rose no further suggests a lack of ambition and contentment with his lot. A plump, clean-shaven, gentle man, he was no dynamic thruster and his job left him plenty of time for his literary pursuits.

Cantarists were required to celebrate mass daily and thus had little time for travel, but Rous managed some prolonged journeys, borrowed and bought books — including some surprisingly up-to-date ones — and built up a considerable library. If in touch with the wider world, his horizons were intensely local. The chantry was for two priests and was idyllically located on the River Avon on the reputed site of the hermitage of the legendary giant Guy of Warwick, who was supposed, mistakenly, to be ancestor of the Earls of Warwick. Rous's situation explains why he wrote his lost works on giants, Guy's Cliff and Warwick, and the two surviving versions of his *Rous Roll* about the earls themselves. Only his *History of the*

Kings of England departs from this pattern. Rous identified himself so much with the earls that his work represents the

> culmination of all previous essays in propaganda on the past of the various families whose estates had merged with those of the Beauchamps to form the powerful earldom of the later middle ages. His yardstick of measurement of the achievements of the earls and their countesses is the extent of their benefactions to the town of Warwick, its churches, priories, hospitals, and chantries.

Valuable though the *Rous Roll* is 'as an indication of how contemporaries saw their own history', its importance 'lies less in the information which it provides than in its evocation of the outlook and interests — the mental climate — of the age when it was written', for which it is indispensable.

Rous has been criticised both as a time-server and historian. Having praised the Warwick heiress Anne Neville and her husband Richard III in 1483, after Bosworth he portrayed his erstwhile patron as a deformed tyrant. If political expediency took priority over historical accuracy, it is hardly surprising given Rous's age and vulnerability. As for his historical stature, all his writings — as Professor Ross scathingly said — are undiscriminating in their use of evidence, credulous of myth and miracles, hopelessly inaccurate, and almost negligible in their achievements. Such charges, however, are strangely reminiscent of those levelled at the indispensable Froissart and moreover ignore Rous's antiquarian significance. He was an enthusiastic and energetic antiquary, who did much more than credulously accept existing written and oral traditions. That he could portray past earls and countesses of Warwick in appropriate clothes and armour is testimony to meticulous research on monuments, seals, and therefore documents. He knew how the past differed from the present. His moral outrage and concerned humanitarianism about enclosure and depopulation does not conceal careful fieldwork and a capacity to analyse changes occurring around him. Ironically it is his flawed published works that have so damaged his reputation. Had we more of his notebooks, like William Worcester's, we *might* hold him in higher estimation. But his notebooks, like his library, are irretrievably lost.

W. H. Courthope, ed., *The Rous Roll*, 2nd edn. 1980.

A. Gransden, *Historical Writing in England* ii, 1982.

E. Mason, 'Legends of the Beauchamps' ancestors: the use of baronial propaganda in medieval England', *Journal of Medieval History* x, 1984.

WILLIAM CAXTON (*c.*1415–91), mercer, merchant and 'the first English publisher', introduced printing to England. There had been earlier oriental experiments in printing, but these had not included the moveable type so essential for the European alphabet. This involved separate metal letters, that could be moved and used repeatedly. The books of medieval Europe had all been written laboriously by hand, one copy at a time, at the pace of the scribe and at a price that had to cover his keep throughout the period he was at work on it. Hence the relative rarity and costliness of medieval books. Printing enabled many copies to be made simultaneously of the same work: books could be made widely available, their cost was reduced, and readership consequently expanded. It was a revolutionary development.

Printing was invented in Germany in the mid 15th century and is usually attributed primarily to Johan Gutenberg of Mainz in 1455–6. It spread extremely rapidly throughout Europe and its introduction to England by Caxton in 1476 is actually rather late. Caxton's enterprise differed from other earlier printers in several respects. First of all, he was primarily a commercial publisher, a merchant dealing in books rather than a typesetter. The German Wynkyn de Worde (of Wörth) managed his printing works, whilst Caxton supplied the capital and commercial acumen. Caxton dealt almost exclusively in English works, many translated specially for the purpose, often by himself. His products were decidedly workaday and no attempt was made to make them look beautiful like contemporary manuscripts. Hand-written books were indeed preferred to printed books in some libraries for precisely this reason.

Caxton was a well-educated Kentishman, who was apprenticed to a distinguished London mercer in 1438. He engaged in trade to the Low Countries and from 1462 was governor of the Merchant Adventurers, who oversaw English trade there. He enjoyed close relations with Edward IV's sister Margaret Duchess of Burgundy and perhaps for that reason was dismissed as governor about 1470 during the Lancastrian Readeption. Subsequently King Edward used him as a commercial diplomat. Recognizing the potential for profit from the new invention, Caxton apparently decided to engage in printing as early as 1468, when he started translating a French *History of Troy* into English for publication. He visited Cologne in 1471, apparently to learn the technology, and published his *History of Troy* at Bruges in 1474. At 700 pages long, this was a major capital commitment in paper alone and a daring beginning to his new career. Returning to England by 1476, he set up his press at Westminster, close to court and the city, where most of his readership probably lived. There he published at least 18,000 pages under 80 different titles. He concentrated on chivalric and religious works and printed 22 that he had translated himself, 21 from the French and another from the Dutch. His production included the first editions of Chaucer's *Canterbury Tales*, Malory's *Morte D'Arthur*, and the poems of Gower and Lydgate. He was an enterprising businessman, who operated on a large scale and took risks. Since his will is lost, we cannot know how profitable his business was, but he certainly held considerable stocks at his death, when some legacies consisted of multiple copies of books. He was a considerable linguist, a quick and hardworking translator, orthodox in religion, and intellectually conventional. Of his private life, nothing is known except that he was married and had a daughter.

N. F. Blake, *Caxton: England's First Publisher*, 1976.
G. D. Painter, *William Caxton. A Quincentenary Biography of England's First Printer*, 1976.

SIR RICHARD CLERVAUX (*c.* 1420–90) of Croft (Yorks.) was one of the Richmondshire affinity on which Warwick the King-maker and Richard Duke of Gloucester based their power. Kept at home by ill-health, Clervaux records in his cartulary the meticulous, time-consuming and expensive acquisitions over thirty years from 1450 that ultimately made him landowner of all of Croft. His motive was not apparently agricultural improvement, but the desire proudly to call himself, albeit incorrectly, lord of Croft. He added to Croft Hall a chapel, which he staffed with chaplains. Fresh food came from a home farm and he acquired hunting rights over all his land. An income of £50, small by southern standards, placed him in the second-rank of Richmondshire gentry, qualified him to marry into county families, brought fees from the Bishop of Durham and Earl of Westmorland, and attracted the attention of the lords of Middleham themselves.

The Richmondshire gentry, to whom Clervaux belonged, were knit harmoniously together by a dense web of relationships: inter-marriage, as they were all cousins; neighbourhood, as mutual executors, trustees, witnesses, and arbiters; and lordship. They and the local baronage were dominated by the lordships of Middleham, which comprised 27 manors worth over £1000, and Barnard Castle. The Nevilles and later Gloucester, in turn wardens of the West March, spent heavily on retaining local gentry. Before 1461, when Clervaux served Henry VI, and after 1485, when he was knighted by Henry VII, other loyalties were possible, but in between they were not. The Nevilles and Gloucester had other lordships and dominated the whole north, but Richmondshire was the nucleus of their power. Thence in 1469 Sir William Conyers led Robin of Redesdale's rebellion and thence Lord FitzHugh led another uprising in 1470. Even after Tewkesbury, in 1471, another rising faltered only for lack of 'any of Warwick's or Neville's blood unto whom they might have rested, as they had done afore'. Richard Duke of Gloucester married Warwick's daughter Anne Neville and thus took over a going concern, which he developed with the advice of Warwick's steward Sir John Conyers as the basis of his hegemony through-out the north, in which even the northern peerage acknow-ledged him as lord. Never actually retained by the duke, Clervaux was a well-willer and naturally turned to him as arbiter in 1478. The Richmondshire gentry helped Richard to his throne, assisted his rule of the rebellious south, and shared the rewards, Clervaux among them. When Richard proposed divorcing Warwick's daughter Queen Anne, he was firmly warned that 'the northerners, in whom he placed the greatest trust, would all rise against him'. He desisted. Following Bosworth, Richmondshire rebelled again in 1486 and it was there in 1487 and 1489 that rebels turned again for support. By then Clervaux and others had accepted the new regime and Henry VII had determined never again to permit an indepen-dent lord, which in 1536 was made a grievance by the nostalgic Pilgrims of Grace. The Richmondshire community of gentry was not unique in fifteenth century England either in its tightly knit texture or its single lord, but it was unusual rather than the normal rule. Only thus could such limited numbers from a small area exercise such a disproportionate influence on national politics.

M. A. Hicks, 'Descent, Partition and Extinction: The "Warwick Inheritance"', *Bulletin of the Institute of Historical Research* lii, 1979.

M. A. Hicks, 'Dynastic Change and Northern Society: The Career of the Fourth Earl of Northumberland 1470–89', *Northern History* xiv, 1978.

A. J. Pollard, *North-East England during the Wars of the Roses*, 1991.

A. J. Pollard, 'Richard Clervaux of Croft: A North Riding Squire in the Fifteenth Century', *Yorkshire Archaeological Journal* l, 1978.

A. J. Pollard, 'The Richmondshire Community of Gentry during the Wars of the Roses', in *Patronage, Pedigree and Power in Later Medieval England,* ed. C. D. Ross, 1979.

THOMAS KEBELL (*c.*1439–1500) serjeant-at-law typifies the successful common lawyer. Lawyers were commonly of gentle stock and trained in the London inns of court. They conducted lawsuits in the central courts in Westminster Hall, or practised locally, or, like Kebell, did both. The younger son of a Leicestershire squire, Kebell went to the Inner Temple, later becoming reader and bencher. The most important of his Leicestershire clients was Lord Hastings, the king's chamberlain, whose man of business he became. He represented a wider range of clients in Westminster Hall. He became J.P. for Leicestershire, counsel (1478) and attorney-general (1483) of the Duchy of Lancaster, and serjeant-at-law in 1486, when the Lord Chief Justice invested him with his insignia: the 'cap of white lawn' (coif), scarlet hood, and livery of blue ray. He would have spent 400 marks (£266.66) on his investiture. 'The greatest honour which the law knew was the call to the coif, and this was demonstrated in the magnificence of the ceremonies which marked the occasion'. Royal judges were chosen from serjeants, all serjeants eventually became judges, and serjeants indeed were reserve judges without specific courts who acted as judges of assize. Of the new serjeants of 1486, Kebell was almost last to assume judicial responsibilities and thus had seven years practice in the court of Common Pleas, the most lucrative court where only serjeants could plead. A judge of assize and king's serjeant handling royal cases in 1495, Kebell became a justice at Chester in 1499, but died before a vacancy for him occurred at any central court.

In payment he received retaining fees and expenses, about which much is known, and fees for cases, about which we know little. Kebell was feed by aristocrats, monasteries, and towns, and in 1494 became recorder of Leicester. He built up a large fortune, which as usual he invested in land, acquiring 20 properties in Leicestershire and others elsewhere. He planned his purchases with a view to ease of administration and improvement by enclosure. From 1476–7 his principal seat was Humberstone manor near Leicester, which was sparsely furnished, apart from the library and notable stores of linen and plate. Kebell succeeded in establishing his son among the county gentry.

Clearly Kebell was able and ambitious. He was fluent in French and Latin and his books included encyclopaedias, fiction, and religious works. The presence among the latter of the Bible and sermons point to a more serious religious understanding than the conventional piety of his chapel and chaplains and projected chantry. He had a strong sense of family and neighbourhood and freely remembered his obligations. His culture, imagination, thoughtfulness, and humanity all figure in his legal career.

It is the law reports in the Year Books that tell us most about Kebell's personality. They record more direct speech than any other source and Kebell features 314 times from 1481, more than anyone else. Even his losing opinions were respected. He is recorded citing 56 statutes and 54 precedents, moving from one to another as it suited him. Supremely self-confident, aggressive and assertive, critical of others, unabashed by strictures, and unimpressed by the opinions of others, he insisted on having his say. Quick to think and to cite authorities, he was a formidable debater, who enlivened cases with his personal reminiscences, droll hypotheses, and linguistic dexterity. Whilst not 'a major or original legal thinker', he worked within the imperfect legal system that he found, seldom making broad points of principle, but impressing with sayings that were remembered long after. He was a master of procedure, who could make much from the smallest technicalities and taxed even a hostile court with his submissions. He demonstrates what vigour and

potential remained in what has often been regarded as a moribund
legal system.

E. W. Ives, *The Common Lawyers of Pre-Reformation England.
Thomas Kebell: A Case Study,* 1983.

SIR WILLIAM STONOR (*c.* 1449–94), the central figure of the
Stonor Letters, represents the normal lifestyle and aspirations of a
country gentleman. The family fortunes had been established by
Chief Justice Sir John Stonor (*d.* 1354) and had not changed much
thereafter. William was the eldest of seven offspring of Thomas
Stonor (*d.* 1474) by Jane (*d.* 1494), apparently a French-born bastard
of the Duke of Suffolk. Although strict parents, who kept a strict
rein on William's initiative, they provided generously for all their
children. Personal profit rather than social advancement explains
William's first two marriages to well-endowed widows of mercantile stock, but it was social climbing and the need for an heir that
prompted his third marriage to Anne Neville, niece of Warwick the
Kingmaker and sister of a former duke. Yet all three marriages
offered affection and mutual support through the childbirth, disease,
and mortality that were constantly recurring themes. William himself lost three wives in seven years. An unusual, but not unique,
experience.

The letters illuminate William's management of his affairs:
everyday estate administration, his involvement in the wool-trade,
ecclesiastical patronage, litigation and legal correspondence. Although he employed a receiver, steward, lawyers and bailiffs,
William was certainly the directing influence. Like previous generations of Stonors, William 'took an active share in such public work
as fell normally to country gentlemen of rank and favour' as sheriff,
knight of the shire (M.P.), and justice of the peace for Oxfordshire.
On one occasion, for example, he exceeded his powers by seizing
corn bought privately before going to the market. He sought to
increase his local authority and perhaps his income too by taking on
stewardships from the Bishop of Lincoln, St Albans Abbey, and St
George's Chapel, Windsor. He may have held a forest appointment
under Lord Lovell, who asked him to care for his deer, whilst the
queen, ironically, accused him of poaching her game. The principal
lordly influence was probably initially the De La Poles, of whom

both duchesses — Alice Chaucer of Ewelme (d. 1475) and Elizabeth of York — feature prominently. After 1480 his main lord was most likely the queen's son Thomas Marquis of Dorset, for William was told — surely an exaggeration — that 'you be the greatest man with my lord (of Dorset) and in his conceit'. Richard Duke of Gloucester also has a walk-on part. Whilst mixing with such people and interesting himself in local politics, William does not actually seem to have been retained by anyone.

Since the days of the chief justice, no Stonor had enjoyed a public career of more than local importance, but in 1478 Stonor was knighted and soon after became a knight of the body. One factor may be his first wife's taste for court-life, another that he was 'the most courteous knight that ever was', but he also needed a patron and we do not know for certain who it was. Court life was costly, as William duly found, but it brought influence. He could not have become steward of Oxford University without court contacts, however generous he had been to impoverished scholars. Although his household office gave him a role at Richard III's coronation, prior loyalties to Edward IV's children and the Wydevilles must explain his participation with so many southern gentry in Buckingham's disastrous rebellion in 1483. Although William escaped alive, his estates were confiscated, but they were restored on Henry VII's accession. William recovered his household office and was made a banneret on the field of Stoke in 1487, without however significantly improving the family's wealth or standing. That pattern was more common than radical transformation in a single generation.

C. L. Kingsford, ed., *Stonor Letters and Papers of the Fifteenth Century*, 2 vols. Camden Society 3rd series, xxix, xxx, 1919.

EDWARD V (1470–83) was in turn Edward of Westminster Prince of Wales, King Edward V (1483), and one of the two Little Princes in the Tower. At his birth his father Edward IV was in exile and his mother Queen Elizabeth Wydeville in sanctuary. Within six months they had resumed thrones made more secure by his existence as male heir. Tragically, however, he did not outlive his childhood.

It is the novel formality of his education that is 'the principal evidence that the royal house of York perceived the importance of education as much as their predecessors, the Lancastrians, had done'. In 1473, aged three, he had outgrown the nursery and he was assigned a separate household at Ludlow. Precisely regulated by ordinances of 1473 and 1483, it was managed by his uncle Earl Rivers as his governor and Bishop Alcock as his teacher. He had 25 councillors and the 50 members of his household included noble youths as his playfellows. Regulated by one of 'the earliest modern timetables in the history of education', his daily routine included three religious services, two sessions of study, and one each for sport and recreation. Doubtless Rivers read him moral stories. He practised riding and archery, heard and perhaps played music, and studied Latin to such effect that at twelve he could pronounce and understand almost all Latin prose and verse. In 1483 new ordinances protected him against undesirable influences, but the damage was already done. Already his uncle Rivers and half-brother Lord Richard Grey had established an ascendancy over him and made his resources into their power-base. They planned to use their influence over him to rule after his father's death. When Edward IV died on 9 April 1483 therefore, the Wydevilles' foes had first to wrest the king from Rivers and Grey. Gloucester and Buckingham did so. They disregarded the boy's defence of his kin, leaving him to cry, and set about ingratiating themselves with him. The political initiative had passed decisively to Gloucester, who made himself king on 26 June following.

Ex-kings were an encouragement to rebellion that no usurper could tolerate. Richard III claimed all Edward IV's children were bastards because their father was already indissolubly committed to another lady before he married their mother. Many people did not believe this and some plotted to restore Edward V as early as July 1483. By October Edward and his brother Richard were rumoured to be dead. There are no subsequent reports that they were alive. Between July and October they probably died, presumably violently, and almost certainly at the hands of their uncle Richard III. Before his accession he had placed both boys in the Tower, where initially they were seen playing and even received visitors. All that had ceased by August. Precisely what happened cannot be shown, because the secret was well-kept. It is quite impossible to confirm or deny the circumstantial tale told later by Sir Thomas More and repeated by Shakespeare. What is clear is that everyone took it for granted that they were dead from the autumn of 1483. Only thus can one explain a rebellion designed to put their *sister* Elizabeth of York on the throne with the obscure Henry Tudor and somewhat later Queen Elizabeth Wydeville's acceptance of Richard III as king. The princes were politically, if not necessarily physically, dead. And whatever befell them, rightly or wrongly, it was their uncle Richard III who has ever since taken the blame for the murder of the innocents and suffered the disastrous political consequences.

L. Attreed, 'From *Pearl* Maiden to Tower Princes', *Journal of Medieval History* ix, 1983.

M. A. Hicks, 'The Changing Role of the Wydevilles in Yorkist Politics to 1483', in *Patronage, Pedigree and Power in Later Medieval England*, C. D. Ross, ed., 1979.

D. E. Lowe, 'Patronage and Politics: Edward IV, the Wydevills, and the Council of the Prince of Wales, 1471–83', *Bulletin of the Board of Celtic Studies* xxix, 1981.

N. Orme, 'The Education of Edward V', *Bulletin of the Institute of Historical Research* lvii, 1984.

C. D. Ross, *Richard III*, 1981.

RICHARD III (1452–85) who ascended the throne in 1483, was the youngest son of Richard Duke of York and his duchess Cecily Neville. The accession of his eldest brother as King Edward IV in 1461 made him into a prince of the blood royal, but the subsequent birth of numerous nephews and nieces shunted him progressively farther down the line of succession. When he took the throne in 1483, he inaugurated what was arguably the most disastrous reign of any English king. It terminated with his defeat, death, and the destruction of the Yorkist dynasty. He has normally been accused of usurping the throne illegally and by force, of murdering his nephews the two Princes in the Tower, of planning to marry his niece Elizabeth of York, and of reigning tyrannically. Only recently have these charges been vigorously and effectively countered. Richard, it is commonly said, was not guilty of any of these charges and certainly cannot be proved to have been at fault. More positively, much play has been made of his loyal and devoted services to his brother Edward IV, his benevolent rule of the north before his accession and the whole country thereafter, and of his

Richard III
(Artist unknown)

evident idealism. Richard was potentially the greatest and best of English kings. At the very least, he was more sinned against than sinning.

Richard can never have had much expectation of succeeding to the crown before 1483. From 1461 he devoted himself instead into making a success of his role as a royal prince and the greatest of subjects. It was during these years that he supported King Edward through all the dynastic vicissitudes of 1469–71, participated in the invasion of France in 1475, implemented the royal will in northern England, and in 1480–3 commanded Edward's war effort against Scotland. King Edward can have had no fears for his loyalty. Such service was a duty. It also served Richard's purpose by advancing his political influence and in enabling him to construct for himself a formidable power-base in the north. This was based on a combination of royal favour and on the inheritance of his wife, Anne Neville, daughter of Warwick the Kingmaker. He exploited each to the full and supplemented them with judicious use of purchase, threats, and force. Richard appears to have been unusually clear-sighted in what he wanted to achieve, particularly singleminded and determined in its pursuit, and utterly ruthless in its implementation. If he could be grasping and uncompromising where he possessed the advantage, he could also be flexible and conciliatory, but he did not lose sight of his ultimate ends and was prepared to wait long for his opportunity. In all this, perhaps, he was unexceptional, though the scale of his self-aggrandisement marks him out from his *immediate* contemporaries and raises the question of where his ambitions would ultimately lead. He had a good working knowledge of the law, was an able administrator, and was militarily formidable as a knight, divisional commander, and commander-in-chief. He met the great on equal terms and the gentry as lord, yet was valued by both as a just arbiter of their quarrels and inspired not merely loyalty but also devotion. At least conventionally pious, he was generous as well as grasping and prudish as well as lecherous. Personal stature and magnetism strengthened the influence of birth and landed power, making him much more than merely his brother's agent. Richard was capable of considerable political independence and his priorities were not always those of Edward. Indeed one may argue that his power, like that of the Wydevilles, was constructed by taking advantage of his brother as much as by the latter's encouragement.

His power in the north was used on Edward's behalf, but need not always have been so.

That Richard was so successful as Duke of Gloucester could have been a great asset as king. He knew all those who mattered politically and yet was untainted by association with any court faction. He could share fully the interests and values of other great noblemen, until recently his equals, and could command their obedience by compelling their respect. Experience as duke had prepared him for managing royal finances, for diplomacy and warfare, for patronage and law enforcement. He could appeal to mutual ideals of nationality, loyalty, lordship, honour, and Christianity. He knew how to command and to reward and could inspire by common ideals and by mutual self-interest. He continued the administrative innovations of his brother, perhaps shared in administrative and legislative reforms, and pursued a foreign policy committed to peace. Such intentions and achievements, however, play only a small part in his activities as king. He merely dabbled in them and did not complete his work, perhaps because his reign was dominated by the struggle for survival, to defeat enemies within and without, and to buy support. He was the king of a narrow faction, that became progressively more restricted as his reign persisted, and lacked the leisure or the consent to make far-reaching changes, if indeed these were ever contemplated. He could never liquidate the opposition that he had created when he became king. Historians cannot disregard this either or confine themselves to what might have been.

Richard became king on 26 June 1483 by setting aside the claims of the sons of his brother Edward IV. Richard justified himself by denying the princes their hereditary right to the crown: their father Edward IV was a bastard, not the legitimate son of Richard Duke of York, and he was not legally married to his queen, the prince's mother. Although serious, such charges were for the church courts—not Richard — to decide. They cannot now be proved, may indeed have been false, and were actually insufficient to justify his case. Kings were kings not purely by hereditary right but by general consent. Edward V had been universally recognized as king, not least by Richard, and therefore *was* king. Subsequent aspersions on his hereditary title, however accurate, could not make him otherwise. Richard undoubtedly usurped the throne of a generally accepted king.

Richard made himself king by eliminating Earl Rivers and Lord Hastings and driving the queen and her son Dorset into refuge with the backing of a northern army. The threat of overwhelming force could not be constantly maintained and almost as soon as he was crowned he was faced by rebellion by erstwhile supporters of Edward IV and Edward V. The princes were still dangerous to him, for there were certainly many who did not believe them to be bastards and not the rightful successors of Edward IV. Like such other deposed kings as Edward II, Richard II and Henry VI, they were surely too dangerous for Richard to let live. By August 1483 it was widely rumoured that they were dead and no evidence, then or since, has been produced to the contrary. Almost certainly Richard was responsible for their destruction, which could be justified in the interests of peace and order, whether or not he believed them genuinely illegitimate. Rightly or wrongly, Richard took the blame. The proposal to marry their sister, his niece, was designed to strengthen his title and again presumes the deaths of her brothers. That it did not occur was apparently due to opposition by ecclesiastical lawyers and his northern supporters, not because Richard saw anything wrong with such an incestuous union.

Richard made himself king by the support of his northern retinue and maintained himself on his throne with their support. He was essentially a northern king. The rebels, many of them retainers of Edward IV and the Wydevilles, came overwhelmingly from southern England, where Richard had little support. After their defeat in Buckingham's Rebellion in the autumn of 1483, Richard had to replace them as landowners, local government, and coastal defence against Henry Tudor by northerners whom he transferred wholesale into the southern counties, where they were regarded, at least by some, as agents of a northern tyranny. Hence partly Richard's poor press even among immediately contemporary chroniclers. Some northerners continued to support Richard's cause even after Bosworth, but it was the desertion of others *at* Bosworth that precipitated his fall. The ambitious egotism that Richard displayed as duke and which might have served him well as a *legitimate* king was not enough once his integrity and morality were questioned. He lost the propaganda war, then and since, and lost his throne and reputation too. Unjust, perhaps, but historical fact.

R. A. Griffiths and J. W. Sherborne, eds., *Kings and Nobles 1377–1529*, 1986.
P. Hammond, ed. *Richard III: Loyalty, Lordship and Law*, 1986.
M. A. Hicks, *Richard III and his Rivals*, 1991.
R. E. Horrox, *Richard III: A Study in Service*, 1989.
C. D. Ross, *Richard III*, 1981.

HENRY STAFFORD, DUKE OF BUCKINGHAM (*c.*1457–83) made Richard III king. He probably resented Edward IV's denial to him of the respect and authority due to his birth, rank and power. A royal prince as senior representative of Thomas of Woodstock, youngest son of Edward III, he was 'head of the wealthiest and most long established of the English magnate families'. Succeeding as a toddler, his marriage to the queen's sister included him in the Yorkist royal family. Hence his early majority in 1473 and his election as K.G. next year. Unfortunately an exaggerated notion of his own importance prompted his assumption of Woodstock's arms and his claim to the Lancastrian half of the Bohun inheritance. Edward's reluctance to lose £1,000 a year to his wealthiest subject was fed by the suspicion that the adolescent duke had designs on his crown. Royal disfavour was only momentarily dispelled in 1477–8, when Edward acted as godfather to Buckingham's son and the duke as high steward sentenced Clarence to death. Lord Hastings' indentured retainers kept Buckingham out of Midlands — he was not even J.P. in his home county of Stafford — and although the greatest marcher lord he was excluded from the Council of Wales, which his Wydeville kinsfolk used to enhance their power at marcher lords' expense. Blaming the Wydevilles and lamenting his marriage to one of them, he feared Edward V's accession would consolidate and increase their influence. He therefore wanted change at the top and had exorbitant demands of his own, which only Richard could satisfy.

Buckingham's role in Richard's revolution was crucial. He shared in the seizure of the young king, dominated the council, and organised Edward V's replacement by Richard III. Clever, eloquent and persuasive, he was in turns shrewd manipulator and honest broker, skilful committeeman and popular demagogue. He revelled in the panoply of power, presiding over the coronation and making himself high steward and constable of England, but the realities of power did not escape him. The coup was risky, took courage and involved bloodshed. Buckingham accepted the necessity for his erstwhile kinsmen to die. Besides honours, he received his Bohun inheritance and the rule of Wales, where he became chief justice and chamberlain of North and South Wales, steward of all the marcher lordships and constable of 53 castles, and military commander of adjacent shires. It was a 'spectacular delegation of royal authority, entirely without precedent in the entire annals of the medieval English monarchy — and was never to be repeated'. Besides such greed and ambition even Warwick the Kingmaker does not compare.

Viceroy in Wales and the king's right-hand man, Buckingham had achieved all he could possibly expect. What next? Later in 1483 he rebelled, ostensibly in support of Henry Tudor, was defeated and executed. Modern historians find this almost inexplicable. For Thomas More the duke wanted the crown for himself, but was persuaded to support Tudor instead. He had known Tudor as a boy, but it is hard to see why he should prefer him to Richard, unless he thought him easier to manage or hoped for the throne himself later. The risks surely outweighed any gains. If Richard had denied any requests, he was unaware of any rift, and anything he denied could hardly match what he had already given. Perhaps Buckingham feared a successful Wydeville-Tudor coup. In any case Buckingham disastrously miscalculated his support, for few followed him and Brecon Castle was sacked behind him, but it was the flooded Severn that isolated him. The main uprising of Yorkist and Wydeville gentry in the southern counties was too poorly co-ordinated and Henry Tudor arrived too late to succeed. Buckingham's overmighty phase was brief indeed.

M. A. Hicks, 'The Changing Role of the Wydevilles in Yorkist Politics to 1483' in *Patronage, Pedigree and Power in Later Medieval England,* C. D. Ross, ed., 1979.

C. Rawcliffe, *The Staffords, Earls of Stafford and Dukes of Buckingham 1394–1521,* 1978.

C. D. Ross, *Richard III,* 1981.

SIR JAMES TYRELL (1445–1502) is reputed to have murdered the Princes in the Tower. Unlike most of Richard III's retainers, he was not a northerner, perhaps because his service to the then Duke of

Gloucester dates back before Richard's acquisition of the Neville inheritance in 1471. James was the son of William Tyrell of Ipswich (Suff.). He was knighted at the battle of Tewkesbury and was certainly one of Richard's retainers in 1472. His activity as witness of ducal charters, trustee, deputy-chamberlain of the exchequer, and under-constable marks him out as one of the duke's most trusted servants. Richard had few if any more important posts in his gift than those of sheriff of Glamorgan and constable of Cardiff, which made Tyrell the chief man in the region. Quite apart from his official fees of £110, he was able to attract a similar income from the Duke of Suffolk, Lord Dudley, and various ecclesiastics, besides his fee as steward of the duchy of Lancaster lordship of Ogmore and the £100 a year profit he made as lessee of the lands of the Abbey of Tewkesbury in Glamorgan. He served in the Scottish war in 1482, when the duke made him a knight banneret, and in 1483 it was to him that Richard confided the custody of Archbishop Rotherham.

Tyrell was thus particularly well-placed to benefit from Richard's usurpation. He was appointed a knight of the body, master of the horse, master of the henxmen, chamberlain of the exchequer, steward of the duchy of Cornwall, steward of lordships and constable of castles in Wales, and lieutenant of Guines by Calais. He was allowed to inherit his brother-in-law's lands in Cornwall — hence his appointment as J.P. for Cornwall — and was granted other confiscated lands. Such posts however carried duties and that Tyrell had incompatible responsibilities for defence in Cornwall, South Wales, and Calais is a measure of Richard III's 'acute shortage of reliable manpower. Many tasks could only be given to men close to him and fully trusted by him'. When Tyrell was sent to take over Guines in 1485 after the commander's defection, he was nevertheless left in command in Glamorgan. Following Henry Tudor's landing, he was therefore unable to organise countermeasures in South Wales.

Clearly Tyrell was the sort of confidential servant that Richard would have trusted with such delicate and secret business as the murder of the Princes in the Tower, if he indeed directed it. Sir Thomas More describes in detail the murder, which he places in the summer of 1483, when the princes probably did die, and Polydore Vergil also attributes the murder to Tyrell. Neither writer was an eyewitness and both were writing thirty years after the events described and indeed after the death of Tyrell himself. The source was allegedly a confession made by Tyrell before his death, which does not survive if indeed it ever existed. There is nothing inherently improbable in the story, but no part of it can be adequately corroborated and it must remain merely the most likely explanation of the princes' fate. There were obvious reasons for the crime to be concealed by the perpetrators before and after 1485.

Because Tyrell was at Guines at 1485, he missed the disaster of Bosworth and continued his career as trusted royal servant to Henry VII. He lost some offices and lands, yet retained his appointments as knight of the body, sheriff of Glamorgan, and lieutenant of Guines. He was frequently at court, was employed on diplomatic and military missions, joined the royal council, and in 1495 was a trustee of the king's will. Almost unique in retaining his offices after Richard's fall, let alone securing further promotion, Tyrell was clearly a man whose remarkable ability demanded recognition. In 1501 however he was implicated in treason with Edmund De La Pole, Earl of Suffolk, the Yorkist Pretender and a nobleman in his home area. He was condemned to death and executed in 1502. It is at this point that he is alleged to have made his notorious confession.

T. More, *History of King Richard III*, ed. R. S. Sylvester, 1963.
C. D. Ross, *Richard III*, 1981.

WILLIAM CATESBY (*c.*1440–83) esquire and Sir Richard Ratcliffe were those favourites of Richard III 'whose wills he scarcely ever dared to oppose'. Their notoriety and that of Viscount Lovell is caught in Collingbourne's scurrilous rhyme:

The cat, the rat, and Lovell the dog
Ruleth all England under a hog.

Lovell was Richard's childhood friend, Ratcliffe the most trusted of his northern retinue, but the reasons for Catesby's influence and his role in government are more difficult to assess. Whereas the others were apparently straightforward and honourable men, Catesby most definitely was not: 'Indeed you would not wish that a man of so much wit should be of so little faith'.

Catesby's father, Sir William Catesby (*d.*1479), was one of the leading gentry of Northamptonshire, five times its sheriff, and four

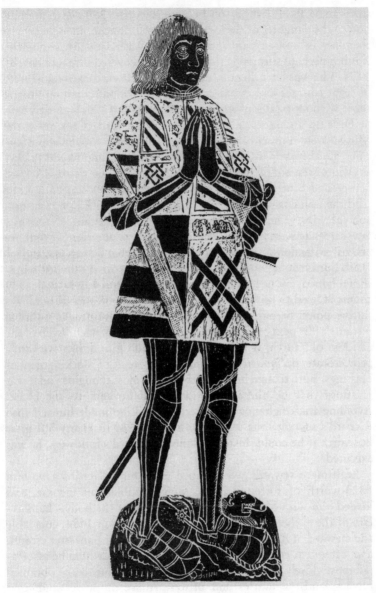

William Catesby
(From his brass in Ashby St Ledgers Church)

times an M.P. He left his son 14 manors worth £250 a year, married him to the daughter of the local baron Lord Zouche, and sent him to the Inner Temple to learn about the law. With a judge for an uncle, it is not perhaps surprising that William discovered a legal talent. By 1474–5 he was lecturing on Magna Carta. He embarked on a career of legal counsel and estate administration more common among those without estates of their own. During the 1470s and early '80s he built up an extensive and lucrative legal practice mainly in the Midlands as counsel of the Duchy of Lancaster, Archbishop Bourchier, Lord Hastings, Lord Lisle, Lady Latimer, and Laund Priory; as estates steward of the Duke of Buckingham, his stepfather Lord Scrope and brother-in-law Lord Zouche, Lord Dudley, Lady Latimer, the Beauchamp feoffees, St Albans Abbey, Sir Ralph Hastings, and John Dyve; and as trustee, executor and annuitant. 'It was as a lawyer, ready with his advice to local aristocratic and other families and as professional land-agent to such like, that he was making his way'. Lords could hope for undivided loyalty from the landed gentry they retained, but not from such professional experts, who had many clients. Catesby, however, was a hybrid: a 'professional administrative expert prepared to run the risks of involvement in political intrigue'. His next professional step up was the chancellorship of the earldom of March, which was conferred on him during Richard's protectorate on *political* grounds as protegé of Buckingham or Hastings. Both trusted him with their innermost thoughts and it was Hastings that he allegedly betrayed and brought to the block. Avoiding Buckingham's fall later in 1483, he made himself into Richard's servant, but would have transferred to Henry VII after Bosworth if he could. Instead, alone of Richard's followers, he was executed.

Legitimate rewards were heaped upon him. Richard gave him £323-worth of forfeited lands, which doubled his income, and loaded him with offices: councillor, esquire of the body, chamberlain of the exchequer, speaker of the Commons in 1484, constable and steward of Rockingham, steward of duchy of Lancaster estates, and a frequent commissioner. From Lovell, with whom he associated most closely, and from those needing his influence, he obtained further lands, annuities and offices. Abuse of power and legal chicanery enabled him to extort yet more property from such victims as the Peyton family and Queens' College Cambridge, some of which troubled his conscience. There is an unbridled quality about his pursuit of personal advantage comparable to the excesses of Walter Langton and the Despensers over a much longer period. It reflects badly on Richard that he did not curb him and it is difficult to see what services were valuable enough to compensate for his lack of principle and notoriety.

J. S. Roskell, *Parliament and Politics in Late Medieval England* ii, 1981.

D. Williams, 'The hastily drawn up will of William Catesby, Esquire, 25 August 1485', *Transactions of the Leicestershire Archaeological and Historical Society* li, 1975–6.

GEORGE CELY (*c.*1458–89) is an example of a minor international merchant. The company of the Staple controlled overseas trade in wool, a principal English export, regulating its quality and routing it in convoys via London to the staple town of Calais. Staplers bought their wool locally in England and sold it in Calais or the Low Countries. The Celys dealt mainly in middle-quality Cotswold wool, bought at Northleach (Gloucs.) from woolbroggers (wholesalers) rather than producers. Unusually they engaged neither in woolbrogging nor in other branches of overseas trade and specialised exceptionally in particular products, sellers and buyers. Some skill was needed to cope with fluctuating prices and exchange rates. The woolbroggers were paid later from income from sales returned to London by bills of exchange, rather like cheques.

A lawsuit after George's death preserved his records: the finest archive of any medieval English firm. From 1472 the firm was headed by Richard the father (*d.*1482), an established stapler from Mark Lane (formerly Mart Lane), London, which was close to the customs house, weighhouse, quays, and Leadenhall market. He was helped by his sons Robert (*d.*1485) and Richard (*d.*1493), while George — the youngest — was learning the trade in Calais. The sons also traded on their own behalf, Richard and George being partners, and in 1478–9 the family exported 172 sacks, placing them eleventh in volume of trade; 95 sacks was their usual total. Whilst the father stood once as sheriff and twice deputised for the mayor of the staple, the Celys were not members of the city or staple elites. Richard and George took over the firm in 1482, both living in Mark Lane, and delegated the Calais office to an employee. Declining trade, political crises, illnesses, and problems in repatriating money worsened trade conditions in 1480s, provoking cash-flow problems and frequent borrowing. Attempts to diversify into shipowning were not profitable. Although undercapitalised, the brothers had a turnover of £1,200 a year and made profits of £100 a year each, enough to live very comfortably as long as the firm remained a going concern. It ceased to be so on George's death, which exposed their weaknesses and plunged Richard into debt and recriminations.

That the eldest brother Robert was disinherited confirms business as a field for talent not seniority, but George and Richard, though abler, were also dangerously lazy and casual. They wrote phonetically and untidily and probably spoke the French and Flemish essential to their calling with little regard for niceties of grammar. George was a poor correspondent and inaccurate accountant, who cannot have known precisely where he stood. Business often took second place to pleasure. He had expensive and indeed aristocratic tastes, keeping a string of horses, dogs, and hawks. Once he organised an archery contest between bachelors and married men. He dressed well, took lessons on the harp, kept several mistresses, and fathered two bastards. Richard also had one. George wrote frankly and openly, showing proper deference to his parents, affection to his brother, generosity to his colleagues, and understanding to his employees. Hence both his popularity and sensitivity to criticism. His brother Richard was even less assiduous, hankering instead after genteel leisure as retainer of the Lord of St John's.

Choosing wives was more serious than taking mistresses. Both Richard and George married heiresses, Richard catching an alderman's daughter and George a stapler's young widow. Both ploughed profits into the security and status of land. Even George held properties in London, Little Thurrock and elsewhere in Essex at his premature death. Their wives moved up to more eminent husbands.

A. Hanham, *The Celys and their world*, 1985.

A. Hanham, ed., *The Cely Letters 1472–88*, Early English Text Society cclxxiii, 1975.

BIBLIOGRAPHICAL NOTE

My collection of material for this book has been enormously assisted by the standard biographical directories and other collections of biographical material, which were often compiled by leading historians in the field. These have been used so frequently that they have not been cited separately under each biography. Where no specific reading is prescribed, they are the only works consulted.

The Dictionary of National Biography.

G. E. C(okayne), *Complete Peerage of England, Scotland, Ireland etc,* H. V. Gibbs, H. A. Doubleday, G. H. White, & R. S. Lea, eds., 12 vols. 1910–59; repr. in 6 vols, 1982.

A. B. Emden, *A Biographical Register of the University of Cambridge,* 1963.

A. B. Emden, *A Biographical Register of the University of Oxford,* 3 vols. 1957–9.

E. B. Fryde, *Handbook of British Chronology,* 3rd edn. 1986.

J. H. Harvey, *English Medieval Architects,* 2nd edn. 1984.

N. Saul, *The Batsford Companion to Medieval England,* 1983.

T. F. Tout, *Chapters in the Administrative History of Medieval England,* 6 vols. 1920–33.

J. C. Wedgwood, *History of Parliament 1439–1509,* 2 vols. 1936–8.

The bibliographies at the end of each biography are designed to indicate where further information about the individual described may be found. For more general information, you should consult one of the excellent textbooks now available for the later middle ages and listed below.

J. L. Bolton, *Medieval English Economy 1150–1500,* 1985.

A. Goodman, *A History of England from Edward II to James I,* 1977.

P. Heath, *Church and Realm 1272–1461,* 1988.

G. A. Holmes, *The Later Middle Ages 1272–1485,* 1962.

M. H. Keen, *England in the Later Middle Ages: A Political History*, 1972.

E. King, *England 1175-1425*, 1979.

J. R. Lander, *Conflict and Stability in Fifteenth Century England*, 3rd edn. 1977.

M. McKisack, *The Fourteenth Century 1307-99*, 1959.

A. R. Myers, *England in the Late Middle Ages*, 8th edn. 1971.

E. Miller and J. Hatcher, *Medieval England: Rural Society and Economic Change 1086-1328*, 1978.

M. Prestwich, *The Three Edwards: War and State in England 1272-1377*, 1981.

C. D. Ross, *The Wars of the Roses*, 1976.

J. A. Tuck, *Crown and Nobility 1272-1461*, 1985.

These may be supplemented by the modern biographies of individual kings, most of them in the Eyre Methuen series, which are now available for every king except Edward II, Edward III, Richard II, and Henry V. Much recent writing has taken the form of articles and is scattered among learned journals, since there is no major journal that specialises in late medieval England. At the very end of the period, *The Ricardian*, the journal of the Richard III society, and the volumes of fifteenth-century conference papers published by Alan Sutton of Gloucester contain much of interest. Hambledon Press has recently collected together the papers of such notable scholars as C. A. J. Armstrong, K. B. McFarlane, A. R. Myers, R. A. Griffiths and J. S. Roskell. Edward Arnold published those of J. R. Lander in *Crown and Nobility 1461-1509*, 1976.

The bibliographical notes to each biography record the date of publication. No attempt has been made to indicate the publishing house, the place of publication, or whether the item in question is still in print.

GLOSSARY

Many of these terms are elaborated in individual biographies. Some are explained at greater length by N. Saul, *The Batsford Companion to Medieval England,* 1983.

Appropriation. Many rectories were appropriated to religious houses. This meant that the institution became rector and received the bulk of the revenues of the living and the parish church was served by a vicar with a smaller income.

Arches. The court of arches was the principal court of the archbishop of Canterbury presided over by the dean of arches.

Assignment. Instead of making payments by cash, the government often assigned payment to some other source of income, e.g. the customs of Hull, frequently from revenues to be paid in the future.

Augustinian, Austin. Augustinian (Austin) canons lived a communal life like monks, but could undertake parochial responsibilities; there was also an order of Augustinian (Austin) friars.

Bastard Feudalism. The name given to the late medieval relationship between lord and retainer, in which the retainer was paid in money rather than by a grant of land.

Benedictine. The oldest order of monks. Benedictines lived strictly enclosed lives in their monasteries. All the largest monasteries and all cathedral priories were Benedictine.

Benefice. Alternative name for a church living, e.g. rectory or deanery, to which the holder was instituted by a bishop. The name stresses the benefits rather than the duties of the post.

Burgundy. A French duchy held from the late 14th century to 1477 by four Valois dukes together with much of the modern Netherlands, Belgium, and north-eastern France.

Canons. Members of a secular (non-monastic) cathedral chapter responsible for conducting services; laws made by ecclesiastical councils. Canon law was the law of the Church.

Cardinal. Titular priests of churches in Rome, who assisted popes in government of the Church and elected each new pope.

Carmelite. Order of friars.

Carthusians. A particularly strict order of monks, who lived in silence and seclusion in individual cells in their monasteries (charterhouses).

Chamber. Originally a bedroom. Because the king often kept his money there, frequently used for a treasury in the household.

373

Chancellor. Royal minister responsible for the king's great seal and chancery; also similar officer serving bishops and other lords.

Chancery. The king's principal writing office, responsible for issuing letters under the great seal under direction of the chancellor. Also the court of the chancellor offering equitable (fairer) and less technical remedies than the common law.

Chantry. Endowment of one or more priests to celebrate mass (holy communion) daily for the souls of the founder forever. The priests were often called cantarists. A chantry of many priests was a college or chantry college.

Chapter. Governing body of an institution, e.g. cathedral chapter, monastic chapter, chapter of the order of the Garter.

Chevauchée. A raid by English armies in France designed to cause maximum damage to the French.

Civil Law. Academic Roman law studied in the universities. Practised in other European countries but not England. Influenced the development of equity in court of chancery.

College. Usually a foundation of secular clergy, often cantarists, who held services in a collegiate church. University colleges also supported scholars through their studies.

Commission. Commissions were used by medieval kings for all kinds of purposes. Commissions of trailbaston, oyer and terminer tried major crimes. Commissioners of the peace (J.P.s) became permanent courts responsible for trying lesser crimes in each county. Commissions of array were for home defence and commissions of sewers for protection against flooding.

Common Law. Law practised in royal courts in England. Based on writs and precedents, not written bills and principles.

Common Pleas. The court of Common Pleas was the royal court of common law at Westminster principally concerned with civil suits between party and party.

Convocation. The convocations of Canterbury and York were the governing assemblies of the two provinces of the English church.

Courts. See Arches, Chancery, Common Pleas, and King's Bench.

Cure of Souls. Responsibility for the spiritual well-being of ordinary people. Rectories and vicarages carried cure of souls and incumbents could not normally hold more than one. Cathedral canonries did not carry cure of souls and clergy could thus hold several at once.

Curia. The court of the popes.

Demesne. The part of a manor occupied by the lord and not rented out. In the later middle ages, demesnes were often leased out as well.

Diocese. Alternative name for bishopric or see.

Escheator. An official who adminstered the king's feudal rights especially those that escheated to the King. Usually responsible for a county or a pair of counties.

Exchequer. Name of royal ministry at Westminster principally responsible for finance presided over by the Lord Treasurer. At this time the chancellor of the exchequer was a second rank official.

Excommunication. Ecclesiastical punishment that denied offenders holy communion and thus threatened their damnation if they were not formally absolved (forgiven).

Feudalism. Ancient system of landownership, whereby all land was held of the king, mainly for military service. Feudal military service was almost obsolete by 1272, but feudalism remained important as a system of land tenure, particularly because under-age heirs to lands held of the king were subject to wardship (guardianship) of his person and lands and marriage as the king chose.

Franciscans. Order of friars.

Friars. Thirteenth century religious orders vowed to poverty and committed to missionary activity among ordinary people. The four principal orders were the Franciscans, Dominicans, Augustinians (Austins), and Carmelites.

Gild. Organisation for regulation of a particular trade in a town. Had religious functions and some gilds or confraternities had purely religious purposes. In London gilds were called livery companies.

Heresy. Unorthodox belief condemned by the church. Heretics might be made to recant and after 1401 could be burnt at the stake for a second offence.

King's Bench. Royal court handling criminal and some civil cases.

Laity. Lay men and women were ordinary people, parishioners, who were not members of the ordained clergy.

Law. See canon law, civil law, common law.

Lollardy. Unorthodox movement derived from doctrines of John Wyclif (d.1384) and condemned by the Church. Lollards were liable to persecution and burning as heretics.

Magnates. Great men. A synonym for the most important members of the nobility, who carried disproportionate weight in English politics.

Maintenance. The exercise of various kinds of pressure and influence to determine the result or prevent legal proceedings.

Marches. The border areas of Wales and Scotland. The Welsh marches were divided into private marcher lordships, where the king's government was replaced by the lord's authority. The marches towards Scotland were defended by wardens appointed by the crown.

Mendicants. Alternative term for friar.

Mystic. Mystics practised mysticism, a form of deeply spiritual meditation in which divine truths were revealed to them.

Oligarchy. Government by the few. Towns were run by oligarchies of the richest citizens, who often co-opted successors of the same type.

Palatinate. The counties of Chester, Durham, and after 1351 Lancaster were palatinates, where the king's writ did not run: i.e. the place of the king and his government were taken by the lord. The Welsh marcher lords also possessed palatine authority.

Papacy. The institution of the popes.

Pope. The popes were bishops of Rome, successors of St Peter, and heads of the Church in western Christendom. They had extensive financial, judicial, and legislative powers in England, particularly over the clergy, but these were largely eroded in the later middle ages.

Privy Seal. A royal seal used to authorise letters under the great seal and to transact the business of the royal council. The keeper of the privy seal (now Lord Privy Seal) ranked third among royal ministers after the chancellor and treasurer.

Rector. Parish priest who had the right to the tithes and other income of his rectory.

Seal. All people of substance used seals to authenticate their formal acts rather than signatures. The king had a great seal, privy seal, and signet.

Secular. Secular clergy were churchmen who did not belong to religious orders of monks or friars. Secular society is another term for lay society.

See. Alternative name for bishopric.

Sheriff. Royal official responsible for royal administration in each county e.g. collecting old revenues, organising parliamentary elections, serving writs and empanelling juries. An unpaid amateur chosen from local notables, who should have changed every year.

Signet. The king's signet ring, used as a seal to authenticate his personal commands by his signet clerk or secretary.

Simony. The purchase of office within the church. An abuse and a sin.

Spiritualities. The spiritual income of bishops and other clergymen derived e.g. from collections and fees for spiritual services. Quite distinct from more valuable temporal income from land.

Temporalities. The temporal income of the clergy. Bishops held their temporalities from the king, who could withhold them if he disapproved of their appointment or conduct.

Translation. Moving a bishop from one see to another. Only the pope could authorise this.

Usury. Lending money on interest. Condemned as sinful.

Wardship. The feudal right of guardianship over the lands and person of an heir, who was under age. Often granted or sold by the crown, together or separately.

INDEX

377